MW01328052

BOOKS WRITTEN IN STONE:

ENOCH THE SEER, THE PYRAMIDS OF GIZA, AND THE LAST DAYS

VOLUME 1

J. Marc. Merrill

AuthorHouse™
1663 Liberty Drive
Bloomington, IN 47403
www.authorhouse.com
Phone: 1-800-839-8640

Published by AuthorHouse 2/29/2012

ISBN 978-1-4685-3171-8 (sc)
ISBN 978-1-4685-3170-1 (hc)
ISBN 978-1-4685-3169-5 (e)

Library of Congress Control Number: 2011962971

Contents

". . . the wisdom of this world is foolishness with God."

(1 Corinthians 3:19)

A NOTE ON DOCUMENTATION:

Although a few minor modifications have been made, for the most part the Modern Language Association (MLA) style of documentation has been chosen for this work so that readers will not have to turn to the end of each chapter or to the end of the book itself in order to find out what sources are being cited.

With the MLA style the reader is given at least the minimum information of authors' and editors' last names (or the titles of sources when no authors or editors are identified) within sentences and paragraphs, along with page numbers, although "page" is included with the page number or numbers only when confusion might result if "page" is left out. If more than one book or article by the same author is cited anywhere within the text, then the title of that book is provided whenever doubts might arise as to which source is being used.

Quite often authors' full names and the titles of their books are mentioned in a sentence; in that case, at the end of the sentence or at the end of the appropriate paragraph, only the page number (or numbers) is enclosed in parenthesis.

Full disclosure of all sources can be found at the end of this book in the "Works Cited" listing. As indicated by "Works Cited", only those sources referred to in the body of this book are included. For a more inclusive bibliography, the reader will need to consult other books that have as their subject the Great Pyramid of Giza.

A WORD ON ADDING TO DIRECT QUOTES:

Whenever it is deemed desirable to add information or to make a comment for purposes of clarification within a direct quote, the words being inserted will be enclosed by brackets [ ]. In those few cases where brackets are used by the author or authors being quoted, a note to that effect will appear at the end of the quote.

A WORD ON SPELLING:

A number of British sources have been used throughout *Books Written in Stone* and for those who might not realize it, British spelling frequently varies from American spelling. For example, the British will write *centre*, *colour*, and *symbolises* whereas Americans will write *center*, *color*, and *symbolizes*. This difference is being pointed out so that only in a few instances will it be necessary to use [sic] in order to indicate that a word in a direct quote is, or at least appears to be, spelled incorrectly.

A WORD ON ITALICIZING TITLES:

Under the MLA system of documentation, the titles of sacred works such as the Bible and its various books are not italicized, nor are they enclosed in quotation marks.

Except when noted otherwise, biblical quotations are from The New King James Version.

THE HEBREW ALPHABET

Name	Transliteration	Numerical Value
’Aleph	’	1
Bêth	B, b, bh,	2
Gîmel	G, g, gh	3
Dāleth	D, d, dh	4
Hē	H, h	5
Wāw	W, w (or v, o, u)	6
Záyin	Z, z	7
Chêth or Hêth	Ch	8
Têth	T, t	9
Yodh	Y, y, I, I	10
Kaph	K, k, kh	20
Lāmedh	L, l	30
Mêm	M, m	40
Nun	N, n	50
Sāmekh	S, s	60
‘Ayin	‘	70
Pē	P, ph	80
Çādhê	Ç, ç, S, s, ts	90
Qoph	Q, q, K, k	100
Rêš	R, r	200
Sin	S, š, sh	300
Tāw	T, t, th	400

The Hebrew alphabet is comprised of twenty-two letters, all consonants. For the letters themselves, see page 11 of *Biblical Hebrew* by R. K. Harrison, or the “Table of Alphabets” in *The American Heritage College Dictionary*.

THE GREEK ALPHABET

Forms	Name	Transliteration	Numerical Value
Α α	alpha	A a	1
Β β	beta	B b	2
Γ γ	gamma	G g	3
Δ δ	delta	D d	4
Ε ε	epsilon	E e	5
* * *	* * *	* * *	
Ζ ζ	zēta	Z z	7
Η η	ēta	H ē	8
Θ θ	thēta	Th th	9
Ι ι	iota	I i	10
Κ κ	kappa	K k	20
Λ λ	lambda	L l	30
Μ μ	mu	M m	40
Ν ν	nu	N n	50
Ξ ξ	xi	X x	60
Ο ο	omicron	O o	70
Π π	pi	P p	80
* * *	* * *	* * *	
Ρ ρ	rho	R r	100
Σ σ ς	sigma	S s	200
Τ τ	tau	T t	300
Υ υ	upsilon	Y U y u	400
Φ φ	phi	Ph ph	500
Χ χ	chi	Ch ch	600
Ψ ψ	psi	Ps ps	700
Ω ω	ōmega	Ō ō	800

Two of the Greek letters became lost over time: *stigma*, which is also called *digamma* by Alexander and Nicholas Humez in *Alpha to Omega: The Life & Times of the Greek Alphabet*, had the numerical value of 6, while *koppa* had the value of 90 (187-188).

1. BREAK-IN

> "He who does not enter the sheepfold by the door, but climbs up some other way, the same is a thief and a robber."
>
> (John 10:1)

In 820 AD the caliph of Baghdad, Abdullah al-Mamun, mounted an expedition to Egypt—which had come under his control that same year—with the intention of directing a team of architects, engineers, stonemasons and laborers in an effort to find a way into the Great Pyramid of Giza. In *Secrets of the Great Pyramid* Peter Tompkins notes that the caliph was acting on claims that the pyramid was a repository of ancient "maps and tables of the celestial and terrestrial spheres" (6), as well as books that dealt with the stars (Ian Lawton and Chris Ogilvie-Herald, *Giza: The Truth* 16).

At that time the Great Pyramid was covered by a polished white limestone casing that Paul Brunton says "reflected the sun's rays with a fierce brilliance [which] justified its old Egyptian name of *The Light*" (*A Search in Secret Egypt* 47). These casing stones not only fit together "with hairline precision, displaying an accuracy of engineering that impresses even present-day builders" (George Constable, editor, *Mystic Places* 48), but they were also impervious to the tools wielded by al-Mamun's crew as they hacked futilely at the north face of the pyramid (Colin Wilson, *From Atlantis to the Sphinx* 57 and 59).

As a last resort, bonfires were used to heat a section of the casing until the stones were red-hot and then they were doused with cold vinegar until they cracked. With the aid of battering rams, the caliph's men broke open an entrance that measured about 5 feet wide and 8 feet high. Now they were able to begin boring into the world's largest man-made building (Richard W. Noone, *5/5/2000*, page 27; J. P. Lepre, *The Egyptian Pyramids* 71).

When they were 100 feet into the interior and about to give up because nothing of value had been found, one of the workers heard something heavy crash to a floor not too far away. Changing direction, the crew tunneled toward the east side of the pyramid until they managed to link up with a dark narrow passage "24 feet left of centre" (Colin Wilson 59) that measured 3½ feet wide and 4 feet high (Lepre 72).

On the floor of this passage, which sloped downwards at an angle of 26 degrees, 31 minutes and 23 seconds, was a block of white limestone shaped like a prism. This stone was obviously the object that had fallen from the ceiling to the floor (I. E. S. Edwards, *The Pyramids of Egypt* 101; Colin Wilson 59).

Ignoring the stone for the moment, al-Mamun's laborers climbed the upward slope of the passage until they reached the end, where they found the original entrance which had been hidden by the exterior casing (Tompkins 9).

With torches flaming, the workers, having to advance bent over because the corridor never changed in height, turned around and worked their way to the bottom, some 350 feet away from the entrance (Colin Wilson 59; W. M. Flinders Petrie, *The Pyramids and Temples of Gizeh* 19). At that point, the passage ran horizontally for 29 feet (Edwards 101), where it finally culminated in what the explorers were looking for—a chamber.

A chamber that had been cut out of solid bedrock "nearly 100′ below ground level" (Lepre 72). To enter the chamber required a step down of 18 inches; however, there was no actual step, only a bumpy uneven drop that demanded caution in order to keep from stumbling (Lepre 114; Rutherford, *Pyramidology*, Book I, 135).

Moving carefully into the chamber, the caliph's men were greeted by an incredible sight—incredible, but not what they had hoped for, and certainly not what they had expected. For the floor of the chamber "rolled up and down like a trench that had been bombarded" (Brunton 62), and in the western half of the 46-foot-long room a rugged chasm divided chunky masses of rock that thrust up toward the low ceiling (Edwards 101; Rutherford, *Pyramidology*, Book III, 1084). It was easy to conclude that "a madman, rather than a master architect, had his hand at. . . giving this chamber a very distorted look" (Lepre 114).

This impression was increased by the discovery of a pit in the floor, the mouth of which was near the east wall. With a diagonal of 100 inches, the pit appeared to go straight down and, despite the torches, was terrifyingly dark and ominous (Graham Hancock and Robert Bauval, *The Message of the Sphinx* 49; Rutherford, Book III, 1084 and 1089).

In the south wall of the chamber was another horizontal passage, which proved to be even more cramped than the previous one. Surely it would lead to hidden treasure. But it did not. Instead, it ran south for about 50 feet and then came to a dead end (Bill Schul and Ed Pettit, *The Secret Power of Pyramids* 27).

Frustrated, but not ready to give up, al-Mamun's men returned to the point where they had broken into the descending passage. Examining that part of the ceiling that had been exposed when the prism stone had been dislodged, they found another stone that was unlike all the others they had seen so far; this one was granite, red granite (Colin Wilson 59).

And, like the casing stones, it too proved to be impervious to their tools. If they wanted to discover what might lie behind this blockage they would have to go around it (Constable 49), but to their surprise—and dismay—the caliph's team, after gouging out a tunnel through the softer limestone on the west side of the granite block, discovered that what lay beyond was another red granite block. And beyond the second block was yet a 3rd one. Altogether, the 3 blocks of granite took up 180 inches (Worth Smith, *Miracle of the Ages: The Great Pyramid of Gizeh* 82; Colin Wilson 60).

The workers' efforts, however, seemed to have been rewarded when they at last forced an entrance into one more passage, this one ascending rather than descending. Working their way up the incline, they found another horizontal passage that led to a second chamber within the pyramid itself. But more disappointment followed when this second chamber, which contained a shallow niche in the east wall, proved to be empty. No mummy, no treasure (Graham Hancock, *Fingerprints of the Gods* 323).

Additional exploration resulted in the discovery of a second ascending passageway that continued upwards at the same angle as the earlier one, but with a major difference. Whereas the first ascending passage had been about the same height and width as the descending passage, this new one opened up into an amazing gallery that measured 7 feet wide, 28 feet high, and 153 feet long (Lionel Casson, *Ancient Egypt* 136; Lepre 79).

Unfortunately, in keeping with the other sloping passageways, the Grand Gallery, as it would come to be called, was a slick ramp and difficult to climb (C. W. Ceram, *The March of Archaeology* 93). But the Caliph's men persevered and eventually reached its south end, where a block of limestone rose up 3 feet from the floor (Lepre 85; Tompkins 13).

At the top of this broad platform was a narrow entrance into an antechamber, then another low but extremely short horizontal passage brought them into a 3rd large chamber. Composed of red granite, this brilliant impressive room was surely the chamber where the pharaoh who had built the Great Pyramid had been buried (Zechariah Sitchin, *Stairway to Heaven* 245).

As expected, there was a sarcophagus. It was near the west wall. But, like the chamber itself, the sarcophagus was empty (Robert Bauval and Adrian Gilbert, *The Orion Mystery* 44).

Where was the pharaoh's body?

And where was the treasure?

2. TREASURE

"Do not lay up for yourselves treasures on earth, where moth and rust destroy and where thieves break in and steal; but lay up for yourselves treasures in heaven, where neither moth nor rust destroys and where thieves do not break in and steal.

"For where your treasure is, there your heart will be also."

(Matthew 6:19-21)

Since al-Mamun's time, many others have entered the Great Pyramid—more often than not by way of the forced passage attributed to the caliph—intent on finding treasure of one kind or another. Among them have been a number of Englishmen, including John Greaves, an astronomy professor who in 1638 discovered a shaft that began near the northern wall of the Grand Gallery on the west side (Constable 51 and 54).

This well shaft, as it is now termed, gave the impression of having been drilled vertically into the pyramid's masonry. At a mere 28 inches square (Petrie 88), it was much narrower than either the descending or ascending passages. Nevertheless, Greaves decided to explore the shaft, which had been provided by its builders with footholds and handholds cut into the opposite sides of the walls, which made it possible to climb down—if one was extremely careful—instead of sliding or falling.

After about 60 feet, Greaves came to a small chamber that opened west off the shaft. Known today as the grotto, this chamber was as empty of treasure as the others. The shaft itself continued downwards but Greaves descended only a little farther before giving up because the air was too foul to breathe (Schul and Pettit 29).

Greaves returned to England puzzled, as Peter Tompkins observes, by the pyramid's having been "built around a single chamber [the King's Chamber] with a single empty coffer [a word frequently used for the sarcophagus]" and by "the complexity of its antechamber where the walls changed mysteriously from limestone to granite" (26).

The next Englishman to probe the well shaft was Nathaniel Davison. He had himself lowered by rope for nearly 100 feet below the grotto, but then he could go no farther because of a blockage formed by sand and debris. Davison, however, would not be remembered solely because of his descent into the well, for he detected yet another chamber that had been known about but had never been found.

Noticing a rectangular hole a little more than two feet wide at the top of the Grand Gallery's east wall "where it joins with the south wall at the ceiling" (Lepre 106), he linked together 7 ladders, climbed up, squeezed into the hole and then crawled for 25 feet through bat dung before he entered a compartment that was directly over the King's Chamber. However, whereas the ceiling of the King's Chamber was composed of 9 granite slabs which weighed up to 70 tons, the ceiling of this compartment was composed of 8 slabs. In addition, the maximum height was no more than 4 feet, and there was nothing of real interest to see. Like the rest of the pyramid, this new find contained no statues, no wall reliefs, no paintings, no hieroglyphs, no indication of its purpose, and no treasure (Lawton and Ogilvie-Herald 32-33; Mark Lehner, *The Complete Pyramids* 45; Tompkins 35-36).

After Davison came the French under the leadership of Napoleon Bonaparte, who, along with his army, brought more than 100 civilian scholars to investigate the Great Pyramid. Greaves and Davison had been partially hindered in their exploration by numerous bats; the French fared no better. As a result, they uncovered nothing new in the interior of the pyramid, but on the exterior, after removing piles of sand, stone fragments and other debris at the northeast and northwest corners, they exposed what came to be known as sockets (Schul and Pettit 31).

There were 2 of them. They were rectangular and measured 10 feet by 12 feet and were sunk 20 inches into the limestone pavement that extended out for several feet north of the pyramid. Believing these sockets had been the sites for the original cornerstones, the French used them to measure the structure's base (Tompkins 44).

Further calculations, combined with information from Greek classical texts, convinced Edme-Francois Jomard, one of the brightest of the "savants", that the builders of the pyramid had the necessary astronomical know-how to measure a geographical "degree and thus the true circumference of the earth, and had developed an advanced science of geography and geodesy [the study of the earth's shape and size] which they had immortalized in the geometry of the Great Pyramid" (Tompkins 48).

Jomard and his colleagues were succeeded by Giovanni Battista Caviglia, a Genoese merchant, who managed to unplug the well shaft and in so doing discovered that it ran from the Grand Gallery all the way down to the descending passage, where an opening had been cut into the west wall (Lemesurier 156-57).

The next important discovery inside the pyramid came from another Englishman, Richard Howard Vyse (sometimes spelled Howard-Vyse). Like others before him, Vyse hoped to find additional passages and chambers. In 1837, after 3½ months of employing gunpowder to force a vertical passage above the King's Chamber, he broke through the east wall of 4 more compartments that were stacked above the one that had been discovered by Nathaniel Davison (Lehner 53).

The 2nd compartment, as Tompkins tells us, presented something entirely new and unexpected: "the floor was covered with a thin black powder which when analyzed turned out to be exuviae, or the cast-off shells and skins of insects" (63). No living insects, however, were in evidence.

If Vyse had been surprised by the black powder on the floor of the second compartment, he was probably even more surprised to find in all 4 compartments cartouches and other marks and symbols on the walls, some of them in red, others in black, and some of them upside down (Sitchin, *Stairway to Heaven* 263-270; Lehner 53).

Vyse considered the cartouches, the marks and symbols to have been for the use of the ancient work gangs; he also considered the 5 compartments to have been built in order to relieve stress on the King's Chamber, which had a flat ceiling (Colin Wilson 68).

Of the 4 compartments discovered by Vyse, the first 3 were similar to Davison's in that their height varied from 2 to 4 feet; however, the topmost compartment was 7 feet high, and its ceiling, instead of being flat, was gabled. In addition, this particular ceiling, unlike the others, was composed of limestone rather than granite (Lawton and Ogilvie-Herald 49; Lepre 108-09).

Not satisfied with the success he had enjoyed so far, Vyse had the rubbish that was still piled high in the middle of the Great Pyramid's north face removed and that brought to light 2 of the original casing stones, which were true to descriptions recorded by Herodotus and other classical writers who had seen the pyramid when all the casing stones had been intact. The stones were highly polished and perfectly joined together, their length being 12 feet, their width 8 feet, and their height 5 feet (Tompkins 2-3 and 67; Worth Smith 61).

Certainly one of the most important benefits to be derived from the casing stones as far as future surveyors of the Great Pyramid were concerned was the opportunity to measure their slope, which proved to be 51 degrees, 51 minutes (Lawton and Ogilvie-Herald 55). That information would help to determine that the ancient builders' use of pi was, in the words of Peter Lemesurier, "basic to the whole design" (*The Great Pyramid Decoded* 25).

An examination of the upper courses of the pyramid's exterior revealed that 2 small openings in the King's Chamber, one in the north wall and one in the south, which had been noticed by Greaves but not examined to any extent, ran through the masonry to exit at the 101st course for the northern shaft and at the 102nd course for the southern shaft (Lemesurier 45).

On May 26, 1837, J. R. Hill, a fellow Englishman hired by Vyse, began clearing the southern shaft, which was blocked at its exit point. After using explosives that demolished "two outer tiers of the stones" (and that also left a gaping hole in the south face of the pyramid), Hill detected an iron plate in "an inner joint" in the shaft, which he retrieved, claiming that it could only have been placed there while the pyramid was being built since there was no other opening or joint that would have permitted the insertion of the plate at a later time. Two civil engineers who were also working for Vyse examined the joint where the iron plate had been found and agreed with Hill's assessment; the plate had to have been left there by the original builders (Hancock and Bauval 105).

As described by Graham Hancock and Robert Bauval in *The Message of the Sphinx*, the plate was "one eighth inch thick, a foot long and four inches wide" (102). Its top edge was wavy lengthwise while the bottom edge was notched and hilly in appearance.

It wasn't much to look at, however "rigorous optical and chemical tests" conducted in 1989 revealed "the odd fact that there were 'traces of gold on one face of the iron plate'" (Hancock and Bauval 106).

Here then, at long last, appeared to be treasure.

But—was it treasure of any real value?

3. ASSAYERS

> "The kingdom of heaven is like a merchant seeking beautiful pearls, who, when he had found one pearl of great price, went and sold all that he had and bought it."
>
> (Matthew 13:45-46)

After an expenditure of more than 10,000 pounds, a fortune to the average Englishman of the 19th century, Vyse returned to England in 1840, where he published a two-volume account of his experiences in Egypt (Tompkins 69; Colin Wilson 71). Drawing on this account, and on information in French publications, a Londoner by the name of John Taylor proffered the idea that the ancient Egyptians had been able to determine the circumference of the earth and had known how far it was from the north pole to the center of the earth. These figures, he asserted, were reflected in the Great Pyramid's perimeter and height (Constable 57; Lehner 57).

Altogether, after 30 years of study and contemplation, Taylor was so awed by the Great Pyramid that he could come to no other conclusion than that its builders had been guided by direct revelation from that same God who had guided Noah in the construction of the ark.

Taylor wrote:

> "It is probable that to some human beings in the earliest ages of society, a degree of intellectual power was given

> by the Creator, which raised them far above the level of those succeeding inhabitants of the earth." (Quoted in Tompkins 75)

Despite the amount of time and thought Taylor had put into his study of the Great Pyramid, London's Royal Society rejected his offer to present his ideas to that august body; however, he won over Charles Piazzi Smyth, who at the time was a member of Edinburgh's Royal Society and, as Scotland's Astronomer-Royal, was well respected—until, as C. W. Ceram points out, "he put forward his [own] interpretation of the Great Pyramid" (101; see also Fatma Turkkan vi and Lehner 57).

In November of 1864, "with little [financial] help from anyone," wrote Smyth in the 1880 edition of *Our Inheritance in the Great Pyramid* (reprinted in 1978 under the title *The Great Pyramid: Its Secrets and Mysteries Revealed*), he and his wife traveled to Egypt so he could measure the Great Pyramid himself. His intent was to prove that Taylor's theories were valid (x). Four months of careful measurements left him accepting wholeheartedly Taylor's idea about the pyramid: the builders had undoubtedly been divinely inspired (Mrs. Smyth 651-52).

Taking the matter a step farther, another Scot, Robert Menzies, proposed that the passages in the pyramid provided a chronological record of important events prophesied in the Bible, with each inch being equivalent to one year. However, like Taylor and Smyth, Menzies saw his ideas ridiculed and rejected by his colleagues (Tompkins 93).

In 1881 William Flinders Petrie took up where Smyth had left off. His contributions to the growing body of information about the Great Pyramid included the undeniable certainty that it was in alignment with the four cardinal points of the compass (Bauval and Gilbert 38). Petrie also observed that the walls of the 350 feet of the descending passage were "under ¼ inch" of being absolutely straight (19); that the King's Chamber incorporated the value of pi "and the 3-4-5 Pythagorean triangles"; and that the sarcophagus had been hollowed out of a solid red granite block (Tompkins 101 and 103).

The next Englishman to spend time at the Great Pyramid was David Davidson (not to be confused with Nathaniel Davison). His initial goal was to disprove Robert Menzies' claim that the Great Pyramid was linked to biblical prophecies, but instead of accomplishing that goal he ended up completely reversing his own position. Max Toth and Greg Neilson relate in *Pyramid Power* how Davidson's exploration of the pyramid resulted in his belief that it revealed "ancient Egyptian messianic prophecies, extending possibly until the end of the world" (109).

Robert Ballard, an Australian engineer, found a different reason for the existence of the Great Pyramid, as well as the 2nd and 3rd pyramids on the Giza plateau. Observing all 3 from inside a passing train, his experienced eye told him they could be used "to triangulate the land anywhere within [their] sight" (Tompkins 117).

On the other hand, August Tournquist has written that the Great Pyramid

> is a sundial, a calendar, and an astronomical observatory. At its original height of 481 feet [meaning that would have been the height if the capstone, which is missing, had actually been in place sometime in the past], the pyramid cast a shadow 268 feet long in mid-winter, diminishing almost to zero in the spring, and could be used to mark the hours of the day, the seasons, and the exact length of the year. (Quoted in Charles E. Sellier, *Mysteries of the Ancient World* 166-67)

More recently, Zechariah Sitchin, author of a multi-volume series titled *The Earth Chronicles*, has maintained that the pyramids of Giza anchored a landing corridor for post-Diluvial spacecraft that used the Sinai peninsula as a spaceport (*The Cosmic Code* 208), and Christopher Dunn argues in his 1998 book *The Giza Power Plant* that "the Great Pyramid was a highly sophisticated machine, with a function that was more fantastic than we have, until now, even dared consider" (22). That function, he says, was to respond "sympathetically with the Earth's vibrations" and to convert "that energy into electricity" which was used to power the ancient Egyptians' highly advanced tools and machinery (151).

As unusual as Sitchin's and Dunn's ideas may seem, they have to give way to the most unexpected thesis ever put forward to explain the existence of the pyramids. That thesis comes from Kurt Mendelssohn, author of *The Riddle of the Pyramids*, who declares—and apparently in all sobriety—that the "pyramids of Egypt are immensely large, immensely ancient and, by general consensus, extremely useless" (9). Later in his book, Mendelssohn modifies his stand somewhat by writing:

> They [the pyramids] reflect a sober and essentially practical society whose mind and reactions were eminently sensible and show little sign of devoting much effort to esoteric issues. Building pyramids, as we suggest, for political and economic reasons seems to fit a good deal better into the picture of this level-headed and sophisticated community than devoting prodigious effort in erecting several gigantic tombs to bury one pharaoh. The pyramids do not represent an aim in itself but the means to achieve an aim: the creation of a new form of society. These huge heaps of stone mark the place where man invented the state. (170)

Opposed to such attempts to explain the purpose of the Great Pyramid, as well as being opposed to the beliefs of Piazzi Smyth and others who have become known as pyramidologists, meaning those who see the Great Pyramid as embodying not only an extremely high technology but a religious message as well, are the orthodox Egyptologists, whose basic point of view is expressed by the following quotes.

> **Barbara Mertz**, *Temples, Tombs and Hieroglyphs*: "There is no way out; the Great Pyramid of Giza was a royal tomb, and nothing else" (68).

> **James Putnam**, *Egyptology*: "Despite many fanciful

> theories, these pyramids were simply tombs of the Pharaohs" (20).
>
> **Mark Lehner**, *The Complete Pyramids*: "It is true that the pyramids are pharaonic tombs" (9).
>
> **John and Elizabeth Romer**, *The Seven Wonders of the World*: "[T]he pyramids were indeed built as tombs for kings as every literate citizen of classical antiquity well knew" (166).
>
> **Ian Lawton and Chris Ogilvie-Herald**, *Giza: The Truth*: "[W]e stand by the theory that the Great Pyramid was primarily designed as a tomb for King Khufu" (144).

Invariably, Egyptologists refer to the Great Pyramid as the final resting place for Khufu—or Cheops, the Greek name for this king—who, according to Michael Hayes, reigned from approximately 2561 to 2538 BC (24). Mark Lehner gives the slightly different dates of 2551-2528 BC (*The Complete Pyramids* 8), while *What Life Was Like: On the Banks of the Nile*, edited by Denise Dersin, lists 2606-2580 BC (141). In contrast, James Henry Breasted, an earlier Egyptologist whose Volume I of *Ancient Records of Egypt* was first published in 1906, dated the beginning of Khufu's 23-year reign to 2900 BC (40).

Nevertheless, the Egyptologists find themselves having to admit, as John and Elizabeth Romer do, that the "great stone monuments. . . are complex symbols" (166). The Romers also admit that many Arabs of the Middle Ages

> thought that the pyramids were especially made to measure time, a belief shared by numbers of European astronomers and mathematicians. To some it seemed that the ethereal simplicity of the pyramids was perfect form made concrete, an idea which gave the ancient stones a theological significance. (176)

Regarding the Great Pyramid itself, the Romers understand that "the pyramid's designers were trying to lock their building into heaven" and that the

> design of the pyramid. . . has its own absolute integrities; an extraordinary geometry. Its triangles and squares are held inside a web of mathematical relationships, some of them based on the subtly simple device of the 8:5 triangle, whose angles render right angles and whose numbers are part of the charmed ratio called the Golden Mean. Such careful numeration does not occur by chance. . . . The pyramid makers, then, caught hold of all the absolutes they could, the durability of stone, the power and harmony of numbers and the very stars of heaven, to lock their building into the natural universe. (179)

Mark Lehner, who has spent many years exploring the Giza plateau, expresses his admiration for the accuracy of the Great Pyramid by noting that

> the base is level to within just 2.1 cm (under 1 in[ch]; the average deviation of the sides from the cardinal directions is 3′6″ of arc; and the greatest difference in the length of the sides is 4.4 cm (1¾ in).

After having recorded such remarkable statistics, Lehner raises the obvious question: "Why such phenomenal precision?" Answering his own question, he states: "For the royal designers such exactitude may have been imbued with symbolic and cultic significance that now eludes us" (109).

In other words, what the orthodox Egyptologists and the pyramidologists have in common is their agreement that the Great Pyramid is, in fact, one of the enduring wonders of the world. After all, as James Putnam points out, the pyramid is of such a vast size that it could "hold the cathedrals of Florence, Milan and St Peters in Rome, as well as St Paul's and Westminster Abbey in London" (21).

The Egyptologists and the pyramidologists have something else in common. As will be seen, not one of them can satisfactorily explain the purpose behind every single feature inside the Great Pyramid.

4. DEGREES

"In My Father's house are many mansions; if it were not so, I would have told you."

(John 14:2)

It should be understood that up to this point only a broad view of the Great Pyramid has been presented. There are many other details to be described, and there are also other voices to be heard in addition to those already introduced. The method now will be somewhat the same as in the last chapter; that is, the findings and opinions of former explorers, researchers and authors will be compared and contrasted. However, a new factor will be added: the real purpose for not just some—or even most—of the pyramid's features, but for all that are described.

As indicated in the previous chapters, the pyramid contains 3 main chambers, which for the sake of convenience have been labeled the subterranean chamber, the Queen's Chamber and the King's Chamber. But why 3? If the pyramid was meant to be a tomb for Egypt's pharaoh, wouldn't one chamber, one burial vault, be enough? How do the Egyptologists respond to this question?

> **John Baines and Jaromir Malek**, *The Cultural Atlas of the World: Ancient Egypt*: "The interior of the Great Pyramid. . . shows that the initial plan underwent at least two alterations in the process of the construction" (158).

James Putnam, *Egyptology*: "The design of the interior only appears complicated because the location of the burial chamber was changed twice during its construction" (29).

Mark Lehner: "Many Egyptologists have long accepted [Ludwig] Borchardt's suggestion that the pyramid's three chambers represent two changes in plan, with the abandonment of the Subterranean Chamber, believed to be the original intended burial chamber of the king, and then the Queen's Chamber, in favor of the King's Chamber" (111; Borchardt, with the assistance of J. H. Cole, an engineer, surveyed the Great Pyramid in 1925 [Tompkins 202]).

John and Elizabeth Romer: "The vast labyrinth of rooms in Cheops' pyramid was the result of three changes in the ancient plan for the location of the royal ritual of entombment" (177).

I. E. S. Edwards: "There is no reason to doubt that the abrupt cessation of work on the subterranean chamber of the Great Pyramid was the outcome of the decision to provide a stone sarcophagus for the burial of the king. The chamber was at the end of the Descending Corridor. . . which was neither wide enough nor high enough for the passage of a sarcophagus as large as the one in the Great Pyramid, which was 7 feet 5 inches by 3 feet 3 inches by 3 feet 1 inch, while the level [or horizontal] section of the Descending Corridor was only 2 feet 8 inches wide and 3 feet 1 inch high. Cheops. . . had no choice but to put his substitute burial-chamber in the superstructure. Practical difficulties precluded any alteration in the Descending Corridor (287).

"That the Queen's Chamber never became the

> King's burial-chamber is not open to doubt. . . but the reason for its abandonment is not easily demonstrable" (289).

Despite the tone of authority struck by the Egyptologists, their claims have not gone unchallenged. Paul Brunton, for example, states bluntly:

> No coffin, no body, no funerary appurtenances have ever been found inside the Great Pyramid. . . . No lengthy hieroglyphic inscriptions, no chiselled bas-reliefs or painted representations of the life of the deceased appear upon any of the inner walls of the Pyramid, as they do upon the walls of every other early burial vault in Egypt. The interior structure is plain, devoid of the embellishment which the pharaohs loved to lavish upon their tombs, free from the ornamentation which one might reasonably expect to find were this one of ancient Egypt's most important tombs. (44)

Ron Charles, an engineer and an archaeologist, is in complete agreement with Brunton. Employing the same tone of authority as the Egyptologists, he emphasizes these points:

> "First, we must clearly understand that no bodies have ever been found in any of the Giza pyramids or in any other Egyptian pyramid for that matter. Furthermore, there is no hard evidence anywhere that the pyramids were ever intended as the burial tombs of the pharaoh kings, although the standard argument is that these tomb chambers were robbed of their contents." (Quoted in Sellier 157)

Addressing the same subject, J. P. Lepre, an orthodox Egyptologist and the author of *The Egyptian Pyramids: A Comprehensive, Illustrated Reference*, maintains that "somewhere within these monuments lies the mummy of at least one of these great kings. That much, at least, we can fairly well assume" (288). Lepre then provides details of the mummy remains that have been found in Egypt's pyramids.

Dynasty III: Djoser

A mummified foot.

Dynasty III: Huni

Full skeleton. (Found in a mastaba, not pyramid.)

Dynasty III: Sneferu

A skeleton found in North (Red) Pyramid (possibly a post Dynasty III interment).

Dynasty IV: Menkara

Mummy fragments (likely a Dynasty XXVI interment).

Dynasty V: Unas

Right arm, fragments of skull, other bones.

Dynasty VI: Teti

An arm and a shoulder.

Dynasty VI: Pepy I

Fragments of body.

Dynasty VI: Pepy II

Mummy wrappings only.

Dynasty XII: Amenemhat III

Charred bones.

Lepre follows up these details by commenting:

> Though it seems difficult to believe, this list of mummy remains constitutes all that has ever been found of the pyramid pharaohs. . . .
>
> This record is truly amazing when one takes into account the fact that each of the pyramid pharaohs was undoubtedly interred with numerous possessions, including the wooden and gold coffins and gold funerary mask [similar to those found in the tomb of Tutankhamen]. (288)

One obvious objection to the theory that a pharaoh was buried in the King's Chamber in the Great Pyramid with his kingly treasure, which was supposedly later removed by tomb robbers, is raised by Graham Hancock in *Fingerprints of the Gods.* Hancock assures us that

> *nothing* was found inside Khufu's Pyramid, making this and the alleged looting of Khafre's monument [i.e. the 2nd major pyramid on the Giza plateau] the only tomb robberies in the history of Egypt which achieved a clean sweep, leaving not a single trace behind—not a torn cloth, not a shard of broken pottery, not an unwanted figurine, not an overlooked piece of jewellery—just the bare floors and walls and the gaping mouths of empty sarcophagi. (301; Hancock's italics)

As for Edwards' claim that the subterranean chamber was abandoned because the sarcophagus was too large and "[p]ractical difficulties precluded any alteration in the Descending Corridor", by which he means the corridor could not have been enlarged to allow the passage of the sarcophagus, a number of questions need to be asked regarding this supposition.

To begin with, what "practical difficulties" does Edwards have in mind? The evidence clearly indicates that the builders of the Great Pyramid had the means, the technology, to alter the descending passage to any size they desired—or they could have simply made the passage larger to begin with. So why didn't they?

Anyone who has assisted in carrying a casket with the dead weight of an adult male inside knows that it is an awkward affair even on level ground, and yet we're supposed to believe that the ancient Egyptians initially planned on carrying their dead king in a casket down a 26-degree slope that was no more than 4 feet high and no more than 3½ feet wide and that ran for 350 feet (for comparison, an American football field is 300 feet, or 100 yards), and then they would have had to go another 29 feet down a horizontal passage that was even narrower than the descending passage before they would have finally reached the burial chamber.

Just how was this to have been accomplished when there would have been room for only one pall bearer at each end of the casket and no room for pall bearers at the sides? Yes, more pall bearers could have lined up either in front of or behind the first two, but these other pall bearers would have been able to help only if ropes had been used. And ropes would have certainly been required in order to keep the casket from running away from the pall bearers if the original floor of the descending passage was smooth. Quite obviously, achieving any dignity or decorum in transporting the king to his final resting place would have been impossible.

What purpose would have been served by such a ludicrous arrangement? And what would have "precluded any alteration" in the sarcophagus itself? What was so important about its dimensions that another sarcophagus could not have been made, especially one that was not from a solid block of stone but prepared instead in 5 different sections that could have been carried down separately to the subterranean chamber? Do the Egyptologists have an answer for this particular question? No, they do not, nor do they ever bring it up themselves.

True, Richard H. Wilkinson does have a chapter on "the symbolism of Numbers" in his book *Symbol & Magic in Egyptian Art*, however, he tries to persuade us that

> Egyptian mathematics lacked even some of the most basic aspects of mathematical understanding. . . . A telling example is found in the many numerological studies of the pyramids, and especially the Great Pyramid of Khufu or Cheops, which has been claimed to show in its dimensions the whole history of the world, past, present, and future. This pyramid does reveal a relatively high level of mathematical competence coupled with careful astronomical observation on the part of its ancient engineers, and these factors are clearly seen in the construction and orientation. . . of the structure —but they should not be exaggerated into claims of advanced Egyptian understanding of astronomy or of important mathematical constants. (126-27)

Lawton and Ogilvie-Herald exhibit the same frame of mind when they write:

> If all the numbers regarded as "significant" by Tompkins. . . et al. [and others] were listed, we would probably have every integer between 0 and 9, and a whole array of other non-whole numbers in between. We are aware that the interplay between and symbolism of, for example, harmonics and geometry is something that has exercised a profound influence on great minds in all civilisations ancient and modern, but this hand is repeatedly and monotonously overplayed. . . .
>
> In summary. . . the primary function of all the monuments was a funerary one—albeit interwoven with much symbolism and ritual. (154)

As a result of the stance that Egyptologists take toward number symbolism not one of them makes the slightest attempt to explain why the ancient Egyptians chose to make the descending passage 3½ feet wide, 4 feet high and 350 feet long or why the sarcophagus was crafted to its particular dimensions.

The pyramidologists, as we have seen, equate each inch of the limestone passages within the Great Pyramid with the passage of one year, but what do they have to say about the pyramid's 3 main chambers?

> **Worth Smith**: The subterranean chamber is "the Pit of Chaos, or Gehenna. Gehenna is that condition of utter destruction, of death from which there is no awakening. . . . One may now understand the known loathsomeness of the Pit. . . its state of absolute darkness, its lack of all ventilation, its dampness and vermin, its fetid odors and other abominations" (100).
>
> "The Queen's Chamber. . . typifies the fate of the Jews. . . . [T]hose who did not accept their Messiah are 'bottled up' within the Chamber. If they should emerge, and in the end *they shall*, they can climb no higher without passing thru [sic] the Grand Gallery. . . . " The Queen's Chamber is also "on the 'Plane of Human Perfection', as it will be at the end of the Millennial Age of Christ's reign of one thousand years of peace on earth" (108-110).
>
> "The King's Chamber is termed. . . 'The Chamber of the Millennial Age', 'The Chamber of Spirit Rebirth' and 'The Chamber of Immortality'. It is also the 'Chamber of the Mystery of the Open Tomb'" (147).
>
> **Adam Rutherford**: "The Subterranean Chamber with its 'bottomless pit' is exceedingly rough and tumble and has no proper floor. It is a chamber of chaos, the Pyramid's 'Chamber of Horrors' and clearly symbolises the smashing, and finally the ultimate destruction in the pit, of the World Order, with all the accompanying

chaos. . . . But the Subterranean Chamber symbolises much more. . . ; it depicts the utter end and throwing down into the pit all institutions—social, civil and ecclesiastical—that are out of harmony with God and His righteousness, and the total abolition of all erroneous scientific theories and false religious beliefs and everything that deceives or misleads humanity" (Book I, 133).

"According to a hitherto widely-held theory," the Queen's Chamber "is supposed to represent a waiting place for the Jews. In view of the fact that there is no exit from the Queen's Chamber to a final apartment beyond it, and that the Queen's Chamber itself constitutes a finality, how can it represent a mere waiting place for the Jews or for anybody else? The King's Chamber and the Queen's Chamber are the two finalities of the Pyramid's interior, and therefore they symbolise destinies. . . of everlasting life, life in its fulness with no death conditions involved—[in other words,] perfection" (Book I, 65).

Tom Valentine: "Every Ego, or Ka as the Egyptians called the discrete bundle of mental energy that makes up a person, descends into incarnation from another plane. . . .

"Those souls or Egos that do not make the struggle to grow upward through the gate of ascent will continue to descend in darkness. . . until finally they reach the 'chamber of upside downness,' the chamber of 'chaos'. There are false indications that lead one to believe there is another way out, but these routes lead nowhere. The Ego in this chamber of chaos has no choice but to die in darkness, or climb all the way back up to the Gate of Ascent and make the struggle. All is not lost when one dies in 'unknowingness' because he will be incarnated again, and again, and again so that he may choose to elevate—the choice must be his own" (quoted in Noone 228).

In "the 'Chamber of New Birth', or 'Second birth' [i.e., the Queen's Chamber]. . . you may take stock of all you have learned during your ascent in darkness, and there will be a realization of what you are struggling toward—new awareness of consciousness of the purpose of all the effort. You will be filled with joy and new resolve to continue the ascent toward the Creator" (quoted in Noone 229).

"Once inside the Hall of Judgment [the King's Chamber], you are initiated into what must be a grand club of joyous, evolved Egoes. You have earned, by your own efforts, this lofty position. At the far end of the chamber sits a huge, empty sarcophagus that signifies that the mystery we call death is no longer. The tomb is open, you are immortal" (quoted in Noone 230).

Peter Lemesurier: "The Great Subterranean Chamber [as distinguished from the "Lesser Subterranean Chamber", which will be discussed later]. . . seems to be cognate with the so-called *Book of the Dead*'s Chamber of Ordeal or Chamber of Central Fire" (134).

The "Subterranean Chamber's Pit is a direct function of the enlightenment of those who experience it. But one can read its overall depth from the Chamber's roof in a downward *or* an upward direction. Thus, falling (downwards) into the Pit from the level of the Plane of Death [which begins with the subterranean chamber's ceiling] must clearly be connected with loss of enlightenment; while climbing (upwards) out of it again to roof-level (surmounting the Plane of Death) must, by the same token, be reflected in a regaining of enlightenment" (142). The pit then "is not final, but has an essentially redemptive function" (143).

"The Great Subterranean Chamber in particular must. . . represent none other than our present age, with all its ups and downs and the warning of a 'bottomless pit' to come" (146).

The "Queen's Chamber represents a chamber of life. And indeed, this is no more than one would expect. The chambers of death of the other pyramids all lie at or below ground level and are approached by downward sloping passages—and for this reason we may well regard the Great Pyramid's own Subterranean Chamber as one such. But the two upper chambers of the Great Pyramid both lie—uniquely —well *above* ground, and are approached by *upward*-sloping passages. It is no more than logical, then, that they, by contrast, should be seen as representing chambers of life" (85).

"Escape [meaning escape from the physical world and its imperfections in order to achieve spiritual perfection] from the Queen's Chamber may. . . lead directly. . . to entry into the King's Chamber.

"Yet the roughly-finished Queen's Chamber floor, contiguous with the base both of the. . . 25th course of masonry, as well as with the top of the 24th course, makes it clear that escape depends upon a return to earth [after death] and a re-learning and re-application of the Messianic teachings."

[As is evident from the preceding comments, Lemesurier, in his treatment of the Great Pyramid, brings into play not just Christianity but "the teachings of Hinduism and Buddhism on the subject of reincarnation and the law of *karma*" as well (29).]

The "King's Chamber floor, which tops the 50th course of masonry. . . presumably signifies the Messianic Millennium" (86).

The "ancient Egyptian *Book of the Dead* seems quite clearly to identify the King's Chamber as the Chamber of the Open Tomb—as though that had always been its intended symbolic function, and the coffer had thus always been empty. . . . "

The "passage-system speaks to us of one who, at death, has succeeded in passing up the Ascending Passage, in entering the King's Chamber and—the upward path having been finally sealed behind him—in 'breaking open' the coffer, escaping from the tomb and thereupon achieving full union with the Divine" (200).

Richard W. Noone: The King's Chamber is "Egypt's oldest temple, the *sanctum sanctorum* [that is, the innermost shrine, the Holy of Holies]" (38).

"In the center of the granite slab [which is identified as the "Granite Leaf" in the antechamber] there is an embossed marker. Measuring from this marker to the granite box [the sarcophagus] in the King's Chamber marks the date of 5 May of the year 2000, a date when. . . [it is believed] a cataclysm of massive earthquakes and *tsunamis* [huge waves]. . . will destroy much of our present civilization" (239).

Unfortunately for Noone's theory, the date of 5 May 2000 came and went without the great destruction he had predicted based on his interpretation of the antechamber and the King's Chamber. Noone, by the way, in contrast to other pyramidologists such as Rutherford, who proclaimed in Book III of *Pyramidology* that inside "the Pyramid, granite never has chronological significance" since it "always has to do with the Divine, the Infinite, the Immortal" (961), decided to ignore such an arbitrary restriction and so assigned dates to those parts of the pyramid where granite was used. At the same time, it should be noted that Rutherford's prediction that "Christ's Millennial Reign is due to be inaugurated in 1979" (Book I, 215) did not come true either.

Paul Brunton deals with other predictions made by pyramidologists that have not fared any better.

> Piazzi Smyth himself gave the date of 1881 as the year of the millennium. One remembers, too, that May, 1928, was for long given by this school as the most fateful month in world history, but it passed uneventfully. The most fateful month was then transferred to September, 1936, which, we were told, had really been indicated by the Pyramid's dimensions. Nevertheless, neither Armageddon nor the Millennium was to be seen on that day. Thereupon the date was altered to August 10, 1953. Once again the prediction proved incorrect. (43)

Turning to those who favor alternate theories regarding the Great Pyramid's three main chambers, Zechariah Sitchin has maintained that they housed "guidance and communications equipment" as auxiliary components of a spaceport that once existed in the Sinai peninsula (*Stairway to Heaven* 288).

Christopher Dunn takes a different tack. Since in his view the Great Pyramid was a power plant, he suggests that the Queen's Chamber was utilized to produce fuel for the King's Chamber, which was the pyramid's power center, while the "equipment that provided the priming pulses was most likely housed in the Subterranean Pit ["Pit" referring to the chamber, not the pit in the floor]" (219-20).

Anyone familiar with the subterranean chamber knows that it was not designed to house even the simplest of machinery, much less sophisticated space-age "guidance and communications equipment". Consider, for example, that not only is the floor rough and "extremely irregular" with the western half resembling "rugged rock formations on a mountain side" while the floor of the eastern half is treacherous because of a "rugged, dangerous hollow 3 to 5 feet deep extending between the east corner of the Pit and the east wall of the Chamber" (Rutherford, Book III, 1084 and 1089), but, again, if the original intention had been to use the subterranean chamber in the manner Sitchin and Dunn suggest, why were the passages made so user-unfriendly and how would such advanced equipment have been transported down to the chamber?

Moreover, how does the vertical pit in the eastern floor or the dead-end passage figure into their schemes? And, to look at the larger picture, why would the shape of a pyramid—and especially one as massive as the Great Pyramid—have been chosen over a square or rectangular design for either an auxiliary unit in a spaceport system or for a power plant? Both Sitchin and Dunn fail to answer such practical questions.

In an update written for a 1990 reprint of William Flinders Petrie's *Pyramids and Temples of Gizeh*, Zahi Hawass, at that time the Director General of the Giza plateau, made the following significant statement:

> [Ludwig] Borchardt saw the three different chambers as an indication of two changes in planning the location of the king's burial place. However, that line of thinking has been altered by later observations that tend to connect a religious motivation to the structural anomalies of the burial chambers inside the Great Pyramid. Thereby, it may be concluded that the physical structure would reflect the dictates of a religious revolution. (99)

While Hawass's belief that the chambers were meant to be sepulchers is as incorrect as all the other Egyptologists, his assigning "a religious motivation to the structural anomalies. . . of the Great Pyramid", as well as his remark that the pyramid reflects "the dictates of a religious revolution", is on target, for the correct meaning of the 3 main chambers in the Great Pyramid can be found in the Bible, in the New Testament.

In the 15th chapter of First Corinthians, Paul the Apostle, who was writing to members of the Church of Jesus Christ in Corinth, Greece, set out to convince those who had come to doubt the reality of the resurrection that Christ had in fact been resurrected. Paul stresses that

> Christ is risen from the dead, and has become the firstfruits of those who have fallen asleep [meaning Christ was the first to be resurrected out of all the people who had lived and died before him; anyone who had been brought back to life previously by Christ or by one of the prophets had not been resurrected but instead had been restored to mortality and would later die again]. (15:20)

In verses 21 and 22 Paul tells the members of the church that because of Adam's transgression in the Garden of Eden all mankind had become subject to death, but because of Christ's resurrection, all mankind would be resurrected—but not all at the same time. Everyone, Paul advises, would be resurrected

> in his own order: Christ the firstfruits, afterward those who are Christ's at His coming [in other words, members of the church who had continued faithful throughout their lives].
>
> Then comes the end, when He delivers the kingdom to God the Father, when he puts an end to all rule and all authority and power. (15:23-24)

In verse 35 of Chapter 15 Paul asks a key question:

> And with what body do they [who are resurrected] come?

Elaborating on Christ's statement in John 14:2 that in his Father's house are many mansions, Paul answers his own question in verses 39-42.

> All flesh is not the same flesh. . . .
>
> There are. . . celestial bodies and terrestrial bodies; but the glory of the celestial is one, and the glory of the terrestrial is another.
>
> There is one glory of the sun, another glory of the moon, and another glory of the stars; for [Paul's meaning would be better understood if *and*, or perhaps *however*, was used instead of *for*] one star differs from another star in glory.

What Paul is describing in these last verses is the broad division that will occur when the various stages of resurrecting the dead have been completed. The first resurrection began when Christ rose from Joseph of Arimathea's tomb. We are informed in Matthew 27:52 and 53 that the

> graves were opened; and many bodies of the saints who had fallen asleep were raised; and coming out of the graves after His resurrection, they went into the holy city and appeared to many.

However, the majority of mankind will not be resurrected until the end of the millennium, the thousand years of peace that will follow the culmination of what is known as the last days, and that culmination will be marked by Christ's second coming.

Paul, then, is indicating that while everyone will eventually be resurrected not everyone will have the same kind of body, not everyone will receive the same reward. There are 3 degrees of glory in the mansions or kingdoms of God, and to make plain their differences Paul compares these 3 degrees to the sun, the moon—which reflects the light of the sun—and the stars, and just as some stars are brighter than others, so will it be with the men and women who share the lowest degree of glory.

The builders of the pyramids of Giza knew about the 3 degrees of glory 3,000 years before Paul was born—and they learned from the same source. And they graphically depicted those 3 degrees in the 3 main chambers inside the Great Pyramid.

With this new understanding, we can see that the subterranean chamber was not left unfinished as claimed by Egyptologists. It was not abandoned in favor of building a burial chamber within the pyramid's masonry, nor does it represent a chamber of chaos. It represents instead the lowest of the 3 degrees of glory. It was constructed on purpose to appear as a desolate wasteland with barren boulders and a narrow chasm and a rugged, uneven landscape to let us know that the lowest kingdom of heaven is not a desirable place to be.

Many researchers have wondered why in the south wall of the subterranean chamber the 30-inch square passage leads nowhere; it simply comes to an end after 53 feet. Lepre describes this passage as being "snakelike" and "tortuous" while at the same time "the cutting through the natural rock is anything but crude, and displays the indelible mark of the ancient quarriers." In other words, Lepre is saying that this passage was not created by "tomb plunderers", and therefore its purpose is "somewhat perplexing" (114-116).

When we realize that the end of this particular passage marks the farthest point away from the entrance to the pyramid it becomes clear that it was constructed to represent the "outer darkness" where Christ said there would be weeping and gnashing of teeth (see Matthew 8:12, 22:13 and 25:30); it also represents the fact that the lowest kingdom is a dead end. What better way to make the point?

What we also need to realize is that after the final resurrection, after the final judgment of everyone who has ever lived on the earth, the people who find themselves in the lowest kingdom will discover they have lost much of their freedom—and that is what the narrow, low-ceilinged passages inside the Great Pyramid represent. They will also learn that they are to be confined to one place and only one place, and that place will not be on the earth. In addition, they will not be reincarnated; they will not be able to advance to a higher kingdom; they will not escape.

Who will be consigned to this lowest degree of glory? What kind of people will they be? Christ identifies some of them for us. In Matthew 22:1-14 the man "who did not have on a wedding garment" represents those who fail to meet the requirements for a higher degree of glory; in Matthew 24:45-51 the "evil servant" who beats "his fellow servants, and" eats and drinks "with the drunkards" is a type for anyone who abuses others and commits self-destruction through dissipation, and as a result will be appointed "his portion with the hypocrites"; in Matthew 25:30 the "unprofitable servant" is typical of people who do not improve on whatever "talents" they are given.

In First Corinthians Chapter 6, verses 9-10, Paul provides a list of others who will be in the lowest degree of glory. This list includes those who engage in fornication, adultery, idolatry, thievery and extortion—in short, those who are unrighteous, disobedient, unwilling to keep the commandments of God, and who are unrepentant.

Such people will reap what they sow during mortality; nevertheless, they will still be heirs of salvation—salvation, but not exaltation. There is a clear distinction between the two, just as there is a clear distinction between the brightness of the stars and the brightness of the sun as seen from the earth.

The pit that is sunk in the floor of the subterranean chamber represents the prison where Satan and his army of evil will be confined during the millennium; however, "when the thousand years have expired, Satan will be released from his prison and will go out to deceive the nations which are in the four corners of the earth" (Revelation 20:1-3 and 7).

The pit also represents the fate of those mortals who sink so far into depravity that they can no longer feel sorrow for what they have done and, because they will have gone beyond the point of redemption, they will become sons of perdition. They, along with Satan, will be bound by "chains of darkness" (2 Peter 2:4; see also Matthew 6:23 and 1 Timothy 6:9).

Like the subterranean chamber, the Queen's Chamber has been judged as unfinished, abandoned, but also like the subterranean chamber it was not. This chamber's rough floor and rough salt-encrusted walls were designed that way in order to represent the 2nd degree of glory—the terrestrial kingdom—which glory is comparable to the moon. While this kingdom is far more desirable than the lowest kingdom, it is not representative of human perfection as Worth Smith and Adam Rutherford thought, nor is it a "Chamber of New Birth" or "Second birth". And those in the terrestrial kingdom will not be permitted to advance any higher; they will, however, enjoy more freedom than the people in the lowest kingdom.

Who will inherit this 2nd degree of glory? A source other than the Bible provides a detailed answer, but it will not be presented at this time; it will, however, be discussed in an upcoming chapter.

The King's Chamber does not signify the "Messianic Millennium", as Peter Lemesurier suggests, neither does it indicate a particular date in the near future; it is rather a representation of the 3rd and highest degree of glory—the celestial glory—which is comparable to the sun and to the glory of God, and that is why, unlike the Queen's Chamber and the subterranean chamber, it was constructed entirely of granite.

The King's Chamber is, then, a representation of not just salvation but of exaltation, which is what Christ's teachings are designed to accomplish.

This subject will be explored in more detail in later pages, but for now another subject needs to be broached. That subject is the builders themselves. Who was responsible for the construction of the pyramids of Giza? Who knew about the 3 degrees of glory before the time of Paul?

And who was their teacher?

5. SEERS

> "To you it has been given to know the mysteries of the kingdom of God, but to the rest it is given in parables, that 'Seeing they may not see,
> And hearing they may not understand.'"
>
> (Luke 8:10)

Mark Lehner mentions a Coptic legend that speaks of a certain king by the name of Surid "who lived three centuries before the flood. His dreams foretold future chaos and only those who joined the Lord of the Boat would escape." In Lehner's judgment this "tale is a blend of both the Judeo-Christian story of the flood and ancient Egyptian themes" (40).

Peter Tompkins adds a little more to the legend, noting that

> Arab historians such as Ibrahim ben Wasuff Shah say that the Giza pyramids were built by an antediluvian [pre-flood] king called Surid or Saurid, who saw in a dream a huge planet falling to earth at the time when "the heart of the Lion would reach the first minute of the head of Cancer."

Two paragraphs later Tompkins refers to the writings of Ibn-batuta, who,

> writing 730 years after the Hegira [about 1352 AD],

> says that Hermes Trismegistos (*the Hebrew Enoch*), "having ascertained from the appearance of the stars that the deluge would take place, built the pyramids to contain books of science and knowledge and other matters worth preserving from oblivion and ruin." (218; italics added)

Exploring the same subject, Erich von Daniken quotes from another Arabian source, the *Khitat*, written by the historian al-Maqrizi in the 15th century:

> There are people who say: the first Hermes, who was called the "triune" because of his function as prophet, king, and wise man (he is the one whom the Hebrews call Enoch, the son of Jared, the son of Mahal'aleel, the son of Ca-i'nan, the son of Enos, the son of Seth, the son of Adam—blessed be his [i.e., Hermes'] soul—and that [Hermes, who is also known as] Idris), read in the stars that the Flood was about to come. So he had the pyramids built and had hidden inside them treasures, learned writings, and all those things which he feared might get lost or disappear, so that they would be protected and well preserved. (214-215)

Ian Richard Netton's *A Popular Dictionary of Islam* contains this entry for "Idris":

> A figure whose name occurs twice in the **Qur'an**. In Surat Maryam. . . he is called a prophet and bears the epithet "true" (*siddiq*), while in Surat al-Anbiya'. . . he is described as patient and righteous. A considerable amount of legend has grown up round his name. Most often Idris is identified with Enoch. (116-117)

The book of Genesis in the Old Testament devotes these few verses to Enoch:

> Jared lived one hundred and sixty-two years, and begot Enoch. (5:18)
>
> Enoch lived sixty-five years, and begot Methuselah.
>
> After he begot Methuselah, Enoch walked with God three hundred years, and had sons and daughters.
>
> So all the days of Enoch were three hundred and sixty-five years.
>
> And Enoch walked with God; and he was not, for God took him. (5:21-24)

The perceptive reader should be struck by the repetition of a key phrase in this extremely brief account: "Enoch walked with God". But what does that mean, to walk with God? *A Commentary on the Holy Bible*, edited by Reverend J. R. Dummelow, gives this explanation:

> [Enoch's] conduct is mentioned in a way which implies that the majority of men lived differently. In all his actions he recognized the duty which he owed to God; from none of his thoughts was God absent; he lived in communion with him. . . . In Jewish tradition Enoch's walking with God was taken to mean initiation into the mysteries of the universe, and the secrets of the past and future. (13)

The expression in Genesis that "God took" Enoch is expounded on in the New Testament:

> By faith Enoch was taken away so that he did not see death, "*and was not found, because God had taken him*", for before he was taken he had this testimony, that he pleased God. (Hebrews 11:5)

One more direct reference to Enoch is recorded in the New Testament in the general epistle of Jude. In the first 13 verses the author identifies himself as a "bondservant of Jesus Christ, and brother of James", who had found it necessary to exhort the members of the church "to contend earnestly for the faith" in the face of opposition from ungodly men. Jude then reminds the members that in times past God punished the wicked and he uses Sodom and Gomorrah, where the inhabitants gave "themselves over to sexual immorality", as an example. As for the evil-minded men of his own time, Jude says in verses 14 and 15:

> Now Enoch, the seventh from Adam, prophesied about these men also, saying, "Behold, the Lord comes with ten thousands of His saints, to execute judgment on all, to convict all who are ungodly among them of all their ungodly deeds which they have committed in an ungodly way, and of all the harsh things which ungodly sinners have spoken against him."

We learn from James C. VanderKam's book, *Enoch: A Man for All Generations*, that Jude's epistle drew on Genesis, Exodus, Numbers, and a source known today as *1 Enoch* (171), which is also referred to as the *Ethiopic Book of Enoch* because it was in Ethiopia that this work was "included in the canon of the Old Testament" (Samuel Terrien, "Books of Enoch" 394).

Fragments of *1 Enoch* were among the scrolls discovered in cave number 4 near Khirbet Qumran in 1952. Lawrence H. Schiffman summarizes the contents of *1 Enoch* in *Reclaiming the Dead Sea Scrolls*:

> Generally, 1 Enoch is understood to have five parts. The first, the Book of the Watchers, portrays the End of Days and the final Judgment, and it relates the story of the fallen angels [which are mentioned in the 6th verse of Jude] and various visions of Enoch. The second, the Parables (or similitudes), deals with the coming

> Judgment, the son of man (taken by many scholars to be the agent of God's salvation in the End of Days), paradise, resurrection, and the punishment of the fallen angels. The third, the Book of Astronomical Writings, is a treatise dealing with the reckoning of time by a solar calendar of 364 days, a calendar virtually identical to that advocated by the Qumran sect. The fourth, the Book of Dream Visions, includes visions of the future (from Enoch's perspective) of the world, Israel, and the Flood, up to the coming of the messiah. The fifth part, the Epistle of Enoch, is a testament discussing the blessedness of the righteous and the punishment of sinners. (182)

The Ethiopic version of *1 Enoch* first became available in Europe in the 18th century. Another book bearing Enoch's name, the *Book of the Secrets of Enoch* or *II Enoch*, was brought to the attention of scholars in 1896 when William Richard Morfill introduced his English translation of the Slavonic manuscript (Terrien, "Books of Enoch" 395). In this narrative Enoch, escorted by two angels, ascends to the 10th heaven where he comes face to face with the Lord. The Lord instructs Michael the archangel to

> "Go and take Enoch from out his earthly garments, and anoint him with my sweet ointments, and put him into the garments of My glory." (Rutherford H. Platt, Jr., *The Book of the Secrets of Enoch* XXII:8)

Afterwards Enoch is permitted to see the books from the Lord's storehouses and then, under the tutelage of another angel, Pravuil, he learns that the souls of all mankind have had places prepared for their eternal inheritance "before the formation of the world." Pravuil directs Enoch to record that fact, as well as the lives of everyone destined to be born on the earth (XXIII:2).

In chapter XXXIII the Lord tells Enoch to return to the earth and inform his sons of all that he has learned; Enoch is also to turn over the books that he has written so his descendants can pass them on from one generation to the next. Further, Enoch is given the writings of his fathers, the former six patriarchs: Adam, Seth, Enos, Cainan, Mahalaleel, and Enoch's own father, Jared (verses 7, 10-11).

In chapter XXXIV Enoch is told of the deluge that the Lord is going to bring "upon the earth [which] will destroy all men, and the whole earth will crumble together into great darkness" because the people have rejected the Lord's commandments and are worshipping idols and "have laden the whole earth with untruths, offences, abominable lecheries, namely one with another, and all manner of other unclean wickedness" (verses 1-2).

Enoch is obedient to the Lord's wishes and upon returning to earth counsels his sons regarding "all that. . . was and all that is now, and all that will be till judgment-day" (XXXIX:2). In the first verse of chapter XL Enoch repeats that he knows "all things", having received that knowledge directly from the "Lord's lips, and this my eyes have seen, from beginning to end."

In the 3rd verse Enoch says, "I have measured and described the stars, the great multitude *of them*."

In verse 9 he reveals that he has

> measured out the whole earth, its mountains, and all hills, fields, trees, stones, rivers, all existing things I wrote down, the height from the seventh heaven, and downwards to the very lowest hell, and the judgement-place, and the very great, open and weeping hell.

In verse 10 he adds,

> And I saw how the prisoners are in pain, expecting the limitless judgement.

In chapter XLIX, verses 4 and 5, Enoch repeats the former declaration of Pravuil, assuring his sons that all men before they were born in the flesh had a place prepared for the[ir] repose. . . .

> Yea, children, deceive not yourselves, for there has been previously prepared a place for every soul of man.

As if to make certain his sons have gotten the message, Enoch says once more in chapter LIII, verse 2:

> You see how I wrote all works of every man, before his creation, *all* that is done amongst all men for all time.

But even then Enoch is not finished. He states in the first verse of chapter LXI:

> And now, my children. . . I know all things, how in the great time [to come] are many mansions prepared for men, good for the good, and bad for the bad, without number many.

In his final comments to his sons, Enoch advises them to

> Walk. . . in long-suffering, in meekness, honesty. . . in faith and in truth. . . loving one another, till you go out from this age of ills, that you become inheritors of endless time. (LXVI:7)

It can be seen from this brief summary and review of *1 Enoch* and the *Book of the Secrets of Enoch* that both have a Christian bent, even though Theodore H. Gastor in his article titled "Books of Enoch", which was written for the 1998 edition of *The Encyclopedia Americana*, specifies that the various sections of the Ethiopic version of *1 Enoch* are generally dated between 170 and 80 BC (472-473), and the introduction to the *Book of the Secrets of Enoch* states that it "was written somewhere about the *beginning* of the Christian era" (Platt, Jr. 81; italics added).

In fact, there is so much Christian doctrine in the *Secrets of Enoch* that Charles Francis Potter was compelled to ask whether or not Jesus was its author. Says Potter:

> Many of the words and phrases in this anonymous Secrets of Enoch are remarkably like the ones Jesus used, as recorded in the four Gospels of the New Testament. Even whole sentences from the book appear in his parables, beatitudes and discussions. (28)

Citing Enoch's use of the phrase "many mansions", Potter observes that the statement by Jesus in John 14:2 now becomes clear; Jesus was saying in effect:

> "Heaven is where my Father lives. In the future time when you go there you will find many mansions, and I am going there ahead of you to prepare a good place for you."

Potter then argues that changing John 14:2 to read "many rooms" instead of "many mansions", as occurs in some translations,

> does violence to the Greek text and rather belittles heaven. The Greek words seem to convey the idea, well expressed in The Secrets of Enoch, of a large settlement—a colony or community of many dwellings. (29)

Commenting on the Dead Sea Scrolls, Potter emphasizes that in

> Cave 4 alone, portions of ten different manuscripts of Enoch were found, each differing in some respects from the others, and from the Ethiopic and Slavonic Enochs. In several of the many caves, other fragments were found, to say nothing of the many apocryphal booklets ["apocryphal" meaning definite authorship is unknown] evidently based on and elaborating the older Enochan books.
>
> The body of Enochan and semi-Enochan literature corroborates what was hitherto suspected by a few

> scholars working in the field of the pseudepigrapha [writings attributed to biblical authors but probably not written by them]: that there were numerous books of Enoch. . . . The Qumran discoveries point to the fact that the so-called Ethiopic Enoch. . . and the Slavonic Enoch are only evidence of a once vast Enochan literature. (54)

Potter's assessment is confirmed by Hugh Nibley, who writes in *Enoch the Prophet* that the 7th patriarch of the Old Testament is

> the colossus who bestrides the Apocrypha as no other. Everywhere we catch glimpses of him. He is identified with more other great characters than any figure of the past. He is the most mysterious, individual, and unique of characters, yet he is the most universal type of them all. (19)

A source that is almost never tapped by those who expatiate on Enoch—and that includes James C. VanderKam and Charles Francis Potter—may help further explain why this prophet became, in Jesus ben Sirach's judgment, "a miracle of knowledge to all generations" (quoted in Terrien, "Enoch" 392). That source, "The Book of Moses", is part of a compilation titled *The Pearl of Great Price.* "The Book of Moses" concentrates first on Moses himself and relates his face-to-face encounter with God at a time "when Moses was caught up into an exceedingly high mountain" (1:1).

Moses, like Enoch before him, is first shown the earth and its inhabitants,

> and there was not a soul which he beheld not; and he discerned them by the Spirit of God; and their numbers were great, even numberless as the sand upon the sea shore. (1:27-28)

After this vision God tells Moses,

> worlds without number have I created. . . and by the Son I created them, which is mine Only Begotten. (1:33)
>
> And as one earth shall pass away, and the heavens thereof even so shall another come; and there is no end to my works. . . .
>
> For behold, this is my work and my glory—to bring to pass the immortality and eternal life of man.
>
> And now, Moses, my son. . . thou shalt write the things which I shall speak. (1:38-40)

Moses is then given an account of the creation of the earth and of man. In Chapter 3 God reveals the fact that all things were created "spiritually before they were naturally upon the face of the earth", and that spiritual creation included "the children of men", who were created in heaven as spirits (verse 5).

Central to this account of man's beginnings on the earth is the role of Satan. In the pre-earthly existence, Satan had offered to redeem all mankind so that not one person would be lost—but he would have accomplished that goal by taking away man's agency, which meant man's freedom to act for himself, to make his own choices, be they good or bad, righteous or evil. Satan was rejected and cast down to the earth, condemned to remain a spirit without a physical body (4:1-4).

In Chapter 6, verses 5 and 6, Moses learns that before the flood "a book of remembrance was kept, in the which was recorded. . . the language of Adam"; he also learns that "children were taught to read and write, having a language which was pure and undefiled."

Enoch makes his appearance in this same chapter, following a genealogy which includes his father, who "taught Enoch in all the ways of God" (verse 21). Two verses later, the narrative has Enoch journeying "in the land, among the people", at which time

> the Spirit of God descended out of heaven, and abode upon him.

> And he heard a voice from heaven, saying: Enoch, my son, prophesy unto this people, and say unto them—Repent, for thus saith the Lord: I am angry with this people, and my fierce anger is kindled against them; for their hearts have waxed hard and their ears are dull of hearing, and their eyes cannot see afar off;
>
> And for these many generations, ever since the day that I created them, have they gone astray, and have denied me, and have sought their own counsels in the dark; and in their own abominations have they devised murder, and have not kept the commandments, which I gave unto their father, Adam.
>
> Wherefore, they have foresworn themselves [that is, they have sworn falsely and have made themselves guilty of perjury], and by their oaths, they have brought upon themselves death [meaning spiritual death or separation from God]; and a hell I have prepared for them, if they repent not;
>
> And this is a decree, which I have sent forth in the beginning of the world, from my own mouth, from the foundation thereof, and by the mouths of my servants, thy fathers, have I decreed it, even as it shall be sent forth in the world, unto the ends thereof. (6:26-30)

Enoch's response to the Lord's calling would be echoed centuries later by Moses himself: "Why is it that I have found favor in thy sight. . . [since] all the people hate me; for I am slow of speech" (6:31; in Exodus 4:10 Moses says, "I am slow of speech and slow of tongue," when he is called by God from the burning bush).

The Lord has an answer for Enoch's problem:

> Go forth and do as I have commanded. . . . Open

> thy mouth, and it shall be filled, and I will give thee utterance. (6:32)

To add to that promise, the Lord lets Enoch know that

> the mountains shall flee before you, and the rivers shall turn from their course. (6:34)

The Lord then directs Enoch to anoint his eyes with clay and wash them so he might "see". After obeying the Lord's instruction, Enoch is able to perceive

> the spirits that God had created; and he beheld also things which were not visible to the natural eye. (6:36)

This vision leads to a saying that spreads throughout the land:

> A seer hath the Lord raised up unto his people. (6:36)

Enoch's subsequent boldness in prophesying draws a challenge from a man named Mahijah, who demands to know who he is and where he is from. Enoch uses the challenge as an opportunity to expound on the fall of Adam, which brought death into the world; however, Enoch explains that God told Adam,

> If thou wilt turn unto me, and hearken unto my voice, and believe, and repent of all thy transgressions, and be baptized, even in water, in the name of mine Only Begotten Son, who is full of grace and truth. . . ye shall receive the gift of the Holy Ghost, asking all things in his name, and whatsoever ye shall ask, it shall be given you. (6:52)

Adam, Enoch relates, was informed that God's name is Man of Holiness

> and the name of his Only Begotten is the Son of Man, even Jesus Christ, a righteous Judge who shall come in the meridian of time. (6:57)

After confirming that Adam "was baptized, and the Spirit of God descended upon him" (6:65), Enoch speaks of himself and describes how he saw the heavens opened and the Lord appeared to him,

> and he talked with me, even as a man talketh one with another, face to face; and he said unto me: Look, and I will show unto thee the world for the space of many generations. (7:4)

As Enoch continues his mission throughout the land, he wins converts but at the same time he makes enemies. When his enemies launch an attack on the Seer and his people, Enoch speaks

> the word of the Lord, and the earth trembled, and the mountains fled, even according to his command; and the rivers of water were turned out of their course; and the roar of lions was heard out of the wilderness; and all nations feared greatly, so powerful was the word of Enoch, and so great was the power of the language which God had given him. (7:13)

Enoch and his people are given a new name by God; he calls them Zion, "because they were of one heart and one mind, and dwelt in righteousness; and there was no poor among them" (7:18). And after Enoch and his people build a city, it too is called Zion (7:19).

In contrast to the righteous citizens of Zion are the "residue of the people". They are under the power of Satan, who has

> a great chain in his hand, and it veiled the whole face of the earth with darkness; and he looked up and laughed, and his angels rejoiced. (7:26)

While Satan laughs, God weeps, knowing that the wicked are "without affection, and they hate their own blood" (7:33). God confides in Enoch that "his indignation is kindled against them" (7:34) and they "shall perish in the floods; and behold, I will shut them up; a prison have I prepared for them" (7:38).

God shows Enoch all the evil doings of the world's inhabitants—and Enoch also weeps. But then he is granted a vision of Noah and his family, and he is permitted to see the future birth of Christ, his ministry and his death on the cross, followed by his resurrection and ascent to heaven, and his return "in the last days, in the days of wickedness and vengeance", when "great tribulations will be among the children of men" (7:60-61). However, God assures Enoch that the righteous will be preserved and that truth will be sent forth

> to bear testimony of mine Only Begotten; his resurrection from the dead; yea, and also the resurrection of all men. (7:62)
>
> And it came to pass that Enoch saw the day of the coming of the Son of Man. . . to dwell on the earth in righteousness for the space of a thousand years. (7:65)

Moses concludes his abbreviated life of Enoch by writing:

> And all the days of Zion, in the days of Enoch, were three hundred and sixty-five years.
>
> And Enoch and all his people walked with God, and he dwelt in the midst of Zion; and it came to pass that Zion was not, for God received it up into his own bosom; and from thence went forth the saying, **Zion is Fled**. (7:68-69)

From the verses that have been cited we can see a definite similarity between "The Book of Moses", *1 Enoch* and the *Secrets of Enoch.* All 3 are concerned with man's rejection of God and the refusal to keep his commandments; with the flood; with the last days, the final judgment and the preparation of different "mansions" for an eternal inheritance; with an emphasis on God's speaking with his own lips, his own mouth, which removes any doubt about the truth having been spoken; and with Enoch's having walked with God, which resulted in Enoch's becoming a scribe, a seer and a prophet who knew all things.

There are, of course, differences between "The Book of Moses" and the two pseudepigraphal works that bear Enoch's name. In *1 Enoch* there is a reference to the Son of Man but he is not specifically identified; in "The Book of Moses" the Son of Man is Christ, the Only Begotten son of God the Father, who is called the Man of Holiness. In addition, it is only in "The Book of Moses" that Adam is baptized and receives the gift of the Holy Ghost, and it is only in "The Book of Moses" that not just Enoch but Zion—which includes both Enoch's people and Enoch's city—are taken off the earth.

At this point a question should be asked: what additional evidence is there to support the claim that Adam, Enoch and Moses actually knew the name *Jesus Christ* thousands of years before Christ was born?

To answer this question, let's begin with the New Testament. In Chapter 4 of the Acts of the Apostles, Peter, having healed a man who had been born lame, is grilled by Annas the high priest and Caiaphas, a Sadducee who did not believe in the resurrection. They demand to know "by what power, or by what name, have you done this?"

Peter answers unflinchingly:

> "let it be known to you all, and to all the people of Israel, that by the name of Jesus Christ the Nazarene [meaning the "hidden one"—this is the interlinear translation from *The NKJV Greek-English Interlinear New Testament*] whom you crucified, whom God raised from the dead, by Him this man stands here before you whole.
>
> "This is the '*stone which was rejected by you builders, which has become the chief cornerstone.*'

> "Nor is there salvation in any other name under heaven given by which we must be saved." (4:7, 10-12)

Hundreds of years earlier, Isaiah, who received his calling as a prophet in about 740 BC (Lockyer, Sr., *Nelson's Illustrated Bible Dictionary* 513), recorded a similar declaration when he quoted the Lord as saying:

> "I am the Lord your God,
>
> The Holy One of Israel, your Savior. . . .
>
> And besides Me there is no savior."
>
> (Isaiah 43:3 and 11)

The Lord who addressed Isaiah was the same Lord who gave Moses the task of delivering the Israelites from the bondage of the Egyptians. Moses, in the beginning, had an important concern regarding this task.

> "Indeed, when I come to the children of Israel and say to them, 'The God of your fathers has sent me to you,' and they say to me, 'What is His name?' what shall I say to them?"
>
> And God said to Moses, "I AM WHO I AM."
>
> And He said, "Thus you shall say to the children of Israel, 'I AM has sent me to you.'" (Exodus 3:13-14)

In the Gospel According to John, during one of the many encounters Christ had with the Pharisees, he tells them, "If anyone keeps My word he shall never taste death." The Pharisees, hostile as ever, fire a series of challenges at Christ.

> "Are you greater than our father Abraham, who is dead? And the prophets are dead. Who do You make Yourself out to be?"

> Jesus answered. . . "Your father Abraham rejoiced to see My day, and he saw it and was glad."
>
> Then the Jews said to Him, "You are not yet fifty years old, and have You seen Abraham?"
>
> Jesus said to them, "Most assuredly, I say to you, before Abraham was, I AM." (John 8:52-54 and 56-58)

The Revell Bible Dictionary makes this observation about the verses just quoted:

> Jewish scholars who heard Jesus say, "Before Abraham was, I am," understood immediately that he was claiming identity with the I AM of the OT [Old Testament]. They "picked up stones to stone him" (Jn. 8:57-59), the penalty for blasphemy (Lev. 24:16). (Lawrence O. Richards 510)

Ian Wilson, author of *Jesus: The Evidence*, discloses the fact that in the earliest texts of the New Testament "there was practically no punctuation or space between words" (26). With this knowledge, we would then be justified in removing the comma after "was", and in that case Christ's statement becomes "Before Abraham was I AM", or to reverse the order of the words, "I AM was before Abraham."

Another point needs to be made, and that is, if Abraham saw Christ's day in vision then he—like Adam, Enoch and Moses—definitely knew who Christ was, knew definitely that Jehovah (or Yahweh) and Christ were one and the same.

Additional confirmation of that truth can be found by comparing another proclamation made by the Lord as recorded in the Book of Isaiah with the first chapter of the book of Revelation.

> "Thus says the Lord, the King of Israel,

> And his Redeemer, the Lord of hosts:
>
> 'I am the First and I am the Last.'"
>
> (Isaiah 44:6)
>
> The Revelation of Jesus Christ, which God gave Him to show his servants. . . .
>
> I [John] was in the Spirit on the Lord's Day and I heard behind me a loud voice, as of a trumpet, saying, "I am the Alpha and the Omega, the First and the Last." (Revelation 1:1 and 10)

There is more. Consider, for example, what Christ says in Chapter 5, verse 39, of the Gospel of John:

> "You search the Scriptures, for in them you think you have eternal life; and these are they which testify of Me."

The scriptures Christ was referring to could not have been the New Testament since nothing had as yet been written by his disciples; no, the scriptures Christ meant were those written by the prophets who had preceded him.

A few verses later Christ is once again responding to those who oppose him.

> "Do not think that I shall accuse you to the Father; there is one who accuses you—Moses, in whom you trust.
>
> "For if you believed Moses, you would believe Me; for he wrote about Me." (John 5:45-46)

In the Gospel of Luke, Christ issues a warning to the Israelites who reject him.

> "There will be weeping and gnashing of teeth, when you see Abraham and Isaac and Jacob and all the prophets in the kingdom of God, and yourselves thrust out." (Luke 13:28)

In other words, the prophets had been taught about Christ, had accepted his teachings and would therefore be exalted with him. But not just the prophets had been taught. In the 3rd and 4th chapters of the Epistle to the Hebrews we're told that the gospel was preached to the Israelites who had been led out of Egypt by Moses. And in the First Epistle of Paul the Apostle to the Corinthians we have this additional commentary:

> Moreover, brethren, I do not want you to be unaware that all our fathers [who were involved in the exodus from Egypt] were under the cloud, all passed through the sea, all ate the same spiritual food, and all drank the same spiritual drink. For they drank of the spiritual Rock that followed them, and *that Rock was Christ.* (10:1-4; italics added)

Having said this much, Paul issues a warning of his own:

> But with most of them God was not well pleased, for their bodies were scattered in the wilderness.
>
> Now these things became our examples, to the intent that we should not lust after evil things as they also lusted.
>
> And do not become idolaters as were some of them. . . .
>
> Nor let us commit sexual immorality, as some of them did. . . nor let us tempt Christ, as some of

> them also tempted, and were destroyed by serpents. (1 Corinthians 10:5-9)

It should be obvious by now that, contrary to what many Bible scholars have taught in the past, when Christ came on the scene in the flesh he was not revealing his teachings for the first time, for he had in fact revealed those teachings to Adam and to all the other prophets who are named in the Old Testament while he was a personage of spirit. Everything Christ taught his disciples during his earthly mission had already been taught over and over down through the millenia.

The same holds true for the church that Christ established, or rather reestablished, as a result of apostasy. Did Enoch, acting under Christ's direction, reestablish the Lord's church as a result of apostasy in his own day? Yes. Did he also build a temple, a House of the Lord? Yes. In fact, he built many temples in many different lands. Did he know everything that Paul knew about the 3 degrees of glory? Yes, he did. It would be safe to assume that since Enoch walked with Christ for more than 365 years he may have known much more than Paul did.

After Christ's resurrection, he commissioned the apostles and other members of the church to go into the world "and make disciples of all the nations, baptizing them in the name of the Father and of the Son and of the Holy Spirit, teaching them to observe all things that I have commanded you" (Matthew 28:19-20). Some 3000 years earlier Enoch and his people had been given the same commission. While some of them no doubt remained in Zion to administer that city's government and to serve in that city's temple, others were sent out to fulfill missions in various parts of the world.

Remember the line in "The Book of Moses" that indicated "all nations feared greatly, so powerful was the word of Enoch"? All nations would not have had cause to fear Enoch unless Enoch had come into their borders and made his presence known. But we don't have to rely on such reasoning alone to document this fact.

In *The World's Last Mysteries*, one of many books to deal with such subjects as the "lost empire of the Indus Valley", Robert Davreu notes that archaeologists have found remarkable

> examples of town planning, with drainage systems that rival those of today. . . [along with] neatly aligned streets that form a modern grid plan.

However, the "social organisation, religion and customs" of the people who were responsible for these impressive innovations "remain a mystery. . . a mystery that will last until their strange picture writing is deciphered" (121).

According to Davreu, the cities of that empire date back to the 3rd millennium BC, as do other ancient cities, monuments, temples and pyramids that have been discovered around the world. They are all evidence of a once highly advanced civilization that colonized much of the world—including the country we know today as Egypt.

And Egypt's remarkable civilization had its beginnings with Enoch the Seer.

6. ALIASES

> ". . . there is nothing covered that will not be revealed, and hidden that will not be known."
>
> (Matthew 10:26)

Adam Rutherford makes a case for Enoch's association with the Great Pyramid, observing that by

> geometric symbolism the representation of Enoch is stamped on the entire Pyramid from top to bottom, inside and outside. No wonder that the Great Pyramid is traditionally associated with Enoch and that Masonic tradition alludes to the Pyramid as "the Pillar of Enoch" (Hanok), even though the Pyramid was not built until the second millennium after Enoch lived. (Book I, 83; "Hanok" is a variant spelling of "Enoch")

While some Masons believe that the beginnings of Masonry can be traced back to the construction of the pyramids, others who have researched the subject have their doubts. John J. Robinson has studied Masonry for a number of years and in *A Pilgrim's Path: Freemasonry and the Religious Right* he states:

> after all manner of investigations by Masonic researchers, Masonic scholars such as Allen Roberts in the United States and John Hamill in England have flatly stated

> that the simple truth is that no one knows how, where, when, or why Freemasonry was founded. (115)

Christopher Knight and Robert Lomas have made their own intensive effort to discover the origins of Freemasonry. That effort is documented in *The Hiram Key*, in which the authors express an interest in ancient "Sumerian references to Enoch, who is important in Masonic lore" (84). They add that the 7th king included in lists of Sumerian kings is depicted "as possessing special wisdom in matters pertaining to the gods and as being the first man to practice prophecy; that seventh [king] is Enoch" (87).

Knight and Lomas link Sumer to Egypt by suggesting the probability that "the first Egyptian builders had originated in Sumer and that these Sumerian immigrants had brought technology and theology to Egypt" (117). They then link Egypt to Freemasonry in a number of ways, one of which involves "the symbolism found on the walls and ceiling of a modern Masonic temple which are based on King Solomon's Temple and, even today, most of the devices are undeniably Egyptian" (178).

Moving forward in time, Knight and Lomas present their case for the Qumran Community being "the spiritual descendants of the Egyptian kings and the antecedents of the [Knights] Templar and Freemasonry" (202). Delving into the Dead Sea Scrolls, the two authors report that some of the

> mysterious works from the Qumran library concern Noah and Enoch, who were said to have been the recipients of divine secrets of Heaven and Earth that had been passed down through certain initiates. There is an ancient belief that the mythical ancestors of the human race were men of superb wisdom, and there are many tales concerning Enoch and Noah as holders of divine secrets. (202-203)

Knight and Lomas followed up *The Hiram Key* with *The Second Messiah*. Here they explore the 33 degrees of the Ancient Scottish Rite, "ruled by the Supreme Council of the 33 degrees in Edinburgh" (61-62). The 13th degree, they explain, "is 'The Royal Arch of Enoch' or 'The Master of the Ninth Arch'".

This degree reveals

> how, in times long before Moses and Abraham, the ancient figure of Enoch foresees that the world will be overwhelmed by an apocalyptic disaster through flood or fire, and he determines to preserve at least some of the knowledge then known to man, that it may be passed on to future civilisations of survivors. He therefore engraves in hieroglyphics the great secrets of science and building onto two pillars: one made of brick and the other of stone.
>
> The Masonic legend goes on to tell how these pillars were almost destroyed, but sections survived the Flood and were subsequently discovered—one by the Jews, the other by the Egyptians. (204-205)

The word "pillar" can, of course, mean different things. For instance, in the Epistle of Paul the Apostle to the Galatians, the apostles Cephas, James and John are called pillars of the church (2:9; Christ gave Peter the name of Cephas when they first met; see John 1:42). Such language is obviously meant to be taken in a figurative sense.

In the Old Testament, Isaiah makes use of the word "pillar". In the future, he prophecies,

> there will be an altar to the Lord in the midst of the land of Egypt, and a pillar to the Lord at its border.
>
> And it will be for a sign and for a witness to the Lord of hosts in the land of Egypt; for they will cry to the Lord because of the oppressors, and He will send

> them a Savior and a Mighty One, and He will deliver them. (19:19-20)

Peter Lemesurier treats this prophecy as a description of "the site, nature and significance of the Great Pyramid of Giza" (215). Lemesurier bases his interpretation of Isaiah's 2 verses on the original Hebrew word translated as "pillar", which he says "means almost any kind of monument" (216).

Manly P. Hall, author of *Freemasonry of the Ancient Egyptians*, makes a similar point in an interview conducted by Richard W. Noone. Hall expresses his opinion that

> the Great Pyramid was a monument or marker of great importance, perhaps an effort to create a structure that would survive practically any disaster that could occur to the world. (190)

As we can see, Rutherford's statement regarding Enoch and the Great Pyramid gains some credibility from other sources, but what of his comment that "the Pyramid was not built until the second millenium after Enoch lived"? In Book I of his series of 5 books titled *Pyramidology* Rutherford claims that "the Pyramid itself. . . gives the precise date of its own construction as beginning in the year 2623 BC" (32).

Other pyramidologists have preferred different dates. Piazzi Smyth, for example, settled on 2170 BC "as the foundation year" (478); Worth Smith's choice of 2644 BC is only a few years later than Rutherford's (27); Noone, however, has gone farther back, favoring 4000 BC (26).

Alternate dates suggested by researchers who would not be classified as pyramidologists range from Manly C. Hall's fifty to sixty thousand BC (Noone 187) to approximately 2450 BC, the figure of choice by Robert Bauval and Adrian Gilbert (172).

As for the Egyptologists, they almost uniformly subscribe to dates of about 2600 to 2550 BC (Casson 129; Hayes 24); however, Lehner reveals in *The Complete Pyramids* that

> in 1984 we radiocarbon dated 64 samples of organic material extracted from the pyramids and associated structures. The dates, after calibration, were on average 374 years earlier than one of the major accepted chronologies. (66-67)

Hancock and Bauval shed a little more light on Lehner's disclosure in *The Message of the Sphinx*:

> Lehner collected fifteen samples of ancient mortar from the masonry of the Great Pyramid. These samples of mortar were chosen because they contained fragments of organic material which, unlike natural stone, would be susceptible to carbon-dating. Two of the samples were tested in the Radiocarbon Laboratory of the Southern Methodist University in Dallas Texas [sic] and the other thirteen were taken to laboratories in Zurich, Switzerland, for dating by the more sophisticated accelerator method. According to proper procedure, the results were then calibrated and confirmed with respect to tree-ring samples.
>
> The outcome was surprising. As Mark Lehner commented at the time:
>
> The dates run. . . significantly earlier than the best Egyptological date for Khufu. . . . Now this is really radical. . . I mean it'll make a big stink. The Giza Pyramid is 400 years older than Egyptologists believe. (301-302)

Charles E. Sellier refers us to

> Dr. Herbert Haas, director of the Radiocarbon Laboratory at Southern Methodist University, [who] is one of the experts who has devoted a great deal of

> effort to establishing accurate dates for the construction of the pyramids. . . . According to Dr. Haas, "Scholars have always insisted that the so-called 'Bent Pyramid' attributed to the pharaoh Zozer was the first pyramid erected in Egypt; that the Great Pyramid was not built until several hundred years after. Now it turns out that. . . the Great Pyramid is *at least* four hundred fifty years older than Zozer's 'Bent Pyramid.' That means that instead of being the seventh or eighth pyramid built in Egypt, the Great Pyramid was the first." (165)

If the results of the radiocarbon dating had been more in line with the ancient Egyptian chronology that Egyptologists had established over the last few decades probably there would have been no more testing conducted on the Great Pyramid. But, as we're told in the article "Dating the Pyramids", published in the September/October 1999 issue of *Archaeology*, the "1984 work raised questions that led to a second project in 1995" (29).

What were the results of samples taken 11 years after the first sampling? For the Great Pyramid, 42 new dates were obtained. "In general," we're told,

> the calibrated dates from the 1995 Old Kingdom samples [which were taken from other monuments in addition to the Great Pyramid] tended to be 100 to 200 years older than the historical dates for the respective kings and about 200 years younger than our 1984 dates. The disparity is particularly glaring for Khufu's pyramid. In 1984, 20 dates on charcoal produced a calibrated average age of 2917 B.C. . . . [T]he 1995 dates are scattered. . . over a range of about 400 years. (31)

The results, then, of the 1995 sampling as they pertain to the Great Pyramid were not much different from 1984. The structure can still be assigned an average date of 2917 BC. Notice the word "average".

Here is the tie-in. Biblical chronology, supplemented by other sources, indicates that Enoch and his people were translated—taken off the earth without experiencing death—about 2958 BC (Skousen, *The First 2000 Years* 191; Skousen's date is actually 2948 BC, but his dates appear to be off by 10 years). If Enoch's last mission was the construction of the pyramids at Giza then the approximate date that has been established by carbon dating is remarkably close.

But, it might be asked, if Enoch played such an important part in Egypt's early history, why isn't he mentioned in any of the ancient Egyptian texts that are extant? The answer to this question begins with the reminder that Enoch, to repeat Hugh Nibley's statement, "is identified with more other great characters than any other figure of the past" (19).

As already stated, he became known as Idris in Arabic histories, and Idris, in turn, was identical to the Greek god Hermes Trismegistos (the Greek spelling of Trisgegistus), but Hermes, according to the *New Larousse Encyclopedia of Mythology*, was also the same as the Egyptian god Thoth (27). Isn't it logical then to form the equation Thoth = Enoch?

A comparison of attributes associated with Thoth and Enoch should clinch the matter. Examine, then, the following quotes, which will alternate between Thoth (or Hermes) and Enoch, with Thoth coming first.

> **Hancock and Bauval** (quoting from "a Hermetic Text, written in Greek but compiled in Alexandria in Egypt some 2000 years ago, that is known as the *Kore Kosmu*"): "Such was all-knowing Hermes, who saw all things, and seeing understood" (270).

> **The Book of the Secrets of Enoch**: "I [Enoch] know all things" (XL:2).

> **James C. VanderKam** (quoting from the *Book of Jubilees*): "he [Enoch] saw everything and understood" (112).

New Larousse Encyclopedia of Mythology: "Endowed with complete knowledge and wisdom, it was Thoth who invented all the arts and sciences. . . and, above all, writing, without which humanity would have run the risk of forgetting his doctrines and of losing the benefit of his discoveries. . . .

"In his quality of lunar divinity Thoth measured the time, which he divided into months. . . and into years, which in turn were divided into three seasons" (27-28).

VanderKam (again quoting from the *Book of Jubilees*): "He [Enoch] was the first of mankind who were born on the earth who learned (the art of) writing, instruction, and wisdom and who wrote down in a book the signs of the sky in accord with the fixed pattern of their months so that mankind would know the seasons of the years according to the fixed patterns of each of their months" (112).

Peter Clayton, *Great Figures of Mythology*: "Because Thoth was impartial and unsusceptible to bribes he was in charge of the scales weighing the hearts of the deceased persons in the Underworld to see if their crimes were too severe for them to enter the realm of Osiris" (181).

The Book of the Secrets of Enoch: "I [Enoch]. . . measured and wrote out every work and every measure and every righteous judgement" (XLIII:1).

"I have put every man's work in writing and none born on earth can remain hidden nor his works remain concealed.

"I see all things" (L:1-2).

"[And all] things will be laid bare in the weighing-scales and in the books on the day of the great judgement" (LII:15).

Richard H. Wilkinson, *Symbol & Magic in Egyptian Art*: "Throughout their history, the Egyptians themselves attributed the origin of their writing system to the gods. This divine source is seen in the very name which the script was accorded: *medu netcher*: 'the words of the gods' or 'divine words.' This meaning was preserved in the word *hieroglyphs* ('sacred writing') which the Greeks later gave to the Egyptian inscriptions. . . .

"Above all, the hieroglyphic script was associated with Thoth" (149).

The Book of Moses: "And Enoch continued his speech, saying:. . . And death hath come upon our fathers; nevertheless we know them, and cannot deny, and even the first of all we know, even Adam.

"For a book of remembrance we have written among us, according to the pattern given by the finger of God" (6:43, 45-46).

Patrick Boylan, *Thoth: The Hermes of Egypt*: "Thoth's part in the semi-historical form of the Osirian drama is chiefly due to essential and independent features of Thoth's own character. That implies that Thoth is not in any way a creation of the Osirian myth, and that we must not take the Osirian drama as a starting point in the analysis of Thoth's personality. He seems, indeed, in many ways to be as ancient and as independent a god as Osiris himself" (25).

"To rule the world as chief minister of Re, Thoth

would require a high degree of intelligence, and a great range of knowledge" (98).

Hugh Nibley, *Enoch the Prophet*: "The combination of certain traits—independence, intelligence, compassion and power—is Enoch's signature, setting him apart from all others by the superlative degree to which he possesses them" (21).

Boylan: "Thoth appears also as Secretary or Scribe of Osiris" (25-26).

Nibley: "Enoch] is the great observer and recorder of all things in heaven and earth. . . . Enoch the Scribe, keeper of the records" (21).

"Thoth/Enoch [stands] at the right side of the throne keeping the record while Anubis [a funerary deity] on the other side brings up the dead for judgment" (64, note # 140).

Boylan: "Pyr. [an abbreviation for the Pyramid texts] 267-268 transforms the king into 'Sia (the bearer of the divine book) at the right hand of Re'. . . . But who is Sia?. . . In the late periods there is no doubt about the identity of Sia and Thoth—Sia being freely used in the Greek period as a name of Thoth" (59).

Nibley: "'Sia,' [R. O.] Faulkner notes, 'is the personification of intelligence and understanding.' He is also the Arabic Idris, who is Enoch. Thoth, like Enoch, is in charge of the rites of initiation, as 'Lord of the Divine Words, Keeper of the Secret Knowledge that is in heaven and earth, the great God of the beginning. . . who established speech and writing, causing the temples to flourish'" (47).

Boylan: "The god who can predetermine length of life

and reign must himself be raised above all limitations of time. Hence, it is not strange to find Thoth described as one that looks into the future and perceives it like the present" (86).

Zecharia Sitchin, *The Cosmic Code*: "Having been given knowledge of the heavens and the Earth and their mysteries, Enoch was told to write down prophecies of future events (according to the *Book of Jubilees*, Enoch was shown 'what was and what will be')" (180).

Boylan: "Thoth appears in Egyptian texts. . . as the All-knowing One, as the dispenser of every kind of strange and mysterious gnosis [meaning knowledge of spiritual truths]" (99).

Nibley: "Enoch [is] the 'first vehicle of. . . the genuine *gnosis*'" (19).

Boylan: "The word of the thinker gives being to his thought, and, hence, the creative power of Thoth is exercised in the utterance of command. . . . The oldest Egyptian texts are familiar with the productive and creative power of certain spoken words. That idea underlies the magical formulae of the Pyramids [sic]" (120).

Nibley: "For his work Enoch is endowed with power—the power of the priesthood. He had but to speak the word of the Lord and mountains shook and rivers turned from their courses" (21).

Boylan: "[Thoth is] 'He who comes to him that calls him'. . . .

"At least in the late texts, therefore, Thoth appears as a. . . saviour, and protector from evil" (132; here we can see a commingling of Enoch and Christ).

Nibley: "Enoch is the great advocate, the champion of the human race. . . . He feels for all and is concerned for all" (21).

Boylan: "In certain texts of the Pyramids Thoth is described as a being of dread aspect who slaughters the enemies of Osiris (Pyr. 635; 962)" (133).

The Book of Moses: "and all nations feared greatly so powerful was the word of Enoch. . . .

"There also came up a land out of the depth of the sea, and so great was the fear of the enemies of the people of God, that they fled and. . . went upon the land" (7:13-14).

"And from that time forth there were wars and bloodshed among them" (7:16).

Bauval and Gilbert: "The Egyptians believed that. . . Thoth himself, had built the Giza pyramids" (118).

Ibn-Batuta: "Hermes Trismegistos (the Hebrew Enoch). . . built the pyramids" (quoted in Tompkins 218).

New Larousse Encyclopedia of Mythology: "After his long reign on earth Thoth ascended to the skies where he undertook various employments" (27).

Nibley: "Even after the removal of Enoch's city, the work of redemption continued among 'the residue of the people'" (264).

More comparisons could be made—and in fact will be made in future chapters—between Thoth and Enoch, but for now what has been presented should be enough to leave little doubt that there exists, as Anthony E. Larson says in the 3rd volume of his prophecy trilogy,

> an intimate relationship between the myths and legends of mankind and the epochs of Enoch and Zion. That connection opens up the world of the ancients and the world of tomorrow in a manner that would not have been possible otherwise. (81)

The last sentence in this quote from Larson will become more meaningful as we return to the Great Pyramid to explore in much greater detail the many additional features Enoch and his people built into its unique exterior and interior systems.

7. DESCENDING

> "O foolish ones, and slow of heart to believe in all that the prophets have spoken!"
>
> (Luke 24:25)

While Egyptologists such as Ian Lawton, Chris Ogilvie-Herald and Richard Wilkinson would have us believe that the various dimensions built into the Great Pyramid's passages and chambers were apparently the result of arbitrary decisions on the part of the ancient Egyptian architect, those dimensions have nevertheless been deemed significant by pyramidologists as well as others who do not fit into either camp but who have personally carried out measurements both within and without the structure. Perhaps that should not be surprising since even a cursory examination of the subject will reveal the fact that certain numbers occur again and again and must therefore have had some special significance to the architect and the builders.

At the same time, it will become evident as this study proceeds that even though Egyptologists offer no explanations for the pyramid's dimensions they have been every bit as obsessed and as diligent as the people they like to call "cranks" when it comes to measuring and remeasuring all of the pyramid's features.

David Furlong goes so far as to claim in *The Keys to the Temple* that number symbolism can be "found in all aspects of Egyptian artistic expression." Referring specifically to the pyramids at Giza, he adds that the ratios involved in their precise construction express "specific religious concepts. In other words, the whole of the Giza complex was based on a coherent design intended to portray a spiritual theme" (89).

His assessment is correct, but it should also be noted that every feature inside the Great Pyramid—as well as outside—that can be dated to ancient times is there as a matter of design, not because of earthquake damage or because of the effects of subsidence, both of which have been used by William Flinders Petrie and other researchers to explain certain anomalies that attracted their attention. (In *The Great Pyramid: Its Divine Message* David Davidson takes Petrie to task for placing too much emphasis on earthquake damage, but he in turn makes far too much of subsidence, since, as architect Greg Pyros tells us, "In *five thousand* years the Great Pyramid, weighing fourteen billion pounds, has settled less than one-half inch" [quoted in Sellier 143].)

As an example of a number being significant, we can begin with the exterior of the Great Pyramid, which covers 13 acres (Lawton and Ogilvie-Herald 11). Why did the ancient architect design the base of the pyramid to be that size?

The answer is in the Epistle of Paul the Apostle to the Ephesians. In this letter Paul tells the members of the church in Ephesus, Greece:

> Now, therefore, you are no longer strangers and foreigners, but fellow citizens with the saints and members of the household of God, having been built on the foundation of the apostles and prophets, Jesus Christ Himself being the chief cornerstone, in whom the whole building, being fitted together, grows into a holy temple in the Lord. (2:19-21)

How many apostles were there? Twelve. Twelve plus Christ makes 13. This is the reason for the 13 acres.

And here is the reason for the pyramid shape as opposed to a square or rectangular structure. In Rutherford's words:

> In a pyramid all the four corners of the building converge in one stone at the top, and thus the crowning stone is

> at once both "the Head-Stone" and "the Chief Corner Stone". (Book I, 48)

In *The Pyramids: An Enigma Solved*, Joseph Davidovits and Margie Morris make the observation that the ancient religious center of Heliopolis, which was across the Nile River from the Giza plateau, was "the holy sanctuary of Egypt, the ground itself [being] religiously symbolic." This center "became the capital of the *thirteenth* Lower Egyptian nome or district" (130; italics added). Heliopolis was undoubtedly the site for Enoch's headquarters while he was in Egypt, therefore this number 13 is no coincidence.

As for the pyramid being a temple, consider what Peter Tompkins says in *Secrets of the Great Pyramid*:

> Several authors have expressed the opinion that there is a close connection between the Great Pyramid and what are known as the Egyptian mysteries, that is to say, the secret knowledge possessed by a hierarchy of initiates which was communicated to those who could prove their worthiness by passing a long period of probationary training and severe trials.

Tompkins cites William Kingsland's belief that

> the secret of the Pyramid is even known to present-day initiates, but is probably "one of those matters which they do not see fit to disclose to the world at large." (259)

There is truth in both quotes from Tompkins' book. The "mysteries", however, were introduced by Enoch and his people only to those Egyptians who joined the church and met all the qualifications. Those Egyptians then received their individual endowments—not in the Great Pyramid itself, for its function is symbolic, but in what is known as the mortuary temple, the floor of which still exists on the east side of the pyramid.

Page 121 of *The British Museum Book of Ancient Egypt*, edited by Stephen Quirke and Jeffrey Spencer, features a photograph of a "sheet of the Great Harris Papyrus". Part of the caption for this photograph reads: "The long roll provides a list of temple endowments throughout Egypt under Ramses III, drawn up by his son Ramses IV".

No doubt the editors would contend that the reference to endowments means financial endowments, but does the ancient document specify that particular meaning? It does not seem to do so; moreover, when it is realized that Ramses III and Ramses IV represent Jacob, who lived the last 17 years of his life in Egypt, and Jacob's 11th son, Joseph, who ruled Egypt for 80 years, then we can be safe in assuming that the phrase "temple endowments" refers not to a financial arrangement but to the spiritual ceremony which is designed to prepare members of the Church of Jesus Christ for eternal exaltation in the celestial kingdom. (More will be said about Ramses III and IV and other names that represent Jacob and Joseph in another volume.)

The Great Pyramid's so-called mortuary temple was a House of the Lord and it was dedicated to the spiritual enlightenment of the living, not the dead, therefore the term "mortuary temple" is inappropriate and misleading, for temple work for the deceased did not begin until after Christ's resurrection.

* * *

In addition to the base of the Great Pyramid representing Christ and the Twelve Apostles, the exterior of the structure also represents the degree of glory that is comparable to the sun. Remember what the ancient Egyptians called the Great Pyramid? It was "*The Light*", because it "blazed out with light like a gigantic mirror" when its "fine, white, smooth, polished limestone casing" was still intact (Brunton 47).

If the Great Pyramid represents the sun, what do the other 2 major pyramids on the plateau represent? What did David Furlong say regarding this matter? The "whole Giza complex was based on a coherent design intended to portray a spiritual theme" (89). Accordingly, the 2nd pyramid represents the 2nd degree of glory, that is, the terrestrial glory, which in turn is represented by the moon, and the smallest of the 3 with its even smaller 3 "satellite" pyramids to the south represents the stars, or the lowest glory of all.

Is there any evidence that the ancient Egyptians knew about the sun, the moon and the stars representing the 3 degrees of glory? Yes, there is. In his examination of the ancient Egyptians' religious beliefs, R. T. Rundle Clark reveals in his book *Myth and Symbol in Ancient Egypt* that the Egyptians believed

> the soul [of the deceased] soared up to join the stars and the sun and moon in their eternal round. . . . In order to reach the heights of the sky the soul had to undergo those transformations which the High God had gone through as he developed from a spirit. . . to his final position as Sun God. (31)

Along the same line, Clark states that "the scribes of the Middle Kingdom provided a Paradise and several Hells" in their description of the afterlife (32), and E. A. Wallis Budge in Volume I of *Osiris and the Egyptian Resurrection* refers to "Gods celestial and gods terrestrial" (92). Budge also refers in the same volume to 3 regions "to which the deceased is said to go" (98). Budge's source for this information is the Pyramid Texts, which are

> the oldest religious literature in ancient Egypt, taking the form of inscriptions on the walls of the pyramids of the 5th and 6th Dynasties. . . . The priests of Heliopolis [in other words, Enoch and his people] are credited with their origin, prompted by a desire to provide the royal deceased with the knowledge of Tuat or the Underworld. The texts include prayers and admonitions concerning the afterlife. (Margaret Bunson, *A Dictionary of Ancient Egypt* 213)

To quote J. P. Lepre regarding the original entrance to the Great Pyramid:

> While the actual aperture or doorway is a mere 4′ high by 3½′ wide. . . there are four [massive portal stones] visible to the naked eye, [and each] is a 10′-long, 15-ton monolith. Together they form an inverted V above the entrance aperture. The striking configuration of these entrance stones seems symbolic of the grandeur which lies beyond, a sort of introduction to a high order of things. (71)

Lepre, an Egyptologist, has struck the right note in this instance. No pyramidologist could have expressed the idea any better.

Turning next to Peter Lemesurier, we learn that the

> Pyramid's Descending Passage is built, uniquely, atop an extraordinary sloping limestone platform known as the Great Basement Sheet. This is some 33 feet wide [from east to west], a fact which perhaps reflects with a special aptness the words attributed to Jesus. (180, footnote)

Jesus, it should be noted, died at the age of 33, and the words spoken by him that can be applied to the "Great Basement Sheet" are recorded in the 7th chapter of Matthew.

> "Enter by the narrow gate; for wide is the gate and broad is the way that leads to destruction, and there are many who go in by it." (7:13)

But, the question should be asked, if that is the case, why is the "gate" only 4 feet high and 3½ feet wide? Why isn't it huge, to be in keeping with the "Great Basement Sheet" and with Christ's saying?

There are two reasons for the opening to be the size it is. One, this opening leads not just to the descending passage but to the ascending passage as well, and the original entrance to the pyramid—as well as the entrance to the ascending passage—represents the "narrow gate" that leads to exaltation; and two, the opening is small to indicate the transition we experience when we are born.

As indicated earlier, Enoch learned that prior to their mortal lives all men and women lived as spirit children of the Lord of spirits, who is the same as the Father that Christ prayed to, and therefore at birth our lives are suddenly cramped, confined, restricted, in contrast to what they had been.

The specific width of 3½ feet, which is 42 inches, was chosen because in ancient Egyptian theology 42 gods kept "ward over those who have done evil" (Budge, *Osiris and the Egyptian Resurrection*, Volume I, 338). The original source for Budge's comment comes from Chapter 125 of the *Book of the Dead*, another compilation of writings that contained instructions "on how to overcome the dangers of the afterlife" by providing "passwords necessary for admittance to certain stages of Tuat or the Underworld" (Margaret Bunson 47).

In this chapter, 42 gods in the "Hall of Justice. . . live [sic] on those who cherish evil" (Faulkner, *The Ancient Egyptian Book of the Dead* 29). And the evil are consigned to the lowest kingdom, as represented by the subterranean chamber, which is linked directly to the descending passage and its entrance.

Along with the *Book of the Dead* and its 42 judges, Graham Hancock tells us that the teachings of Thoth were "handed down from generation to generation in the form of forty-two books of instruction", and it was to these books that the ancient Egyptians "ascribed their renowned wisdom and knowledge of the skies" (439).

Lemesurier, discussing the significance of the number 42, observes that

> forty-two seems an oddly arbitrary number to choose. . . unless we interpret the number in terms of the mathematical function 6 x 7. [This, he goes on to say,] is the Pyramid-code for the preparation of spiritual perfection. . . . Meanwhile we find this same figure reflected in the forty-two settings-up of the Israelites'

> tabernacle during their exodus through the wilderness—
> the "test" which they likewise had to pass. (169)

Also related to the entrance to the Great Pyramid is the length of Christ's mortal ministry—3½ years (Hoyt W. Brewster, Jr., *Behold I Come Quickly: The Last Days and Beyond* 101), and 3½ years equal 42 months. Christ is identified in Chapter 10 of the Book of Acts as *the* "Judge of the living and the dead." Which verse in Chapter 10 contains this identification? It is verse number 42.

The 4′ height of the entrance has additional symbolism in that the number 4, as Hans Biedermann relates, "is associated with the cross and the square; there are four seasons, four rivers of paradise. . . [and] four points of the compass" (143). In scriptural terms, 4 "is emphatically the *number of Creation*; of man in his relation to the world as created". Four is also "the number of things that have a beginning" (Bullinger 123).

Converting 4 feet to 48 inches brings into play *The Book of Enoch the Prophet* as translated by Richard Laurence. And while Laurence dated the manuscript which he translated to a time before the New Testament but not earlier than the Babylonian captivity of the Jews, Lyman Abbott, who wrote the Introduction to *The Book of Enoch the Prophet*, regarded the work as having been written before the biblical flood (ix and xxxiv). We can, in fact, be certain that the original text (as opposed to the copy which Laurence had access to) was written by Enoch himself.

Now, the number 48 in *The Book of Enoch the Prophet* is prominent because Chapter 48 is repeated twice. In the first version of this chapter, in the first verse, Enoch draws our attention to "a fountain of righteousness, which never failed"; in the second verse the fountain is equated with the "Son of man", and in the 3rd verse Enoch writes:

> Before the sun and the signs were created, before the stars of heaven were formed, his name was invoked in the presence of the Lord of spirits. A support shall he [the Son of Man] be for the righteous and the holy to

> lean upon, without falling; and *he shall be the light of nations.* (Italics added)

Christ, the Light, was the architect of the Great Pyramid, and Enoch was the foreman who carried out his designs.

* * *

The descending passage begins in the middle of the "Great Basement Sheet" (Rutherford, Book III, 952). The stones that make up the walls of the passage are laid so that their joints are perpendicular to the floor; however, 40 feet from the entrance is an anomaly which Lepre describes:

> there are, on either wall side, two joints which rise vertically—the only such ones in the entire passage. Also, close to these two joints, on both walls, is a single chiseled line running. . . perpendicular to the passageway. Yet these are not joints proper, comprising a "seam" between two wall stones, but lines that are actually inscribed into the stones at these points. (73-74)

Lepre suggests that these inscribed lines, which are exactly opposite each other and which extend from floor to ceiling, might indicate the presence of a secret chamber waiting to be discovered. His suggestion is based on the existence of another line that is inscribed in the floor farther down the passage and that serves to signal the beginning of the ascending passage (74).

In contrast to Lepre, Rutherford contends that the "absolutely straight knife-edge" lines in the side walls "are intended as a clear cut zero-line. . . from which to take measurements and thus ascertain the periods of the Pyramid's chronological prophecies" (Book I, 91).

Drawing on information supplied by the English astronomer Sir John Herschel, Rutherford asserts that the Dragon Star, Alpha Draconis, "shone exactly straight down the Descending Passage" in 2141 BC, and that date establishes the "correct reading of the whole range of inch-year chronology in the Pyramid" (Book I, 93).

Piazzi Smyth was the first explorer to notice these "scored lines", as they are frequently designated, but it was his friend Waynman Dixon who took the measurements to determine the mean distance between them and the vertical masonry joints, which, because they stand out from the other joints, are clearly meant to be combined with the lines in order to represent a particular function or idea.

Dixon reported that on the east wall the distance was 9 inches, and on the west wall—13 inches (Piazzi Smyth 471).

Dixon's measurements had nothing to do with guiding explorers to a secret chamber or with "the astronomical fixing and correct reading of the whole range of inch-year chronology" as believed by Rutherford.

Turning to other authors, Sitchin has nothing to say about this particular feature of the Great Pyramid. And Dunn—who alleges that any "theory about the Great Pyramid should both satisfy the demands of logic and provide answers for all the relevant discoveries that have promoted so much perplexity in the past" (45)—what does he have to say? Perhaps he deems the scored lines and the unique vertical joints as irrelevant since he, like Sitchin, never mentions them in *The Giza Power Plant.* And yet, he says on page 47,

> When searching for a solution to the enigmas of the Great Pyramid, assuming that all other explanations do not satisfy us, we must take all the evidence into consideration, even the most trivial details.

So then, even if the scored lines and the vertical joints are trivial, what is their purpose?

Here is the answer: the 9 inches between the scored line and the vertical joint on the east wall correspond to the 9 months that most of us spend in our mothers' wombs before we are born.

That this interpretation is correct is reinforced by the fact that the scored lines are beneath the limestone gable that marks the entrance to the pyramid (Lemesurier 53). This positioning of the scored lines is made possible by the exterior slope of the pyramid, by the gable being recessed in the north face of the pyramid, and by the descending passage's angle of 26 degrees.

Taking into consideration the fact that the scored lines are in the same vertical plane as the entrance to the pyramid and that, in conjunction with the floor and the ceiling of the descending passage, they form a rectangle, they are clearly intended to function as another entrance—an entrance into mortal life.

In addition, the correlation between the 9 inches and 9 months is evident from the 9 inches being on the east wall while the west wall has the larger number of 13. The east wall in the pyramid's system of passages and chambers represents earthly or carnal matters as contrasted to heavenly or celestial matters for the west wall. This east-west symbolism, as will become evident, is consistent throughout the entire pyramid. At the same time, it should be pointed out that when going from north to south inside the pyramid, east is to the left and west is to the right, therefore east-west symbolism is also left-right symbolism, which is similarly employed in the Bible.

Along with discovering the scored lines, Piazzi Smyth also counted the number of joints in the floor of the descending passage. From the inscribed lines on the walls to the beginning of the ascending passage there are 13 (Smyth 475). The meaning of this number 13 as well as the 13 inches associated with the scored line on the west wall is the same as it is for the 13 acres.

Or to put a little different slant on the matter, we, as spirits, are accompanied to the earth by one or more celestial beings who have the authority to represent Christ and the Quorum of the Twelve Apostles, and when we are born, our companions, who then serve unseen, continue to accompany us throughout our lives however long we might live. And while these companions are usually called guardian angels, that label is not entirely correct; it is more correct to refer to them as recording angels, for their primary task is to record our mortal lives. Their records will one day be recognized as the "books" that are to be opened to determine what our final judgment will be (see the book of Revelation 20:12).

As for the meaning of the 40 feet of passage that precede the scored lines, we turn again to the Bible, where the number 40 signifies a period of preparation and of trial. For example, Moses spent 40 years away from Egypt, during which time the Lord was preparing him for his role as the great deliverer (Lockyer, Sr., *Nelson's Illustrated Bible Dictionary* 728); Moses also spent 40 days and nights on Mount Sinai before the Lord gave him the Ten Commandments (Exodus 24:18 and 31:18); the Israelites spent 40 years in the wilderness before they were permitted to enter the land promised to them:

> you shall remember that the Lord your God led you all the way these forty years in the wilderness, to humble you and test you, to know what was in your heart, whether you would keep His commandments or not. (Deuteronomy 8:2)

Christ spent 40 days and nights in the wilderness preparing for his mortal ministry. During that time he was tried by Satan (Matthew 4:1-10). And after his resurrection, Christ spent 40 days preparing his disciples for the labors they were to perform after he departed from them (Acts I:1-3).

The first 40 feet of the descending passage represent the preparation of the Father's children during their pre-mortal existence for their experience in mortality. The primary trial involved in the pre-mortal existence was the war of ideas proposed by Christ and Satan. As indicated previously, all those who sided with Christ were appointed to come to this earth in order to have the opportunity to advance farther than they could as spirits.

Besides the scored lines in the descending passage, there are "at various points. . . three large fissures, evidently," says Lepre,

> the results of earthquake activity. The middle of these fissures is so wide as to admit the body of a grown man,

> and must have been filled in at one time by the original builders. If this were ever the case, though, the blocks have now been removed. The speculation that they were once shored up is based on the fact that they present visual eyesores along a stretch of wall that has otherwise been finely cut and smoothed. . . . Where the fissures do occur, they encompass the entirety of walls, floor and ceiling. (75)

These 3 fissures are not the result of earthquake activity, nor were they ever shored up. They were built into the descending passage to depict in a graphic way the 3-part division of Christ's Parable of the Sower, which relates how

> "[1] a sower went out to sow his seed. And as he sowed, some fell by the wayside; and it wastrampled down, and the birds of the air devoured it.
>
> "[2] Some fell on rock; and as soon as it sprang up, it withered away because it lacked moisture.
>
> "And [3] some fell among thorns, and the thorns sprang up with it and choked it." (Luke 8:5-7)

To the apostles, Christ explained that this parable pertained to the word of God, which was represented by the seed.

> "Those by the wayside are the ones who hear [the word]; then the devil comes and takes away the word out of their hearts, lest they should believe and be saved [and thus frustrate the devil's plan to destroy God's kingdom].
>
> "But the ones on the rock are those who, when they hear, receive the word with joy; and these have no root, who believe for a while and in time of temptation fall away.
>
> "Now the ones that fell among thorns are those

> who, when they have heard, go out and are choked with cares, riches, and pleasures of life, and bring no fruit to maturity." (Luke 8:12-14)

The fissures, then, illustrate how rejecting Christ's teachings can completely disrupt our lives and open up huge cracks in our moral behavior that can easily engulf us. The end result is that the people described in the first part of this parable are, for the most part, destined for the lowest kingdom of heaven which, as already stated, is portrayed in the subterranean chamber. However, the Parable of the Sower does have a final part, a more positive part, that will be applied to another section of the Great Pyramid in an upcoming chapter.

* * *

The descending passage runs 150 feet from the original entrance to ground level (Tompkins 101). From there the passage continues on for another 200 feet. Dealing first with the number 200, we read in "The Testament of Benjamin", which is included in *The Lost Books of the Bible and the Forgotten Books of Eden*, that when Cain "was two hundred years old he began to suffer" from murdering his brother Abel (Platt, Jr. I:44-45). And in *The Book of Enoch the Prophet*, we read of 200 angels who transgressed and defiled the earth by marrying mortal women and having children who began to devour the earth, for which they were condemned by God (Laurence VII:1-14 and X:15).

And 200 years passed from the time Abraham was forced to leave Egypt by an enraged pharaoh, who had lusted after his wife Sarah only to learn that she was married to the great patriarch, to the time Joseph, Abraham's great-grandson, was imprisoned by Potiphar. (Abraham left Egypt in 1957 BC and Joseph was cast into prison in 1757 BC.)

The significance of the number 150 is linked to the number 350, the total number of feet in the descending passage. Why did Enoch and his people go to the trouble to attain that length, especially considering that in order to do so they not only had to prepare the passage through the 150 feet of masonry but also drill through 200 feet of solid bedrock.

The answer lies in the number of years that Noah lived after the biblical flood—which was 350 years (Genesis 9:28)—and how long did the water from the flood cover the earth? The answer: 150 days (Genesis 7:24).

Now, all the people who died in the flood—and these were people who were warned over and over beginning with Enoch and continuing up until the last minute, nevertheless they chose not to hear and to reject God no matter what he tried to do to get them to keep the commandments, not to curse them but to bless them—these people cheated themselves out of the 350 years that were granted to Noah.

The descending passage has "a slope of about 1 in 2" (Noone 341). Why? Because that ratio is related to Christ's warning that in the last days, at the moment of extreme crisis,

> "two men will be in the field: one will be taken [off the earth] and the other left [to be burned as stubble—see Malachi chapter 4].
>
> "Two women will be grinding at the mill: one will be taken and the other left." (Matthew 24:40-41)

Those who are left—and half of humanity is the indication—will end up in the lowest kingdom.

This is the heart of the message being delivered by the descending passage.

* * *

At the end of the 350 feet a horizontal passage begins, however, in comparison to the descending passage this one decreases in size, with the width shrinking from 42 inches to 32 inches and the height from 48 inches to 37 inches (Edwards 287). This passage runs south for 18 feet (the number 18 is important both inside the Great Pyramid and outside and will be the subject of further discussion later on); then, as reported by Lepre, the horizontal section

> passes through a small recess or niche cut into the corridor's west wall. This niche was most likely planned

> to be an antechamber. . . . Yet the builders ceased working on this niche when they abandoned the idea of using the subterranean chamber to contain the mummy of the pharaoh. . . . Said antechamber measures 6′ long by 6′ wide by 4′ high. (75)

As should be anticipated, this antechamber never figures in either Sitchin's or Dunn's discussion of the Great Pyramid. Its true purpose will be examined shortly, but first, we need to ask what purpose was served by reducing the width and the height of the passage once the horizontal section began? For that matter, what need was there for the descending passage to level out? Why didn't Enoch and his people simply run the descending passage straight into the subterranean chamber?

Do the Egyptologists deal with these questions? Do Sitchin and Dunn deal with them? No, they do not.

The horizontal section and the antechamber described by Edwards and Lepre are related to statements made by Christ and by Simon Peter the Apostle in the New Testament.

Christ first:

> "Most assuredly, I say to you, the hour is coming. . . when the dead will hear the voice of the Son of God; and those who hear will live. . . .
>
> "Do not marvel at this; for the hour is coming in which all who are in the graves will hear His voice and come forth—those who have done good, to the resurrection of life, and those who have done evil, to the resurrection of condemnation." (John 5:25 and 28-29)

Simon Peter states:

> it is better, if it is the will of God, to suffer for doing good than for doing evil.

> For Christ also suffered once for sins, the just for the unjust, that He might bring us to God, being put to death in the flesh but made alive by the Spirit, by whom also He went and preached to the spirits in prison, who formerly were disobedient, when once the Divine longsuffering waited in the days of Noah, while the ark was being prepared, in which a few, that is, eight souls, were saved through water. (1 Peter 3:17-20)

In the next chapter Simon Peter adds:

> the gospel was preached. . . to those who are dead, that they might be judged according to men in the flesh, but live according to God in the spirit. (4:6)

Dummelow's *Commentary on the Holy Bible* offers this explanation of Simon Peter's statements:

> The whole passage clearly means that Christ, as a spirit, preached to certain spirits, who had been disobedient to the end of their earthly life. This preaching took place between His death and resurrection, and its purpose was that, by hearing the gospel, these men might have an opportunity of repentance. . . .
>
> Thus the judgment of these dead men did not take place till Christ preached in the spirit to them. Then they could choose their side, for or against Him. (1046)

The horizontal section that leads to the subterranean chamber represents the spirit prison mentioned by Simon Peter—and that is why its width and height are less than the descending passage, which represents mortality. In earthly prisons, people who break the law are confined, their freedom restricted; it is no different in the spirit prison. It should be understood, however, that the spirit prison is not a final stop;, it is, instead, a temporary place of habitation that stands in between mortality and the final judgment which will determine the degree of glory everyone will inherit for eternity.

As for the antechamber, it represents one part of the prison that has been referred to by spirits of the dead who have been permitted to contact living relatives. One such case is reported in *Hello from Heaven!* by Bill and Judy Guggenheim, who surmise that

> there are many who fail to make amends before they die for the suffering they have caused others. Following their death, it seems they are temporarily restricted to lower levels of existence, not for punishment but for their spiritual healing and growth. Apparently they receive ongoing opportunities to advance to the higher levels of the spiritual dimension as they experience deep remorse, sincere repentance, and true rehabilitation. (239)

Having made these prefatory remarks, the Guggenheims quote from the case of Wanda, a 37-year-old woman whose occupation was in real estate and who had an after-death encounter with her husband Norm, who had taken his own life.

> A year after my husband passed away, I had a very vivid dream. Norm was in a place with other people. It was not a very cheery place—it was kind of dark and a little bit depressing. I remember feeling uncomfortable there, and I didn't have a very good feeling when I saw him.
>
> I approached him and asked, "Where are you? What are you doing here?" He told me he was in a holding place. That he had to be there until his life would have been over on earth. (240)

George Ritchie saw another part of the spirit prison in 1943 while he was in basic training at an army base in Texas. Hospitalized with a high fever, his spirit separated from his body and he was met by a man who seemed to be made of light; Ritchie identified the man as Jesus, the Son of God.

With Jesus as his guide, Ritchie was given a tour of the spirit world, a tour which included a wide flat plain where he saw

> hordes of ghostly discarnate beings. . . . And they were the most frustrated, the angriest, the most completely miserable beings I had ever laid eyes on.
>
> "Lord Jesus!" I cried. "Where are we?"
>
> At first I thought we were looking at some great battle-field; everywhere people were locked in what looked like fights to the death, writhing, punching, gouging. It couldn't be a present day [sic] war because there were no tanks or guns. No weapons of any sort, I saw as I looked closer, only bare hands and feet and teeth. . . .
>
> Although they appeared to be literally on top of each other, it was as though each man was boxing the air; at last I realized that of course, having no [physical] substance, they could not actually touch one another. They could not kill, though they clearly wanted to, because their intended victims were already dead, and so they hurled themselves at each other in a frenzy of impotent rage.
>
> . . . These creatures seemed locked into habits of mind and emotion, into hatred, lust, destructive thought-patterns. Even more hideous than the bites and kicks they exchanged were the sexual abuses many were performing in feverish pantomime. Perversions I had never dreamed of were being vainly attempted all around us. It was impossible to tell if the howls of frustration which reached us were actual sounds or only

> the transference of despairing thoughts. Indeed in this disembodied world it didn't seem to matter. Whatever anyone thought, however fleetingly or unwillingly, was instantly apparent to all around him, more completely than words could have expressed it, faster than sound waves could have carried it.
>
> . . . [H]owever, no condemnation came from the Presence at my side, only a compassion for these unhappy creatures that was breaking his heart. Clearly it was not His will that any one of them should be in this place. (Ritchie and Sherrill 63-65)

Many others besides Wanda and George Ritchie have seen portions of the spirit prison. In *The Eternal Journey* Craig R. Lundahl and Harold A. Widdison review the personal accounts of people who, during what is called a near-death experience, felt

> extreme fear or panic, emotional and mental anguish. . . being lost and helpless; intense feelings of loneliness. . . coupled with a great sense of desolation; and a dark, gloomy or barren and hostile environment. (222)

Lundahl and Widdison credit Angie Fenimore with the observation that "most people who are dying today are going to a place of darkness" (223).

In another near-death experience related by Lundahl and Widdison,

> It was black and there was a terrible wailing noise. There were a lot of other beings there, wailing and full of desperation. (225-26)

The 2 authors also cite Harriet Lee, who

> saw a region of the otherworld inhabited by millions

> of miserable and unhappy occupants. She said, "They were in great confusion, wringing their hands, holding them up, and tossing their bodies to and fro in fearful anguish." My [spiritual] guide said, "These are the spirits in prison; they know the punishment that awaits them and they are in great distress by reason of their knowledge." (235)

The parallels between these various accounts and the descriptions of the spirit prison presented from other sources should be obvious. In addition, the emotional turbulence that is an inevitable element of this prison is reflected in the ceiling of the antechamber, which, like the floor of the subterranean chamber, appears to be the result of some violent explosion (Rutherford, Book III, 1084).

However, it should be pointed out that since the horizontal passage measures 32 inches wide and 37 inches high while the antechamber is 6 feet square and 4 feet high, and since the antechamber is on the west side of the passage—west indicating movement to the right and therefore toward God—it represents, as perceived by Bill and Judy Guggenheim, the possibility of spiritual growth within the spirit prison.

That possibility became a reality when Christ himself entered the spirit world. Prior to that, as revealed by Christ's parable of the rich man and a beggar named Lazarus, there was a division between the wicked and the righteous spirits. In this parable, found in Luke 16:19-31, the beggar dies first and is "carried by the angels to Abraham's bosom"—which means he went to that part of the spirit world known as paradise—then the rich man dies and he ends up in the spirit prison. He sees Abraham and Lazarus far off and begs Abraham to send Lazarus to him so he can

> "dip the tip of his finger in water and cool my tongue; for I am tormented in this flame."

Abraham informs the rich man that he cannot send Lazarus because

> "between us and you there is a great gulf fixed, so that those who want to pass from here to you cannot, nor can those from there pass to us."

While he was in the spirit world Christ bridged that gulf, and at the same time he commissioned the spirits of the righteous who had been members of his church throughout the ages to begin teaching those in the spirit prison who were ready to listen. Christ himself would not have been able to do the necessary teaching in 3 short days. Why? Because of the number of people that would have been involved.

Consider, for instance, that during Enoch's lifetime alone the earth's population was probably close to 6 billion. To demonstrate that such a figure is not impossible, W. Cleon Skousen in *The First 2,000 Years* begins with Adam and Eve in 4,000 BC and then takes them up to their first fifty years, allowing for the conservative figure of 10 sets of parents as their descendents. Now, if "each of those couples had ten surviving children during the next 50 years" there would have been 100 surviving children in all. Continuing to base population growth on the ever-increasing number of couples, Skousen comes up with the figure of 4,882,812,500 people at the end of 650 years (143-44). If we then factor in Enoch's 365 years after that, 6 billion is certainly a feasible number.

Plus, we also have to consider the earth's population from the time of the great flood to the death of Christ. Could Christ have taught so many spirits in 3 days what he had taken 3½ years to teach the living in the relatively small country of Judea? No, of course not.

Continuing to focus on the antechamber, other factors ought to be considered before taking another look at the subterranean chamber. Among them is the fact that the numbers 4 and 6 (derived from the dimensions of the antechamber) have a symbolic significance that relates to the antechamber's function. Adding to what has already been said about 4, Richard H. Wilkinson writes in *Symbol & Magic in Egyptian Art*:

> the number 4 probably appears more frequently in

> Egyptian art and ritual than any other number—in contexts ranging from the four sides of pyramids and altars to groups of gods and ritual objects and activities. (133)
>
> [But the] number four was primarily related to the concepts of totality or universality through its relation to the four cardinal points. (144)

Remembering that the height of the descending passage is 4 feet and therefore the same as the antechamber, we can conclude that people from all 4 quarters of the earth will be in the spirit prison.

Six, on the other hand, implies incompletion and imperfection, especially when compared to the number 7. For instance, as Vicki Alder comments in *Mysteries in the Scriptures: Enlightenment Through Ancient Beliefs*, the earth was created in 7 creative periods, the 7th day was sanctified by God, "King Solomon completed his famous temple in *seven* years (1 Kings 6:38)", the "number seven was also used in the completion of a number of religious feasts in ancient times"—in short, the number 7 "appears to have significance in denoting perfection or final completion" (120-122 and 125).

Six, then, falls short of perfection and completion. In addition, as pointed out by E. W. Bullinger, "*six* is also the number of man in his opposition to and independence of God" (123), and so the 6-foot-square measurement of the antechamber is appropriately symbolic of the spirits confined in the spirit prison.

Here is one more thought on the antechamber. Joseph, the son of Jacob, was 17 when his older brothers sold him as a slave to Ishmaelite traders who carried him off to Egypt (Genesis 37: 2 and 28). There, we are told in "The Testament of Joseph", he served Potiphar for 7 years until, at the age of 24, he was imprisoned (Platt, Jr. I:29; all of *The Testaments of the Twelve Patriarchs*—the patriarchs being the sons of Jacob—which are included in *The Lost Books of the Bible and the Forgotten Books of Eden*, should be part of the Bible, for even though the translations are based on copies, and even though the copies are bound to be abbreviations of longer works, they are nevertheless authentic and provide valuable details about these 12 brothers that are not in the Bible as we currently have it).

At the age of 30, Joseph was set free and made the ruler of all Egypt, second in power only to the pharaoh (Genesis 41:46). If we subtract 24 from 30, the result is 6—the number of years Joseph was in prison. Moreover, Cleon Skousen advises us that the "administrative quarters [were] above ground for those in charge while prisoners were confined below the ground in a dungeon" (*The Third Thousand Years* 98; see also Genesis 40:15).

In addition, it was the king's prison where Joseph was kept; this is known because sometime before the end of his 4th year the pharaoh's chief butler and "chief baker"—who was not actually a baker but rather "chief of the butchers" (Skousen, *The Third Thousand Years*, 96; "chief of the butchers" means he butchered people, not animals)—were confined in the same dungeon (Genesis 40:1-3).

It was at the end of Joseph's 4th year of imprisonment that these 2 political prisoners had prophetic dreams which Joseph correctly interpreted and which 2 years later resulted in his release from prison.

With Joseph, then, we have the numbers 4 and 6 associated with his stay in an underground prison which was under the king's personal control, just as the spirit prison is under Christ's personal control.

But we should not make the mistake of thinking that Joseph was guilty of any crime so severe that he deserved to be in prison. Just the opposite was true; he was imprisoned because of a lie, and as a result he was numbered with the transgressors, just as Christ would be many centuries later.

With Joseph, we might add, there are more connections with Christ, especially when we consider the number 13. For instance, in verse 9 of Chapter 37 of Genesis, Joseph dreams that 13 astronomical figures bow down to him; the figures—listed as the sun, the moon and 11 stars—represent his father, his mother, and his 11 brothers. (Incidentally, it is in verse 33 of this chapter that Jacob comes to believe Joseph has been killed by a wild beast. How old was Christ when he died? He was 33.)

Additionally, Jacob had been married to his second wife Rachel for 13 years when she gave birth to Joseph; Joseph had lived in Egypt for 13 years when he became the governor of the land; and his story is told in 13 chapters in Genesis (i.e. chapters 37 and 39-50).

It is also interesting to note that Joseph's life ends with verse 26 of the last chapter of Genesis. What is the angle of the descending passage? It is 26 degrees (Edwards 101).

Another measurement to be considered while discussing the horizontal passage is its height of 37 inches. If we subtract 37 inches from 48 inches, the height of the descending passage, the result is 11 inches—and Joseph was the 11th son of Jacob.

But there is another reason for the height having been set at 37 inches. In *Jesus Christ: the* [sic] *Number of His Name*, Bonnie Gaunt emphasizes the fact that the letters in both the ancient Hebrew and Greek alphabets "were used as numerals" (4), and therefore words and names in the Old and New Testament have "a number equivalent"—in other words, she is talking about gematria (6-7). And she demonstrates quite convincingly that the number 37 is "basic to the names and titles of Jesus" (179).

To validate her claim, Gaunt lists examples from the Bible that add up to 37 when the letters are converted to their numerical values. These examples include:

He lives (Isaiah 33:5)

He rules (Psalm 66:7)

Judge of all the earth (Genesis 18:25)

I am Alpha and Omega

Nazarene

The Rock

Son of Man (Matthew 8:20)

The Door (John 10:9)

Lord of Hosts (I Samuel 1:3)

The Holy One of Jacob (Isaiah 29:23)

The God of Israel

I am the life

The resurrection (Philippians 3:1)

Chief cornerstone (I Peter 2:6)

The Son of God (Galatians 2:20)

(180-186, 188 and 193)

The number 37 is also associated with Joseph, since, as pointed out above, it is in Chapter 37 of Genesis that he is first introduced. This introduction occurs in verse 2, where we're told Joseph was feeding his father's flock of sheep with his brothers; afterwards he gave his father a "bad report" of his brothers. In "The Testament of Gad", who was the 9th son of Jacob, we learn why:

> Joseph told our father that the sons of Zilpah and Bilhah [2 of Jacob's 4 wives] were slaying the best of the flock and eating them against the judgement of Reuben and Judah [Reuben being Jacob's first son and Judah the fourth]. (Platt, Jr. I:6)

In *The Book of Enoch the Prophet*, 37 shepherds fail to protect their sheep, meaning the Lord's people, "while the sheep were eaten up by the dogs. . . until their bones alone remained; until their bones fell upon the ground." The Lord's response is to take "in his hand the sceptre of his wrath" and shake the earth so that it is "rent asunder", after which the shepherds are tried, found guilty and thrust into an abyss—which "was on the right" side of a "house" that is immerged, meaning it is sunk into the earth (Laurence LXXXIX:1, 6, 26, 33, 36 and 38).

* * *

It has been observed that there is a difference of 11 inches between the height of the horizontal passage and the descending passage. There is also a difference between the width of the horizontal passage and the descending passage, that difference being 10 inches (42 minus 32). The number 10 brings to mind the 10 commandments. Breaking those commandments leads to the lowest degree of glory when repentance is lacking.

The exit from the antechamber is 5 feet from the entrance to the subterranean chamber (Rutherford, Book III, 1071). The number 5, according to David Furlong, "finds expression through the five senses and is associated with communication and movement as portrayed by the god Hermes [who, as a reminder, is Enoch; however, Hermes—and Thoth as well—can also represent Christ in certain contexts]" (297).

The Masons employ the number 5 in the ceremony that is required to attain the Third Degree, which "is calculated to bind men together by mystic points of fellowship, as in a bond of fraternal affection and brotherly love". During this ceremony the candidate is symbolically resurrected from the dead by the Worshipful Master gripping his wrist "and raising him on the five points of fellowship" (Knight and Lomas, *The Hiram Key* 10 and 13).

The 5 feet between the antechamber and the entrance to the subterranean chamber are illustrative of a statement made by Melvin J. Ballard:

> no man or woman will come forth in the resurrection until they have completed their work, until they have overcome, until they have done as much as they can do. (Quoted in Crowther 22)

By the time of the final judgment, then, the people in the spirit prison should have reached a point where they can live together in peace and fellowship.

* * *

In Book III of *Pyramidology* Rutherford gives one of the most detailed descriptions of the subterranean chamber that can be found in the literature about the Great Pyramid. This chamber, he states,

> is roughly divided into two halves, eastern and western. The eastern half lies much lower down and varies from 12 to 18 feet below the roof. The bottom of the northeast corner is roughly and irregularly from 1½ to 2 feet below the floor of the entrance doorway. (1089)
>
> The western half of the bottom of the Subterranean Chamber rises, at first abruptly, then gradually towards the west wall. This half has high ridges of rock lying practically east and west and thus almost parallel to each other and, at some points, reaching almost to the roof. Right along the east-west centerline or axis of the Chamber, in this western half, there runs a sort of open passage way [sic] sunk down between the ridges and dividing them into two sections. (1091)
>
> The entrance to the Dead End Passage is at the eastern extremity of the south wall of the Subterranean Chamber, and is opposite to the entrance into the Chamber at the eastern extremity of the north wall, although at a different level. . . . The floor of this Dead End Passage lies at a level 41 inches lower down than that of the Subterranean Chamber Passage and at the entrance it is only a few inches above the uneven bottom of the Chamber. (1092)
>
> The Dead End Passage floor is covered throughout its entire length with a very fine dark limestone mould to a depth of several inches. (1093)

Mold ("mould" is a British spelling), being a fungus that breaks down organic matter, is an apt symbol for the degenerative, depraved, decadent people who will be cast out into outer darkness.

A woman who tried to commit suicide at the age of 26 had an experience that brings to mind both the dead-end passage and the subterranean chamber. She says she suddenly felt herself

> slipping down, not straight down, but on an angle, as if on a slide. It was cold, dark, and watery. When I reached the bottom, it resembled the entrance to a cave. . . . The inside of the cave was gray and brown in color.
>
> I heard cries, wails, moans, and the gnashing of teeth. I saw these beings, that resembled humans, with the shape of a head and body. But they were ugly and grotesque. . . . They were frightening and sounded like they were tormented, in agony. No one spoke to me.
>
> I never went inside the cave, but stood at the entrance only. I remember saying to myself, "I don't want to stay here." I tried to lift myself up as though trying to pull myself (my spirit) up out of this pit. That's the last thing I remember. (Quoted in Greyson and Bush 225)

There is more description of the subterranean chamber in Rutherford's book, but what is being omitted will fit better with a discussion of other parts of the Great Pyramid as well as the other 2 major pyramids on the Giza plateau. In addition, numbers such as 41 will be linked to other discoveries such as the boat pit that was found on the south side of the Great Pyramid in 1954 (see Volume 2 of *Books Written in Stone*). In the meantime, what has been quoted provides a visual depiction of Paul's statement regarding the lowest kingdom of glory.

Despite the barren and forbidding appearance of the subterranean chamber, the lowest kingdom still constitutes a positive afterlife. In fact, a source that is usually identified by the shortened title of *Doctrine and Covenants* calls this lowest kingdom the telestial kingdom and specifies that its glory "surpasses all understanding" (section 76, verse 89).

At the same time, however, we should keep in mind that the subterranean chamber is "nearly 100′ below ground level" (Lepre 72) and Enoch meant for that fact to send a clear message that the telestial kingdom is not a kingdom to strive for. However, since the subterranean chamber "is by far the largest chamber in the Great Pyramid, being larger than the others put together" (Rutherford, Book III, 1084), it is painfully obvious that the lowest kingdom is where the majority of mankind will spend their immortal lives.

8. ASCENDING

> "I say to you, if you have faith as a mustard seed, you will say to this mountain, 'Move from here to there,' and it will move; and nothing will be impossible for you."
>
> (Matthew 17:20)

The whereabouts of the prism stone that once concealed the beginning of the ascending passage is unknown, however, what it symbolized is known. It symbolized faith, and that is why the stone was shaped like a prism. Prisms are multisided, which suggests the fact that faith can be developed in many different ways; in addition, glass prisms can separate white light into a spectrum and they can reflect light, and prisms in the form of crystals have three or more similar surfaces that are parallel to a single axis, all of which is similar to the way families should be structured, with the faith of the mother and father spreading out to their children, their children then reflecting their faith, and the entire family functioning around a single axis—faith in God the Father and in Christ, his son.

But there is more to the missing stone than that since it also represents the "narrow gate" that "leads to life, [unfortunately,] there are few who find it" (Matthew 7:14). Christ's declaration is especially apropos when we recall that the beginning of the ascending passage went undetected for almost 4000 years, and then when it was finally revealed, explorers such as J. P. Lepre found that the ascending passage was somewhat funnel shaped, with the narrowest point of the funnel enclosing the 3 granite stones that were concealed behind the prism stone (77).

Much nonsense has been written about these 3 stones. According to Egyptologists, they were originally stored in the Grand Gallery and then, after the pharaoh's mummy was placed in the King's Chamber, they were slid down the ascending passage in order to plug its entrance so that tomb robbers would not be able to plunder the pharaoh's treasure (Lehner 113).

However, in the first quarter of the 20th century David Davidson came to realize that

> the depth and width of the granite plugs closing the lower end of the 1st Ascending Passage clearly show that the plugs were built into the passage when the Pyramid masonry had reached the height of the plugs. This is certain from the fact that half an inch of clearance at the sides and top in the 1st Ascending Passage would not be sufficient to ensure the granite plugs being lowered from the Grand Gallery without risk of jamming in the descent of the 1st Ascending Passage. [According to Richard W. Noone, the clearance is "less than one-sixteenth of an inch" (181).] It is clear, then, that the granite plugs were in position before the Pyramid courses had reached the height of the lower end of the Grand Gallery. (180)

Davidson's argument is echoed by Peter Lemesurier who confirms that "the Pyramid's design shows that the blocks of the Granite Plug *cannot* be 'taken down'. They are built into the Ascending Passage as a permanent feature" (56). Adam Rutherford, sharing that point of view, expresses his opinion that the 3 granite stones symbolize "the perfect Law of God as given to the Israelites through Moses" (Book III, 963).

Christopher Dunn has a different explanation, claiming that the 3 plugs had served to provide feedback on what was happening as energy was building up in the Grand Gallery, where he says sound was generated by an assembly of resonators that ran the full length of the passage (164-168). He adds:

> the ancient Egyptians may have cancelled out excess vibrations by using an out-of-phase interference sound wave. My inquiry began with the Ascending Passage, for it is the only feature inside the Great Pyramid that contains "devices" that are directly accessible from the outside. If the operators of the machine found it necessary to cancel out vibrations, they would have to be able to *quickly respond* to this need from the machine's exterior. (175-76; italics added)

Quickly Respond? Dunn is silent on just how near—or far—the beginning of the ascending passage is from the pyramid's original entrance. Petrie supplies the figure: it is 1110.64 inches, or 92.5533 feet (18). Admittedly, not a great distance, but in order to get to the granite stones from outside the pyramid the Egyptian technicians—assuming they were between 5 and 6 feet tall—could not have run down the descending passage, not with its 4-foot high ceiling. And even if they had been midgets or dwarves they still would have had problems coping with the passage's 26-degree slope, which even in 1865 caused Piazzi Smyth's measuring rods to go shooting down the floor "with a velocity increasing every moment" if he wasn't careful (475).

If Dunn's theory had any merit, would not the ancient Egyptians have installed some kind of control at the base of the pyramid? After all, the original entrance is 55 feet above the base (Lawton and Ogilvie-Herald 19) and unless the Egyptians had a permanent guardhouse built right outside the entrance and kept it manned, the impossibility of responding quickly to any emergency inside the Grand Gallery is all too obvious.

To give Dunn some credit, he does bring up a weakness in the Egyptologists' assertion that the stones were meant to keep out tomb robbers. He charges that

> it was not necessary to use granite to block this passage. . . limestone would have been sufficient. Realistically, limestone would have been better. The

> very fact that the stones "blocking" this passage are granite contradicts their effectiveness at securing the inner chambers from robbers. . . . In fact, they had the opposite effect, drawing Al Mamun's attention to the existence of the Ascending Passage and, subsequently, to the entire internal arrangement of passages and chambers. (176)

Rutherford's reason for the granite stones is much closer to the truth than the hypotheses of Dunn or the Egyptologists. As Rutherford says, the stones are symbols, but they do not symbolize the Mosaic Law; instead, they symbolize repentance, baptism by immersion in water, and baptism by fire, which is the gift of the Holy Ghost or Holy Spirit.

In general, the use of granite in the Great Pyramid signifies—as Rutherford recognized correctly this time—a connection with "the Divine, the Infinite, the Immortal" (Book III, 961). And the ascent toward God begins first with faith, which, to be truly effective, needs to be followed by repentance, which in turn needs to be followed by baptism and by the laying on of hands for the gift of the Holy Spirit.

This pattern is made explicit in the Acts of the Apostles. On the day known as Pentecost, Jews from various nations who had gathered in Jerusalem took part in a miracle; though they spoke different languages, they were suddenly able to understand what Christ's disciples were saying in their own individual tongues. Perplexed by what was happening, they began asking each other what it meant.

Simon Peter then rose up to explain that God, as the prophet Joel had predicted, was pouring out his spirit on his servants. Peter then went on to testify of Christ, affirming his resurrection and his

> being exalted to the right hand of God, and [as a result of] having received from the Father the promise of the Holy Spirit, He [has] poured out this which you now see and hear. (2:33)

Peter was so persuasive that the Jews who were not members of the church asked what they should do. Peter replied,

> "Repent, and let every one of you be baptized in the name of Jesus Christ for the remission of sins; and you shall receive the gift of the Holy Spirit." (2:38)

In a later chapter in Acts, we're told that

> when the apostles who were at Jerusalem heard that Samaria had received the word of God, they sent Peter and John to them, who, when they had come down, prayed for them that they might receive the Holy Spirit.
>
> For as yet He had fallen upon none of them. They had only been baptized in the name of the Lord Jesus.
>
> Then they laid hands on them, and they received the Holy Spirit. (8:14-17)

The account doesn't end there, for a man named Simon, who is identified as a sorcerer, becomes involved.

> And when Simon saw that through the laying on of the apostles' hands the Holy Spirit was given, he offered them money, saying, "Give me this power also, that anyone on whom I lay hands may receive the Holy Spirit."
>
> But Peter said to him, "Your money perish with you, because you thought that the gift of God could be purchased with money!" (8:18-20)

The power and the authority to perform baptisms and the laying on of hands cannot be purchased, nor can they simply be assumed by someone who has had a spiritual experience and therefore thinks he or she has been called by God to be his servant. Paul is a perfect example of what has to be done to obtain the authority to act in Christ's name.

Paul, who was first known by his Jewish name of Saul, became a fervent enemy of the Church of Jesus Christ because, as an orthodox Jew, he believed the powerful teaching of the apostles threatened to overturn the law of Moses by which he lived. As an orthodox Jew he failed to realize that the law of Moses was meant to prepare the Israelites for the fulness of Christ's teachings. However, while he was on the way from Jerusalem to Damascus to persecute members of the church who resided there, Christ appeared to him in a vision and Saul was instantly and completely converted. Nevertheless, for him to obtain the priesthood, which is the authority to act in the name of Christ, he had to be baptized first and then receive the gift of the Holy Spirit. To bring that about, a member of the church named Ananias was directed by Christ himself to go to Saul and perform the necessary ordinances (Acts 9:9-18).

Baptism and the laying on of hands for the gift of the Holy Spirit *and* for ordination to the priesthood, as well as priesthood blessings, have to be performed by authorized servants of Christ, otherwise they are of no force. That fact was conveyed by Christ when he told his disciples,

> "Not everyone who says to Me, 'Lord, Lord,' shall enter the kingdom of heaven, but he who does the will of My Father in Heaven.
>
> "Many will say to Me in that day, 'Lord, Lord, have we not prophesied in Your name, cast out demons in Your name, and done many wonders in Your name?'
>
> "And then I will declare to them, 'I never knew you; depart from Me, you who practice lawlessness!'" (Matthew 7:21-23)

Along with the prism stone and the granite plugs serving as symbols, consider the fact that the passage dug out of the limestone around the plugs is on the west side, not the east side (Edwards 103). West, it should be recalled, means moving toward God. Additionally, each of the 3 granite stones is 5 feet long (Lepre 75), and the number 5, as discussed in the previous chapter, is related to fellowship, and baptism and the laying on of hands for the gift of the Holy Spirit—and for confirmation as a member of the church, which actually precedes the gift of the Holy Spirit—make new members "no longer strangers and foreigners, but fellow citizens with the saints and members of the household of God" (Hebrews 2:19).

Taken together, the 3 granite stones have a combined length of 180 inches (Worth Smith 82). In addition, 180 inches is the vertical distance from the Great Pyramid's pavement to the beginning of the ascending passage (Petrie 31).

The number 180 leads us to the 21st patriarch of the Old Testament: Isaac. In the New Testament, the Epistle to the Hebrews points to Isaac, along with his father and mother—Abraham and Sarah—as an example of faith:

> By faith Abraham obeyed when he was called to go out to the place which he would receive as an inheritance. And he went out, not knowing where he was going.
>
> By faith he dwelt in the land of promise as in a foreign country, dwelling in tents with Isaac and Jacob, the heirs with him of the same promise. (11:8-9)
>
> By faith Sarah herself also received strength to conceive seed, and she bore a child when she was past the age [of childbearing], because she judged Him [God] faithful who had promised. (11:11)
>
> By faith Abraham, when he was tested, offered up Isaac, and he who had received the promises offered up his only begotten son. (11:17)

This last verse refers to the dramatic events described in the 22nd chapter of Genesis. In verse 2 of that chapter the Lord commands Abraham to offer up his son Isaac "as a burnt offering on one of the mountains of which I shall tell you."

To reach the mountain Abraham had to travel a good distance. "Then on the *third* day Abraham lifted his eyes and saw the place afar off" (22:4; italics added). As the narration continues:

> Abraham built an altar there and placed the wood in order; and he bound Isaac his son and laid him on the altar, upon the wood.
>
> And Abraham stretched out his hand and took the knife to slay his son. (22:9-10)

At the last moment "the Angel of the Lord", who was Enoch, commanded Abraham to stop (22:11-12).

> Then Abraham lifted his eyes and looked, and there behind him was a ram caught in a thicket by its horns. So Abraham went and took the ram, and offered it up for a burnt offering instead of his son. (22:13)

Isaac, as Abraham's "only begotten son" who was faithfully offered up as a sacrifice and then restored to life on the 3rd day, was clearly a Christ-figure. And he was, like Christ, a child of promise who fulfilled prophecy.

And he lived to be 180 years old (Genesis 35:28).

Returning to the 11th chapter of the Epistle to the Hebrews, we read: "By faith Isaac blessed Jacob" (verse 20).

As we have learned, the distance from the original entrance to the beginning of the ascending passage is 92 feet. Jacob's name was changed to *Israel* by the Lord when Jacob was 92. This is determined by the fact that Jacob was 130 when he went to Egypt (Genesis 47:9) while Joseph was 39 (he began to rule Egypt when he was 30 and it was 9 years later that he was reunited with his father; see Genesis 41:46-47 and 45:11), and 39 from 130 equals 91, Jacob's age when Joseph was born. It was during the next year, after Jacob led his family out of Haran back to the land of Canaan, the land promised to Abraham and his descendants through Isaac, that his name was changed (see Genesis chapters 30-32; Jacob's name is changed in 32:28).

Bible scholars have tried to determine the meaning of Jacob's new name by referring to the statement that follows his renaming, which reads, "for you [Jacob] have struggled with God and with men, and have prevailed." Because of this statement Dummelow's *Bible Commentary* says *Israel* means "Perseverer with God", *perseverer* being a synonym for *prevailed* (37). *Nelson's Illustrated Bible Dictionary* offers the following comment on this subject:

> The name Israel has been interpreted by different scholars as "prince with God," "he strives with God," "let God rule," or "God strives." (Lockyer, Sr. 519)

None of these definitions is entirely correct. To understand the significance of the name *Israel* we have to separate it into its syllables: Is/ra/el. Now, let's capitalize Ra and El. Ra, Veronica Ions asserts, "was the [Egyptian] god personifying the sun" (41). He was known by other names; as Auf-Ra or simply Auf he wore a crown with a sun disk "borne between *the horns of a ram*. . . . Ra was also represented as the divine child". And he was revered as the "upholder of truth on earth and as judge of the dead" (*Egyptian Mythology* 45; italics added).

The god of the Hebrews was also known by various names, but the "root name for God in the Old Testament is El." Examples of the use of El include Abraham's planting

> a tamarisk tree at Beersheba "and there [he] called on the name of the Lord (Yahweh), the Everlasting God (El Olam) (Gen. 21:33). Jacob built an altar on a piece of land he purchased at Shechem and called it "El Elohe Israel" ("God, the God of Israel"). . . (Gen. 32:28-30;

> 33:20). (Lockyer, Sr., *Nelson's Illustrated Bible Dictionary* 428)

The name *Israel* means, in essence, *Ra is El*, or *El is Ra*; they are one and the same God. (This is one explanation of *Israel*; there is another explanation, and it, plus the meaning of *Is* in *Israel* will be given in Volume 2 of *Books Written in Stone*.)

At the beginning of the ascending passage, then, we have an association with Abraham, Isaac and Jacob, the 3 patriarchs whose names were always linked by the Israelites to the Lord.

> God said to Moses, "Thus you shall say to the children of Israel: 'The Lord God of your fathers, the God of Abraham, the God of Isaac, and the God of Jacob, has sent me to you. This is My name forever, and this is My memorial to all generations.'
>
> "Go and gather the elders of Israel together [the elders being holders of the higher priesthood and not necessarily elderly], and say to them, 'The Lord God of your fathers, the God of Abraham, of Isaac, and of Jacob, appeared to me, saying, "I have surely visited you and seen what is done to you in Egypt"'". (Exodus 3:15-16)

From Acts 3:13 we have:

> "The God of Abraham, Isaac, and Jacob, the God of our fathers, glorified His Servant Jesus".

Accepting the theory that the 3 granite blocks were slid down the ascending passage, Edwards hypothesizes that the

> existence of a small gap between the first two plugs shows that the free fall of the second had been well judged, perhaps by reducing the lubrication of the

> corridor near the bottom end [which lubrication he and others say would have been necessary in order to move the heavy granite blocks, which Lepre estimates weighed seven tons each (75), down the full 129-foot length of the passage (77)]. (290)

In making such a claim, Edwards, as well as other Egyptologists, is ignoring one important fact mentioned by none other than Petrie. During his close examination of the ascending passage Petrie found "a bit of granite still cemented to the floor some way farther south of" the 3rd granite block (21). Considering the extremely small allowance between the ceiling of the ascending passage and the height of the 3 stones, how did they get past this bit of cemented granite without knocking it loose?

It could be argued, of course, that the bit was cemented to the floor of the passage after the blocks were slid into place, but then it would be necessary to ask not only how that could have been done with the passage being completely sealed but also *why* it would have been done.

Petrie recorded one other important detail pertaining to the 3 blocks. He wrote: "the faces next [to] each other are never very flat, being *wavy* about + or - .3 [inches]" (21; italics added).

There is a gap between the first 2 stones because repentance is one act while baptism is another, and the faces of the stones are wavy to represent the waters of baptism. However, there are people who are sorry for certain things they have done but are not baptized. Without baptism, they will never pass through the door that leads upward to exaltation in the highest kingdom of heaven.

What did Christ say?

> "[U]nless one is born of the water and of the Spirit, he cannot enter the kingdom of God." (John 3:5)

Christ meant that one has to be baptized by water and by the Holy Spirit in order to be exalted. Even he was no exception, having told John the Baptist that he had to be baptized if he was to "fulfill all righteousness" (Matthew 3:15).

In contrast to the first 2 stones, the 2nd and 3rd stones are butted together (Lemesurier 55). That is because in the Church of Jesus Christ anyone who is baptized by water will always receive the gift of the Holy Spirit by the laying on of hands. The two ordinances are inseparable.

With this understanding of the purpose behind the 3 granite blocks, we can also understand another important point that Petrie makes about the 3rd block and the bit of granite cemented to the floor of the ascending passage. The 3rd block, he notes, was roughly broken off at its upper end, and that, combined with the position of the bit of granite, indicated "that originally the plug was 24 inches beyond its present end" (21).

How far offset is the original entrance to the pyramid? It is 24 feet to the east of center (Lehner 111). Why was it offset that way? Because it illustrates our moving away from the Lord when we come to this earth. We return to the center, meaning to the Lord, by keeping the commandments, which include developing faith, repenting, being baptized and receiving the gift of the Holy Spirit to guide us in our activities and in our thoughts. And that is why the 3rd granite stone was originally "24 inches beyond its present end."

* * *

One of the most mysterious features in the entire pyramid is the existence of what are called girdle stones, several of which appear in the ascending passage. Relying on information reported by Petrie, Edwards states:

> all the stones which he [Petrie] could see in the. . . part of the corridor occupied by the [granite] plugs were girdle-stones—a name used to describe either single stones or two stones, laid one above the other, with a rectangular hole in the middle through which the

> corridor passed. Each stone thus provided the ceiling, the walls and the floor of the corridor.

Edwards adds that

> Much of the corridor beyond the plugs also consists of girdle-stones, but further on they were laid at regular distances of about 17 feet 2 inches apart. (103)

Lepre also depends on Petrie for his observation that the wall blocks in the ascending passage "were set horizontally for the first half of the length of the passageway, but were inclined to the rising angle of the passageway for the second half of its length." Lepre sees the change in the way the wall blocks were laid as a sign that "the builders had now initiated a dramatic change of direction", but then he says that the builders at this point "conceived of incorporating an ascending passage system into their ultimate plan" (78).

He's not quite correct about the "dramatic change of direction" and not correct at all about the construction plan being altered. One of John Anthony West's comments in *Serpent in the Sky* sheds some light on this matter. West writes:

> nowhere in Egypt is there a scene showing an architect at work. Nothing indicates the manner in which the prodigious monuments of Egypt were planned, designed or executed. A few fragmentary plans laid out carefully on papyri set out in grids prove that plans existed—which comes as no surprise. But not a word of the knowledge underlying those plans. That architectural knowledge existed. There is the architecture to prove it. The technical skill of the Egyptians has always been self-evident. It is now equally evident that this was matched by a profound knowledge of harmony, proportion, geometry and design. And it is clear that all

> of this knowledge, technical and theoretical, was secret and sacred, and that those secrets were kept. (27-28)

West's insightful deduction is borne out by the fact that Enoch was given the design of the Giza pyramids, both inside and out, by Christ, just as King David, hundreds of years later, was given the design of the temple which his son Solomon would build (see I Chronicles 28:11-13), and so there were no changes in the plan either before or after construction began. And, knowing that Christ was the architect helps us to appreciate Worth Smith's deduction that the creator of the Great Pyramid was "a towering intellectual and spiritual giant" (52).

Before detailing the purpose behind the girdle stones and the horizontal wall stones in the first half of the ascending passage, it is necessary to establish a point that has already been touched on but has not been developed at length. That point is the contention that the Great Pyramid, even though it was built approximately 5,000 years ago, was intended to be understood not by earlier generations but by this generation, the generation of the last days.

Consider these remarks:

> **David Davidson**: "the designer of the Pyramid deemed he was projecting his knowledge into a future stage of civilisation that could interpret his intention" (139).
>
> **Worth Smith**: "The Great Pyramid we have found was 'sealed up' until nearly 'the time of the end'" (137).
>
> **Peter Lemesurier**: "the Pyramid's designer appears to have taken precautions against the decipherment of the Pyramid's message at too early a date" (36).
>
> **Wilfred J. Gregson**, an architect quoted in *5/5/2000* by Richard W. Noone: "*I know of no architect today* who would have the knowledge necessary to build what we know of the Great Pyramid, let alone what we don't know. . . . [T]here is more concealed within the structure

> than we have discovered, and I think that the purpose of the Great Pyramid was to pass on to later generations what they did discover" (116; Noone's italics).

Compare the remarks just quoted to this statement from the beginning of *1 Enoch*:

> "Enoch a righteous man, whose eyes were opened by God, saw the vision of the Holy One in the heavens, which the angels showed me, and from them I heard everything, and from them I understood as I saw, but not for this generation, but for a remote one which is to come." (Quoted in Robinson and Robinson 151)

Here is James H. Charlesworth's translation of this same passage:

> The blessing of Enoch: with which he blessed the elect and the righteous who would be present on the day of tribulation at (the time of) the removal of all the ungodly ones. And Enoch, the blessed and righteous man of the Lord, took up (his parable) while his eyes were open and he saw, and said, "(This is) a holy vision from the heavens which the angels showed me: and I heard from them everything and I understood. I look not for this generation but for the distant one that is coming. I speak about the elect ones and concerning them. (Volume 1, 13)

VanderKam, in his analysis of *1 Enoch*, comes to the understanding that the "future will be a literal return to the conditions of the first people", which includes the time of Enoch before he and his people were translated (56).

That "return to the conditions of the first people" began in earnest in 1820 when a boy of 14, who had been taught to have faith in God by his parents, and who had no doubt that God would answer his prayer, wanted to know which church he should join. This was an important issue to him because the churches where he lived in upstate New York were making a push for new members and the various ministers were at odds with each other, some, for instance, teaching that baptism was essential for salvation while others insisted just the opposite was true.

That 14-year-old did have his prayer answered—in person, when God the Father and his son Jesus Christ appeared to him. As a consequence, when the boy matured into a young man he was commissioned by Christ to restore his church with the same foundation it had enjoyed in former ages, that foundation being prophets and apostles, with Christ himself being the chief cornerstone.

But the restoration of the church did not end there. Along with the return of the proper foundation came the return of the priesthood, and, just as there had been temples—Houses of the Lord—in the days of Enoch and at various times throughout the Old and New Testament periods, so temples were soon being built in what has come to be known as the Dispensation of the Fulness of Times. (For those who are interested, there are numerous books that give an account of the restoration of the Church of Jesus Christ, but one of the best, and an excellent place to begin, is *A Marvelous Work and a Wonder* by LeGrand Richards.)

The washings and anointings, the endowments and the sealings performed in these temples were—and are—basically the same as they were anciently. That is so because Christ himself restored the sacred knowledge that was crucial to the House of the Lord, knowledge that had been taken from the earth in the past whenever total apostasy occurred, as it had among the Israelites—and among the Egyptians as well.

The boy who was instrumental in fulfilling a prophecy by Peter that in the "times of refreshing" God would "send Jesus Christ. . . whom heaven must receive until the times of restoration of all things, which God has spoken by the mouth of all His holy prophets since the world began" (Acts 3:19-21), was named after his father, Joseph Smith.

It is because of the restoration of the Church of Jesus Christ—now known as the Church of Jesus Christ of Latter-day Saints—and the restoration of the temple ordinances, that it is possible to understand not only who built the pyramids of Giza but why they were built. And that means the opinions that were recorded above and the statement in *1 Enoch* are on the mark.

But before returning to the girdle stones in the ascending passage, a little more information has to be provided. In these last days, as the forces of evil have continually increased, the Church of Jesus Christ of Latter-Day Saints has, under direct inspiration from Christ, instituted certain programs to spiritually strengthen the younger members. One of these programs is the Young Women's organization. Twelve-year-old girls are brought into the program as Beehives; 14-year-old girls are called Mia Maids, and 16-year-old girls advance to become Laurels. The young women learn to become leaders by participating in lessons and in various activities that are supervised by adult women.

For the boys, there is the priesthood. Twelve-year-olds who are judged worthy by their bishop receive the Aaronic Priesthood—the lesser or Levitical priesthood spoken of by Paul in Hebrews 7:11—and are ordained to the office of a Deacon. Fourteen-year-olds are ordained to the office of a Teacher, and 16-year-olds are ordained Priests—but not High Priests, for that office pertains to the higher priesthood, the Melchizedek Priesthood (Hebrews 7:12-28).

To spiritually strengthen the adult women, there is the Relief Society, an organization which was established by Joseph Smith in 1842 (Brooks 409) and which is today the world's largest organization for women; for the men there is the Melchizedek Priesthood, with the offices of Elder, Seventy, High Priest, Apostle and Prophet.

And now, back to the girdle stones, which Edwards speculates must have been intended to strengthen the masonry in the ascending passage (290). Lepre agrees, believing that "they insured a greater support than regular stones would" (78). Lehner refers to Ludwig Borchardt, who theorized that "the so-called 'girdle stones'. . . represent the accretions of an inner step pyramid" (219).

The pyramidologists take the position that the ascending passage, in Lemesurier's words, begs "specific identification with the historical development of Judaism"; however, Lemesurier allows that "other, parallel, evolutionary paths may equally well be alluded to." After that qualifier, he is honest enough to concede that the "historical significance of the three girdle-stones is none too easy to ascertain" (59).

There are actually more than 3 of these special stones, for Lepre lists 3 that he labels as "half-girdles" and 4 that are full girdles. The "half-girdles" are "split at their midsections to form a top and a bottom portion rather than one continuous, unbroken block" (78). Though Lepre avoids pointing out the obvious, the fact that there are 3 "half-girdles" makes it clear that these peculiar stones were not meant to strengthen the masonry.

In that case, what purpose do they serve?

Rutherford notes that for 24 feet beyond the 3 granite blocks the girdle stones "are crowded thickly together touching each other" (Book III, 969). This additional occurrence of the number 24 is intentional, for this first group of stones represents the Young Women's organization, the adult women's Relief Society, the Aaronic Priesthood, and the office of Elder in the Melchizedek Priesthood.

The 3 half-girdles, which are in this group, are linked specifically to the Aaronic Priesthood and its three offices of Deacon, Teacher and Priest. Like the half-girdles, this lesser priesthood is incomplete; it has its limitations; it does not hold all the keys needed to administer the affairs of the church. Priests, for example, may perform the ordinance of baptism, but they cannot participate in the laying on of hands for the gift of the Holy Spirit. That ordinance, as well as all the ordinances associated with the temple, requires the higher priesthood. The Aaronic Priesthood is to prepare the young men for the Melchizedek Priesthood, which they are eligible to receive at the age of 18, assuming they are worthy of advancement.

It is the stones in this contiguous group that are horizontal or vertical to the ground. This feature tells us that the members of the church who are progressing spiritually are upright and moving in the right direction, as opposed to those who are on a downward slide, as represented by the descending passage.

Moving on up the ascending passage past the group of contiguous girdle stones, there are 3 more that are complete and that are also vertical to the ground, however, the first of these 3 is separated from the lower group by "10 Royal Cubits", or by 17 feet, as recorded by Edwards. The 2nd stone is separated from the 1st by the same figure, as is the 3rd from the 2nd (Rutherford, Book III, 969).

These 3 girdle stones represent 3 other offices in the Melchizedek Priesthood: in particular, Seventies, High Priests, and Apostles, and in that order as the passage continues upwards toward the Grand Gallery.

There are, however, additional features in the ascending passage that need to be dealt with. They are described in detail by Rutherford in his 3rd book on the Great Pyramid:

> Accompanying each of the last three Girdles there are inset stones resembling pointers let into the side wall just in front of the north side of each Girdle. In the case of the central Girdle of these three, the Pointer is on the east wall of the Passage, whilst in the case of the other two the Pointers are on the west wall. There can be little doubt that the purpose of these Pointers is to draw attention to the Girdles because of their symbolic significance. (969)

Rutherford quotes Morton Edgar, who explored the Great Pyramid in 1914, in order to focus on one more feature that is associated with the 3 complete girdle stones:

> "Almost exactly in the centre of the double space between the upper end of the passage and the first Girdle's lower joint-line, the joints in the floor and both walls are nearly continuous with each other, forming, therefore, what we might term a *Girdle Joint.* [Edgar's 1st girdle is listed in this book as the 3rd girdle as a result of counting upwards instead of downwards.] Let into the east wall

> immediately below this Girdle Joint, and as if to call attention to it, are two small inset stones, somewhat similar to the pointers immediately below the three important Girdles. . . It is interesting to notice that the inset-pointer stones alternate, first on the east wall below the Girdle Joint, then on the west wall". (969-70)

(For illustrations of the ascending passage with its girdle stones and inset "pointers" or "markers" see pages 962 and 968 of Rutherford's *Pyramidology*, Book III.)

After paying such close attention to these inset stones, Rutherford says no more about them; he simply includes them in his assertion that the "entire life of Christ on Earth from Bethlehem to Calvary [is] portrayed at the upper end of the First Ascending Passage" (Book III, 970).

At one point in *The Great Pyramid Decoded* Lemesurier says the "markers" on the west wall are "favourable" physical obstacles, while the ones on the east wall are "unfavourable" as far as human evolution is concerned (58). However, later in his book he seems to reverse his position, concluding that there is no "convincing reason for the use by the Pyramid's designer of the principle of horizontal 'insets'" (180).

Lepre, continuing to be honest, confesses that the presence of these inset stones

> is somewhat puzzling, but one is tempted to conclude that they somehow must have been used in conjunction with the lowering of the granite plug stones. Perhaps they were in some way employed to facilitate the manipulation of these blocks, acting as chocks to control the sliding process. All of this is pure speculation, though, and their specific purpose still remains a mystery. (78)

After reading these lines by Lepre, at least one obvious question should spring to mind: how could *inset* stones act "as chocks to control the sliding process" of the granite stones?

Now, what about Sitchin and Dunn? Do they have an explanation for these inset stones? No, they never mention them.

Illustrations of the inset stones on the west wall, starting with the 1st of the 3 complete girdle stones in the lower end of the passage, reveal an upright rectangle, followed by a water jar that is a little larger than the rectangle. A horizontal bar links these two figures together, with the south end of the bar touching the north end of the girdle stone.

As already indicated, the rectangle and the jar are on the north side of the girdle stone, the side that symbolizes coming from God's presence. On the south side, which symbolizes being distanced from God, is a small square.

Higher up the passage, still on the west side, and to the north of the 3rd girdle stone, are 2 upright rectangles equal in length and width to the rectangle depicted at the 1st girdle stone. The pair of rectangles identify the 3rd stone as representing the Quorum of the Twelve Apostles, who are special traveling witnesses for Christ. Verse 7 of Chapter 6 in the Gospel According to Mark reads:

> And He [Christ] called the twelve to Himself, and began to send them out two by two.

The 2 rectangles represent the Twelve Apostles traveling in pairs.

Verse 12 adds:

> So they went out and preached that people should repent.

The apostles are missionaries.

So are the Seventies, who are represented by the first of the 3 girdle stones. The Seventies are mentioned in the Gospel According to Luke, where we're told:

> the Lord appointed seventy others also, and sent them two by two before His face into every city and place where He Himself was about to go.

> Then He said to them, "The harvest truly is great, but the laborers are few; therefore pray the lord of the harvest to send out laborers [missionaries] into His harvest.
>
> "Go your way; behold, I send you out as lambs among wolves." (10:1-3)

In verse 17 we learn that "the seventy returned with joy, saying, 'Lord, even the demons are subject to us in Your name.'"

Dummelow's *Bible Commentary* has this to say about these verses:

> Another step in the organization of the Church. The Seventy receive a subordinate commission, similar to that of the apostles, to preach and to cast out devils. . . .
>
> The charge to the Seventy reads like an abridged report of St. Matthew's charge to the Twelve. . . . The close similarity of the two charges is best accounted for by supposing that Christ gave nearly the same directions to the Seventy as to the Twelve. (751)

Nelson's Illustrated Bible Dictionary offers this entry under the heading "The Seventy":

> Jewish writings often spoke of the Gentile nations as numbering 70. Among the four gospels, Luke is known as the one with a universal, world-wide view. By speaking of the 70 disciples, Luke probably wanted to show that the gospel of Christ is not only for the Jews, the 12 tribes of Israel, but also for the Gentiles, the "70 nations" of the world. (Lockyer, Sr. 968)

Regarding both the Twelve Apostles and the Seventy, section 107 of the *Doctrine and Covenants* states:

> The twelve traveling councilors are called to be the Twelve Apostles, or special witnesses of the name of Christ in all the world—thus differing from other officers in the church in the duties of their calling. (Verse 23)
>
> The Seventy are also called to preach the gospel, and to be especial witnesses unto the Gentiles and in all the world—thus differing from other officers in the church in the duties of their calling. (Verse 25)
>
> The Twelve are a Traveling Presiding High Council, to officiate in the name of the Lord, under the direction of the Presidency of the Church, agreeable to the institution of heaven; to build up the church, and regulate all the affairs of the same in all nations, first unto the Gentiles and secondly unto the Jews.
>
> The Seventy are to act in the name of the Lord, under the direction of the Twelve, in building up the church and regulating all the affairs of the same in all nations, first unto the Gentiles and then to the Jews. (Verses 33-34)

By now the symbolism of the square on the south side of the first stone, the Seventies' stone, should be obvious, but if it isn't then Barbara Walker's statement that the square is "'emblematic of the four corners of the earth'" (61) will make it clear: the Seventies' mission is to cover the entire globe. Moreover, the square is also "emblematic of down-to-earth honesty and truth" (Walker 61), and the message delivered by the Seventies is the truth as taught by Christ.

But, it should be asked at this point, what does the water jar that is connected to the Seventies' rectangle symbolize? First, when combined with the rectangle, it represents the Seventies being sent out in pairs, just like the apostles; second, it is related to a number of scriptures that specifically refer to water in a metaphorical or symbolical sense. The following passage is a good example:

> How long can rolling waters remain impure? What power shall stay the heavens? As well might man stretch forth his puny arm to stop the Missouri river in its decreed course, or to turn it up stream, as to hinder the Almighty from pouring down knowledge from heaven upon the heads of the Latter-day Saints. (*Doctrine and Covenants* 121:33)

That knowledge, of course, is to be shared with the people of all nations, so that Isaiah's prophecy that "the earth shall be full of the knowledge of the Lord as the waters cover the sea" will be fulfilled (Isaiah 11:9).

A similar prophecy comes through Enoch in "The Book of Moses" when the Lord tells him,

> And righteousness will I send down out of heaven; and truth will I send forth out of the earth, to bear testimony of mine Only Begotten; his resurrection from the dead; yea, and also the resurrection of all men; and righteousness and truth will I cause to sweep the earth as with a flood, to gather out mine elect from the four quarters of the earth, unto a place which I shall prepare, an Holy City, that my people may gird up their loins, and be looking for the time of my coming. (7:62)

Christ frequently used water as a symbol for himself. For instance, what did he do for the first miracle recorded by John? He changed water into wine.

> On the third day there was a wedding in Cana of Galilee, and the mother of Jesus was there.
>
> Now both Jesus and His disciples were invited to the wedding.

> And when they ran out of wine, the mother of Jesus said to Him, "They have no wine."
>
> Jesus said to her, "Woman, what does your concern have to do with Me? My hour has not yet come."
>
> His mother said to the servants, "Whatever He says to you, do it."
>
> Now there were. . . six waterpots [or jars] of stone, according to the manner of purification of the Jews, containing twenty or thirty gallons apiece.
>
> Jesus said to them, "Fill the waterpots with water." And they filled them up to the brim.
>
> And He said to them, "Draw some out now, and take it to the master of the feast." And they took it.
>
> When the master of the feast had tasted the water that was made wine, and did not know where it came from. . . the master of the feast called the bridegroom.
>
> And he said to him, "Every man at the beginning sets out the good wine, and when the guests have well drunk, then the inferior. You have kept the good wine until now!" (John 2:1-10)

E. Keith Howick, author of *The Miracles of Jesus the Messiah*, sees this early demonstration of Christ's power as one of "declaration, kindness, joy, and testimony" (203). But "declaration" and "testimony" of what? Of his identity as the Son of God, as the Messiah. John makes the same point when he states that with this miracle Christ "manifested His glory; and His disciples believed in him" (2:11).

Out of the many other occasions when Christ used water as a symbol perhaps the most memorable one involved the woman of Samaria, who came to draw water from Jacob's well. Christ engaged her in conversation and took the opportunity to convince her that

> "Whoever drinks of this water will thirst again, but whoever drinks of the water that I shall give him will never thirst. But the water that I shall give him will become in him a fountain of water springing up into everlasting life." (John 4:13-14)

Today, the Seventies, along with the Twelve Apostles, are canvassing the earth to take that "fountain of water springing up into everlasting life" to everyone who is willing to accept it.

Before ending this discussion of water symbolism, it is worth noting Joseph Davidovits' discovery "that whereas the bedrock of Giza is dry, the pyramid blocks are full of moisture." He explains this anomaly by claiming that only "concrete would be full of moisture" (Davidovits and Morris 15 and 95), but by doing so he fails to perceive the consistent symbolism built into the blocks themselves.

This symbolism becomes especially evident when we recall that during the Israelites' wandering in the Wilderness of Sin they became desperate, fearing they would die from thirst, but Moses, following instructions from Christ, used his rod to strike a *rock—twice*—out of which came life-saving water (Exodus 17:1-6; also Numbers 20:1-11).

Turning now to the girdle joint near the top of the ascending passage that Morton Edgar described, it is positioned appropriately to represent the First Presidency of the Church. This "Presidency of the High Priesthood," which is a quorum of 3 presiding high priests "after the order of Melchizedek, have a right to officiate in all the offices in the church" (*Doctrine and Covenants* 107:9 and 22).

At this girdle joint, as stated above, are 2 "pointers" or "markers" on the east wall. They are squares that are the same size as the square next to the Seventies' stone, but since they are on the east wall they are obviously meant to be associated not just with the Seventies' square but also with 2 rectangles set lower down in the east wall next to the girdle stone that stands for the high priests. Like the rectangle and the water jar on the west wall, these 2 rectangles are on the north side of the girdle stone and they are similarly linked by a horizontal bar, with the south end of the bar touching the north end of the girdle stone.

Barbara Walker reveals that the rectangle known as the "Golden Section"

> was long regarded as the perfectly proportioned building plan, especially for any structure of religious significance. . . .
>
> This rectangle has been called the most rational, secure, and regular of all geometric forms. (23)

This symbol couldn't be more fitting. At the same time, however, it should be pointed out that high priests have a calling somewhat different from the Seventies and the Twelve Apostles. Among other things, they officiate in the temples under the direction of the First Presidency, and so there is a link between them just as there is between the Seventies and the Twelve. This is confirmed by Hans Biedermann's observation that the square—and remember, there are two squares associated with the First Presidency's girdle joint—is "a form associated. . . with the heavenly powers." And, he adds significantly, the "design of many temples is based on the square" (320).

But why are the symbols for the Seventies and the Twelve on the west wall while those for the high priests and the First Presidency are on the east wall? And why do the Seventies have only one square instead of two like the First Presidency?

The answer has to do with the Seventies and the Twelve doing missionary work for the living, who are represented by the west side, whereas the high priests engage in temple work for the dead, who are represented by the east side. As for the single and double squares, again, the Seventies are responsible for teaching the living, but the First Presidency holds all the keys for administering to the living *and* the dead in all 4 quarters of the earth as well as in the spirit world.

After Christ bridged the gulf between the spirits of the dead, he was resurrected. He then spent 40 days with the disciples, "speaking of the things pertaining to the kingdom of God" (Acts 1:3) In his first letter to the Corinthians, Paul, responding to doubts raised about the resurrection of all mankind, revealed part of what Christ taught during those 40 days when he asked,

> what will they do who are baptized for the dead, if the dead do not rise at all? Why then are they baptized for the dead? (15:29)

Christ had made it clear in his teachings to the Jews that baptism was the door to the celestial kingdom, but spirits cannot be baptized. To overcome that obstacle, Christ instituted proxy baptism for the dead, thus making it possible for the living to be baptized in behalf of the dead, who would then have the opportunity, along with being taught in the spirit world, to accept or reject the temple work that was done for them by authorized temple workers serving under the direction of the First Presidency (LeGrand Richards 170-175).

Because the dead are usually buried in the ground, baptismal fonts for the explicit purpose of baptizing the living for the dead are placed underground in the temples (*Doctrine and Covenants* 128:13). These special fonts are typified by the one in the temple at Salt Lake City, Utah, which is mounted on the backs of

> twelve life-sized oxen, of cast iron. . . . The oxen face outward in groups of three. . . . The font is of cast iron enameled in white, elliptical in form, of ten and six feet in its longer and shorter axes respectively, and four feet deep; its capacity is over four hundred gallons. (Talmage, *The House of the Lord* 155)

Lepre, in his careful exploration of the Giza plateau, came across "a huge cavity cut into the rock foundation" that was once part of the so-called "mortuary temple of the Pharaoh Khufu". This cavity "exists at the point where [the] inner sanctuary once stood", therefore, Lepre argues, it

> could not have been a natural chasm, present at the time of the construction of the Great Pyramid, or it would

> have been filled with square blocks of stone throughout by the builders. It has been cemented over with a roof or cover of a sort in modern times and has an iron grating at its entrance which is rusted shut and obviously has not been opened for quite a long period of time.

So far so good. But then Lepre suggests that this cavity

> may have represented an access route into the subterranean sections of the pyramid (275).

Not so. This cavity was an underground room in the temple where the baptismal font was located. It would have been used for baptisms for the dead during the New Testament period when, in Rosalie David's words, "Egyptians eagerly adopted Christianity" (*Handbook to Life in Ancient Egypt* 132).

Nothing has yet been said about the thickness of the complete girdle stones. The one that represents the elders is 58 inches thick, the two that represent the Seventies and the Twelve are identical at 32 inches, and the one for the high priests is 33 inches (Piazzi Smyth 432).

The elders' stone is so much thicker than the other 3 because the elders make up the majority of the Melchizedek Priesthood holders as well as the majority of the church's missionary force. Notice that if you separate the 5 and the 8 in the number 58 and then add the two numbers, you have 13—the foundation of apostles and prophets plus Christ, which foundation keeps the elders solid spiritually. Knowing this, isn't it interesting that the thickest of all the exterior courses of the Great Pyramid is the very first course, which measures—58 inches (Lemesurier 44).

Using the number 13 in such a positive way may surprise some readers since 13 is traditionally regarded as unlucky. Examining that tradition, E. W. Bullinger, in his extremely detailed book *Number in Scripture*, devotes page after page to demonstrating that the "enemies of God and His people as named in Scripture are generally multiples of *thirteen*" (219).

However, Bullinger is wise enough to realize that the Bible employs comparison and contrast, and so he includes the fact that Christ's

> names in the Old Testament, before the work of Atonement was entered on or accomplished, are all multiples of **13**, just as His names, afterwards in the New Testament and when the work of Atonement was carried out, are all multiples of **8**. (228)

The number applicable to the Seventies and the Twelve, 32, if separated into 3 and 2 and then added, yields the sum of 5—the number for fellowship. And again, isn't it interesting that the beginning of the ascending passage is on the level of course number 5 (see the diagram between pages 95 and 96 of Petrie's *Pyramids and Temples of Gizeh*).

The high priests' stone is 33 inches (which corresponds to the 33 foot width of the "Great Basement Sheet" on which the Pyramid's entrance is founded); separate the 3's and add them and what do you have? Six. The number of incompletion and imperfection, which applies to the living as well as to the spirits of the dead who have not yet benefitted from the ordinances of the temple.

The girdle joint, representing the First Presidency, when measured from the north side of the 3rd girdle stone to the upper end of the ascending passage is 35 feet in length (Piazzi Smyth 432). The reason for including the stone that represents the Twelve Apostles is that the First Presidency administers the affairs of the church in conjuction with the Quorum of the Twelve. Moreover, the members of the First Presidency, while being high priests, are also former members of the Twelve.

If we separate the two numbers in 35 and add them, the result is 8. The name *Jesus*, when spelled with Greek letters—*Ιησους*/*Iēsous*—has a numerical value that adds up to 888, and Christ is represented by the 3 presiding high priests of the First Presidency.

To make certain we didn't miss the point, Enoch placed 8 stones in the floor and 8 in the ceiling between the Twelve Apostles' girdle stone and the top of the passage, which serves as the south end of the section that represents the First Presidency. Appropriately enough, there is also a total of 8 stones in the floor and 8 in the ceiling between the Twelve and the Seventies, the traveling witnesses for Christ.

Backing up momentarily to the row of contiguous girdle stones in the lower part of the ascending passage, we learned earlier that they cover 24 feet. Twenty-four is 3 times 8—three 8s, the number for *Jesus.*

Now, as also noted earlier, the complete girdle stones are separated by a distance of 17 feet. Why was that distance chosen? It was chosen because, as we have seen, Joseph, the son of Jacob, was sold into slavery at the age of 17 and taken to Egypt. Years later when famine struck the land of Canaan where his father and brothers continued to live, they came to Egypt looking for food, and Joseph, who had risen to become 2nd only to the pharaoh, held their lives in his hands.

Fortunately for them, Joseph was a model of virtue and righteousness, and he was forgiving. He not only fed his father, his brothers and their families with the grain he had stored up in anticipation of the famine, but he also persuaded the pharaoh to permit them to stay in Egypt, which they did, settling in the land of Goshen, the best land Egypt had to offer (Genesis 47:6).

Three more points in regard to this famous episode related in chapters 37-50 of Genesis are worth reviewing: (1) Jacob lived in Egypt for 17 years (47:28); (2) when he brought his extended family into that land the total number of men and children was 70 (46:27), which is to be related to the 70 of Luke 10:1; and (3) it was through Jacob's son Judah that Christ's ancestral line was to be traced.

We have now accounted for 2 of the 3 occurrences of the number 17 in the ascending passage. The 3rd occurrence can be explained by turning to the 8th chapter of Genesis, which is concerned with the last phase of the flood.

> Then the ark rested in the seventh month, the *seventeenth* day of the month, on the mountains of Ararat. (8:4; italics added)

The 7 that is combined with the 17 in this verse has a counterpart in the 2nd of the 3 granite stones in the lower end of the ascending passage, for it is located at course number 7 (Lemesurier 44; Petrie, diagram between pages 95 and 96). As a reminder, that 2nd stone is the one that represents baptism, and in the verse just quoted, the earth, having been swept clean, had also been baptized.

Now, some reader with an excellent memory will no doubt recall that Edwards did not give an exact length of 17 feet between the girdle stones, but of 17 feet 2 inches. So, what are the 2 inches for? Let's start with the 17 that represents the ark coming to rest on the 17th day. Here, the number 2 stands for Christ, the 2nd member of the Godhead. He was the one who called Noah to warn the world what was coming; he was the one who controlled the elements—just as he did during his mortal ministry—to bring on the flood to ritually cleanse the earth.

With the other occurrences of 17.2 we have a link to Joseph's sons Manasseh and Ephraim (Exodus 48:1). These 2 sons are also closely associated with their grandfather, who adopted them. Skousen explains why the adoption took place:

> Jacob's problem was that his two oldest sons, Reuben and Simeon, had both disgraced themselves. Reuben had been guilty of incest many years before [this is confirmed in "The Testament of Reuben"]. . . and Simeon was guilty of being the leader in the murderous attack on the settlement of Shechem [in the land of Canaan] which had wiped out the entire male population of that community and nearly precipitated the massacre of Jacob and his family. . . .
>
> Now, as Jacob approached the end of his life, he felt he must take formal action against these two eldest sons. He felt that as far as the covenant was concerned, he must formally disinherit them. Jacob had made up his mind to replace them with his two grandsons, Ephraim and Manasseh. (*The Third Thousand Years* 130; see also Genesis 48:5)

Today, most of the members of the Church of Jesus Christ of Latter-day Saints are descendants of Ephraim, while a much smaller number are from Manasseh.

* * *

While the subject may seem to have been exhausted, there are in fact other important numbers to be gleaned from the ascending passage, which was designed to obviously contrast with the descending passage since both have slopes of 26 degrees. However, the descending passage has an angle of 26 degrees plus 31 minutes and 23 seconds, while the ascending passage has an angle of 26 degrees plus 2 minutes and 30 seconds (Petrie 19 and 22).

We have a difference of 29 minutes in the 2 passages. Why? Because Joseph was 29 when his grandfather Isaac died. This is easily figured. Isaac died at the age of 180 (Genesis 35:28); his son Jacob was 60 years younger (Genesis 25:26), making him 120; Joseph was 91 years younger than Jacob, making him 29.

And Joseph, at the age of 29, was still in prison. Notice that the passage with the additional 29 minutes is the descending passage which leads to the spirit prison as represented by the connecting horizontal passage.

The horizontal passage itself has a total length of 29 feet (Edwards 101), which is matched by the total of 29 floor stones in the ascending passage (Rutherford, Book III, see the illustration on page 968), but the 29 feet are exactly 100 feet less than the 129 feet that make up the total length of the ascending passage (Lepre 77). The +100 in the ascending passage is obviously meant to be a positive figure since the passage is leading upwards toward the celestial kingdom as represented by the King's Chamber.

The difference in seconds in the slope of the 2 passages is 7, with the + going to the ascending passage. And 7, as Bullinger and numerous other sources tell us, pertains to spiritual perfection.

The number 31 in the minutes of the descending passage takes on meaning when we read in the Book of Joshua that he conquered 31 kings in the land of Canaan (12:7-24). These kings had been judged to be ripe for destruction by the Lord because of their evil practices (see Deuteronomy 20:16-18). Moreover, in 1 Kings 16:23-25, we read:

> In the thirty-first year of Asa King of Judah, Omri became King of Israel, and he. . . did evil in the eyes of the Lord and sinned more than all those before him.

The number 23 in the seconds of the descending passage has a connection with the prophet Jeremiah, who warned the people of Judah for 23 years that if they didn't repent they were going to be led into captivity (Jeremiah 25:3-5). They did not repent and those who survived the destruction of Jerusalem ended up prisoners of the Babylonian king Nebuchadnezzar.

The number 2 in the minutes of the ascending passage once again refers to Christ. The number 30 in the seconds refers to Joseph and Christ, for Joseph began to rule Egypt at the age of 30 and Christ began his earthly ministry at the same age (Genesis 41:46; Luke 3:23), but in addition, 30 men lifted Jeremiah out of a dungeon where he had been imprisoned because of his prophecies of destruction and captivity (Jeremiah 38:10).

Here is one more important comparison: the passage that snakes south off the subterranean chamber is 53 feet long; the upper end of the ascending passage is 53 inches high (Lepre 73). The serpentine-like passage is a dead end; the ascending passage, on the other hand, opens up into the Grand Gallery. Is there any greater contrast in the Great Pyramid than this? This contrast, by the way, is made even more so by the fact that the lower end of the ascending passage is 47¼ inches in height (Lepre 73), which means the upper end is increased by 5¾ inches.

There is also a change in the width of the ascending passage. At the lower end the measurement is 38½ inches; at the upper end it is 42 inches, an increase of 3½ inches (Lepre 73). Lawton and Ogilvie-Herald assure us, "we must conclude that this taper of 5¾ inches in height and 3½ inches in width. . . is deliberate" (533). They use the word *taper* because they accept the theory that the 3 granite blocks were slid down the ascending passage from the Grand Gallery. Like Joseph Davidovits and so many others, they have no perception of the symbolism that is involved.

We are not intended to view the ascending passage as a means of descent but of ascent. It is typical of Egyptologists that they turn things upside down and so miss the point entirely, and in the process they mislead virtually everyone who reads their articles and books.

Look at the number 5¾. We know what 5 represents—fellowship. But 5 is also 3 + 2: 3 for the Godhead, 2 for husband and wife joined by God. The gematria of the Hebrew word translated as "'the heavens'. . . is 395, a multiple of *five*" (Bullinger 135). The number 5, Lemesurier says, "is the Pyramid number *par excellence*" and it "seems to be intimately linked up with the function of the Pyramid itself" (29).

He is absolutely right.

As for the number ¾, when we convert it to .75 it has special significance because after Joseph revealed his true identity to his brothers when they came to Egypt a 2nd time for food, he

> sent for his father Jacob and his whole family, *seventy-five* in all. (NIV, Acts 7:14; italics added)

It is rather amazing to see how the numbering of the chapters and the verses in the Bible tie in with crucial events, as in this case. Chapter 7, verse 14—the 7 ties in with the pharaoh's dream of 7 fat cattle and 7 thin cattle; the 14 ties in with the 14 special years that the cattle symbolized; and it was Joseph's interpretation of the pharaoh's dream that led to his release from prison and the reunion with his family.

The increase in width of 3½ inches is an undeniable link to Christ and his earthly mission of 3½ years, and the ultimate goal of the Son of God is to reunite families in this life and in the next.

* * *

Besides discovering moisture in the Great Pyramid's blocks, Davidovits also uncovered other symbols of Christ in the ascending passage. He reports in *The Pyramids: An Enigma Solved*:

> I observed marks on core masonry. . . unlike those made with a chisel. Some appear to be impressions made by reeds. I also noticed long, sweeping impressions that fan out exactly like a palm leaf. Using a microscope, I was clearly able to see wood-grain impressions on a sample from the ascending passageway of the Great Pyramid. (Davidovits and Morris 76)

As with the moisture in the blocks, Davidovits accounts for the presence of these marks and impressions by contending that the pyramid's masonry is not stone quarried from the Giza plateau or from anywhere else in Egypt but rather it is "geopolymeric concrete" cast in wooden molds, and when the molds were removed a block was still relatively soft. A covering

> of reeds or palm leaves was probably applied to the blocks, affording an optimum amount of ventilation. This was required to harden (carbonate) the lime and protect the blocks from becoming brittle from evaporation. (75)

Since Davidovits was probing for evidence to support his particular thesis he once again failed to notice the symbolism inherent in his findings. To point up that symbolism we look to Christ's scourging prior to his crucifixion. The Roman soldiers

> stripped Him and put a scarlet robe on Him.
>
> When they had twisted a crown of thorns, they put it on His head, and a *reed* in His right hand [*Nelson's Illustrated Bible Dictionary* defines "reeds" as "Gigantic hollow-stemmed grasses which grew along river banks

> and in moist areas of Egypt and Palestine" (Lockyer, Sr. 855)]. . . .
>
> Then they spat on Him, and took the reed and struck Him on the head. (Matthew 27:28-30; italics added)

Palm leaves, of course, are associated with Christ because on the day he rode a donkey into Jerusalem "a great multitude. . . took branches of palm trees and went out to meet Him" (John 12:12-13). And certainly wood has a link to Christ because of his wooden cross and because he referred to himself as a green tree (Luke23:31; in the marginal translation of The NKJV Greek-English Interlinear New Testament "green wood" is used whereas in the interlinear translation "tree" is preferred).

Davidovits has to be credited with one more intriguing find in the ascending passage. He reports:

> Another substance was not vital to the chemistry [needed to create the blocks of masonry] but may have been added because it symbolized the highest spiritual essence. The product was gold, the metal of the Sun. During my analysis, I found flecks of gold dust in [the] sample [of limestone] from the Great Pyramid. It is possible that the gold did not occur naturally and was ritually added. Divine eternal qualities were attributed to gold. . . . [A]nciently its value was purely sacred. (123)

Davidovits is correct in his evaluation of this discovery, except for linking gold to the sun. Change the spelling to *Son*, meaning the Son of Man, and the symbolism becomes what Christ and Enoch meant it to be.

* * *

Before moving on to the next section of the pyramid, it might be worthwhile to respond to a criticism that is bound to arise from some readers. That criticism will have to do with the supposition that it is possible to know the future before it happens. How, it will surely be asked, could Enoch or Moses or anyone else "see" the future, especially for thousands of years in advance?

Let's return to "The Book of Moses" for a crucial statement that Christ made to this prophet. "Worlds without number have I created," the Lord says, then adds,

> there are many worlds that have passed away by the word of my power. And there are many that now stand, and innumerable are they unto man; but all things are numbered unto me, for they are mine and I know them. (1:33 and 35)

The *Doctrine and Covenants* contains a similar quote:

> through him [Christ], and of him, the worlds are and were created, and the inhabitants thereof are begotten sons and daughters unto God [the Father]. (76:24)

The Pearl of Great Price, which contains "The Book of Moses", also contains another brief excerpt from a different prophet, Joseph's great-grandfather, Abraham. After Abraham is shown so many worlds that he "could not see the end" of them (3:12), he writes:

> Now the Lord had shown unto me, Abraham, the intelligences that were organized before the world was; and among all these there were many of the noble and great ones;
>
> And God saw these souls that they were good, and he stood in the midst of them, and he said: These I will make my rulers; for he stood among those that were spirits, and he saw that they were good; and he said unto

> me: Abraham, thou art one of them; thou was chosen before thou wast born.
>
> And there stood one among them that was like unto God, and he said unto those who were with him: We will go down, for there is space there, and we will take of these materials, and we will make an earth whereon these may dwell. ("The Book of Abraham" 3:22-24)

In the chapter that focused on Enoch, it was noted that the pre-mortal existence of all mankind was taught in the books of Enoch. The same concept is made explicit in *The Pearl of Great Price* and in the Bible. It is also made explicit in Betty J. Eadie's bestselling book *Embraced by the Light*, in which she tells us that during her near-death experience she was escorted

> to a place where many spirits prepared for life on earth. They were mature spirits. . . [and] I saw how desirous these spirits were of coming to earth. They looked upon life here as a school where they could learn many things and develop the attributes they lacked. I was told that we had all *desired* to come here, that we had actually chosen many of our weaknesses and difficult situations in our lives so that we could grow. (89-90)

In *The Eternal Journey* Lundahl and Widdison, after recounting the near-death experiences of a number of men and women who also learned that we existed as spirits before we were born on the earth, come to the conclusion that in "the pre-earth life, we associated with many people for eternities" (46).

All well and fine, but what is the point?

The point is that if earthly parents are able to predict what their children will do under certain circumstances as a result of observing them for a few years, and they usually can, then the Father of our spirits, who has perhaps known us for thousands of years, can certainly predict what we will do while we are experiencing mortality. In addition, with this earth being one of millions that have already gone through a similar "schooling", God can certainly use those other earths as models for this one.

Then, too, it is surely no problem for God to put into key positions around the world all the translated people who are needed to bring about the fulfillment of all genuine prophecies.

As for showing prophets like Enoch actual scenes of the future, well, ever hear of movies? God must have a marvelous catalog of films to draw on for revealing what for him has already happened. After all, superior intellects like Albert Einstein have realized that the past, present and future are really one (Sellier 58).

God would have no argument with that revelation.

9. SALT

> ". . . unless you are converted and become as little children, you will by no means enter the kingdom of heaven."
>
> (Matthew 18:3)

At the top of the ascending passage, the Grand Gallery begins, as does the horizontal passage that leads to the Queen's Chamber. (For a photo of this junction see pages 972 and 973 of Rutherford's *Pyramidology*, Book III).

According to Lemesurier the entrance to the horizontal passage involves a downward step of 5 inches (64). The passage itself measures 3 feet 5 inches wide and 3 feet 9 inches high (Edwards 104; Tompkins 11).

During a close survey of the same passage, Lepre was struck by an oddity: out of the 130 stones that made up the passage 122 of them were

> either of the same relative size or oriented in the same direction.
>
> Yet eight of the 130 stones did not obey this basic rule. Two of them, although of the same general dimensions as the majority of other blocks in the corridor, were floor stones which represented the area of a single block,

> with a joint separating them which ran in the opposite direction of the joints of the other floorstones [sic].

Lepre correlates this unusual feature with the line inscribed in the floor of the descending passage which marked the beginning of the ascending passage. He then continues by noting that

> [i]mmediately beyond these two stones lie six other blocks which are different from the others. . . in that they are much larger in size, being double the length of the average stone. Not only this, four of the six are exactly parallel to one another, two situated on the east wall and two on the west wall.

To this observation Lepre adds that 22 inches above the floor "straight red-ocher lines" one-eighth inch thick, "finely painted and leveled," could be seen running almost "the entire length of the corridor on the east and west walls". Salt encrustations, which "were so common to this section of the pyramid", could also be seen (105 and 110).

For more details, Rutherford once again quotes Morton Edgar:

> For a length of 64 feet from the beginning of the roof at the Grand Gallery end, each wall [of the horizontal corridor] is built in two equal courses. In each of these courses there are 15 stones of uniform size, namely, 41¼ inches. . . in length and half the height of the passage in breadth. The vertical joints in the upper course are in line with those in the lower; and those on the east are in direct opposition to thosc on the west wall. (Book III, 1029)

Following this quote, Rutherford states that past "these long blocks the walls are built in one course only," up to the point where the floor of the passage suddenly drops nearly 2 feet while the ceiling remains the same. From the beginning of the passage to the drop is 109 feet;

from the drop to the entrance of the Queen's Chamber is 18 feet (Book III, 1029-1030).

These 2 figures combined give a total length of 127 feet, which is 2 feet or 24 inches less than the length of the ascending passage. This 24 then, like the 24 connected with the pyramid's offset entrance, is negative in its symbolism and is to be equated with imperfection. Remember the number 6 and its link to imperfection? Twenty-four is, of course, 4 x 6, and 4 represents all quarters of the earth, which means people from every nation are involved in the path that leads to the terrestrial kingdom as represented by the Queen's Chamber.

But 24 is also 3 x 8 and since three 8s is the number for Jesus, we know that Jesus will continue to try to elevate these people to the next level before the final judgment.

With that much said, let's see how the Egyptologists and pyramidologists evaluate the other details that have been listed for the Queen's Chamber passage.

Starting with Lemesurier, we're told that the passage is "a spiritually static path of continuing mortality and reincarnation" (66). On the subject of dating, he relegates the downward step to the year 58 AD, and at the same time wonders if the 5 inches indicate an "initiate or Messianic leader" who would establish "an inferior offshoot. . . of the true Messianic path" (68-69). He suspects that leader was Paul the Apostle, who, he says, was arrested in 58 AD, "prior to his last journey and death in Rome." He goes on to say that if this is so, then the passage also represents "the particular teaching which Paul propounded, namely the ancestral form of Christianity as we know it today", and that "form" naturally infers that Paul's Christianity was "an *offshoot*, or deviation, from the teachings of Jesus of Nazareth" (70).

Lemesurier offers no comment on the 8 unusual stones described by Lepre, but then Lepre himself does not go beyond correlating the one really noticeable joint with the line inscribed in the floor of the descending passage. He does, however, speculate on the red-ocher lines. In his opinion they are "construction lines" that were "used as a rough guide in the positioning and leveling of the various stones" (111).

Concerning the basic measurements of the passage, Rutherford writes:

> the first portion of the passage is very low (similar height to that of the Descending Passage) so that we have to stoop heavily while going along it, representing our stooping under the burden of sin, whilst the final portion of the passage terminating at the entrance into the Queen's Chamber is high, so that an average man can walk upright, symbolising complete resurrection. (Book I, 153)

For the rest of his analysis, Rutherford takes a broader approach in order to inform us that

> the beginning of this Queen's Chamber Passage portrays sin entering into the World by Adam and the date when that occurred and although the length of the passage reveals the duration of the period of the reign of sin and death from Adam right to the Millennium, nevertheless the ages and great events during that period are not revealed therein. The symbolism discloses that the passage represents the process of deliverance from sin and death of all who have lived since the time of Adam's transgression (5407 B.C.), but this does not take place until the Millennium. (Book 1, 152)

Just what symbolism Rutherford had in mind is not disclosed. As for the millennium, in Rutherford's view it was "due to be inaugurated in Jerusalem in the autumn of A.D. 1979" (Book I, 145). The evidence for that date, he was certain, had been built into the entrance to the Queen's Chamber (Book I, 152).

Since he was mistaken about the date for the millennium was he also mistaken in his other interpretations?

One of Rutherford's predecessors, Worth Smith, does no more than point out that the sunken section of the passage is one-seventh of the total length and that, he argues, is important because 7 is "the number of perfection, typifying the perfect man" (88).

David Davidson relies on Marsham Adams, author of *The Book of the Master*, to explain that, according to the *Book of the Dead*, the horizontal passage from the Queen's Chamber to the top of the ascending passage is identified as "the Path of the coming forth of the Regenerate Soul" (370). Marsham Adams, in other words, traces the passage back to its beginning in order to determine its meaning.

Likewise, Richard W. Noone, by drawing an imaginary line from the drop in the floor back to the beginning of the passage, comes up with the date of "4 B.C.—the Birth of Jesus." However, the drop itself is, for him, simply an unexplained mystery (238).

Graham Hancock, observing that the drop results in an increase in the height of the passage to 5 feet 8 inches, remarks that no one has "come up with a convincing explanation for this particular feature" (323). And Colin Wilson asks, "why a two-foot step at that point?" Then he remarks: "The Pyramid would prove to be full of such absurd and arbitrary mysteries" (60).

Back to Lemesurier. He proposes that the downward step represents an "inferior alternative to" the Grand Gallery (63). Rutherford says basically the same thing:

> A rising step indicates a rising scale, that is a larger scale, whilst a descending step represents a descent in scale, i.e., a smaller scale than that of the inch-year general chronograph. The step in this horizontal passage simply constitutes a vertical drop in the horizontal floor from one level to a lower one. (Book I, 143)

Sitchin, as we should expect, is silent on this issue. In fact, since he does not concern himself with such matters there will be no more reason to refer to him again until the compartments above the King's Chamber are discussed in some detail in Volume 2 of *Books Written in*

Stone. Dunn, on the other hand, does have a theory regarding the drop in the passage.

He conjectures that "chemicals were introduced to the Queen's Chamber" in order to cause "a reaction that filled all the cavities within the Great Pyramid with hydrogen" (205), then, viewing the drop in the floor of the passage as a step up rather than a step down, he surmises that this feature was to "allow chemicals to pool inside the chamber and 'wick' up the evaporation tower" (207), which he suggests was anchored inside the niche in the east wall of the Queen's Chamber (199).

There are 2 major problems with this particular theory. First, he says the narrow shafts in the north and south walls of the Queen's Chamber "could have been supply shafts for chemicals. . . to enter the chamber and prevent evolving gases from escaping" (207). He claims that even though these shafts were not originally connected with the chamber—that is, they were sealed up for a length of 5 inches until they were broken into by Waynman Dixon in 1872 (Piazzi Smyth 427)—a small hole in the sealed section permitted "a specific amount of fluid" to be metered "into the channel over a period of time" (198). However, there was no hole in the sealed section. On the south wall there was merely a crack which allowed Dixon "at one place to push in a wire to a most unconscionable length". Dixon then had a carpenter take a hammer and chisel to the wall at that spot and that led to the discovery of the southern shaft.

There is no mention of even so much as a crack in the north wall. Dixon simply measured "off a similar position" on that wall and the carpenter set to work again, opening up the northern shaft (Piazzi Smyth 428). How then could these shafts have been used to meter chemicals into the chamber?

The second major problem with involving the shafts in Dunn's theory is the fact that there are no known outlets for either of them (Edwards 104; Hancock 321), so how would the ancient Egyptians have been able to access them?

As for the drop in the floor of the passage, if it was meant to function as Dunn maintains, why was it placed 18 feet away from the entrance to the chamber? Why wasn't it installed right at the entrance? Dunn, of course, doesn't bring up these bothersome points and so we will find no response from him in his treatment of the subject.

Before revealing whether or not Lemesurier and Rutherford have satisfactorily answered Colin Wilson's query—"Why a two-foot step at that point?"—let's examine the other details in the order in which they were presented.

First detail: why is there a downward step of 5 inches at the beginning of the horizontal passage?

Answer: this downward step is in obvious contrast to the ascending passage where there is an increase of 5 inches from the halfway point, which measures 48 inches high (Lepre 73), to the upper end with its height of 53 inches. The drop of 5 inches is clearly a negative symbol, indicating that those people who step off the upward path that leads to the celestial kingdom are in for a letdown if they end up in the terrestrial kingdom. The horizontal passage does indicate a leveling off, a failure to meet all the requirements, all the sacrifices required in order to keep growing spiritually. In short, the people who inherit the terrestrial kingdom will prove to be resistant to the fellowshipping of the saints and as a consequence the majority of them will not join the Church of Jesus Christ.

So Lemesurier's assessment of the passage is partly correct; it is "a spiritually static path", however, reincarnation is not a factor, nor is any specific date such as 58 AD. As for Paul, his teachings came from Christ and Christ's authorized servants and that eliminates their being an "offshoot" or a "deviation" from the truth. Paul is frequently criticized for supposedly corrupting "original" Christianity mainly because those who do the criticizing are not members of the Church of Jesus Christ of Latter-day Saints and therefore do not understand his references to such doctrines as the 3 degrees of glory or baptism for the dead.

Second detail: why is it that out of the 130 stones that make up the passage, eight stand out as being different? And why do the 2 floor stones that represent "the area of a single block" have "a joint separating them which [runs] in the opposite direction of the joints of the other floorstones"?

Answer: the 2 floor stones that appear to make up "a single block" and that have a distinguishing joint running "in the opposite direction" represent Noah and his wife. As a couple they had become "one flesh" (see Genesis 2:24), joined by the sealing power of the higher priesthood (see Matthew 18:18). And because they kept the commandments of God, they were going "in the opposite direction" of the rest of mankind during their lifetimes, with the exception of 3 of their sons and their sons' wives. It is those sons and their wives who are represented by the 6 stones that "are much larger in size, being double the length of the average stone." The unusual size of these 6 stones tells us that the 3 sons and their wives were, like Noah and his wife, spiritual giants in comparison to everyone else.

The 8 stones that stand out, then, represent the 8 special people who survived the great flood (see 1 Peter 3:20).

Third detail: why are "four of the six" stones "exactly parallel to one another" with two being "situated on the east wall and two on the west wall"?

Answer: the 2 stones on the west wall represent Noah's 2nd son Shem and his wife: the 2 on the east wall represent the 3rd son, Ham, and his wife. Keeping in mind the different symbolism of east and west, Ham is on the east side because Noah "blessed him with the blessings of the earth, and with the blessings of wisdom, but cursed him as pertaining to the Priesthood" ("The Book of Abraham" 1:26). Shem, however, held the priesthood (Skousen, *The First 2,000 Years* 200), plus Christ's lineage is traced through Shem (Luke 3:23-36), and that is why he is represented by the west wall.

Does this symbolism mean that Ham was condemned to inherit a lower kingdom while Shem would be in the highest kingdom? Not at all. Ham simply had a different mission in life to fulfill. If he proved faithful the day would come when he would be allowed to receive all the blessings of the priesthood, as will everyone else who is worthy of those blessings.

Fourth detail: what is the meaning of the 122 stones that are "of the same relative size or oriented in the same direction"?

Answer: in Genesis 6:3 the Lord says, "My Spirit shall not strive with man forever. . . yet his days [before the flood] shall be one hundred and twenty years." This verse accounts for 120 of the 122 stones; the other 2 represent the two prophets who warned about the coming of the flood: Enoch and Noah.

In connection with this answer is the height of the horizontal passage. It is 45 inches (which equal 3 feet 9 inches) because Noah's ark was 45 feet high (NIV, Genesis 6:15).

Fifth detail: why are there "straight red-ocher lines" in the horizontal passage?

Answer: an explanation will be given when the top 4 compartments above the King's Chamber are discussed in Volume 2 of *Books Written in Stone.*

Sixth detail: why is there salt in the passage?

Answer: during the Sermon on the Mount, Christ told his disciples, "You are the salt of the earth; but if the salt loses its flavor, how shall it [the earth] be seasoned? It [the salt] is then good for nothing but to be thrown out and trampled underfoot by men" (Matthew 5:13).

The men and women on their way to the terrestrial kingdom have the potential to be the salt of the earth, to set and preserve high standards for others to follow, to be spiritual giants as Noah and his family were, but they are not living up to their potential. This assessment of the salt in the passage is supported by the fact that there is salt also in the Queen's Chamber, and Richard W. Noone had a sample of that salt tested by the state of Arizona's Bureau of Geology and Mineral Technology. In his book, Noone reproduces a letter addressed to him by Robert T. O'Haire, Associate Mineralogist, who determined that the sample was "predominantly calcite (calcium carbonate) with some halite (sodium chloride) and gypsum (calcium sulfate)" (100). To put it another way, as Noone himself does, the salt inside the pyramid has a "surprisingly low salt content" (99).

Noone refers to the Queen's Chamber as "an extraordinary crystal-producing factory" (99). Hoping to learn more about this phenomenon, he interviewed William A. Tiller, an authority on "the formation and perfection of crystals" (89).

> **Noone**: Dr. Tiller, why would the Middle Chamber of the Great Pyramid be such a magnate, or a repository for these crystals?
>
> **Tiller**: That's really tough to imagine, because you basically have got to have (a) either some salt water which was in there and evaporated and then deposited this [i.e., the crystals] because it got very hot, or (b) it [the chamber] was at some time under the ocean and [the water] seeped in, or (c) somehow the [Pyramid's] "energies" converted what was in the walls to sodium chloride. None of these, however, makes any sense at all to me. (99)

Dunn explains the salt on the walls of both the horizontal passage and the Queen's Chamber as the

> natural by-product of the reaction designed to produce hydrogen. It would form when the hot, hydrogen-bearing gas reacted with the calcium in the pyramid's limestone walls. The orientation of the passage leading from the Queen's Chamber would take the chemicals down into the Well Shaft and into the Subterranean Pit. (194)

Dunn must have forgotten that he had made this statement when he later wrote on page 220 of his book that the "equipment that provided the priming pulses was most likely housed in the Subterranean Pit." Did the subterranean chamber serve both purposes, to provide "the priming pulses" and to collect the waste from the Queen's Chamber? Does this explanation make any sense? Does it provide the reason for the salt crystals continuing to be produced today in the chamber?

Seventh detail: why is the first part of the horizontal passage "built in two equal courses" with "15 stones of uniform size"? And why are the vertical joints on the east wall "in direct opposition to those on the west wall"?

Answer: the 2 courses with the opposing joints represent the 2 opposing camps that formed during the time of Enoch and Noah, meaning those who kept the commandments of God and those who did not. However, remembering that Christ, in between his death on the cross and his resurrection, organized a missionary force in the spirit world so that those who had lost their lives in the flood could be taught and then afterwards decide to accept or reject him, we can understand that the courses on the east wall represent those who will accept Christ in the spirit world and as a result will inherit the terrestrial kingdom. In contrast, the courses on the west wall represent those who led decent lives during mortality and who believed in God or Christ enough to merit the middle kingdom.

But that is not all; the 2 courses also represent the "clean animals" (symbolized by the west wall) and the "unclean" (symbolized by the east wall), which went 2 by 2 "into the ark to Noah" (Genesis 7:8-9).

Also related to the ark and the flood is the number 15 that occurs in the "15 stones of uniform size". In the biblical account of the flood we read: "The waters prevailed fifteen cubits upward, and the mountains were covered" (Genesis 7:20).

Do the 64 feet of the two courses tie in with the flood? Yes, they do, because verses 1-3 of Chapter 64 (in Roman numerals LXIV) of *The Book of Enoch the Prophet* records how Noah

> saw that the earth became inclined, and that destruction approached.
>
> Then he lifted up his feet, and went to the ends of the earth, to the dwelling of his great-grandfather Enoch.
>
> And Noah cried with a bitter voice, Hear me; hear

> me; hear me: three times. And he said, Tell me what is transacting upon earth; for the earth labours, and is violently shaken.

Enoch replies in verse 6:

> A commandment has gone forth from the Lord against those who dwell on the earth, that they may be destroyed; for they know. . . every oppressive and secret power of the devils.

Enoch was prophesying the flood, as proven in the first 2 verses of the next chapter where Noah is the narrator, as he is in Chapter 64:

> After this he [Enoch] showed me the angels of punishment, who were prepared to come, and to open all the mighty waters under the earth:
>
> That they may be for judgment, and for the destruction of all those who remain and dwell upon the earth.

Incidentally, since both Tiller and Dunn relate heat to the salt crystals in the Queen's Chamber, it should be pointed out that in Chapter 66 of *The Book of Enoch the Prophet*, Noah reveals that the waters of the flood would be mixed with fire and heat (see verse 6 and especially verse 7 where reference is made to "rivers of fire. . . to which those [rebellious] angels shall be condemned who seduced the inhabitants of the earth"; "rivers of fire" would have come from volcanic activity).

The number 64 has another important tie-in—and that is with Moses. The mother of Moses was Jochebed and her father was Levi, the 3rd son of Jacob. And Levi was 64 when Jochebed was born. His age can be calculated by drawing on information provided in Genesis, Exodus and the "Testament of Levi".

Levi was, of course, one of Joseph's brothers, and from Joseph's death to the birth of Moses there was a passage of 64 years (Joseph died in 1671 BC and Moses was born in 1607.)

Now, Moses is known for one of the greatest miracles recorded in the Bible, and that is the Israelites' crossing of the Red Sea on dry ground while the waters of the sea formed walls "on their right hand and on their left" (Exodus 14:22). And the Red Sea, as *Nelson's Illustrated Bible Dictionary* informs us, "has the reputation of being one of the. . . saltiest on earth" (Lockyer, Sr. 903).

Nelson's Illustrated Bible Dictionary also advises us that the "name Red Sea has found its way into the Bible as a translation of the Hebrew *yam suph*, which means 'sea of reeds' and not 'Red Sea'" (903). And so the argument is made that the Israelites did not cross the Red Sea after all but instead made their escape from the pursuing Egyptians by crossing a marshy area in northern Egypt where reeds grew.

This argument is invalid, for there has been a misunderstanding as to what the "sea of reeds" means. It does not mean a marshy area where reeds grew. The correct meaning is found in Matthew 11:7 where Christ refers to a reed "shaken by the wind", using it as "a symbol of weakness" (Lockyer, Sr., *Nelson's Illustrated Bible Dictionary* 855). The Israelites who followed Moses to the shore of the Red Sea were a sea of people "shaken by the wind" when they saw the pharaoh's soldiers bearing down on them in "six hundred choice chariots" (Exodus 14:7). Terrified, the Israelites cried out to Moses,

> "Was it because there were no graves in Egypt that you brought us to the desert to die? What have you done to us by bringing us out of Egypt? Didn't we say to you in Egypt, 'Leave us alone; let us serve the Egyptians'? It would have been better for us to serve the Egyptians than to die in the desert!" (NIV, Exodus 14:10; notice that there is no mention of a marsh in this passage)

Clearly, the Israelites themselves were the "sea of reeds", shaken by every threat, despite the miracles that had been performed in their behalf in Egypt (including the miracle that had happened the night before the exodus began when the Israelites were passed over by the Lord's destroying angel while the firstborn children of the Egyptians were slain). And even after they had crossed the Red Sea and the pharaoh's army was drowned when the walls of water came crashing down on them—walls of water that could not have been formed in a marshy area—the Israelites still remained weak in the faith and were quick to be washed under like the Egyptians as demonstrated by their convincing Aaron, Moses' older brother, to make them a golden calf to worship while Moses was on Mount Sinai for 40 days and nights (see Chapter 32 of Exodus).

Now, at first what follows may not seem to be related to the above discussion, but it is.

Lawton and Ogilvie-Herald report that in 1986 a design technician and an architect, both from France, drilled 3 holes in the horizontal passage to the Queen's Chamber hoping to find "a hidden system of passages and chambers." They had been drawn to the passage because

> some of the stone blocks in the walls. . . were laid in a different way from all the others: "The walls of the long, very low, passage leading to the chamber are lined with a crosswise [or cross-shaped] arrangement of stones, the perfect symmetry of which is illogical [and certainly not a feature that fits in with Dunn's theory].". . . [T]he blocks in the passageway were laid one above the other so that the joints formed a cross-shaped pattern, and this arrangement was totally unlike that in any other passage in the Great Pyramid. (301; the addition of the phrase "or cross-shaped", which is inside brackets, is by Lawton and Ogilvie-Herald)

After drilling the 3rd hole the 2 Frenchmen discovered "a cavity behind the west wall" that contained "sand of a very fine quality" (301-02). A year later a "Japanese team using microscopic observation and X-ray photography" compared the sand from the cavity to "samples of sand from the Giza and Saqqara areas [Saqqara being just south of the Giza plateau]." The sand from the cavity, they learned,

> was composed of more than 99 per cent quartz grains between 100 and 400 microns in size, whereas the samples taken outside the pyramid and from Saqqara were composed of calcite, quartz and plagioclase, with the grain size much smaller at between 10 and 100 microns. Further investigation revealed that this type of sand is termed "weeping", "whispering" or "musical" sand, because of the sound it makes when walked on or blown by the wind. So from where had it come?
>
> The Waseda [University] researchers were informed by a local Egyptian about an area where a deposit of sand was known to make similar sounds. This area turned out to be near El Tur, *in southern Sinai, a few hundred miles southeast of Giza across the Red Sea*. . . . Waseda team members also noted that the formation and deposition of the quartz sand in the region of El Tur was probably caused by the weathering of granite deposits originating at *Mount Sinai or its immediate area*. (304; italics added)

Lawton and Ogilvie-Herald follow up this revelation by stating:

> The observations made by the Japanese researchers raise several important questions. Why did the Ancient Egyptian architects choose to transport a potentially large quantity of quartz sand to Giza, and place it in a cavity behind the Queen's Chamber passage? (304)

After raising this question, they add:

> it has been suggested that the sand was placed in the Great Pyramid to act as a "shock-absorber" against

> earthquakes—although why local sand could not have been used is not readily apparent. (305)

Sand from Sinai was stored inside the Great Pyramid because it was in "the *third* month [compare to the 3rd drilling in the wall of the horizontal passage] after the children of Israel had gone out of the land of Egypt, on the same day [which was the 15th day of the month—another reason for the 15 stones in each wall], that they came to *the wilderness of Sinai* (Exodus 19:1; italics added).

As for the sand being "musical", we read in the 32nd chapter of Exodus, verses 17-18, that after Aaron had made the golden calf, Moses, coming down from Mount Sinai, was met by Joshua. Hearing

> the noise of the people as they shouted, he said to Moses, "There is a noise of war in the camp."
>
> But he [Moses] said: "it is not the noise of a shout of victory,
>
> Nor the noise of the cry of the dead,
>
> But *the sound of singing* I hear." (Italics added)

The joints in the horizontal passage were intentionally designed to be cross-shaped in order to represent Christ, for it was Christ, as we learned earlier, who accompanied the Israelites during the exodus. Paul, who supplies that information, also tells us that all the Israelites

> were under the cloud [which also represented Christ], all passed through the sea, [and] all were baptized. . . in the cloud and in the sea. (1 Corinthians 10:1)

Now, getting back to Noah and the flood, it may puzzle some Latter-day Saints that both are represented in the horizontal passage to the Queen's Chamber, the representative of the terrestrial kingdom. Shouldn't Noah and his family be associated instead with the King's Chamber, the representative of the celestial kingdom?

Noah and the flood are in evidence in the horizontal passage because the flood not only swept the earth clean but it also baptized the earth (Melvin R. Brooks, *L.D.S. Reference Encyclopedia* 141), and that raised the earth—but not its inhabitants—from a telestial level to a terrestrial level. It won't be until after the final judgment that the earth is celestialized.

Eighth detail: why are the 2 courses followed by one course?

Answer: the New International Version (NIV) of the Bible renders Genesis 8:15, 18 and 19 as follows:

> Then God said to Noah, "Come out of the ark. . . . "
>
> So Noah came out, together with his sons and his wife and his sons' wives. All the animals and all the creatures that move along the ground and all the birds—everything that moves on the earth—came out of the ark, *one kind after another.* (Italics added)

Chapter 9 contains the covenant God made with Noah that "never again will all life be cut off by the waters of a flood; never again will there be a flood to destroy the earth" (verse 11). According to God's promise, after the flood life would proceed uninterrupted by any more worldwide catastrophes until Christ's second coming. When that time arrives, only those who are worthy of inheriting either the terrestrial or the celestial kingdom will be spared. All others will be destroyed, as they were in Noah's day (Brooks 442-448).

The change from 2 courses of stones to one course in the horizontal passage reflects what is recorded in chapters 8 and 9 of Genesis. The flood was such a crucial event in human history that its inclusion in this part of the Great Pyramid is perfectly apropos.

But, since the world is filled with skeptics, and since numerous books have been written about the flood, many of them claiming that it was only a local event, more will be said about this subject in another volume in this series. For now, however, it's time to explain the real reason why there is a drop in the floor 18 feet before the entrance to the

Queen's Chamber. (For a photograph of this step-down see Rutherford's 3rd book; the photo follows page 1051.)

As already noted, the drop results in an increased height in the passage, taking it from 47 inches to 68 inches, which is the 5 feet 8 inches mentioned by Hancock. Worth Smith, it will be recalled, figured that since the sunken part of the passage was one-seventh of the total length it represented perfection, and therefore typified "the perfect man." Lemesurier, voicing an opposite opinion, saw it as an "inferior alternative to" the Grand Gallery, and Rutherford was of the same frame of mind, believing that the drop indicated going from a higher level to a lower level. Marsham Adams and Richard W. Noone found meaning in the total passage by tracing it backwards to its beginning.

None of the above speculation is correct.

At the point where the drop occurs, we are to understand that mortal life has ended for those living on a terrestrial level. The 18-foot section that follows represents a level of the spirit world that Christ refers to as "paradise" in Luke 23:43.

Notice the contrast between this representation of the spirit world and the one depicted in the horizontal passage that leads to the subterranean chamber. That passage is even more confined, more restricted than the 350-foot-long descending passage, that is, until it cuts through the 6-foot-square antechamber with its 4-foot-high ceiling. However, in the Queen's passage, which is above the base of the pyramid, the height is 5 feet 8 inches and the ceiling, unlike the one in the antechamber, does not give the impression of having been formed by some violent explosion.

Those who will be in this part of the spirit world will enjoy considerably more freedom—including the freedom to grow in knowledge—than the spirits destined for the lowest kingdom, and that is the reason for the increased height.

The sharp contrast between the 2 levels in the spirit world has been vividly described by George Ritchie, who, after witnessing the plain where "hordes of ghostly discarnate beings" engaged in battle, was taken to what he perceived as a different realm altogether.

> Enormous buildings stood in a beautiful sunny park and there was a relationship between the various structures, a pattern to the way they were arranged, that reminded me somewhat of a well-planned university. Except that to compare what I was now seeing with anything on earth was ridiculous. It was more as if all the schools and colleges in the world were only piecemeal reproductions of this reality. (Ritchie and Sherrill 68-69)

Ritchie goes on to describe how peaceful this realm was in comparison to the plain and how absorbed in studying everyone seemed to be inside the buildings.

> Through open doors I glimpsed enormous rooms filled with complex equipment. In several of the rooms hooded figures bent over intricate charts and diagrams, or sat at the controls of elaborate consoles flickering with lights. I'd prided myself on the beginnings of a scientific education; at the university I had majored in chemistry, minored in biology, studied physics and calculus. But if these were scientific activities of some kind, they were so far beyond anything I knew, that I couldn't even guess what field they were in. Somehow I felt that some vast experiment was being pursued, perhaps dozens and dozens of such experiments. (69-70)

Next, Ritchie was permitted to visit a studio where incredibly complex music "was being composed and performed"; that was followed by "a library the size of the whole University of Richmond" (70), then he entered yet another "building crowded with technological machinery" and "into what might have been some kind of space observatory" (71).

At last Ritchie felt compelled to ask his guide,

> "Is this. . . heaven, Lord Jesus?. . . When these people were on earth did they grow beyond selfish desires?"

> *They grew, and they have kept on growing.* The answer shone like sunlight in that intent and eager atmosphere. But if growth could continue, then this [realm] was not all. Then. . . there must be something even these serene beings lacked. And suddenly I wondered if it was the same thing missing in the "lower realm." Were these selfless, seeking creatures also failing in some degree to see Jesus? Or perhaps, to see Him for Himself? Bits and hints of Him they surely had; obviously it was the truth they were so single-mindedly pursuing. But what if even a thirst for truth could distract from the Truth Himself, standing here in their midst while they searched for Him in books and test tubes. (71)

Compare what Ritchie learned in this higher realm to these verses from section 76 of the *Doctrine and Covenants*:

> again, we saw the terrestrial world. . . these are they. . . whose glory differs from that of the church of the Firstborn who have received the fulness of the Father, even as that of the moon differs from the sun in the firmament.
>
> Behold, these are they who died without law [meaning they did not know about Christ's teachings during mortality];
>
> And also they who are the spirits of men kept in prison, whom the Son visited, and preached the gospel unto them, that they might be judged according to men in the flesh;
>
> Who received not the testimony of Jesus in the flesh, but afterwards received it.
>
> These are they who are honorable men of the earth, who were blinded by the craftiness of men.

> These are they who receive of his glory, but not of his fulness.
>
> These are they who receive of the presence of the Son, but not of the fulness of the Father. (71-77)
>
> These are they who are not valiant in the testimony of Jesus; wherefore, they obtain not the crown over the kingdom of our God. (79)

The last verse pertains to members of the Church of Jesus Christ of Latter-day Saints who fail to live according to all the standards of the church, who do not accept callings to serve in various positions, who fail to boldly stand up for the church when the opportunity arises, and yet are good people who commit no serious crimes, who are responsible citizens and who certainly deserve more in the afterlife than the lowest kingdom.

Now, reference needs to be made one more time to the length of the "spirit world" passage, which is 18 feet, and which also contrasts with the 29 feet of the lower horizontal passage found in the bedrock. What the shorter length tells us is that the candidates for the terrestrial kingdom will not have to spend as much time in the spirit world as the candidates for the telestial kingdom before they are resurrected.

One more number needs to be considered in relation to the 2 passages that represent the spirit world. The difference in height between the last 18 feet of the horizontal passage to the Queen's Chamber and the horizontal passage to the subterranean chamber is 31 inches (68 inches minus 37 inches). This 31 is a positive number since it is the passage to the Queen's Chamber that is 31 inches higher than the subterranean passage.

In the Old Testament, Josiah, one of the kings of Judah, ruled in Jerusalem for 31 years (2 Kings 22:1). He stood out because

> he did what was right in the sight of the Lord. . . he did not turn aside to the right hand or to the left. (2 Kings 22:2)

> Now before him there was no king like him, who turned to the Lord with all his heart, with all his soul, and with all his might, according to all the law of Moses. (2 Kings 3:25)

Here then is another connection with Moses in the passage to the Queen's Chamber.

The number 31, combined with 68, also provides a connection with Christ. How? By the fact that "the latitude of Bethlehem is 31.68° North" (Gaunt 44). Bethlehem was, according to the Gospel of Matthew, the birthplace of Christ. What is more, in gematria, using Greek letters, the name and title "Lord Jesus Christ" add up to 3168 (Gaunt 9). Christ should be represented in the passage to the middle chamber since, as we read in the *Doctrine and Covenants*, the terrestrial kingdom will "receive of the presence of the Son".

In contrast to the positive 31, there is a negative 31 if we compare the width of the last 18 feet of the Queen's Chamber passage to the width of the niche or antechamber in the subterranean passage, for 6 feet = 72 inches and 72 - 41 = 31.

Turning once more to the Old Testament, we discover that Joshua conquered 31 kings "on the west side of the Jordan [River]" (Joshua 12:7). And where is the niche in the subterranean passage? It is on the west side.

In addition,

> In the thirty-first year of Asa king of Judah, Omri became king of Israel. . . .
>
> But Omri did evil in the eyes of the Lord and sinned more than all those before him. (NIV, 1 Kings 16:23 and 25)

The contrast is explicit in both the passages and in the 2 kings, Josiah and Omri.

Finally, one of the Hebrew names for God—*El*—has a gematria of

31 (Aleth = 1 and Lamedh = 30; see Bullinger 265)), and 31 gives us a link to the exterior of the Great Pyramid, for the capstone, which is currently missing, will measure 31 feet high when it is installed (Edwards 100). As noted previously, the capstone is a symbol of Christ. The time to install the capstone will come at the end of the millennium when Christ will have completed his work "to bring to pass the immortality and eternal life of man" ("The Book of Moses" 1:39).

10. TALENTS

"For the kingdom of heaven is like a man traveling to a far country, who called his own servants and delivered his goods to them.

"And to one he gave five talents, to another two, and to another one, to each according to his own ability; and immediately he went on a journey.

"Then he who had received the five talents went and traded with them, and made another five talents.

"And likewise, he who had received two gained two more also.

"But he who had received one went and dug in the ground, and hid his lord's money.

"And after a long time the lord of those servants came and settled accounts with them.

"So he who had received five talents came and brought five other talents, saying, 'Lord, you delivered to me five talents; look, I have gained five more talents besides them.'

"His lord said to him, 'Well done, good and faithful servant; you were faithful over a few things, I will make you ruler over many things. Enter into the joy of your lord.'

"He also who had received two talents came and

said, 'Lord, you delivered to me two talents; look, I have gained two more talents besides them.'

"His lord said to him, 'Well done, good and faithful servant; you have been faithful over a few things, I will make you ruler over many things. Enter into the joy of your lord.'

"Then he who had received the one talent came and said, 'Lord, I knew you to be a hard man, reaping where you have not sown, and gathering where you have not scattered seed.

'And I was afraid, and went and hid your talent in the ground. Look, there you have what is yours.'

"But his lord answered and said to him, 'You wicked and lazy servant, you knew that I reap where I have not sown, and gather where I have not scattered seed.

'So you ought to have deposited my money with the bankers, and at my coming I would have received back my own with interest.

'Therefore take the talent from him, and give it to him who has ten talents.

'For to everyone who has, more will be given, and he will have abundance; but from him who does not have, even what he has will be taken away.

'And cast the unprofitable servant into the outer darkness. There will be weeping and gnashing of teeth.'"

(Matthew 25:14-30)

While the word *talent* in this parable is defined by *Nelson's Illustrated Bible Dictionary* as "the largest unit of silver" that was in use in Judea during Christ's time (Lockyer, Sr. 724), the Lord was not concerned with our ability to increase our income. Instead, he was emphasizing once more the necessity to perform, to engage in worthwhile activities, to improve ourselves, to increase our talents whatever they might be. Why? Because we are going to be held accountable for what we do with our lives, but if we do well we will be amply rewarded for our efforts. On the other hand, if we do not improve ourselves, if we attempt to justify our failure to perform by blaming God, then we will lose what we have been given.

The Reverend J. R. Dummelow addresses this issue by observing that it is not ability as such that is rewarded, "but faithful diligence"; furthermore, it "is a law of the natural as well as of the spiritual world, that the disuse of a faculty finally leads to its complete loss, whereas the due use of it leads to its development and increase." Dummelow also points out another lesson to be gained from this parable: "the reward of faithful work lies, not in rest only, but in enlarged activity" (706-07)).

Now, how does all this apply to the Great Pyramid, and in particular, to the Queen's Chamber?

The answer has to do with realizing that with the Parable of the Talents we once again have a series of 3 being dealt with: (1) the servant with 5 talents who doubles that amount, (2) the servant with 2 talents who also doubles what he has been given, and (3) the servant with one talent who buries it rather than put it to use.

The 3rd servant is unprofitable, wicked and lazy, and is to be cast out into outer darkness—as represented by the subterranean chamber and its dead-end passage. The 2nd servant is far more acceptable to his lord, and yet he does not receive the one talent that is taken from the 3rd servant; that extra talent goes to the 1st servant. So it should be obvious that the 2nd servant in the parable has reached his limit; his increase is at an end. Obvious also is the fact that he stands between the highest producer and the non-producer.

Where in the pyramid does the Queen's Chamber stand in relation to the King's Chamber and the subterranean chamber? It is in the middle—exactly at the "midpoint between the north and south sides of the Pyramid," according to Max Toth and Greg Nielsen (71). The middle servant, then, is related to the middle chamber, which represents the middle kingdom of heaven. He is a producer, but clearly not on the same level as the 1st servant, and that same comparison between the middle chamber and the highest, the King's Chamber, is made visually evident by their different features.

Toth and Nielsen remind us of a claim made by Egyptologists when they state, "The Queen's Chamber shows indications that work was abandoned before completion" (71). A number of factors give rise to this claim. Colin Wilson lists some of them:

> The floor was rough, and looked unfinished.
>
> . . . [The chamber] was not quite square, which was odd, since the pyramid builders showed themselves obsessed with precision and accuracy, and the wall niche was slightly off-centre. [Furthermore, w]hy should the architect of the Pyramid build two "air vents" that failed to reach the outside air, and then seal them off at the lower end so they were not visible? (60-61)

It was explained in the chapter titled "Degrees" that the Queen's Chamber was purposefully built with these features because it represents the terrestrial kingdom, which, even though it is vastly superior to the telestial kingdom, is not perfect. As for the supposed air vents, the true reason for their inclusion will be revealed in Volume 2 of *Books Written in Stone.*

In the meantime, there is more in the Queen's Chamber that needs to be accounted for. For example, the niche in the east wall, which, as noted by Wilson, is not centered on the wall, but instead, as reported by Rutherford, it is 25 inches "to the south of the vertical axis of the [gabled ceiling]." The niche is corbelled in 5 sections, having "four overlaps in the. . . north and south sides", with each overlap measuring 5 inches (Book III, 1038; a photo of the niche follows page 1084).

The niche is 5 feet 2 inches wide at its base. Its height is 15 feet 4 inches, and its depth is 3 feet 5 inches (Edwards 104; Rutherford,

Book III, 1038); however, a tunnel begins at the back of the niche and continues "for well over 38 feet through solid core blocks ending in a large bulb-shaped cavern" (Noone 98). Lawton and Ogilvie-Herald, who cite the more precise figure of 40 feet as the length, attribute this dead-end passage to al-Mamun (21). Other Egyptologists simply assign it to "treasure-seekers" (Edwards 104). If they are correct, then those treasure-seekers were most unusual in that they carefully carved out the tunnel with a "flat, level floor" and an "almost perfect right-angled left" wall (Noone 98).

Since the Egyptologists, as usual, are unable to find a valid reason for the tunnel's existence, they drag in a convenient excuse so they can write it off; Noone, on the other hand, is astute enough to agree with Edward Kunkle, who, after researching the pyramid for 50 years, concluded that the tunnel "was an original part of the construction" (98).

Unfortunately, Kunkle's insight in this instance is all but negated by his book, *Pharaoh's Pump*, in which he argues that the pyramid's passages and chambers functioned as a hydraulic ram pump. In his view, the subterranean pit was the pump's "compression chamber" where compressed air forced water into the upper levels of the pyramid. By this means, he says, the ancient Egyptians were able to employ a series of locks to float the stones into position as they were building the pyramid (Noone 344 and 355). But, like all the other theories presented so far, Kunkle's cannot possibly explain all the unique features built into the passages and chambers.

Back to the tunnel. What is its purpose? It is one more element in the pattern of contrasts utilized by Enoch. In the subterranean chamber, for instance, we have a dead-end passage that runs south for 53 feet. Here, in the Queen's Chamber, we have one that runs east for 40 feet. The subterranean passage simply ends in a blank wall. The Queen's tunnel ends "in a large bulb-shaped cavern". The subterranean passage represents outer darkness. The Queen's tunnel with its cavern represents a degree of freedom and growth—but there is a limit to that freedom and growth, which is evident not just from the tunnel and the cavern but also from their being on the east side of the chamber, which still signifies being distanced from God.

The niche itself carries a similar significance, but before proceeding any farther, what do the Egyptologists have to say about it? Since they all tend to favor the same hypotheses, we'll let Mark Lehner be their spokesman:

> The Queen's Chamber was. . . characteristic of a *serdab*, a room for the *ka* statue—the king's spiritual double. . . . With a total height of 4.7 m[eters] (15 ft 5 in), a corbelled niche in the east wall could certainly have contained a larger-than-life statue of the king. (111)

Lehner's definition of *ka* is typical nonsense from Egyptologists; the correct understanding of "*ka*" will be given at another place. Lehner's height for the niche is one inch more than the figure given by Edwards and Rutherford; that difference may be accounted for by the unevenness of the floor or by the salt crystals on the wall, which make exact measurements of certain features difficult in the Queen's Chamber.

Regarding the Egyptologists, Graham Hancock maintains they have "been unable to come to any persuasive conclusions about the original function of the niche, or, for that matter, of the Queen's Chamber as a whole" (323). He is right. Lehner is simply making an assumption that cannot be supported by any convincing evidence.

Now, what do the pyramidologists say?

> **Rutherford**: "The Niche is the most easterly feature in the entire interior of the Great Pyramid and it runs eastward, so its symbolism is therefore very sinister. . . . [T]hose entering the Niche have failed to reach the Divine standard and requirements necessary to obtain life in the Millennial Age" (Book III, 1040-1041).

> **Lemesurier**: "The Niche speaks of five successive

'lives'—and thus of four opportunities to move up the ladder of enlightenment at rebirth" (84).

Worth Smith: "The Great Pyramid treats extensively. . . of the science of numbers and numerical symbolism. . . . P]rominence [is] accorded the three mystic numbers, namely the three, five and seven, the numbers of Israel, and which are also dealt with in Freemasonry. In the Queen's chamber. . . the mystic five is accented thus:

(1) The Queen's Chamber (floor plane) is situated on the level of the 25th (5 X 5) tier of masonry;

(2) All measures in this recess. . . answer to a single standard, that of the Ancient, Sacred Hebrew Cubit of 25 (5 X 5) Pyramid inches;

(3) The Great Niche in the east wall of the room is 15 feet (3 X 5) high;

(4) The Great Niche is composed of 5 strongly marked stories, the top story of which is 25 inches (5 X 5) in width;

(5) The top story of the Great Niche is 25 inches (5 X 5) removed from the perpendicular center of the wall into which it is deeply cut." (89)

Although it isn't mentioned in this quote from Worth Smith, it was mentioned in the previous chapter that the 2 shafts in the north and south walls were originally sealed off to a depth of 5 inches. Therefore, even though some of Smith's numbers are in disagreement with the findings of Petrie and others, with that pair of 5s added to the others that are certain, there is no denying the frequency of this particular number in the Queen's Chamber and in the niche itself.

In a manner similar to Smith's examination of the Queen's Chamber, Bullinger studied the description of the tabernacle built by Moses, which is found in Exodus, and concluded that the tabernacle also "had *five* for its all-pervading number; nearly every measurement was a multiple of *five*" (140).

Here are a few excerpts from Chapter 26 of Exodus that support his conclusion:

> "Moreover, you shall make the tabernacle with ten [5 x 2] curtains." (Verse 1)
>
> "Five curtains shall be coupled to one another, and the other five curtains shall be coupled to one another." (Verse 3)
>
> "Fifty [5 x 10] loops you shall make in the one curtain, and fifty loops you shall make on the edge of the curtain. . . .
>
> "The length of each curtain shall be thirty [5 x 6] cubits. . . .
>
> "And you shall couple five curtains by themselves." (Verses 8-9)
>
> "Ten cubits [5 x 2] shall be the length of a board." (Verse 16)
>
> "And you shall make the boards for the tabernacle, twenty [5 x 4] boards for the south side.
>
> "You shall make forty [5 x 8] sockets of silver." (Verses 18-19)
>
> "And you shall make bars of acacia wood: five for the boards on one side of the tabernacle, five bars for the boards on the other side of the tabernacle, and five bars. . . for the far side westward." (Verses 26-27)
>
> "And you shall make a screen for the door of the tabernacle. . . .

> "And you shall make for the screen five pillars of acacia wood, and overlay them with gold; their hooks shall be gold, and you shall cast five sockets of bronze for them." (Verses 36-37).

Despite the frequency of the number 5 in the Queen's chamber, Worth Smith made no additional statements to specify why he thought that number was significant. His reference to the "numbers of Israel" and to Freemasonry is rather vague. But, by recalling the "5 points of fellowship" associated with Freemasonry, we can determine that the terrestrial kingdom will be one of greater harmony and friendship than the telestial kingdom, where imperfection and opposition to God are symbolized by the number 6.

There is, however, more to be gained by making a further comparison between the niche and the tabernacle, as will be demonstrated shortly. But for now we turn to Lemesurier, whose evaluation of the niche relies on reincarnation. Those who believe that every single person born on this earth is reincarnated should consider the following information.

According to *The World Almanac and Book of Facts: 2004*, in 1 AD the earth's population is estimated to have been 300 million; in 1250 AD the estimate is 400 million; in 1500 AD, 500 million; in 1804, 1 billion; in 1927, 2 billion; in 1960, 3 billion; in 1974, 14 years later, 4 billion; in 1987, 13 years later, 5 billion; in 1999, 12 years later, 6 billion (McGeveran, Jr. 479).

How can such huge increases in the 20th century be explained if everyone who dies is then reincarnated in a different body? In such an event, the world's population should remain basically the same, should it not?

Proponents of reincarnation say its purpose is to help us to progress, to become more and more enlightened as we experience life after life until we reach a stage where we do not have to be reincarnated in order to keep progressing towards perfection. If that is so, what has gone wrong? After all, who would argue that the human race—speaking in general terms—has significantly improved in morality, in spirituality, over the last 4000 years? In fact, we seem to be heading at an ever increasing speed in the opposite direction. Instead of climbing toward God, humanity is for the most part descending toward the pit, just as Angie Fenimore learned during her near-death experience (Lundahl and Widdison 223).

Lemesurier's interpretation of the niche is as untenable as Rutherford's. One mistake Rutherford makes is to ignore the tunnel that extends east from the niche. Like the Egyptologists, he assigns that feature to treasure-seekers and as a consequence misreads the purpose of the niche, equating it with the dead-end passage that snakes south off the subterranean chamber.

But one of the most significant differences between the two passages is in their length: 53 feet for the one that comes to a dead-end and 40 feet—if we accept the figure given by Lawton and Ogilvie-Herald—for the other. That is a difference of 13 feet, and even though this 13 may seem to be negative, if we consider that the shorter passage represents the least distance away from God, it becomes positive.

The number 13, as previously explained, represents the Twelve Apostles plus Christ in the Great Pyramid's number symbolism. And since Christ's presence will be a part of the terrestrial kingdom so will the Twelve and other authorized servants of the Lord minister to the people of the 2nd glory.

This is borne out by the number 40 itself. How long did the Israelites have to wait after they left Egypt before they entered the land promised to them? It was 40 years (Exodus 16:35), and shortly before they crossed over the Jordan River, what happened to Moses? He was translated and joined Enoch and his people in their ongoing ministry (Skousen, *The Third Thousand Years* 466), and that ministry, as Joseph Smith taught, is "of the terrestrial order" (Joseph Fielding Smith, *Scriptural Teachings of the Prophet Joseph Smith* 194).

Now, getting back to the tabernacle, it is most important to realize that it was a portable temple, a House of the Lord, "set up with its only entrance toward the east" (Lockyer, Sr., *Nelson's Illustrated Bible Dictionary* 1024)—which provides an obvious correlation with the niche being in the east wall.

In addition, the tabernacle was set up in "three distinct zones of increasing holiness: the courtyard, the holy place, and the holy of holies" (Metzger and Coogan, *The Oxford Companion to the Bible* 729).

Note that the holy place is the 2nd of the 3 zones; in other words, the holy place represented the terrestrial glory.

The niche in the Queen's Chamber, then, as affirmed by the numerous occurrences of the number 5 and by its location in the Queen's Chamber, is solidly linked to the tabernacle built by Moses—and built during the 40-year period that followed the exodus from Egypt. And who gave Moses the plan for the tabernacle? It was, of course, Christ, the great I Am (see Exodus 25:8-9).

Is there more evidence to support this claim, that the niche is linked to the tabernacle? There is. How far off-center is the niche? It is 25 inches south of the chamber's east-west axis (Lemesurier 81). Its placement was arranged that way because south symbolizes being distanced from God and 25 was the age at which Levite priests could begin "to perform service in the work of the tabernacle of meeting" (Numbers 8:24). The purpose of the tabernacle was to provide a place where the Lord could dwell among the Israelites, who were, as a nation, distanced from him in a very real and physical sense (Exodus 25:8; 19:20-23; 20:18).

How high is the niche? Lepre measured it at 15 feet (110). How high was the tabernacle? It was 10 cubits (Exodus 26:15-16), and since the common cubit of the Bible is considered to be equivalent to 18 inches or 1½ feet (Lockyer, Sr., *Nelson's Illustrated Bible Dictionary* 1098), 10 cubits equal 15 feet.

But now a question arises: how does the niche's corbelled design relate to the tabernacle? *The Zondervan Pictorial Encyclopedia of the Bible* supplies the tie-in by noting that at the west end of the tabernacle

> a pair of frames [were] joined at each corner of the. . . rear of the framework, sloping upward and inward from their bases to a point under the top bar. (Tenney, Vol. 5, 576)

The west end of the tabernacle utilized a total of 8 frames (Exodus 26:22-23), which would mean 4 frames on each side, or in other words, 4 overlaps on each side, just as there are in the niche.

Certainly one of the most compelling pieces of evidence that connects the niche with the tabernacle comes from Peter Tompkins' *Secrets of the Great Pyramid.* Tompkins reveals a little known fact about the niche that seems to be ignored by virtually all other 20th-century authors who take up the subject. He writes:

> In the Queen's Chamber Colonel Howard-Vyse had relays of men work day and night digging up the floor in front of the niche, but all they found was an old basket: so they refilled the hole. (63)

Why would anyone go to the trouble to bury a basket at the entrance to the niche? The answer is in Exodus 29:31-32, where the Lord instructs Moses to

> "take the ram of the consecration and boil its flesh in *the holy place.*
>
> "Then Aaron and his sons shall eat the flesh of the ram, and the bread that is in *the basket, by the door of the tabernacle of meeting.*" (Italics added)

We can relate the 2nd verse just quoted to the 9th division of what is called *The Book of the Tuat,* Tuat being the spirit world. There, "three deities, seated on baskets. . . provide food, or offerings, for the gods [or the spirits] who are in the Division" (Budge, *The Egyptian Heaven and Hell,* Volume III, 156).

Unlike the baskets described in Exodus and *The Book of the Tuat,* the basket that was buried by the niche had no bread in it; it was empty —signifying what? Christ tells us in John 6:35:

> "I am the bread of life. He who comes to me shall never hunger"

All of this is meant to be interpreted in a symbolic sense. Take away the bread, the food—the nourishment—and the "gods" will starve spiritually. Along with confirming the link between the niche and the tabernacle, that is ultimately what the buried basket in front of the niche was meant to symbolize.

But, is *buried* the right word to use here? Perhaps *hidden* is more appropriate. Consider, for example, Christ's statement in Chapter 5 of Matthew:

> "A city that is set on a hill cannot be hidden.
>
> "Nor do they light a lamp and put it under *a basket*, but on a lampstand, and it gives light to all who are in the house." (Verses 14-15; italics added)

"They" in verse 15 refers to the elect, meaning those who will inherit the highest kingdom. What about those who do just the opposite, who do, in fact, put their light under a basket—speaking symbolically—and therefore in effect bury their light, their talent (like the servant in Christ's parable), their God-given gifts which are meant to elevate them to the celestial kingdom? They will surely end up in a lesser kingdom.

The basket which was buried—or hidden—in the Queen's Chamber has other associations. For example, when Moses was born, was he not placed in a basket by his mother, who then placed the basket among the reeds by the bank of the Nile, where it was discovered by the pharaoh's daughter, and this she did because the pharaoh, fearing that the Israelites were becoming too numerous and therefore posed a threat, had ordered that all male babies of Israelite blood be killed at birth.

However, before the mother of Moses put him in the basket she hid him for 3 months (see Exodus 1:8-16 and 2:1-10). Petrie gives the width of the niche's base in terms of the Egyptian cubit of 20.6 inches, which results in a measurement of precisely 3 cubits (24).

Another significant association with the basket is found in Matthew 14:19-20:

> He [Christ] commanded the multitude to sit down on the grass. And He took. . . five loaves and. . . two fish, and looking up to heaven, He blessed and broke and gave the loaves to the disciples; and the disciples gave to the multitudes.
>
> So they all ate and were filled, and they took up twelve baskets full of the fragments that remained.

Note the numbers in verse 19; they are 5 and 2. What is the width of the niche's base in feet and inches? It is 5 and 2 respectively.

And now note that if we convert the 5 feet 2 inches of the niche's base into 62 inches, we get another association, for Abraham went to Egypt at the age of 62 in order to escape the famine that was ravaging Mesopotamia and Canaan ("The Book of Abraham" 2:14).

There is more. According to Petrie, at a height of 13 feet (156 inches), the width of the niche narrows to just 20 inches (24). Abraham was in Egypt for 13 years (Skousen, *The First 2000 Years* 295), and he was the 20th Old Testament patriarch.

There is still more. If we take Petrie's figure for the highest point of the gabled ceiling—20.4 feet—and deduct from it the height at which the ceiling begins—15.4 feet—the difference is 5 feet or 60 inches (23). Isaac was 60 when Jacob was born (Genesis 25:26).

What about Joseph, Jacob's son? Is he associated with the Queen's Chamber? He is, in the angle of the northwest corner of the roof, which is 30 degrees 14 minutes (Petrie 23). Joseph was 30 when he began to rule Egypt under the pharaoh, and he was granted that power after he interpreted the pharaoh's prophetic dream that involved 14 cattle.

It is a curious thing that not one of the 4 corners of the roof has exactly the same angle. For instance, the southwest corner is 30 degrees 10 minutes. This 30 is for Christ, who began his ministry at the age of 30; the 10 is for Pontius Pilate, who governed Judea for 10 years (Lockyer, Sr., *Nelson's Illustrated Bible Dictionary* 841). Pilate's unwillingness to defy the Jews who wanted Christ dead resulted in his crucifixion, which took place *southwest* of the temple. The tomb where Christ's body lay from Friday until Sunday morning was nearby. (The evidence for this claim will not be presented here but in the second volume of *Books Written in Stone.*)

The southeast corner is 30 degrees 33 minutes; Christ's ages when he began his ministry and when he died on the cross.

The northeast corner is 30 degrees 48 minutes. The 30 once again refers to Christ; the 48 refers to the lesser priesthood, where 48 priests make a complete quorum. Priests, as pointed out in the discussion of the half-girdle stones in the ascending passage, have the authority to baptize but not to administer the higher ordinances that are required for an inheritance in the celestial kingdom.

The ceiling reveals something else of importance.

In 1837, Vyse managed to expose one of the ceiling stones in the northwest corner of the chamber and "found it to extend beyond the wall face for" just over 10 feet (Rutherford, Book III, 1035). Petrie says

> this, coupled with the thickness of these blocks. . . throws the centre of gravity of each of the slabs well behind the wall face, so that they could be placed in position without pressing one on another. Hence there is never any arch thrust so long as the blocks are intact; they act solely as cantilevers, with the capability of yielding arched support in case they should be broken. (23)

The ceiling was constructed in this fashion to establish beyond a doubt that this middle chamber symbolizes a definite degree of growth and freedom, and yet at the same time there is the suggestion of mutual support, all of which defines the terrestrial kingdom quite well.

In addition to Petrie's description of the ceiling, Rutherford observes that the ceiling blocks "have an overall length of over 240 inches" or slightly more than 20 feet (Book III, 1037). Why would that particular length have been chosen?

Concerning the flood, the New International Version of the Bible gives this translation of Genesis 7:20: “The waters rose and covered the mountains to a depth of more than twenty feet.”

More than twenty feet?

Coincidence? Not very likely when the 350 feet of the descending passage match the 350 years that Noah lived after the flood. Not when the subterranean chamber lies “600 feet beneath the apex of the pyramid” (Hancock 317), and 600 was Noah’s age when the flood began (Genesis 7:11). Not when the 8 special stones in the passage to the middle chamber relate to Noah and his family. Not when there is salt in both the passage and the chamber. And not when the figure of 20+ is in the ceiling.

It remains to give the width and length of the middle chamber. Edwards lists their dimensions in *The Pyramids of Egypt*: “18 feet 10 inches from east to west and 17 feet 2 inches from north to south” (103).

The measurement of “17 feet 2 inches from north to south” is the same as the distance between the complete girdle stones in the ascending passage and so we have another reference to Joseph and his two sons. But we also have another reference to the flood which started

> on the *seventeenth* day of the *second* month—on that day all the springs of the great deep burst forth, and the floodgates of the heavens were opened. (NIV, Genesis 7:11; italics added)

The 18 feet in the east-to-west measurement provide a link to the 18 feet that make up the “spirit world” section of the horizontal passage to the Queen’s Chamber. Keeping that in mind, we should consider the Lord’s instruction to Noah to “finish the ark to within 18 inches of the top” (NIV, Genesis 6:16)—and those 18 inches should remind us of the 18-inch drop at the entrance to the subterranean chamber.

But along with the length of 18 feet in the east-west measurement of the Queen’s Chamber we also have the number 10. Why? Because after "the rain had stopped falling from the sky" the water began to recede, and it "continued to recede until the *tenth* month, and on the first day of the tenth month the tops of the mountains became visible" (NIV, Genesis 8:2-3 and 5; italics added).

Moreover, there were 10 antediluvian patriarchs—and Noah was number 10 (see Genesis, chapter 5).

* * *

Now, this chapter began with Christ's Parable of the Talents in which the 2nd servant who was given 2 talents increased them to 4. We have seen the number 4 in the measurements for the height of the ceiling where it begins and for the height of the ceiling's peak (15 feet 4 inches and 20 feet 4 inches respectively).

There is another 4 to consider. Petrie informs us that

> all round the chamber, and the lower part of the passage leading to it, is a footing of fine stone, at the rough floor level; this projects 1 to 4 inches from the base of the walls, apparently as if intended as support for flooring blocks which have never been introduced. (23)

This number 4 that is associated with the imperfect floor, along with the other 4s just mentioned—plus the 4 overlaps in the niche and the 30 stones in the horizontal passage that are 41 and ¼ inches long—confirm the connection between the middle servant in the parable and the middle chamber in the Great Pyramid.

11. BREAKOUT

> "If anyone would come after me, he must deny himself and take up his cross and follow me."
>
> (Matthew 16:24)

Paul Brunton explains why the well shaft received that name:

> for nearly two thousand years it was thought to have water at the bottom. Not till it was cleared out by [Giovanni Battista] Caviglia of the mass of debris which had accumulated in it was the bottom discovered to be perfectly dry. (60)

The well shaft has two openings, one near the end of the descending passage and the other at the north end of the Grand Gallery. In both cases, the openings are on the west side, but other features are not so similar. (A view of this shaft can be found between pages 1084 and 1085 of Rutherford's Book III.)

The bottom of the shaft is sunk lower than the short section that leads to it off the descending passage (Lemesurier 94-95). In addition, according to Rutherford, that short section is "rough and irregular with a mean height of about 31 inches and is not at right-angles to the Descending Passage but lies at an angle of approximately 65 degrees and runs north-west by west for 6 feet to the lower mouth of the Well-Shaft" (Book III, 1028).

In contrast, Rutherford describes the top entrance as having a shorter connecting passage that is "precisely constructed and lies due east and west at right-angles to the main passages [i.e., the horizontal passage to the Queen's Chamber and the Grand Gallery]", plus the upper mouth is square, measuring 28 inches across (Book III, 1028).

One other difference that Rutherford perceives between the two entrances—or exits, depending on the point of view one takes—is that the top one appears to have been blasted open by some "tremendous force from within", and yet it is partly covered by a roof, formed when part of the bottom stone in the west ramp was broken up (Book III, 1023).

Lawton and Ogilvie-Herald disagree with Rutherford's description of the well's upper mouth. They present the following argument:

> Apart from the physical improbability of attempting to dislodge a well-cemented and sizeable block from below in a cramped space, a close examination of the chisel marks on the *topside* of the blocks that surround the upper entrance to the shaft reveals that it was *chiselled out from above.* (137-38)

We'll come back to this subject.

Moving upwards from the lower entrance, the well is built in 4 sections, with the first section slanting steeply to the north; the second section is much longer than the first and is not as steep, but it also slants to the north; the third section "passes vertically through [the] irregularly shaped natural 'grotto' before bending northwards;" and the fourth section ascends straight up (Lemesurier 91).

There are then, as Lepre notes, "five different directions" included in the four sections, two being "vertical and three oblique" (116). Again, counting upwards from the lower entrance, Lepre cites the following figures for the 5 directions: 30 feet, 100 feet, 10 feet, 35 feet, and 25 feet, which add up to a total of 200 feet. In the "uppermost area" of the 100-foot section, 2 of the 3 fissures found in the descending passage can be seen (116).

The purpose of the well has, of course, generated a variety of comments. Brunton, for example, assures us that, based on his own research,

> the shaft and the Grotto had been cut at the same time as the building of the Pyramid, but. . . the Well did not descend any farther than the Grotto itself at the time. For thousands of years there was no direct link between the upper passages and the subterranean one. . . .
>
> Working at their task, the last tenants cut the lower section of the Well through solid rock as a way of escape for themselves. When the work was finished and they had made their retreat, it was only necessary to block up the exit of the newly cut section securely, at the point where it joins the descending passage, and then ascend the 300-feet slope to the original entrance. Thus, the Well, although originally created as a means of reaching the Grotto, finally became a means of leaving the blocked-up Pyramid. (61)

Egyptologists offer a similar explanation for the well's existence, as seen in this quote from Edwards:

> Once the first [granite] plug had begun its descent [to block the beginning of the ascending passage], the well-shaft from the lower end of the Grand Gallery to the bottom of the Descending Corridor provided the only possible exit for the workmen who had lowered [all three of] the plugs. Initially, it may have served to ventilate the bottom end of the Descending Corridor and the subterranean chamber. . . when they were being constructed, but that need ceased when the internal plan was changed. It was only, as Petrie showed, after much of the superstructure had been built that the upper part of the shaft was hewn downwards through

> the masonry. It could, however, have had no practical function before the closure of the Ascending Corridor. (290-91)

Regarding the use of the well as an escape shaft by the pyramid's workmen, Piazzi Smyth asks:

> "In what state would they have left the ramp-stone over the well's mouth?"
>
> Certainly not blown from within outwards, as if by uncontrollable explosive force, breaking off part of the wall with it, and leaving the hole's mouth exposed; for that would have defeated their whole object. They would, on the contrary, have contrived a temporary support. . . [so] that when the last man had come away, the prop would be easily withdrawn and the stone would fall neatly into a seat already cut for it, and cemented round the edges with freshly applied lime to make the work permanent and secure. For then such stone would be flush with the rest of the ramp, and would utterly conceal from any one who should ever enter the Grand Gallery by the regular method of the first ascending passage, that there was any well-mouth whatever behind the surface of the ramp.
>
> The original builders, then, were not those who knocked out, from within on the well side, that now lost ramp-stone. . . .
>
> Who then did burst out that now missing ramp-stone?. . .
>
> Either some fanatics of the later dynasties of Ethiopic intruders, or the following Persian conquerors, are considered to have been those spoilers. . . .

> *Precisely* who those earlier men were, as Colonel Howard-Vyse well remarks, who committed that first spoiling, "will never be known". (455-57)

Smyth has nothing else to say about the well, having accepted the Egyptologists' reason for the well's existence.

Worth Smith, on the other hand, regards the well's "narrow, jagged, vertical" design as demonstrating "the impossibility of anyone ascending that route from the Way of Rebellion to the higher planes of Human Perfection and Spirit Rebirth, or even as high as the Plane of Justification, except by faith" (101).

Smith also regards the well as a symbol of Christ's "descent into the death-state (Hades) into which Jesus went in His ransom sacrifice at 33½ years of age". Smith cites the 33½ inches that separate the top entrance to the well from the beginning of the Grand Gallery as correlating to the 33½ years that he believed Jesus had lived.

The condition of the well's upper mouth is seen as a representation of Christ's resurrection since it illustrates

> the tremendous spiritual force that He generated within himself prior to expiring and which He used with such great effectiveness in raising himself from the dead. (106)

But the

> Well signifies, additionally, the sudden drop into the Hell-state by those who, climbing up, refuse to accept the Atonement of Christ. (106-07)

Rutherford takes the position that the well is one of the few places in the pyramid where dating cannot be applied, so he adopts basically the same view as Worth Smith: "the Well-Shaft represents the Way of Life through the death and resurrection of Christ" (Book III, 1027).

He adds that the narrow width of the shaft prevents two people from climbing it abreast of each other, and that tells us

> it is an individual matter between each one of the human race and the Creator. If we are agile we might climb some parts of the Well-Shaft unaided, but in its upper part which is vertical we all need help from above. So no one can succeed in his own strength. (Book II, 420)

Lemesurier regards the well as

> a path of self-redemption [which] will be available to any souls who manage to regain sufficient enlightenment. . . to rise above the deathly level to which they have sunk. . . . [T]his path will eventually have the effect of transforming them into "living beings" pursuing, even in the midst of hell, one of the upper paths to immortality. (89)
>
> This upward spiritual path. . . will be a difficult, fourfold one. . . . None the less [sic], once a start has been made, progress will become easier. (92)
>
> The fairest assessment would therefore seem to be that the Well-Shaft represents a *potential* opportunity to join the path of the enlightened ones—an opportunity which, even if not fully profited from, will still lead at very least to the path of the semi-enlightened. In either event, then, the Well-Shaft represents a Path to Life for those ascending it.

But, Lemesurier warns, the well is "a kind of two-way highway", for it "just as clearly represents a pit of physical death for those descending it" (93).

Noone's book, *5/5/2000*, contains two illustrations of the pyramid's interior (one of them being a reproduction from David Davidson's *The Great Pyramid: Its Divine Message*) and both illustrations suggest that the well was constructed so the fissures could be inspected in order to determine if they were a threat to the pyramid's stability (58 and 227).

As usual, the Egyptologists have no understanding as to why the well was included in the pyramid's internal plan, and, as usual, some of the pyramidologists are only partly right, while others are completely wrong.

Dunn, enlarging somewhat on his earlier theory, says the

> *Well shaft bored from the juncture of the Grand Gallery and the Horizontal Passage down to the Grotto. . .* was probably either a waste removal shaft or an overflow shaft. (207)

He also alleges that at some point in time there was an explosion in the King's Chamber, and with that as his premise he would have us believe that

> the only explanation for the constructed portion of the Well Shaft near the Grand Gallery is that it was enlarged to allow the guardians access to the Grand Gallery after the explosion in the King's Chamber, and this excavation resulted in the thin block of limestone on the south side. (213-14)

In the last part of his statement Dunn is referring to Petrie's observation that

> the sides of the [well's upper] mouth are very well cut, quite as good work as the dressing of the gallery walls; but on the S. side there is a vertical joint in the gallery side, only 5.3 inches from the mouth. Now, great care is always taken in the Pyramid to put large stones at

> a corner, and it is quite inconceivable that a Pyramid builder would put a mere slip 5.3 [inches] thick beside the opening to a passage. It evidently shows that the passage mouth was cut out after the building was finished in that part. It is clear, then, that the whole of this shaft is an additional feature to the first plan. (87)

While Petrie's measurements and descriptions are of great value, his lack of understanding when it comes to the symbolism built into the Great Pyramid caused him to draw the wrong conclusions. And the same lack of understanding has led all the Egyptologists who have followed him to do the same.

Before exploring more of the individual features of the well, a question should be asked. If the well originally went only to the grotto, as Brunton says, what was in the grotto to warrant the linkup? Brunton offers no clues to answer this question, nor does he indicate what research in particular led to his determining that the continuation of the well down to the descending passage occurred thousands of years later.

Another question needs to be asked. If the well was meant to be an escape shaft, why was it made so narrow and so difficult to climb either up or down? And why was it made so long? A quick look at the layout of the pyramid's interior makes it obvious that a much shorter route could have been taken to the descending passage.

As for the claim that the well was constructed so the fissures could be inspected, that doesn't add up. If inspecting the fissures was the goal, it would have been better to have gone into the fissures themselves, or to have cut a shaft that would have closely paralleled them so they could have been tapped into and checked in numerous places.

Graham Hancock reveals how weak the argument is that the well had to be used as an escape shaft because of the 3 granite stones blocking the entrance to the ascending passage by pointing out that "if the objective had been to deny intruders admission" it would have been "much easier and more efficient to have plugged the *descending* corridor" (318). In fact, plugs could have been placed at the top of the descending passage at the very entrance to the pyramid, so why weren't they?

* * *

Now we'll examine the well more minutely, starting at the lower end, and starting with Lepre, who contends it "was dug out from the top down. This," he is convinced, "is indicated by the fact that its bottom end penetrates a few feet below its lower-most doorway. If it had been hewn from the bottom up, this bottom section would surely have been level with its doorway at that point" (117).

Here is one more example of an Egyptologist reaching a conclusion based on an incorrect premise. It would have actually made no difference from which end the well was dug. The result would have been the same because the well is a symbol. It was not built to ventilate the "Descending Corridor and the subterranean chamber" as proposed by Edwards.

One reason it was not constructed for that purpose can be taken from the Egyptologists themselves who argue that the subterranean chamber was abandoned and only after that were the ascending passage and the Queen's Chamber built, so to reverse things and say the ascending passage was built first makes no sense.

Nor was the well built as an escape shaft, for no one was ever buried inside the pyramid. Enoch and his people simply laid down the various roofs as they worked their way to the top so there was never any concern about being trapped inside.

The bottom of the well is lower than its entrance for a specific reason, but before giving that reason it will be better to give one of the reasons why the first section of the well measures 30 feet. Most likely it is obvious by now, but in case it isn't, we're told in Genesis that Joseph's older brothers, before he was sold as a slave,

> cast him into a pit. And the pit was empty; there was no water in it. (37:24)

What did Brunton say about the well shaft? He said,

> for nearly two thousand years it was thought to have

> water at the bottom. Not till it was cleared out. . . was the bottom discovered to be perfectly dry. (60)

In Egypt, Joseph was bought by Potiphar, who, after Joseph had served him faithfully for 7 years, cast him into an underground prison where he remained for 6 years. How long is the short section that links the descending passage to the first 30 feet of the well? It is 6 feet.

And this part of the well is underground, for it is only "the top third of the shaft [that] runs through the [pyramid's] superstructure" (Lawton and Ogilvie-Herald 537).

The first 30 feet of the well is one more connection to Joseph's becoming the ruler of Egypt at the age of 30. Using Joseph as an example, Vicki Alder finds the number 30 significant "in regards to mourning, sacrifice and service." To add weight to her statement, she points out that "the children of Israel mourned after the death of Aaron for *thirty* days. (Num. 20:29) When Moses was taken from them, the people mourned again for thirty days" (129).

But these are not the only biblical connections to be made, for, as stated previously, Christ began his ministry at the age of 30. Now, in Matthew 11:18-19 we read: "John [the Baptist] came neither eating nor drinking, and they say, 'He has a demon.' The Son of Man came eating and drinking, and they say, 'Look, a glutton and a winebibber, a friend of tax collectors and sinners!'" In Isaiah 53:12 we read: "And He [the Messiah] was numbered with the transgressors/And he bore the sin of many,/And made intercession for the transgressors."

And in the *Doctrine and Covenants* we read that Christ, the Messiah, "*descended below all things*, in that he comprehended all things, that he might be in all and through all things" (88:6; italics added).

In particular, it is the verses from Matthew, Isaiah and the *Doctrine and Covenants* that lend meaning to the fact that the bottom of the well is lower than its entrance, for this feature represents the presence of the Savior, who descended below all things by taking on himself the sins of those who would repent, and who will not give up on anyone who has not gone past the point of redemption.

There are 2 more verses in the Bible—one from the Old Testament and one from the New Testament—that involve the number 30 and that have a bearing on this subject, but they won't be discussed until later in this chapter.

The 2nd section of the well is the one that runs for 100 feet. With that in mind, consider this verse from Ecclesiastes in the Old Testament:

> Though a sinner does evil a hundred times, and his days are prolonged, yet I surely know that it will be well with those who fear God. (8:12)

Consider also these verses from Matthew:

> "the Son of Man has come to save that which was lost.
>
> "What do you think? If a man has a hundred sheep, and one of them goes astray, does he not leave the ninety-nine and go to the mountains to seek the one that is straying?" (18:11-12)

The reference to "mountains" may not seem to fit the Great Pyramid, however, the pyramids of Giza have frequently been called man-made mountains. In fact, Leonard Cottrell's book on the pyramids is titled *The Mountains of Pharaoh.*

With the quotes presented so far from the Bible and the *Doctrine and Covenants* we see a continuity that is consistent and appropriate for the symbolism of the well, which does not represent Christ's "descent into the death-state" as suggested by Worth Smith, but rather it has to do with those people who recognize that it is time to turn their lives around before it is too late. To do so they have to get off the downward path they're on; they have to turn back toward God, and that is why the section that connects the descending passage to the well is at an angle of 65 degrees. The number 65 is associated with Enoch, for he was 65 when he began to build the city of Zion (Skousen, *The First 2000 Years* 172), and he was 65, the Bible says, when his son Methuselah was born and afterwards "Enoch walked with God" (Genesis 5:21-22). Those who ascend the well are beginning to follow in Enoch's footsteps.

Turning back toward God is also the reason that the well, from the bottom up, slants to the north. Our spirits came from that direction when we left our Father so we could be born into mortality.

Lemesurier is not correct in everything he has to say about the well; for example, his statement that those souls who ascend the well are "pursuing, even in the midst of hell, one of the upper paths to immortality" (89) needs to be rephrased. Everyone born on this earth will gain immortality in the flesh because of Christ's resurrection (see 1 Corinthians 15:21-22), so it is not immortality that is symbolically involved, but rather the potential of being exalted in the celestial kingdom.

With that clarification, we can see that Lemesurier's perception of the well as "an upward spiritual path" and his understanding that "once a start has been made, progress will become easier", are precisely what is being depicted in the first two sections.

The 3rd section of the well is the vertical 10 feet that pass through the grotto. The number 10 was important in the Queen's Chamber and it is important here, where the 10 commandments again come to mind. Those who keep the 10 commandments are on an upward path.

Bullinger reminds us of another important use of 10. In Exodus, when Christ identified himself as *I Am*, he provided only one subject complement. That is, he completed only one meaning of the *I Am* clause. In the Gospel of John, however, we have 10 subject complements for *I Am* (248). These include:

> "I am the door. If anyone enters by Me, he will be saved". (10:9)
>
> "I am the good shepherd. The good shepherd gives His life for the sheep." (10:11)
>
> "I am the true vine. . . . you are the branches. He

> who abides in Me, and I in him, bears much fruit; for without Me you can do nothing." (15:1 and 5)

David Furlong adds to the symbolism of 10 by asserting that it "is the number of God in the Hebrew system of Gematria" (298). The Hebrew word for "to be united", *ohad* (Aleph-Hē-Daleth), has a gematria of 10 (for the spelling of *ohad* and its definition see James Strong's *The New Strong's Complete Dictionary of Bible Words* 299, entry # 161).

At this point it should not be too surprising to learn that Christ is represented in the grotto as well as in the 10-foot vertical section of the well.

Lepre describes the entrance to the grotto as being composed "of roughly hewn and squared limestone blocks"—10 in number. He adds that the grotto is "situated just below the monument's ground level [and] constitutes what appears to be the hollowing-out of a once-smaller, natural pocket of earth at the center of the pyramid plateau." Lepre then confesses his inability to explain why the grotto was "uniquely located in the very middle of an otherwise solid rock foundation" (117).

That rock foundation, according to Rutherford, "is practically 24 feet above. . . the [pyramid's] casing-stone base" (Book III, 1025). Rutherford also mentions that the width of the well where the grotto begins is "28 inches square" (Book III, 1028), which is identical to the mouth of the well where it exits at the beginning of the Grand Gallery.

The grotto itself, Rutherford continues,

> is longer from east to west than from north to south [as are all the chambers inside the pyramid], but it is so irregular that it has no definite shape, and therefore dimensions would be difficult to state. It is about 10 Royal Cubits long [the equivalent of 17.2 feet], but is low, although at one part towards the western end, where there is a deep hole in the floor, even a tall man could stand upright with plenty of room to spare. (Book III, 1027)

A cutaway illustration on page 193 of the Reader's Digest edition of *The World's Last Mysteries* shows the deep hole in the grotto, which is beneath the horizontal passage to the Queen's Chamber.

Rutherford also cites Marsham Adams' assertion that in "the ancient Egyptian texts the grotto is alluded to as the *Well of Life*" (Book III, 1027). Finally, Rutherford observes that the grotto "is on the same level as the beginning or lower end of the Granite Plug" in the ascending passage, and as we learned earlier, that granite plug represents repentance.

Even though the grotto is within natural rock and the ascending passage is within the pyramid, this match-up is possible because "the rock rises to a slightly higher level in the central part of the pyramid's base" (Book II, 419).

Because of that rise, the top of the grotto, like the 2nd of the 3 granite blocks in the ascending passage, is on the same level as the pyramid's 7th course (Lemesurier 44). The number 7 is one more link to Enoch, the 7th patriarch, while the 2nd granite block represents baptism.

Returning to Lepre, we learn that the grotto's

> ceiling is composed, not of packed earth as would be expected, but of gravel packed in damp, caked sand. Whereas the earthen walls of this cavity are relatively hard to the touch, the ceiling of small stones is so loosely packed that one has only to reach up and dig in with one's fingers in order to extract whole handfuls of this material. . . .
>
> The ceiling is also unusually damp to the point where there is actually a perceptible coating—like a light frost—over the pebbles themselves. This unusual composition naturally temps one to speculate about the existence of a nearby water source. Yet a water source—and especially one so very cool—does not seem likely

> in the middle of a solid rock foundation at the edge of a barren section of desert. (117)

No, not likely at all—and certainly no more likely than tapping a rock twice, as Moses did, and then having water flow from it.

Lepre follows up this description of the ceiling with 2 more bits of information worth recording.

> Located in the center of the Grotto is a single block of granite with a 3½″ drill hole bored through it; its dimensions are 21″ by 18″ by 17″. . . .
>
> The shape of the grotto is unorthodox, displaying several levels. . . . It curves or bends in its configuration, and forms a rough L-pattern.

Lepre then makes this comment:

> Although seemingly insignificant when compared to the other, much more commanding, apartments of the Great Pyramid, the grotto nevertheless had a special purpose which we are not presently familiar with.

He also reveals that the grotto is "neglected by nearly all researchers and explorers," and many authors do no more than mention it "in passing within the context of their treatises on the subject of the Great Pyramid" (118).

Lepre is right. The purpose of the grotto is not understood—especially by Egyptologists—and yet it is one of the most important of the pyramid's many symbols. Part of that symbolism has been explained, but now it's time to back up and start over again, in order to supplement the points that have already been made and to establish even more firmly the specific, unified message being presented by the odd lengths of the well's various sections.

The short passage that links the bottom of the well to the descending passage is 6 feet and these 6 feet can be linked to this quote from Proverbs:

> These six things the Lord hates,
>
> Yes, seven are an abomination to Him:
>
> A proud look,
>
> A lying tongue,
>
> Hands that shed innocent blood,
>
> A heart that devises wicked plans,
>
> Feet that are swift in running to evil,
>
> A false witness who speaks lies,
>
> And one who sows discord among brethren.
>
> (6:16-19)

One of the 7 in this list does not belong with the other 6, and that is "hands that shed innocent blood". Anyone who is guilty of shedding innocent blood—of committing cold-blooded murder—is in a separate class because the murderer, after taking a life, cannot restore it, cannot make restitution, no matter how much he or she might try to repent (Kimball 128-29).

On the other hand, the remaining 6 can be repented of and restitution can be made at least in part, if not in whole, for whatever is done. It is these 6, and others like them, that have to be overcome by breaking away and starting over again.

Rutherford gives the height of this 6-foot link as 31 inches. That is just one inch higher than the height of the dead-end passage that runs south off the subterranean chamber. What that tells us is that nearly all sins, including adultery, can be repented of in mortality, and it is repentance that will keep us from being sent into the outer darkness.

Once repentance occurs, those who are then moving toward God can be compared to the Israelites who followed Moses into the wilderness, where the tabernacle was erected to the Lord's specifications. The tabernacle, as already said, was meant to be a sanctuary so the Lord could "dwell among" his people (Exodus 25:8). The fact that "entry into the courtyard was through. . . the narrow, eastern end" (Gower 341) immediately establishes the same east-west symbolism that we see in the Great Pyramid.

When the tabernacle was set up,

> Moses took his tent and pitched it outside the camp, far from the camp, and called it the tabernacle of meeting. And it came to pass that everyone who sought the Lord went out to the tabernacle of meeting which was outside the camp. (Exodus 33:7)

The repetition of "outside the camp" should be noticed, for in a like manner the well is "outside" the descending passage, where the masses of mankind are represented.

The first section of the well measures 30 feet. There is a corresponding number in the tabernacle. Moses was instructed to "make curtains of goats' hair to be a tent over" it. The curtains were to be "*thirty* cubits" in length (Exodus 26:7-8; italics added).

Goats' hair, it should be mentioned, was used in biblical times to make tunics, which "were very uncomfortable because they caused skin irritation. They were therefore worn in times of mourning and repentance" (Gower 12).

The second section of the well measures 100 feet. There is a corresponding number in the tabernacle. Moses was instructed to "make the court. . . *one hundred* cubits long for one side" (Exodus 27:9; italics added). Incidentally, the court represented those who were living on a telestial level.

The 3rd section, which contains the doorway to the grotto, measures 10 feet. There is a corresponding number in the tabernacle. For this sanctuary, Moses was instructed to make "boards of acacia wood, *standing upright*." And "*ten* cubits shall be the length of a board" (Exodus 26:15-16; italics added).

Concerning acacia wood, *Nelson's Illustrated Bible Dictionary* contains this entry for the Valley of Acacias:

> a dry valley where only the acacia tree grows (Joel 3:18). According to Joel's prophecy, in the end time a fountain of refreshing water will flow from the Temple ("the house of the Lord") and give new life to the parched and barren valley. (Lockyer, Sr. 11)

The width of the well at the doorway to the grotto is 28 inches. There is a corresponding number in the tabernacle, which was to be made "with ten curtains of fine woven linen. . . . The length of each curtain shall be *twenty-eight* cubits" (Exodus 26:1-2; italics added).

When Moses entered the tabernacle a

> pillar of cloud descended and stood at the door of the tabernacle, and the Lord talked with Moses. (Exodus 33:9)

An illustration of the grotto on page 118 of Lepre's *The Egyptian Pyramids* shows the block of granite near the doorway.

Dunn would like to persuade us that the

> granite, being more impervious to erosion than the limestone, may have served to catch the chemical flow from the Queen's Chamber and direct it into the deep hole to the side of the Well Shaft. (214)

Come now. Are we really to believe that engineers who are supposed to have had advanced resonators and who knew about microwave energy could devise no better system than this to dispose of a chemical overflow?

Granite, as Rutherford says, represents the divine; this block of granite, in particular, represents Christ at the door.

Now, Moses wanted to see not just the "pillar of cloud" but the Lord himself. Christ told him,

> "Here is a place by Me, and you shall stand on the rock.
>
> "So it shall be, while My glory passes by, that I will put you in the cleft of the rock, and will cover you with My hand while I pass by." (Exodus 33:21-22)

Those who enter the grotto are standing in the cleft of a rock. That rock measures 24 feet. Twenty-four is 3 x 8 or three 8s, the number for *Jesus*. And, as Rutherford states, "towards the western end [of the grotto]. . . there is a deep hole in the floor [where] even a tall man could stand upright with plenty of room to spare" (Book III, 1027).

P. M. H. Atwater has had two near-death experiences; she describes them in her book *Beyond the Light*. During her 2nd experience she says she met Jesus.

> He was *tall*, swarthy complexioned, had red-gold hair, and the softest blue eyes I had ever seen. (184; italics added)

A Roman by the name of Lentulus saw Christ during his ministry in Jerusalem. Lentulus wrote of Christ, and what he had to say

> was found in Jerusalem by Emperor Theodosius the Great in the public registers of Pontius Pilate. These were translated in the nineteenth year of Tiberius Caesar, emperor of the Romans in the seventeenth year of the government of Herod, the son of Herod, King of Galilee.

Lentulus, in a handwritten statement, recorded the following:

> There hath appeared in our time and is yet among us, a person of great virtue called Jesus Christ who is said by the people to be a prophet and his disciples call him the Son of God, he raiseth the dead and healeth the diseased; he is a man of *tall stature* of comely presence. His looks strike a veneration on those that behold him and there is something that a man sees in him which affects one with awe and love. (Quoted in Robinson and Robinson 54-55; italics added)

The grotto was designed so a tall person could stand upright to the *west* of its entrance. Now we know which tall person Enoch had in mind when he shaped the grotto the way he did.

Rutherford compares the grotto to the Well of Life which is spoken of in ancient Egyptian texts. He could have also compared the grotto and the well itself to Proverbs 10:11—"the mouth of the righteous is a well of life"—or to Proverbs 16:22—"understanding is a wellspring of life to him who has it"—as well as to these verses from Isaiah:

> in that day [when the Lord delivers you] you will say:
>
> "O Lord, I will praise You;
>
> Though You were angry with me,
>
> Your anger is turned away, and You comfort me.
>
> Behold, God is my salvation,
>
> I will trust and not be afraid;
>
> 'For Yah, the Lord, is my strength and song;
>
> He also has become my salvation.'"
>
> Therefore, with joy you will draw water
>
> From the wells of salvation.

(12:1-3)

Lepre's description of the grotto's damp ceiling should call to mind the depiction of a water jar in the ascending passage. The comments made about that symbol apply here. But there is now a new element: the ceiling "crumbles when touched" (Morton Edgar, quoted in Lepre 117).

Paul the Apostle warned us to "work out [our] salvation with fear and trembling" (Philippians 2:12). The warning is justified, for we live in a world of great temptations and anyone can fall spiritually at any moment. The loose pebbly ceiling, where "one has only to reach up and dig in with one's fingers in order to extract whole handfuls of this material" can be related to Paul's admonition.

In other words, achieving a certain height in our struggle to get back to God is no guarantee that we cannot fail, that our "salvation" is made fast and certain. Yes, we are saved by grace, as Paul says in Ephesians 2:5, but we also have to "work out our salvation", or exaltation, by being obedient to Christ's teachings.

As soon as we turn away from those teachings we are once again plunging downwards, away from God. And that possibility is clearly illustrated in the downward slope of the well, which understandably leads southward instead of northward. It is also illustrated by the two fissures that pass through the well, and it is illustrated by the fact that the distance between the grotto and the upper mouth of the well is 60 feet (Lawton and Ogilvie-Herald 31).

We encountered the number 60 in the distance between the beginning of the ceiling in the Queen's Chamber and the peak of the ceiling. There, 60 was a positive figure, but here in the well it is both positive and negative. Why is that? Because, as in the Queen's Chamber, 60 directs us to Isaac, who was 60 years old when Jacob was born, however, Jacob had a twin. The twin was named Esau and Esau was born first (Genesis 25:25). That meant that by

> Old Testament custom, he would have inherited most
> of his father's property and the right to succeed him as

> family patriarch. But in a foolish, impulsive moment, he sold his birthright [which "represented a high spiritual value"] to Jacob in exchange for a meal (Gen. 25:28-34). This determined that Jacob would carry on the family name in a direct line of descent from Abraham and Isaac, his grandfather and father. (Lockyer, Sr., *Nelson's Illustrated Bible Dictionary* 351)

In the New Testament, Esau stands as a symbol of rebellion against God:

> Make every effort to live in peace with all men and to be holy; without holiness no one will see the Lord. See to it that no one. . . is sexually immoral, or is godless like Esau, who for a single meal sold his inheritance rights as the oldest son. (NIV, Hebrews 12:14-16)

And so the number 60 and its association with Esau and Jacob are another indication of the 2-way nature of the well.

Two more observations need to be made about the grotto. The length of 17.2 feet provides another reference to Joseph and his sons Manassah and Ephraim. And, as in the ascending passage, we are to understand that here in the grotto not only is Christ on hand to "talk face to face" with those who have come looking for him, but so are his authorized servants, and the scriptures ascertain that whether we are ministered to by Christ or by his authorized servants, it is the same (see Luke 10:16 and *Doctrine and Covenants* 1:14).

As support for this interpretation, from the "summit of the Well-Shaft" to "the base of the Pyramid", according to Rutherford, "is approximately 70½ feet" (Book III, 1025). The number 70 is an obvious reference to the 70 elders of Israel who, on Mount Simai,

> saw the God of Israel. And there was under His feet as it were a paved work of sapphire stones.

In what chapter of Exodus do we find this account? Chapter 24. Which verse? Number 10.

The 70 feet also refer to the Seventy who were among the Savior's authorized servants. In what chapter of Luke do we find this reference? Chapter 10. Which verses? Numbers 1-17.

Concerning the ½ of 70½, it can be written as .5 and 5 is once again a reminder of the "five points of fellowship".

It is the implied presence of Christ's servants that is depicted by the different levels within the grotto. As for the L-shaped pattern detected by Lepre, it suggests a carpenter's square—a symbol for upright behavior—and it will be linked to similar patterns in the Grand Gallery in the next chapter.

The stones that comprise the entrance to the grotto are described by Lepre as being "roughly hewn and squared limestone blocks" that give the impression of being crude (117); Rutherford describes the same stones as "small blocks" (Book III, 1028). The entrance was constructed this way to reflect the tabernacle, which was "crude" in comparison to the temple that Solomon later built in Jerusalem.

Unlike the tabernacle, the temple did not use goats' hair in its construction. In addition, the temple was twice the dimensions of the tabernacle and was overlaid with gold throughout (see the 3rd chapter of 2 Chronicles). The difference between the two is brought out in the rest of the 3rd section and the 4th section of the well, plus the Grand Gallery, which is meant to be the correct course to follow by those who exit from the top of the well.

The continuation of the 3rd section beyond the grotto slants once more to the north and measures 35 feet. It "is hewn through the masonry in a very rough fashion," but the 4th section, at 25 feet, "is composed of the pyramid's core masonry blocks, and is fairly well squared and level" (Lepre 116).

The transition taking place between these 2 sections is obvious. What they are leading to is the entrance to that part of the pyramid that represents a permanent House of the Lord rather than a temporary one.

The numbers 35 and 25 provide another link to the temple. From 2 Chronicles 3:15, for instance, we learn that Solomon "made in front of the temple two pillars *thirty-five* cubits high" (italics added). And, as pointed out in the last chapter, the Levites "from *twenty-five* years old and above" were permitted to serve in the tabernacle (Numbers 8:24).

The number 25 is combined with the number 30 in this quote from the Gospel of John:

> when they [the disciples] had rowed about five and twenty or thirty furlongs, they see Jesus walking on the sea, and drawing nigh unto the ship; and they were afraid.
>
> But He saith unto them, It is I; be not afraid." (KJV, 6:19-20)

The number symbolism in this instance is quite remarkable since the top section of the well is 25 feet and the bottom section that begins the well is 30 feet; in other words, we have a balance struck by Christ's presence at both the beginning and the end of the climb back toward God.

In a similar manner, if we convert 25 feet to 300 inches we have a balance struck with Enoch being represented in the short connecting section that has a slope of 65 degrees and in the top section of the well, for Enoch walked with God for 300 years after he began building the city of Zion at the age of 65.

The number 25 is, of course, a multiple of 5. John Anthony West explains in *Serpent in the Sky* that 5 "is the key to the vitality of the universe, its creative nature." It is also

> the number of "potentiality". Potentiality exists outside time. Five is therefore the number of eternity and of the principle of eternal creation, union of male and female—and it is for this reason. . . that the ancients

> came to hold Five in what looks to us like a peculiar reverence. (42)

West's comments are particularly appropriate in this instance, since the well's higher exit is at the beginning of the Grand Gallery, and it is the Gallery that represents the permanent House of the Lord.

And now we know why "there is a vertical joint in the gallery side, only 5.3 inches from the mouth [of the well]" (Petrie 87).

The 3 in the 5.3 is for the 3rd day on which Christ was resurrected, and now we know why the stone that once blocked the upper mouth of the well shaft appears not only to have been forced out from below but also to have been chiseled out from above. The force applied from below, as Worth Smith believed, does represent Christ's rising from the tomb and forcibly breaking the seals that his enemies had applied to the stone that blocked the tomb's entrance (see Matthew 27:62-65). And the ineffective chisel marks represent Christ's declaration that without him we could do nothing ((John 15:5). He is the one who must remove the stone on our own tombs—be they symbolic or real—if we are to rise to the highest heights that can be attained spiritually.

12. LIGHT

> "If you abide in My word, you are My disciples indeed.
>
> "And you shall know the truth, and the truth shall make you free."
>
> (John 8:31-32)

In addition to what has already been said about the 24 feet of rock in which the grotto lies, it can also be related to Chapter 24 of First Chronicles where we learn that 24 priests served in "the temple of the Lord" (verses 7-19). The temple referred to was the one built by Solomon, and it was built with hewn limestone (Wright 222). It was also built on a mound of rock called Mount Moriah (Lockyer, Sr., *Nelson's Illustrated Bible Dictionary* 1035).

"In order to build his Temple to the Israelite God, Yahweh," say Leen and Kathleen Ritmeyer, the authors of *Secrets of Jerusalem's Temple Mount*, "Solomon needed to construct a level platform on the highest hill of Jerusalem" (15). The platform was square (61).

The base of the Great Pyramid is, of course, square, and the pyramid is built on a platform. Also square is the upper mouth of the well. "Inherent in the square," writes Hans Biedermann, "is an ordering principle that seems innately present in all humans; the figure forms a DUALITY with the CIRCLE, a form associated rather with the heavenly powers" (320). This symbolism is in keeping with the Grand Gallery's symbolism.

We learned in the last chapter that the total length of the well's 5 sections is 200 feet, and it should be clear that the well primarily represents a symbolic climb upward toward God, but at the same time it represents the very real possibility of falling away and plunging downward into spiritual darkness.

With this in mind, consider the following, for they all tie in with the well and the 6-foot-long section that connects it to the descending passage.

In the *Doctrine and Covenants* we are told that Jared, patriarch number 6 in the Old Testament, was 200 years old when he was ordained by Adam (107:47; see also Genesis 5:18). And Jared, the father of Enoch, taught him "in all the ways of God" ("The Book of Moses" 6:21). Jared's teachings prepared Enoch for his ascent through the various levels of the heavens, which occurred in a manner that should remind us of the upward ascent of the well. During his ascent Enoch saw "two hundred angels, who rule the stars" (Platt, Jr., *The Book of the Secrets of Enoch* IV:1; a number such as this is meant to be seen as symbolic and therefore not to be taken literally).

In the "Testament of Benjamin", Jacob's youngest son informs us that Cain, the murderer of his brother Abel, was 200 years old when he began to suffer for this worst of all criminal acts (Platt, Jr. I:44-45).

Counting from the time that Abraham was forced to leave Egypt until Joseph was imprisoned by Potiphar, 200 years passed (1957 BC to 1757 BC).

The First Book of Samuel contains an account of a woman named Abigail who, by offering "two hundred loaves of bread. . . and two hundred cakes of figs" to King David (25:18), caused him to repent and therefore prevented him "from coming to bloodshed and from avenging" himself by killing her husband (25:33), a man who was "harsh and evil in his doing" (25:3).

Here we have a link with the number 200 as well as 2 symbols of Christ in the bread and in the figs (see Matthew 26:26 and Luke 21:29-31).

In the Second Book of Samuel, King David once again receives 200 loaves of bread, not from Abigail this time but from a man named Ziba, and as a result Ziba gains favor in the king's eyes (16:1-4). Sacrifice and generosity in this case bring forth blessings.

The First Book of the Kings tells us that the 2 pillars placed in front of Solomon's Temple had capitals which were decorated with "two hundred. . . pomegranates in rows. . . all around" (7:20). Pomegranates, according to *The Revell Bible Dictionary*, were "a symbol of the fruitfulness of Canaan" (Lawrence O. Richards 802).

One support for this interpretation can be found in the account of Moses, who, as he led the Israelites "toward the land of Canaan, sent scouts, or spies, into the territory on a fact-finding mission. They returned with grapes, pomegranates, and figs to verify the fertility of the land" (Lockyer, Sr., *Nelson's Illustrated Bible Dictionary* 204).

The Second Book of Chronicles includes the sacrifice of 200 lambs at the time temple worship was restored (29:32). The lamb is a symbol of Christ (John 1:29). In a similar passage, a sacrifice of 200 rams is recounted in the Book of Ezra (6:17). The ram is a male sheep and another symbol of Christ.

John 6:7 has an allusion to the number 200 and it is again associated with bread; John 21:8-9 is similar and will be quoted later in this chapter.

The Sea of Galilee, where Christ spent much of his mortal ministry, "is about two hundred feet in depth" (Talmage, *Jesus the Christ* 165).

And the wall of the New Jerusalem is described as being 144 cubits or about 200 feet thick. In addition, the city is laid out like a square (NIV, Revelation 21:15-17).

The number 200, then, serves the same purpose as the smaller numbers connected to the well: it relates, in particular, to Christ, to those who serve him, to sacrifice, to becoming spiritually productive, to repentance, to mercy and generosity, to forgiveness—and to the city and the House of the Lord.

It has been pointed out that the upper exit of the well appears to have been forcefully blown open, and to some of the pyramidologists that represents Christ's resurrection. They are correct. But the upper exit of the well also represents the power of repentance and coming to a knowledge of the truth regarding Christ, and that knowledge bursts the bonds of sin, of ignorance, of blind prejudice, and as a consequence, freedom in its most important sense is born.

That sense of freedom is also captured in the width and the height of the Grand Gallery in comparison to all the other passages in the pyramid.

For example, what is the width of the well? It is 28 inches (Petrie 88). In contrast, the total width of the Gallery at floor level is 84 inches (Lepre 79)—an expansion of 56 inches. And the height of the Gallery is 336 inches, or 28 feet (Evans 91; Edwards 104). If that isn't enough, the length of the Gallery is 28 feet more than the ascending passage—129 feet for the ascending passage as opposed to the overall length of 157 feet for the Gallery (Tompkins 13).

It is this dramatic difference in size and scale that makes the Gallery so impressive. And yet the matchup of the number 28 between the well and the Gallery indicates that those ascending the well are expected to continue ascending by way of the Gallery.

To return momentarily to the upper exit of the well, it has a partial roof over it. The purpose of this roof, combined with the short passage that connects the exit to the floor of the Gallery, is to direct those coming out of the well to the east as they enter the gap between the end of the ascending passage and the raised floor of the Gallery; that way the east-west symbolism is maintained.

The same symbolism, as mentioned earlier, was built into the portable tabernacle of the Israelites, but in addition, the Temple of Solomon, which was in the shape of a rectangle that ran east to west, was also entered from the east (Metzger and Coogan 732).

Now, because the horizontal passage to the Queen's Chamber branches off the ascending passage, there is a gap between the top of the ascending passage and the narrow, central floor of the Grand Gallery, and we're told in *Giza: The Truth* that it would take a bridge 17 feet long in order to span that gap (Lawton and Ogilvie-Herald 533).

This is especially interesting because Petrie, as noted in the chapter on the ascending passage, observed that the 3rd granite block at the beginning of the ascending passage had originally extended 2 more feet into the passage. These 2 feet would have made the 3rd block 7 feet long instead of 5 feet, and, more importantly, the 3 granite blocks together would have had a total length of 17 feet.

The gap between the top of the ascending passage was designed to suggest that at one time it was in fact filled in by the 3 stones but then they were ripped out and placed at the lower end of the passage, and that is why the 3rd granite block appears to have been broken off, thus creating the impression that it was once attached to the low end of the Gallery.

Symbolically, we are to regard the blocks as still in place in the gap. This is confirmed by Max Toth and Greg Nielsen in *Pyramid Power*: "The peculiar fact about these plugs is that they would fit just as tightly the depth at the upper end of the [ascending] passage as they [do] the lower end" (70).

As a reminder, the 3 granite blocks represent repentance, baptism, confirmation in the Church of Jesus Christ and the laying on of hands for the gift of the Holy Spirit. In the layout of the pyramid, these ordinances must be performed in order to achieve the upward progress that culminates in entering the House of the Lord.

If those who have successfully climbed to the top of the well forego these ordinances, they will be putting themselves on the horizontal path to the middle kingdom, or, if former destructive habits are resumed, they will plunge back down the well and their condition will be worse than before.

Peter had this in mind when he wrote:

> [Corrupt people] are *wells without water*. . . .
>
> [And] when they speak great swelling words of [spiritual] emptiness, they allure through the lusts of the flesh, through lewdness, the ones who have actually escaped from those who live in error.

> While they [the corrupt ones] promise them liberty, they themselves are slaves of corruption; for by whom a person is overcome, by him also he is brought [back] into bondage.
>
> For if, after they have escaped the pollutions of the world through the knowledge of the Lord and Savior Jesus Christ, they are again entangled in them and [are] overcome, the latter end is worse for them than the beginning. (2 Peter 2: 17-20; italics added)

It has to be kept in mind, of course, that we're not talking about researchers or tourists or anyone else actually going through the pyramid; we're talking instead about the symbolic function of the passages and chambers, and symbolically, in our time only those people who become members of the Church of Jesus Christ of Latter-day Saints and who are found worthy as a result of observing the standards of the church—standards established by Christ himself through direct revelation—will be permitted to continue their upward path by climbing up to the floor level of the Grand Gallery, where they can then proceed toward the antechamber and the symbolism that awaits there.

It is worth noting that if the gap was filled in, the floor between the ascending passage and the Gallery would be continuous and the passage to the Queen's Chamber would be blocked off (Rutherford, Book III, 1021). This clearly suggests that the Lord wants us to progress steadily toward the highest kingdom, thus bypassing the way to the middle kingdom.

But before going any farther with this discussion, let's hear from the Egyptologists, starting with Edwards, who provides a rather detailed description of the Gallery.

The base walls, he says, are composed of "polished limestone" and they

> rise vertically to a height of 7 feet 6 inches; above that level each of the seven [additional] courses projects

> inwards about 3 inches beyond the course on which it rests, thus forming a corbel vault of unparalleled dimensions. The space between the uppermost course on each side [in other words, the ceiling], measuring 3 feet 5 inches in width, is spanned by roofing slabs, every one of which is laid at a slightly steeper angle than the gradient of the gallery. Sir Flinders Petrie, commenting on this method of laying the slabs, says it was done "in order that the lower edge of each stone should hitch like a pawl into a ratchet cut in the top of the walls; hence no stone can press on the one below it. . . and each stone is separately upheld by the side walls across which it lies". At the foot of each wall a flat-topped ramp, 2 feet in height and 1 foot 8 inches in width, extends along the whole length of the gallery. A passage measuring, like the roof, 3 feet 5 inches in width runs between the two ramps [this passage, or floor, is sometimes called a "slot" or a "channel" by Colin Wilson and other writers]. (104-05)

The 2 ramps, Edwards states, were designed with

> fifty-six horizontal sockets, fifty-four of which were cut in two rows of twenty-seven, one row on the upper surface of each ramp. The two remaining sockets were cut on each side of the high step at the upper end of the gallery. They alternated in size, the longer being about 1 foot 11¼ inches and the shorter about 1 foot 8½ inches. . . . [T]wenty-five vertical sockets [were carved] in each of the side-walls directly above the horizontal sockets, apart from two neighboring pairs at the lower end of the gallery and the pair on the high step [i.e. the Great Step]. . . [There is also] a continuous groove running the whole length of the gallery on both sides in the lower part of the third projecting lap from the

> bottom of the corbel roof. . . . The vertical sockets had been filled with insets of stone, which suggested that they had been superseded by those cut horizontally. Across each inset and extending beyond it on both sides are some shallow incisions. (108 and 110)

Petrie theorized that the primary purpose of the Grand Gallery had been to store the 3 granite blocks that would be needed to seal the beginning of the ascending passage after the pharaoh's body had been placed in the sarcophagus in the King's Chamber. "But," he says, "we are met then by an extraordinary idea," that is, the funeral procession "must have gone up the gallery, on the narrow-side [sic] ramps or benches, past the plug-blocks four feet high standing between them" (88).

Today, researchers and tourists can climb the Gallery without too much trouble thanks to the installation of side rails and wooden flooring with slats (see the photo that precedes page 1005 in Rutherford's 3rd book), but before they were installed, getting up the Gallery was a challenge. To prove the point, C. W. Ceram quotes from Johannes Helfrich's journal, which is dated 1579 AD:

> "We climbed a high corridor which lay straight before us, with great difficulty, because this corridor was both wide and extremely high. On the sides the wall is set back at about a man's height [he's referring to the width of the Gallery], with holes a good pace distant from the next; we had to hold onto these and climb up as best we could." (93)

The "holes" were the sockets or slots in the ramps.

John Greaves, who explored the interior of the pyramid in 1638, said of the Gallery's polished limestone walls and floor: "that which adds grace to the whole structure, though it makes the passage the more slippery and difficult, is the acclivity and rising of the ascent" (quoted in Piazzi Smyth 363). Smyth himself measured the Gallery in 1865 and described it as being "dangerous and slippery" (118). And the ramps, besides being every bit as dangerous and as slippery as the floor, had the added hindrance of the 54 slots cut into their sides.

How difficult it would have been to have transported a coffin down the descending passage has already been stressed, but now, if we seriously consider Petrie's theory, after a descent of 92 feet, the pall bearers would have been required to heft the coffin up to the original entrance of the ascending passage; however, now, instead of going down at 26 degrees, they would have been going up at 26 degrees, with, once more, room for no more than one pall bearer in front of the casket and one pall bearer behind it, so obviously, one or more ropes would have been needed to pull the casket up the full 129 feet to the end of the ascending passage.

And then, still going up at the same angle, because the 3 granite blocks would have been sitting in the middle of the Gallery, and because the floor between the ramps measures only 41 inches (3 feet 5 inches), the pall bearers would have been forced, as Petrie says, to climb up the ramps—without the aid of handrails—and, since the slots in the ramps are 6 inches wide (Lemesurier 98), they would have had a space of only 14 inches (1 foot 8 inches or 20 inches minus 6 inches) in which to walk.

How was it possible for someone like Petrie, who took pride in what he believed was his superior intelligence—superior especially when he compared himself to the pyramidologists—to ever seriously propose such an absurd state of affairs? And what is just as absurd is that so many others who came after him accepted his proposal with only slight modifications, as we are going to see.

* * *

In the side walls between the top of the ascending passage and the Gallery, as well as in the lowest part of the 2 ramps, there are 5 holes per side. Lehner observes that these holes "are regularly spaced" and those on the east side match the ones on the west side. He goes on to say that they

> are generally believed to be sockets for large wooden

> beams for holding back the blocks which sealed the Ascending Passage—which would make this beautiful construction [i.e., the Grand Gallery] a parking space and slipway. (113)

Kurt Mendelssohn expresses basically the same idea:

> This impressive high passage. . . was for a long time believed to have served ritualistic purposes until it was discovered by Flinders Petrie that its real object was to serve as a store for a series of large limestone blocks. These blocks, when the tomb chamber was to be sealed, were let down into the ascending passage where, in fact, three of them are still in position. (52)

Mendelssohn, in this quote, fails to distinguish between limestone and granite, which is perfectly understandable since in his case he sees no significance in the Great Pyramid other than its having served to "mark the place where man invented the state".

Tompkins, in his treatment of the Grand Gallery, reviews ideas put forth by Ludwig Borchardt and Leonard Cottrell, whose book *The Mountains of Pharaoh* maintains that the Gallery was created when the decision was made not to bury the pharaoh in the middle chamber but higher up in the pyramid.

Tompkins points out that Cottrell, like the other Egyptologists, fails to explain "why the Grand Gallery should have been raised to 28 feet, when less than half that height would have been ample for the bearers [of the king's coffin] and for the storage of the plugs" (239).

Borchardt did challenge one part of Petrie's theory, arguing

> that the granite and limestone plugs which filled the Ascending Passage could not have been stored on the Grand Gallery floor between the ramps, because they would have provided an "undignified obstacle" for the funeral train to clamber over. As the plugs were too large

> to be brought in or out of either the Queen's Chamber or the King's, Borchardt theorized that the blocks were raised onto a wooden platform which was fitted into the grooves which appear halfway up the walls of the Gallery.

Tompkins agrees that this

> would have allowed the funeral cortege to move beneath them; though how this would have been any less undignified than having to crawl up the low and narrow Ascending Passage is not explained, nor is it explained how the heavy blocks [which weigh seven tons, according to Lepre (83)] were brought down from the level of the wooden planking to the level of the pavement on which they were to slide. (240)

Edwards adds a few more details to this matter. Borchardt's platform, he says, had it actually existed, would have been

> supported by single uprights. . . attached at the base to the vertical sockets. If that interpretation is accepted, it was probably because the structure proved to be unstable that the uprights were increased in number and were set in the horizontal sockets on the ramps, three lashed together side by side in the longer sockets and two in the shorter.

Edwards continues:

> Notwithstanding its ingenuity, Borchardt's explanation is open to some clear objections. . . . His explanation of the use of the vertical sockets also is not convincing. (110)

Jean Philippe Lauer, says Edwards, has a different idea regarding the

Gallery's supposed scaffolding: it was "a device for enabling the plugs, which were stored on the floor of the Grand Gallery passage, to be hauled to the top of the gallery so that they could be used as building material for constructing the antechamber and the King's Chamber" (110).

Now, back to Cottrell. Tompkins credits him with the theory that

> the notches [i.e. the sockets or slots—the terminology varies] in the ramp[s] of the Grand Gallery were cut to hold cross beams of wood or limestone to keep each of the massive plugs from prematurely sliding. (240-41)

Regarding Cottrell's theory, Tompkins remarks that it

> raises the question as to what became of the wooden or limestone crosspieces. Had they been made of wood they might conceivably have pulverized and completely disintegrated in the thousands of intervening years. They might also have been carried down the well by the escaping operators, though this would have been something of an ordeal, if indeed possible. The material might also have long since been disposed of by grave robbers. Still the question is puzzling. (241)

Richard Anthony Proctor, a British astronomer, found another use for the holes in the ramps. He wrote in *The Great Pyramid, Observatory, Tomb and Temple* that the Grand Gallery had been "perfectly aligned on the [earth's] meridian through which they [the pyramid builders] could observe the apparent movement of the stars" (Sellier 153). Proctor claimed that the holes in the ramps "served to hold some sort of scaffolding" since observers, "to function effectively," would have needed "cross ramps or reclining benches. . . positioned at different levels of the Gallery" (Tompkins 153).

But enough of the Egyptologists. It's time to hear from the pyramidologists, beginning with Lemesurier, who equates the Grand

Gallery with the *Book of the Dead*'s "Hall of Truth in Light" (95). He also sees "the significance of the Gallery [as] that of the Ascending Passage 'expanded telescopically'" (98). And he equates the holes in the ramps with mortality, while the "vertical sockets" above the ramps symbolize the "millennial souls. . . [who are] 'fit for the kingdom'" being "'borne up-wards'". The slots or grooves that appear halfway up the walls and that extend along their full length are, in his view, "apparently for a 'sliding floor'" (99).

Lemesurier assigns the date of 33 AD to the floor of the Gallery where it runs under the north wall; 58 AD to the "north edge of [the] Well-Shaft, and [the] beginning of [the] Grand Gallery roof proper" (100); and 1845 AD to the "riser", meaning the north face of the Great Step (102).

With that information as a base, Lemesurier gives the following "reading" for the Gallery:

> The souls of those who learn fully to accept the Messianic enlightenment between A.D. 33 and A.D. 58 will enter an upward evolutionary path reserved for the spiritually perfect enlightened ones of mankind.
>
> First, however, they will have to. . . accept physical death as the price of their initiateship [sic]. But, as a result of this, they will succeed in partially breaking out of the reincarnation cycle in the physical world. Indeed, through the power of the Messianic initiative the truly enlightened ones will not again taste death and mortality until they rejoin millennial mankind in incarnations of appropriate enlightenment from the year 1845 onwards. . . .
>
> For the rest of the enlightened, the upward path will lead directly towards the eventual culmination of mortality—i.e. the perfection of mortal man, the consummation of the evolutionary process—through

> the perfection of the coming Millennium. . . . The great step leading to these events will have its beginnings in the year A.D. 1845, and will be complete by the summer of 1914. (104)

The year 1914, Lemesurier alleges, is to be found at the top end of the Gallery's floor, which is actually beneath the Great Step (102).

J. Clemishaw, in his Introduction to *The Great Pyramid: Its Divine Message*, makes reference to H. Aldersmith, the book's co-author, and "the Rev. Dr. Denis Haran", who were in agreement that "if the Grand Gallery symbolised the Christian Dispensation, then the commencement of the Gallery must necessarily symbolise the date of the Crucifixion or that of the Pentecost of the Crucifixion year" (vi).

For Worth Smith, the beginning of the Gallery "marks the birth of Jesus Christ. . . [on] October 6, B.C. 4" (101), while the Gallery itself "portrays the history of Jesus Christ's Church," along with typifying "the fulfillment of the plan of salvation as written in the Scriptures." Furthermore, the holes in the ramps symbolize miniature "graves, *every one of which is open*" (110)!

Furthermore, he believes the

> vertical stones [that are inset over the horizontal holes], are a symbol of standing uprightly, and proclaim as strongly as words ever could. . . that the tenant of each of the graves is risen! There are 8 times 7 (56) of these empty graves. In the symbolism of numbers eight is the number of resurrection and new life, while seven is the number of dispensational fulness. (111)

Smith dates the north face of the Great Step at 1844 AD and claims that

> almost the whole lot of the discoveries and inventions in common usage have come into existence since [then]. Therein is seen verification abundant of the fact that

> there was a great upward step taken by humanity at that time, just as prophesied [by the Great Step]. (115)

Switching to Rutherford, his dates for the Grand Gallery are the same as Lemesurier's, and he regards the years from 33 AD to 1914 as "the duration of the Christian Dispensation or Gospel Age from its inception until the beginning of its closing down" (Book III, 979-80). He finds 1914 to be especially significant because it "pertains to matters in connection with the overcoming saints, those who are 'called and chosen and faithful'" (Book III, 980).

Noone, in his discussion of the Grand Gallery, quotes from *A New Model of the Universe* by P. D. Ouspensky:

> This corridor is the key to the whole pyramid. What strikes you first is that everything in this corridor is of very exact workmanship. The lines are straight, the angles are correct. At the same time there is no doubt that this corridor was not made for walking along. Then for what was it made? (147-48)

Ouspensky made a stab at answering his own question. Taking into consideration the slots in the ramps, he decided that "up and down this 'corridor' some kind of stone or metal plate, or 'carriage', must have moved, which, possibly, in its turn, served as a support for some measuring apparatus and could be fixed in any position" (Noone 148).

Possibly? Then again, possibly not.

Dunn, as previously noted, envisioned resonators installed in the ramps' slots. Then,

> [a]s the Earth's vibration flowed through the Great Pyramid, the resonators converted the vibrational energy to airborne sound. By design the angles and surfaces of the Grand Gallery walls and ceiling caused a reflection of the sound, and its focus into the King's Chamber.

Consequently, he says, "the entire granite complex, in effect, became a vibrating mass of energy" (160). He goes on to suggest that "'shot' pins" were installed in the grooves in the walls of the Gallery to hold the resonators in place, and he justifies the walls stepping inward by saying that design was intended to "increase the resonators' frequency" (166).

Dunn, like others before him, detected signs that the Grand Gallery's walls had been

> subjected to heat and, as a result, the limestone blocks calcinated or burned. The disaster that struck the King's Chamber, therefore, may have been responsible for destroying the resonators. (212)

And so Dunn manages to answer the question, "What happened to the resonators? Where is the evidence that they ever existed?" However, Dunn, who insists that "*everything* [his italics] in the Great Pyramid has as explanation" (35), says nothing about the purpose for the vertical slots above those in the ramps, nor does he specify why the ramps were needed. After all, slots could have been cut into the floor.

Nor does he tell us why it was necessary to construct the Gallery to an overall length of 157 feet. What is more, there are other features yet to be described—such as the little-emphasized fact that the floor between the ramps is on 2 different levels—that neither he nor the Egyptologists or the pyramidologists bother to explain.

In order to reveal the reason behind all the features of the Gallery it will be best to begin with its low end and the 5 holes in each side wall, which Lehner tagged as "sockets for large wooden beams" that were supposedly meant to hold "back the blocks which sealed the Ascending Passage" (113).

But no blocks, either limestone or granite, were ever stored in the gap between the top of the ascending passage and the Grand Gallery, nor were any stored in the Gallery itself. The 5 holes in each wall, like the Gallery itself, are symbolic. Since 5 was the subject of considerable discussion in Chapter 11, and since what was said there applies here as well, only 3 more points need to be made regarding the significance of the 2 sets of 5 holes.

First point: the symbolism involving the servant who increased his 5 talents to 10 in the Parable of the Talents can certainly be applied.

Second point: in Solomon's Temple the entrance to the sanctuary had double doors that measured 5 cubits per side (each was one-fourth of 20 cubits; see 1 Kings 6:2 and 33-34).

Third point: in the temple seen in vision by Ezekiel the prophet, "the side walls of the entrance [to the sanctuary] were five cubits on this side and five cubits on the other side" (Ezekiel 41:1-2).

The beginning of the short section of the floor at the low end of the Gallery is 38 inches above the ceiling of the horizontal passage to the Queen's Chamber (Lemesurier 72). What is important about the number 38?

In the Book of Deuteronomy we learn that after 38 years of wandering in the wilderness "all the generation of men of war was consumed from the midst of the [Israelites'] camp", so that those who remained were at last permitted to resume their original trek to the land promised to them.

In the Gospel of John we read:

> Now there is in Jerusalem by the Sheep Gate a pool, which is called in Hebrew, Bethesda, having *five* porches.
>
> In these lay a great multitude of sick people, blind, lame, paralyzed, waiting for the moving of the water.
>
> For an angel went down at a certain time into the pool and stirred up the water; then whoever stepped in first, after the stirring of the water, was made well of whatever disease he had.
>
> Now a certain man was there who had an infirmity *thirty-eight* years.

> When Jesus saw him lying there, and knew that he already had been in that condition a long time, He said to him, "Do you want to be made well?"
>
> The sick man answered Him, "Sir, I have no man to put me into the pool when the water is stirred up; but while I am coming, another steps down before me."
>
> Jesus said to him, "Rise, take up your bed and walk."
>
> And immediately the man was made well, took up his bed, and walked. . . .
>
> Afterward Jesus found him in the *temple*, and said to him, "See, you have been made well. Sin no more, lest a worse thing come on you." (5:2-9 and 14; italics added)

The appropriateness of applying the verses just quoted from the Old and the New Testament to the upward height of the Grand Gallery's northern cut-off, as Lemesurier calls it, should be obvious (72).

The same can be said of the Hebrew word *galah*, which means "to reveal" (Strong 340, entry # 1540). *Galah* is spelled Gimel-Lamedh-Hē. Gimel = 3, Lamedh = 30, Hē = 5. The 3 letters have a combined total of 38. A key purpose of the temple is to reveal the secret—and sacred—signs and tokens that enable the righteous to return to their Father, the Lord of Spirits.

Thirty-eight is also the gematria for the name *Abel* in Greek. The spelling is Alpha, which = 1, Beta, which = 2, Epsilon, which = 5, and Lambda, which = 30 (see Strong 567, entry# 6). The total of these 4 figures is 38. Abel was a precursor of Christ. In "The Second Book of Adam and Eve" he is called the "just one", and after he is murdered by Cain "a smell of sweet spices" issues from his body "by reason of its purity" (Platt, Jr. I:3). In The Acts of the Apostles Christ is the "Just One" murdered by the descendants of those who murdered the prophets of old (7:52). And when Christ died spices were brought to anoint his body (Mark 16:1).

Now, if we combine the height of the cut-off with the height of the horizontal passage to the Queen's Chamber, we have a total figure of 83 inches (38 inches plus 45 inches). Aaron was 83 when he became the spokesman for Moses (Exodus 7:7), and Aaron's name was later used to identify the lesser of the 2 priesthoods. In present-day temples, during the endowment, Melchizedek priesthood holders put on a robe that symbolizes the Aaronic priesthood.

Once we are on the floor of the Gallery, we find that its first section measures 40 inches in length from north to south (Lemesurier 72). In Solomon's Temple the "sanctuary was *forty* cubits long" (1 Kings 6:17; italics added). The sanctuary is also called the main hall, the main room, the central room, the Holy Place, or the *hekal*. According to *The Anchor Bible Dictionary*, the term *hekal* "is sometimes used to designate the Temple as a whole" (Freedman, volume VI, 357).

Coinciding with the 40 cubits of the sanctuary in Solomon's Temple is Christ's 40 days of sacred instruction to the apostles following his resurrection. During those 40 days the Savior taught "things pertaining to the kingdom of God" (Acts 1:3). In particular, he revealed the true purpose of the House of the Lord, which includes the temple endowment, and it is the endowment that is represented by the span of 40 inches.

But what is the endowment?

After members of the church have been baptized, confirmed and given the gift of the Holy Spirit, and after they have consistently demonstrated their willingness to keep the commandments, they become eligible at certain ages to attend the temple for their own individual endowment. For example, young men who are ordained elders and who have been called to serve a full-time mission are eligible, as are young women who have reached the age of 21 and are similarly called to serve a full-time mission. Adult members who return to church activity after a prolonged absence, as well as converts who have been active in the church for at least one year and who are found worthy, can attend the temple.

James E. Talmage explains the endowment in *The House of the Lord*:

> The Temple Endowment. . . comprises instruction relating to the significance and sequence of past dispensations, and the importance of the present as the greatest and grandest era in human history. This course of instruction includes a recital of the most prominent events of the creative period [meaning the creation of the earth], the condition of our first parents in the Garden of Eden, their disobedience and consequent expulsion from that blissful abode, their condition in the lone and dreary world when doomed to live by labor and sweat, the plan of redemption by which the great transgression may be atoned, the period of the great apostasy [after the deaths or the translation of Peter and the other apostles], the restoration of the Gospel with all its ancient powers and privileges, the absolute and indispensable condition of personal purity and devotion to the right in present life, and a strict compliance with Gospel requirements. . . .
>
> The ordinances of the endowment embody certain obligations on the part of the individual, such as covenant[s] and promise[s] to observe the law of strict virtue and chastity, to be charitable, benevolent, tolerant and pure; to devote both talent and material means to the spread of truth and the uplifting of the [human] race; to maintain devotion to the cause of truth; and to seek in every way to contribute to the great preparation that the earth may be ready to receive her King,—the Lord Jesus Christ. With the taking of each covenant and the assuming of each obligation a promised blessing is pronounced, contingent upon the faithful observance of the conditions. . . .

> The blessings of the House of the Lord are restricted to no privileged class; every member of the Church may have admission to the temple with the right to participate in the ordinances thereof, if he [or she] comes duly accredited as of worthy life and conduct. (83-84)

Why aren't the temples open to everyone? The same question could have been asked of Solomon's temple, of which Joan Comay writes,

> It must be borne in mind that the interior of the Temple was not a place of assembly for the congregation, as in a Jewish synagogue today, a Christian church or a Moslem mosque. The Temple was primarily God's house, a dwelling for the *Shechinah*, the Divine Presence, as the old desert Tabernacle had been. The worshippers gathered in the great courtyard outside. (47)

And the same question might be asked of the ancient Egyptian temples. In Egypt, Christine Hobson writes in *The World of the Pharaohs*, "except during the great festivals, the ordinary people would have little contact with the temple, and would never, in any case, be permitted to go beyond the front open courtyards" (131).

Lewis Spence adds more details regarding ancient Egyptian temples and the Egyptian priesthood in his book *Egypt*:

> Individuals of the priesthood were generally alluded to as *hen neter* ("servant of the god") or *uab* ("the pure"). . . .
>
> A most stringent and exacting code had to be followed so far as cleanliness and discipline were concerned. Constant purifications and lustrations [purification ceremonies] succeeded each other, and the garb of the religious must be fresh and unspotted. It consisted entirely of the purest and whitest linen. (53)

Today, both male and female patrons and officiators in the temples of the Church of Jesus Christ of Latter-day Saints also wear all-white clothing, which symbolizes purity (Charles 57).

As in ancient times, temples are not open to the public because they are not regular meeting houses; they are sacred edifices used only for certain ordinances. New temples are temporarily open to the public for a limited time before they are dedicated to the Lord, and so are older temples that are refurbished, but afterwards they are not. But even if they were open to the public nothing would be accomplished. Why? Because without the necessary preparation, and without the accompaniment of the Spirit of the Lord, the endowment would not be properly understood, nor would it be appreciated.

And sacred things are not to be taken lightly. That is why Christ told his disciples, "Do not give what is holy to the dogs; nor cast your pearls before swine, lest they trample them under their feet, and turn and tear you to pieces" (Matthew 7:6). The word *pearls*, of course, does not refer to the actual gems, but rather to spiritual knowledge and ordinances derived from the Lord.

Just as the living are baptized in behalf of the dead in modern temples, so the living are endowed in behalf of those who are in the spirit world and who were not endowed during mortality. However, as Talmage remarks in *The House of the Lord*,

> the administration of ordinances in behalf of departed spirits [does not] interfere with the right of choice and the exercise of free agency on their part. They are at liberty to accept or reject the ministrations in their behalf. . . in accordance with their converted or unregenerate state, even as is the case with mortals to whom the Gospel message may come. (68)

Doing vicarious work for the dead, then, brings with it no guarantees; it is, therefore, a labor of love, and of hope that at least some of the people in the spirit world will accept the temple work done in their behalf so they can advance to a higher level. (It should also be understood that no one serving in a House of the Lord is paid to labor in behalf of the dead; just the opposite, for to be worthy of serving in the temple members of the church are required to pay a tithing of 10%.)

The ultimate purpose of the endowment, as John D. Charles states in *Endowed from On High*, is to empower "us to return to God's presence and receive our exaltation" (45). What exaltation means is explained by Talmage:

> In the Kingdom of God there are numerous degrees of exaltation provided for those who are worthy of them. The old idea, that in the hereafter there will be but two places for the souls of mankind,—a heaven and a hell, with the same glory in all parts of the one, and the same terrors throughout the other,—is wholly untenable in the light of Divine revelation. (*The House of the Lord* 80)

Now, for a minute we need to redirect our attention to the north wall of the Gallery. In contrast to the east, west and south walls, the north wall has only 6 courses or tiers of stone instead of 7. This wall is "over the entrance into the Gallery" (Rutherford, Book III, 975).

Here, again, we have a link with Ezekiel's temple, which was measured by "a man whose appearance was like the appearance of bronze" (Ezekiel 40:3), and who used "a measuring rod *six* cubits long. . . and he measured the width of the wall structure, one rod; and the height, one rod [which means 6 cubits each]" (40:5; italics added). He also measured "the gateway which faced east" and its threshold "was one rod wide" (40:6), plus "the gate chamber", which "was one rod long [again, six cubits]" (40:7). One more measurement included the sanctuary's "doorposts, six cubits wide" (41:1).

The number 6 represents here, as it has elsewhere in the Great Pyramid, incompletion and imperfection, and that is why above "the N. doorway of the gallery the stone is left roughly in excess" (Petrie 86). Dove-tailed in with this symbolism is the omission of vertical slots or inset stones above the holes or notches in the extreme low end of the two ramps (Lepre 85). That omission was intentional and again represents incompletion. The incompletion in this instance has to do with the endowment, which is represented *after* bypassing the north wall and the initial holes in the ramps.

Moreover, in case it isn't obvious, there is a match between the north wall and the short connecting section in the lower end of the well shaft. Both incorporate the number 6—6 courses, 6 feet.

Resuming the discussion of the Grand Gallery's floor, Petrie's measurements revealed an "average variation from a straight line" of five-tenths of an inch (24). Was this variation also intended? Yes, it was. Five out of 10 recalls the parable of the 10 virgins; 5 of them were wise, meaning they were prepared for the coming of the bridegroom (i.e. the Lord), but 5 were foolish and were not prepared and so they were shut out of the wedding (Matthew 25:1-13). In like manner, only about half of the members of the Lord's church live so that they are worthy of entering the temple where they are in the presence of the Lord.

At the end of the 40-inch span, it is necessary to step up to the next level of the Gallery's floor. How high is the step? Eight inches (Lemesurier 72). Eight is the number for "the work of the New Beginning" (Gaunt 74). It is also the number for Christ and for resurrection, and, says Herbert Lockyer, Sr. in *All about the Second Coming*, for "the sign of eternity" (230).

With the endowment complete, as symbolized by the step-up, the remaining notches in the ramps have the accompanying inset stones. Lepre describes these as "inverted L-shaped cavities filled in with mortar" (83). He also makes the observation that "the smaller cavities within which the cement was placed" are positioned at "45-degree angles". He adds that "diagonal grooves were cut into the surface of the inset stones and the adjacent wall sections. . . nearly two inches deep" (84).

Lepre's illustrations of these inset stones on page 84 of *The Egyptian Pyramids* make it clear that what is involved is not two L-shapes but one L-shape and an inverted V. The inverted V represents a drafting compass and the L-shape represents a carpenter's square.

The drafting compass is used to form a perfect circle and so it is, Biedermann asserts,

> a symbol for geometry, cosmic order, and. . . [it] is one of the three "great lights" of the symbology of FREEMASONRY, referring to the ideal circle of "all embracing love for others" and thus indicating the appropriate attitude toward fellow Masons and humanity in general.
>
> . . . [T]he angle between the two arms of the compass is also significant (a right angle symbolizing the ideal balance between body and spirit). (75)

The carpenter's square is one of the other "great lights" of the Freemasons and "stands for that which is right, for justice, the true law." It also represents practicing "every virtue of which a person is capable" (Biedermann 321).

Basically, the endowment incorporates this same symbolism, and since the endowment began with Adam and Eve, we know where the Freemasons' symbols ultimately trace back to. However, there are major differences between the endowment and the ceremony that takes place in a Masonic lodge. Knight and Lomas, for instance, describe "the three levels of Masonic ritual" as "inexplicable activities" which "by any standards. . . are bizarre" (*The Hiram Key* 16). The reason for this state of affairs has to do with the founders of Freemasonry having known only part of the endowment and therefore they had to make up the rest.

In contrast, the endowment is straightforward and takes members of the church through the 3 degrees of glory, culminating "in the celestial room, which represents the highest degree of heaven, a return to the presence of God, a place of exquisite beauty and serenity" (Charles 96).

The diagonal groove that is incised across the inset stones represents the altar or table "that is before the Lord" (Ezekiel 41:22), and "on which was the showbread" (2 Chronicles 4:19). In Leviticus we have the

Lord's specific instructions regarding the 12 loaves of showbread which were to be baked with "two-tenths of an ephah [of fine flour]. . . in each cake." When the loaves were ready they were set out "in two rows, six in a row, on the pure gold table before the Lord." Additionally, the Lord instructed the priests:

> "you shall put pure frankincense on each row, that it may be on the bread for a memorial, an offering made by fire to the Lord.
>
> "Every Sabbath he [Aaron] shall set it in order before the Lord continually, being taken from the children of Israel by an everlasting covenant.
>
> "And it shall be for Aaron and his sons, and they shall eat it in a holy place; for it is most holy to him from the offerings of the Lord made by fire, by a perpetual statute." (24:5-9)

Showbread was first baked for the tabernacle, then later for Solomon's Temple (Lawrence O. Richards, *The Revell Bible Dictionary* 917). The twelve loaves, according to Biedermann, "stand for spiritual nourishment" (Biedermann 48).

Bread, of course, became a symbol for Christ. In the Gospel of John, Christ miraculously multiplies 5 loaves of barley bread so that 5000 are fed; afterwards he tells the multitude,

> "My Father gives you the true bread from heaven.
>
> "For the bread of God is He who comes down from heaven and gives life to the world."
>
> Then they said to him, "Lord, give us this bread always."
>
> And Jesus said to them, "I am the bread of life.

> He who comes to Me shall never hunger, and he who believes in Me shall never thirst." (6:32-35)

In ancient Egypt, Barbara Walker reports, "**[b]read** and **wine** were substituted for the flesh and blood of numerous ancient savior gods, such as **Osiris**" (177). Focusing on Osiris, she declares that he

> was one of the earliest of the dying gods whose worshippers ate his body in the form of **bread**, confident that this sacrament would make them divinities in the afterlife by partaking of the divine essence. He was the Egyptian form of "the god-man who suffered, and died, and rose again, and reigned eternally in heaven." (216)

The "religion of Osiris," says Budge in *An Introduction to Ancient Egyptian Literature*,

> spread all over Egypt. This religion promised to all who followed it, high or low, rich or poor, a life in the world beyond the grave, after a resurrection that was made certain to them through the sufferings, death, and resurrection of Osiris, who was the incarnation of the great primeval god who created the heavens and the earth. (12-13)

For the Egyptians, then, Osiris became the "Savior of the World. His 'body' is the **ankh** or Cross of Life" (Walker 216).

Osiris is obviously another name for Christ.

The word *ephah* in the above quote from Leviticus is important. It was "a unit equal to one-tenth of a homer" (Lockyer, Sr., *Nelson's Illustrated Bible Dictionary* 1097). In another verse from Leviticus we read that a "homer of barley seed shall be valued at fifty shekels of silver" (27:16). The instructions for the showbread included "two-tenths of an ephah", which would have amounted to 100 shekels of silver.

We will see how the number 100 becomes significant when the

King's Chamber is discussed, but immediately applicable is the shekel, since it was the "most common weight in the Hebrew system. . . [and] the shekel of the sanctuary [was]. . . the same weight as the common shekel" (Lockyer, Sr., *Nelson's Illustrated Bible Dictionary* 1097). In other words, "common" people may receive the blessings of the temple, just as they received Christ's blessings during his mortal ministry.

The frankincense that was put on the showbread is also important. Biedermann reveals that in "the Jewish tradition, incense [which "is traditionally frankincense"] was burnt only as a sacrifice to God—a symbol of worship that also served to placate divine anger" (184). Frankincense was also "part of the sacred anointing oil (Ex. 30:34)" (Lockyer, Sr., *Nelson's Illustrated Bible Dictionary* 851). Members of the Church of Jesus Christ of Latter-day Saints are washed and anointed with water and sacred oil before they are endowed. These ordinances "signify the cleansing and sanctifying power of Jesus Christ applied to the attributes of the person and to the hallowing of all life" (Charles 47).

In a similar fashion, Margaret Bunson states in *A Dictionary of Ancient Egypt* that incense "was a purifying element in all Egyptian observances, as well as the material used to bestow honor upon the gods or the dead or living kings" (123). Richard Wilkinson expands on the use of incense, indicating that "in religious rituals" incense was symbolic "of the interaction between the human and divine spheres" (103).

* * *

The depth of the diagonal groove is "nearly two inches" (Lepre 84). The number 2 appears in the "two-tenths of an ephah" and in the 2 rows of bread—more evidence that the interpretation of this particular symbol is correct.

But what about the holes in the ramps? Do they in fact represent empty graves? No, they do not. But the holes are definitely empty, which suggests something is missing.

The holes have a symbolic function that is joined to the inset stones above them. The showbread, it will be recalled, was, according to Biedermann, a symbol of "spiritual nourishment". The empty holes in the ramps are a reminder that the body, the mind and the spirit have to be nourished—not just once in a while but constantly. And that is why all 4 symbols—the holes, the altar or table, the carpenter's square and the drafting compass—run all the way up to the Great Step.

What did Christ say? "[H]e who endures to the end shall be saved" (Mark 13:13). The word "endures" means enduring in faithfulness, enduring in keeping all the commandments, enduring in the covenants made in the House of the Lord. And the way to endure is to seek proper nourishment—not once a year, say at Christmas time or Easter, and not even once a week, but daily. In other words, Christ's teachings have to be a way of life; anything less will mean facing the possibility of falling away and, like the servant who failed to make use of his one talent, ending up losing all.

Addressing the subject of the holes in the ramps, Colin Wilson asks,

> why are the holes of two different lengths, alternately long and short, and why do the short ones slope, while the long ones are horizontal? And why does the sloping length of the short holes equal the horizontal length of the long holes? It is as if the place had been designed by an insane mathematician. (73)

Dunn isn't troubled by this peculiar design. He simply states: "In either scenario, it appears that the slots were prepared to accommodate a vertical structure, rather than to restrain weight that would exert shear pressure from the side" (168). How, we must ask, would the structure he is referring to—the resonators—have stood up vertically in a slot with a bottom that inclined at a 26-degree angle? Has Dunn really solved the problem presented by Wilson? Plainly, he has not.

The holes are different because there are different ways to find the nourishment needed to live a righteous life. But additionally, not everyone moving upwards toward the celestial kingdom is moving at the same pace; not everyone is equal in spirituality. This concept is borne out by more details regarding the inset stones above the holes, details provided by the ever-vigilant Lepre, who says they are not all vertical as supposed by most researchers. After a careful investigation he found that

> all the inset stones on the east wall, except for one (vertical) set, were in a slightly slanted position from true vertical; and. . . all of the others on the west wall, except for one (slanted) set, were in a true vertical position. The twenty-sixth set on the east wall is on the vertical, and the thirteenth set on the west wall is slanted. (83)

What is illustrated by this arrangement is the 2nd part of Christ's Parable of the Sower:

> "these are the ones sown on good ground, those who hear the word [of God], accept it, and bear fruit: some thirtyfold, some sixty, and some a hundred." (Mark 4:20)

The 3 groups listed in the parable are represented by the symbols in the ramps and on the walls. The members of the Church of Jesus Christ of Latter-day Saints who produce thirtyfold and sixtyfold are represented on the east wall, and that is the reason for all but one of the inset stones being slanted. The thirty and sixty percenters are outstanding people but they are not performing on the same level as those who are producing at nearly 100 percent. The fact that no one has reached perfection—as represented by the west wall—is spelled out by the one set of symbols that is slanted. Those who are approaching 100 percent are missing something. That something will be explained shortly.

In the meantime, why is there a total of 56 sockets (54 in the ramps and 2 in the top of the Great Step)? So far no one has been able to answer this question. It will be answered now. There are 56 because Joseph was 56 years old when his father Jacob died. (Jacob was 147 at his death [Genesis 47:28]; Joseph was 91 years younger, and 91 subtracted from 147 is 56.)

Why are there 54 sockets in the ramps? Because Joseph lived another 54 years after Jacob died. (He lived to be 110 [Genesis 50:26]; 110 minus 56 equals 54.) The separation of Joseph from his father reflects the fact that being endowed in the House of the Lord does not guarantee that family members will be together in the afterlife. Something else is required, and because this subject is vitally important it will be dealt with in more detail in this chapter as well as in the next.

The mean angle of the Grand Gallery's floor is 26 degrees, 17 minutes and 37 seconds (Piazzi Smyth 424). Verse 26 from Chapter 50 of Genesis was just cited. As indicated, that verse relates Joseph's death; Joseph was 17 when he was taken to Egypt; and 37 was his age at the end of the 7 years of plenty. Storage facilities throughout Egypt were then full; it was a time of incredible abundance, of ample nourishment for all—but 7 years of famine were coming. The obvious tie-in with the symbolism of the slots in the ramps should be beyond arguing.

Incidentally, why are there 27 slots in each ramp? The answer: Joseph had been in Egypt for 27 years when the famine ended. (He was 44 at that time; we deduct 17—his age when he entered Egypt—from 44 in order to obtain the 27.)

But there are 2 other reasons for the 27. One: the table for the showbread that was prepared for the tabernacle measured 2 common cubits long, one cubit wide, and one and a half cubits high (Exodus 25:23). Two cubits = 36 inches; one cubit = 18 inches; and one and a half cubits = 27 inches. Two: with the number 27 there is a planned contrast between the Gallery and the subterranean chamber, where the north-to-south measurement is 27 feet (Lawton and Ogilvie-Herald 19).

For 2 more numbers associated with Joseph we take another look at the inset stones on the west wall. The single slanted set, as Lepre has informed us, is at number 13, and since that leaves 14 sets from that point up to the Great Step, the slanted set clearly serves as a dividing marker. Here is why it was done that way: Joseph had been in Egypt for

13 years when he became that country's co-ruler, and 7 years of famine plus 7 years of abundance add up to 14 years.

But that still does not end the matter, for Edwards' figure of 1 foot 11 inches for the longer sockets in the ramps can be written as 23 inches, and Joseph was the 23rd patriarch of the Old Testament period.

If we include the 2 sockets in the Great Step, then we have another occurrence of the number 28 represented by the total of 28 sockets on both the east and west sides of the Gallery. While Joseph was in prison at the age of 28, his eventual freedom was assured when his prophecies concerning the pharaoh's butler and the "butcher" were fulfilled.

Both of these prophecies involved the number 3. For instance, the butler dreamed about a vine with 3 branches that budded and produced grapes, from which he made a fresh grape drink for the pharaoh. The 3 branches, Joseph told him, meant that within 3 days the pharaoh would restore him to his former position. The "butcher", on the other hand, dreamed that there were 3 white baskets on his head. In the topmost basket there were baked goods for the pharaoh, however, birds ate them. This dream meant that in 3 days the "butcher", in punishment for his crimes, would have his head cut off and impaled on a stake where birds would peck at his flesh (see Genesis 40:9-22).

And now, how far do the 7 courses above the base wall project into the Gallery? Three inches (Lemesurier 98).

Related to the symbols discussed up to this point are the grooves that run

> the entire length of the Gallery on both side walls (east and west walls). The lower edge of these grooves is 5¼ inches above the third overlap from the bottom [that is, the base wall] and is approximately midway between the floor and roof with which the grooves are parallel. Each of the two grooves has a mean depth of ¾ of an inch and is 6 inches wide. (Rutherford, Book III, 975)

These grooves function as another dividing marker; they separate the 2 halves of the walls, and that is in keeping with the 30 and 60 percenters being separate from the 100 percenters. And the number 6 continues to have the same meaning: incompletion and imperfection. In the next chapter we will see the ¾ of an inch duplicated in the antechamber to the King's Chamber and its significance will then be explained.

In addition to his query about the slots in the ramps, Colin Wilson wonders why "there has to be a sunken channel between two low walls [meaning the ramps], instead of a flat floor". This, he says, "is another of those unsolved mysteries of the Pyramid" (62). Along the same line, he also wonders why the King's Chamber has "to be approached by a long, slippery gallery of smooth limestone rather than a sensible staircase" (72).

The Revell Bible Dictionary points out that in Exodus 20:26 God "forbids climbing steps to approach an Israelite altar. A broad main ramp and smaller side ramps are important features of the altars at Ebal [a mountain in Israel] and outside the Jerusalem Temple" (Lawrence O. Richards 51).

Where is the altar in the Grand Gallery? Graham Hancock supplies the clue to that answer when he describes the Great Step as being "[s]omewhat like an altar in appearance" (327). An altar is exactly what the Great Step represents.

And the floor of the Grand Gallery leads directly to the Great Step. The Grand Gallery is the "strait gate" and the narrow way that leads to eternal life, but "few there be that find it" (KJV, Matthew 7:13). The word *strait* is defined by *The American Heritage College Dictionary* as a "narrow channel" and as "difficult"; in archaic language it also means "righteous" (1341).

Rutherford and Lemesurier list the measurements of the Gallery in inches (which are placed in parenthesis), but they prefer to use the "royal cubit", which equals 20.6 inches, a figure that Petrie himself agreed on, although he chose to call it the "regular cubit" (Rutherford, Book III, 979; Petrie 24). Each of the ramps is 1 royal or regular cubit in width; the channel or floor between the ramps is 2 cubits.

The number 2, as should be apparent by now, appears frequently in the Gallery. As a reminder, we have 2 holes at the low end of the ramps that do not have inset stones above them; we have the diagonal grooves above the other holes in the ramps that are 2 inches deep; we have 2 grooves halfway up the walls; we have 2 ramps that are 2 feet high; we have 2 cubits in the width of the central channel, and 2 cubits in the width of the ceiling; and we have 2 holes in the top of the Great Step.

So what is the significance of the number 2?

The number refers to Christ, the 2nd member of the Godhead, but it also refers to 2 people—husband and wife.

The central channel is wide enough for 2 people to ascend side by side, whereas the ramps are only wide enough to accommodate one person. That arrangement is on purpose. It reflects the 3 levels—the 3 heavens—of the highest degree of glory. The lowest level of this highest degree will be composed of those who receive their endowments, remain single and perform at 30 percent of their overall potential; the middle level will be composed of those who receive their endowments, remain single and perform at 60 percent; and the highest level, which Paul the Apostle calls the 3rd heaven (2 Corinthians 12:2), will be home to husbands and wives who have not only received their endowments but have also been married in the House of the Lord for time and for all eternity. Marriages that will endure beyond death and the grave are performed at altars in sealing rooms in the temples.

During his mortal ministry, Christ told the apostles,

> I will give you the keys of the kingdom of heaven, and whatever you bind on earth will be bound in heaven. (Matthew 16:19)

Christ was referring to this binding power, which is exercised in the sealing rooms, when he said,

> "Have you not read that He who made them at the beginning 'made them male and female,' and said, 'For this reason a man shall leave his father and mother and

> be joined to his wife, and the two shall become one flesh'?
>
> "So then, they are no longer two but one flesh. Therefore what God has joined together, let not man separate." (Matthew 19:5-6)

These special binding or sealing keys were restored, along with the church, in 1830 (see section 27 of the *Doctrine and Covenants*). The keys are delegated to high priests who officiate in the temples and who represent the Lord when they bind or seal couples for eternity (Brooks 393).

As represented by the slanted set of symbols on the west wall of the gallery, it is the lack of this sealing that is keeping husbands and wives from reaching the goal of 100 percent, but once the top of the Great Step is mounted that lack has symbolically been eliminated, as evidenced by the two rectangular holes in the southeast and southwest corners of the Step.

Lemesurier describes these holes as being "1 RC [royal cubit] long like the ramp-holes and of similar width [which is 6 inches (98)], [however, they] have no inset-stones [vertical slots] in the wall above them." Lemesurier continues by speculating that if "the inset-stones represent a series of 'skipped incarnations'. . . [then] the holes in the Great Step could well refer to an incarnation that *cannot* be skipped, i.e. a return to mortality" (100).

The 2 holes in the Great Step have nothing to do with "an incarnation that *cannot* be skipped". In the temples, when ordinances such as baptism for the dead are performed, "it is required that, beside the recorder and the officiating elder, two witnesses be present, and that they attest the ceremony as duly performed" (Talmage, *The House of the Lord* 78-79).

To digress for a minute, a Frenchman by the name of Georges Goyon has noticed at the beginning of the ascending passage "indications on the lowest granite block of 2 slots 7 centimeters [about 3 inches] wide intended for wedges." The wedges, he argues, were used to control the "downward movement" of the granite block as it was lowered into position (Tompkins 253).

On the contrary, the slots are symbols of the 2 witnesses required for baptisms of the living, the requirements for the living being the same as for the dead.

Now back to the 2 holes in the Great Step, which, as stated by Lemesurier, are one cubit long, and just as each ramp is one cubit wide and represents one individual, so the 2 holes represent the 2 witnesses required for temple ordinances. It is for this reason that they have no inset stones above them. In other words, it is not the need for nourishment that is being symbolized by these particular slots.

Because the Church of Jesus Christ of Latter-day Saints is a missionary church, many husbands and wives who are converted join the church and then qualify to go to the temple. Since they have already been married, when they enter the sealing room they do not have to be remarried but only sealed together. If there are children, they are sealed to their parents. However, children born to couples who have already been sealed are "born in the covenant", meaning they are automatically sealed to their parents in the Lord's eyes (Talmage, *The House of the Lord* 88 and 91).

The 3rd heaven of the celestial kingdom is for families. The primary purpose of the temples is to bind families together for eternity, going all the way back to Adam and Eve, which will be possible by means of adoption where gaps in family lines exist due to certain family members having rejected the teachings of Christ.

It is interesting to note that in *People of the Pharaohs* Hilary Wilson says the "family was so central to Egyptian life that prayers were said for a man to be reunited with his family in the next world." She goes on to say that in

> some scenes showing the banquet at which all the family gathered together to celebrate the transition of the tomb-owner from mortal to everlasting life, several generations are shown together and no distinction is made between

> those who were still alive at the time of the funeral and those who had passed on many years before. A prime example of this is the scene from the tomb of Paheri at el-Kab where *four generations* are depicted, together with close friends and nurses, showing that the term "family" was interpreted in its very broadest sense. (73; italics added)

Members of the Church of Jesus Christ of Latter-day Saints are urged to record all the vital information they can for relatives going back 4 generations so the temple work can be done for their ancestors, thus binding them together as an extended family. But besides this parallel, Abraham was told by the Lord:

> "Know certainly that your descendants will be strangers in a land that is not theirs [the Lord was talking about Egypt], and will serve them [the Egyptians], and they [the Egyptians] will afflict them four hundred years.
>
> "And also the nation whom they [Abraham's descendants] serve I will judge; afterwards they shall come out with great possessions.
>
> "Now as for you, you shall go to your fathers in peace; you shall be buried at a good old age.
>
> "But in the *fourth generation* they shall return here [to the land of Canaan]. (Genesis 15:13-16; italics added)

Jacob, before he died, had Joseph swear that he would take his body back to Canaan so he could be buried with his parents and his grandparents, Abraham and Sarah (Genesis 47:29-31 and 49:31). Joseph did as requested and that made 3 generations joined together. Decades later, when Moses led the Israelites out of Egypt, he took Joseph's bones with him so he too could be laid to rest in Canaan (Exodus 13:19), and that made 4 generations.

With so many parallels between the beliefs and practices of ancient Egypt and the Church of Jesus Christ of Latter-day Saints, it's no wonder that Arthur Wallace, in his independent study titled *LDS Roots in Egypt*, came to the unavoidable conclusion that both "had common origins" (24).

* * *

The top edge of the north face of the Great Step appears to have seen heavy use. It is generally assumed that the limestone has been worn down from people climbing on it, but Worth Smith rejects that assumption, declaring that the Step's appearance was "chosen by the builders to portray the near-collapse of the tenets of the Master in the hearts and minds of men *en masse*" (117).

Smith's interpretation is a complete misunderstanding of what Enoch meant to tell us by the worn appearance. The Seer meant for us to understand that even though few of the earth's total number of inhabitants will find the strait gate and the narrow way to the celestial kingdom, nevertheless millions of couples will, and the worn edge of the Great Step is a symbolic reflection of that fact.

At the end of 2010 the total membership of the Church of Jesus Christ of Latter-day Saints was more than 14,000,000. During 2010 there were 272,814 converts baptized into the church, and full-time missionaries numbered 52,225. In addition, 134 temples were in operation throughout the world (Brook P. Holes, "Statistical Report, 2010" (29). For a comparison, in 1999 the total membership was nearly 10,700,000 and 68 temples were in operation (Watson, "Statistical Report, 1999" (22).

In comparison to the present, what was the membership of the church during Enoch's 365 years of missionary activity? No precise figures are available at this time, however, Hugh Nibley, citing the 4th volume of the Jewish source *Bet ha-Midrash*, says more than 800,000 men were translated with Enoch (253). No doubt, many—if not most—of those 800,000 men would have had wives and children who would have joined them.

There is no way to confirm the number of 800,000, but if we consider that Enoch was as Christ-like as a man could become during mortality, and if we consider what the membership of the church might have been if Christ had been able to extend his mission to 365 years, then 800,000 is likely to be a low figure.

And what of the future? Present-day members anticipate thousands of temples being built during the millennium; they also anticipate a tremendous increase in church membership. What is the purpose of the millennium, the 1000 years of peace? It is largely to permit the temple work for the dead to be completed (Brewster, Jr. 211-12). With this understanding it is possible to see why the symbolic altar in the Great Pyramid appears to have had much use.

There is one more feature in the Grand Gallery that Lepre relates to the Great Step. He says he has detected "[h]undreds of rough chisel marks" above the grooves that are cut into the 3rd overlapping section of the Gallery's east and west walls (82). A few paragraphs later he notes that "above the Great Step. . . there are *no* chisel marks" (83; italics added).

Accepting the theory that a platform once supported the 3 granite stones in the ascending passage and that something once traversed the Gallery's walls, Lepre suggests that

> intruders climbed. . . to the top of the platform. From this location they chiseled downwards, in order to break into the grooves and thus remove whatever was lodged within. (83)

Lepre reasons that the "material must have been of some value (more than plain wood or stone) for intruders to have wanted to extract it" (83).

Were intruders responsible for the chisel marks above the grooves that run the length of the Gallery?

No. There were no intruders.

Here is the reason for the chisel marks.

But first, more description from Lepre:

> Majestic, exalted and noble are a few of the words which spring to the mind of men and women who view the Grand Gallery. "The glory of the workmen who built the Great Pyramid"... say Perrot and Chipiez, in their *Ancient Egyptian Art*, "is the masonry of the Grand Gallery. . . . The faces of the blocks of limestone of which the walls are composed have been dressed with such care that it is not surpassed even by the most perfect example of Hellenistic architecture on the Acropolis at Athens."
>
> ... The overall appearance is that of a long, exalted tunnel of a sort.
>
> Although the gallery is very much blanketed by soot deposits from torches having been passed through here for over 1000 years, and is further darkened by lack of adequate lighting, in its original, pristine state it was quite white, having been constructed of unblemished limestone blocks. (79)

Switching to the book of Revelation, we read: "To him who overcomes I will give... a *white stone*, and on the stone a new name written which no one knows except him who receives it" (2:17; italics added). The new name mentioned in this verse is given in the House of the Lord. It is a key word used during the endowment in order to symbolically enter the Lord's presence. The new name, then, symbolizes a "new relationship with God" (Charles 63). As for the white stone, Joseph Smith taught that it would be a means "whereby things pertaining to a higher order of kingdoms will be made known" (*Doctrine and Covenants* 130:10).

The chisel marks on the walls of the Gallery represent individual white stones being carved out so they can be given to those who inherit the celestial kingdom.

* * *

Noone has observed that "between the huge blocks forming the walls of the Grand Gallery, the joints are precision-cut. The joints are almost invisible. It is impossible to insert a needle anywhere" (170). And like Dunn, Noone has observed evidence of intense heat having been applied to the walls at some point in the past. Describing one section of wall as exhibiting "signs of calcination", he adds:

> Limestone does not melt like wax, but when subjected to intense heat it is reduced to a. . . powder and [the surface] falls away, leaving the undersurface appearing as if melted, dissolved, or fused. (168)

This feature was created by Enoch to represent fire being used to purify that which is impure. With that in mind, Hoyt W. Brewster Jr., author of *Behold, I Come Quickly*, offers this quote from Harold B. Lee, a latter-day prophet: "We must be cleansed and purified and sanctified to be made worthy to receive and abide [the Lord's] presence" (181). Related to this quote is a passage from the short but important book of Malachi in the Old Testament:

> "But who can endure the day of His coming?
> And who can stand when He appears?
> For He is like a refiner's fire. . . .
> He will sit as a refiner and a purifier of silver;
> He will purify the sons of Levi,
> And purge them as gold and silver,
> That they may offer to the Lord
> An offering in righteousness."
> (3:2-3)

Silver, when associated with the House of the Lord, symbolizes the terrestrial kingdom, while gold symbolizes the celestial kingdom. As for the sons of Levi, they officiated in the tabernacle and in the temples that were built in Jerusalem.

Another passage that applies to Noone's description of the Gallery's walls is this one from 2nd Peter:

> the day of the Lord will come as a thief in the night, in which the heavens will pass away with a great noise, and the elements will *melt with fervent heat*; both the earth and the works that are in it will be burned up.
>
> Therefore, since all these things will be *dissolved*, what manner of persons ought you to be in holy conduct and godliness. (3:10; italics added)

Puzzling over some of the features of the Gallery, Hancock asks why it was necessary for the pyramid builders to have the central channel or slot of the floor "mirror so precisely the width and form of the ceiling, which also looked like a 'slot' sandwiched between the two upper courses of masonry" (324). The answer is: the floor and the ceiling combine to illustrate the ideal of following a constant, undeviating course toward exaltation.

Even though the ceiling of the Gallery has already been described, it may be beneficial to present this account by Rutherford:

> The roof is comprised of slabs, each tilted at a slightly deeper angle than that of the magnificent passage itself. To receive the lower ends of each roof-slab, the tops of the side walls are cut like ratchet teeth, each tooth being about 2 inches deep. [Note that this number 2 could have been added to the list of 2s given earlier.]

Rutherford, like virtually all other authors who have commented on the ceiling, says its "arrangement is to avoid cumulative pressure" (Book III, 976). Is he stating a fact or an assumption?

He is stating an assumption.

The side walls, we are told, support each of the ceiling stones. How many sections are there altogether in each wall? There are 8—7 overlaps plus the base. The number 8 represents Christ. (While it hasn't been mentioned yet, the gematria for the word *Lord* in Greek—*κυριος*—is 800, or 8 x 100 (Gaunt 9), and quite frequently in the New Testament *Lord* is combined with *Jesus Christ*, as in the closing salutation of the book of Revelation: "The grace of our Lord Jesus Christ be with you all" [22:21].)

Among other things, the ceiling illustrates Christ's assurance that if we are weighed down by the cares of the world we can lighten our load by turning to him. His invitation to do so is in the Gospel of Matthew:

> "Come to Me, all you who labor and are heavy laden, and I will give you rest.
>
> "Take My yoke upon you and learn from Me, for I am gentle and lowly in heart, and you will find rest for your souls.
>
> "For My yoke is easy and My burden is light." (11:28-30)

The stones of the ceiling do not press down on each other. Independently, they fulfill their function, and individually their weight is comparatively light. Similarly, by learning the truth, by accepting Christ's teachings, by trusting in him and by keeping the covenants made in the House of the Lord, we become independent and free of enslaving addictions, of false theories and false religions, and especially of fear, including fear of failure, fear of not being worthy, fear of being rejected by the Lord.

This chapter began with the quote from John 8:32, which reads, "And you shall know the truth, and the truth shall make you free." Dimitri Meeks and Christine Favard-Meeks write in *Daily Life of the Egyptian Gods*: "it was Osiris's servants who enjoyed the greatest freedom of movement" (88). Freedom is what is depicted by the design of the Gallery's ceiling.

There are 7 additional courses above the base walls in order to represent Enoch. Recalling that Thoth is one of Enoch's names, we learn from Christiane Desroches-Noblecourt that the solar god departed "for celestial horizons" and was replaced by Thoth, the divine scribe, god of the moon. . . who governs the world in his stead" (264). The solar god is Christ; departing "for celestial horizons" refers to his ascension.

Thoth, Patrick Boylan says, had a "special endowment of mysterious knowledge" (98). Moreover,

> Thoth is described at an early period, as the founder of the cult carried on in the temples—as the originator of divine sacrificial worship. (88)
>
> [T]he erection, internal arrangement, and decoration of the temples were regarded as designed by him. (89)
>
> It is Thoth. . . who pronounces the formulae of "glorification". (136)

Glorification is an acceptable synonym for exaltation.

Now, was Thoth associated with the number 8? Of course he was. Thoth's city, Hermopolis (another Greek name being substituted for the Egyptian name), was called the "City of the Eight", and "sacred formulae were sought" there (Boylan 157).

Thoth was also associated with the numbers 5 and 15: "his chief priest in Hermopolis [was]—'Great of the Five'" (Boylan 157), and the city itself "was the capital of the 15th nome of Upper Egypt" (Margaret Bunson 113). Fifteen has been an important number so far in this investigation of the Great Pyramid with the 3 granite blocks in the ascending passage adding up to 15 feet, plus the connection with the Queen's Chamber and its 15-foot-high niche. Then, too, on which day of the month did the Exodus begin? The 15th.

* * *

Tompkins, as reported previously, informs us that the "overall length of the Grand Gallery. . . is 157 feet" (13). Compare this figure to

Rutherford's "total *vertical* distance of 157 feet [as opposed to the *overall* distance of 200 feet]" for the well shaft (Book III, 1025; italics added). The figures are identical and therefore provide additional evidence that the well was not created to be an escape shaft but instead was meant to connect with the Gallery in a symbolic way.

From the step-up at the end of the first 40 inches at the beginning of the Gallery's floor to the north face of the Great Step is 153 inches (Edwards 104). An odd number. What can it relate to? The pyramidologists supply the answer, having found a match in the Gospel of John.

After Christ was resurrected he appeared one morning at the Sea of Tiberias—another name for the Sea of Galilee—where Peter, James and John, plus 4 other disciples (making 7 in all), had been fishing during the night but had not caught a single fish.

Without being recognized, Christ called to them while they were still in the boat.

> "Children, have you any food?" They answered Him, "No."
>
> And He said to them, "Cast the net on the right side of the boat, and you will find some." So they cast, and now they were not able to draw. . . [the net] in because of the multitude of fish. (21:5-6)

Peter, being told by John that it was Christ on the shore, "plunged into the sea" to go to him (21:7).

> But the other disciples came in the little boat (for they were not far from land, but about *two hundred* cubits), dragging the net with fish.
>
> Then, as soon as they had come to land, they saw a fire of coals there, and fish laid on it, and bread.

> Jesus said to them, "Bring some of the fish which you have just caught."
>
> Simon Peter went up and dragged the net to land, full of large fish, *one hundred and fifty-three*; and although there were so many, the net was not broken. (21:8-11; italics added)

Because the number 153 is so unusual (it occurs only once in the entire Bible), anyone who is not blinded by a certain mind-set, by a predetermined interpretation of the Grand Gallery's purpose, should be able to see the undeniable connection between the 153 feet in the Gallery and the 153 fish listed in the Gospel of John.

At the same time, precisely because the number 153 is so unusual, it has puzzled Bible scholars and they have tried to explain its significance in various ways. As an example, Reverend J. R. Dummelow suggests that "the number of the fishes are [sic] to be mystically interpreted. But the meaning. . . is uncertain" (811).

Lewis Spence reveals that in the *Book of the Dead* "we find password and countersign and all the magical material necessary to the existence of. . . a secret cult" (59). The *Book of the Dead*, then, as the pyramidologists have perceived, does have some connection with the Great Pyramid. This is especially true of Chapter 153, for in this chapter fishermen use a "great and mighty net" that has the name "The All-embracing". The fisherman who uses the net for himself is termed "the great prince who dwells in the eastern side of the sky." The narrator of this chapter identifies himself with Osiris and says he is "the Lord of Light" (Faulkner, *The Ancient Egyptian Book of the Dead* 152).

In the Gospel of John, emphasis is placed on the fact that the net is unbroken despite the number of large fish caught in it. According to Dummelow, this

> draught, in which. . . every fish is brought safe to shore, symbolises the Church triumphant in heaven, freed at last from all earthly imperfections, and *embracing*

> in its membership *all* genuine servants of God whose salvation is now for ever assured. (811; italics added)

Dummelow's interpretation is not entirely correct. The draught does not symbolize "the Church triumphant in heaven"; Christ's concern was with the earthly church, not the one in heaven, nor is salvation "for ever assured" until the servants of God have endured to the end. However, Dummelow's use of the words *embracing* and *all* is appropriate.

The "All-embracing" net in the *Book of the Dead* is a reference to Christ, for the "Father loves the Son and has given *all things* into His hand" (John 3:35; italics added). This same declaration is repeated in John 13:3 and 16:15, 1 Colossians 1:19, and in the *Doctrine and Covenants* where Christ says:

> he that receiveth me receiveth my Father;
>
> And he that receiveth my Father receiveth my Father's kingdom; therefore *all that my Father hath shall be given unto him*. (84:37-38; italics added)

The "Lord of Light" in the *Book of the Dead* is also Christ, who was—and is—the light of the world (John 8:12), and he is "the great prince who dwells in the eastern side of the sky." When Christ was born a star signifying that momentous event shone in the eastern sky (Matthew 2:2; that "star" was actually the city of Zion), and when Christ comes again he will appear as lightning coming "from the east" (Matthew 24:27).

Bullinger offers some interesting information concerning the number 153. After noting that students of the Bible "have felt there must be something deeply significant and mysterious in this number", he reviews some of the commentary found in the writings of Augustine and others who have seen in the "number some connection with the saved" and who have therefore concluded that "the number of the elect is fixed and pre-ordained" (273).

Bullinger then proceeds to examine some of the various ways of dealing with the number in mathematical terms. For instance, 153 is 3 squared x 17, or, to put it another way, 9 x 17. Three squared, Bullinger says, represents the Godhead (274), while 17 is "one of the *prime* (or indivisable) numbers. What is more, it is the *seventh* in the list of prime numbers." In addition, 17, expressed as 7 plus 10, combines 2 perfect numbers and as a result it signifies "spiritual perfection, plus ordinal perfection, or *the perfection of spiritual order*" (258).

Bullinger also points out that in gematria, the phrase "Sons of God", when written in Hebrew, adds up to exactly 153. This same phrase, when written in Greek, adds up to "3213, or 3 x 7 x 153." Similarly, "joint-heirs" in Greek "amounts to 1071, the factors of which are 153 and 7" (275). And in

> the record of the miracle itself there are some remarkable phenomena:—
>
> The word for "fishes" [in Greek], is by gematria 1224, or 8 x 153.

The same is true for "the net" (276).

What all of this adds up to is not that "the number of the elect is fixed and pre-determined", but that Christ, the architect of the Great Pyramid, knew that the elevated portion of the Grand Gallery's floor measured 153 feet and so he arranged for the number of fish that were caught in the net to number that same amount. The "large fish", or the "great fish" as they are described in the King James Version, symbolize the members of the church who become endowed in the House of the Lord and who, if they remain faithful to their covenants, will become sons and daughters of God and "joint heirs with Christ" in the highest kingdom of heaven (Romans 8:17).

* * *

In addition to the number 153, we should look at the other parallels between the verses in the Gospel of John and the Gallery. In John we have Christ plus 7 disciples; in the Gallery we have the base wall plus 7 overlaps. In John we have the disciples initially without food; in the

Gallery we have the empty holes in the ramps, and at the low end of the ramps no inset stones above the holes. In John we have the disciples catching a multitude of fish when they follow Christ's instructions; in the Gallery we have a multitude of holes with inset stones above them that represent, among other things, reminders to nourish our bodies, minds and spirits by following Christ's teachings. In John we have a fire of coals; in the Gallery we have evidence of fire and heat. In John we have bread; in the Gallery the symbolic altar or table is like the one that held the showbread in Solomon's Temple. In John we have the net heavy with fish, but the net remains strong and intact; in the Gallery we have the ceiling that remains strong and intact.

In John the fish symbolize people being brought to Christ—but only "some", and the fish are "large", or "great", and they were caught "on the right side of the boat". In the Bible, as we know, the right side symbolizes righteousness. In the Gallery we have a great hall with large stones in the walls and on the right side we have the vertical inset stones that represent some of the members of the church living uprightly.

In addition, the 200 cubits mentioned in John provide another connection with the 200 feet of the well, which symbolizes people either moving down and away from the Grand Gallery—where Christ's presence is depicted—or upwards toward it.

When Christ contacts the 7 disciples who are fishing and coming up empty, they are on their way down; for instead of being faithful and believing and anxiously waiting for their Messiah to direct them in their work of representing him, they are back doing what they had done before they were called to become fishers of men.

After the fish are brought to Christ, he feeds the 7 disciples, and then in the next verse John lets us know that this was "the third time Christ showed Himself to His disciples after He was raised from the dead" (21:14).

When breakfast is finished, Christ asks Peter,

> "Simon, son of Jonah, do you love Me more than these?"

> He [Peter] said to Him, "Yes, Lord; You know that I love You." He [Jesus] said to him, "Feed My lambs."
>
> He said to him a second time, "Simon, son of Jonah, do you love Me?" He said to Him, "Yes, Lord; You know that I love You." He said to him, "Tend My sheep."
>
> He said to him the third time, "Simon, son of Jonah, do you love Me?" Peter was grieved because He said to him the third time, "Do you love Me?" And he said to him, "Lord, You know all things; You know that I love You." Jesus said to him, "Feed My sheep." (21:15-17)

First comes the specific notice that this was the 3rd time Christ had appeared to his disciples after his resurrection, then Christ tells Peter 3 times to feed or tend to his sheep, meaning, of course, the members of the church plus those who would become converted when they were taught the truth.

In the Grand Gallery, the width of the overlaps in the 7 courses is 3 inches, and the grooves that run the length of the Gallery are in the 3rd course up from the base walls. The number 3 is another direct link to the 21st chapter of John.

But the walls of the Gallery also tie in with measurements in Solomon's Temple. For instance, each of the temple's 2 bronze pillars had a capital that was 5 cubits high, which was the equivalent of 7½ feet (1 Kings 7:16). The base walls in the Gallery are 7½ feet high.

Then, too, consider this: "for the door of the sanctuary he [Solomon] made doorposts. . . one fourth of the wall" (1 Kings 6:33). The base section of the Gallery is one-fourth of the wall. Solomon also "built the inner court with *three* rows of hewn stone" (1 Kings 6:36; italics added). The width of the overlaps in the Gallery, as already noted, is 3 inches, and the overlaps are made of hewn stone.

Anything else? Yes. It took Solomon 7 years to build the temple (1 Kings 6:38). How many sections are there above the base wall in the Gallery? Seven.

The number 7 suggests additional associations. For example, in the book of Joshua the Israelites are given their inheritance in the Promised Land. Here is part of that account:

> Now the whole congregation of the children of Israel assembled together at Shiloh. . .

Before finishing the quote, a comment about Shiloh needs to be made. Shiloh, according to *Nelson's Illustrated Bible Dictionary*, was

> a city in the territory of Ephraim which served as Israel's religious center during the days before the establishment of the United Kingdom [under Saul, Israel's first king]. . . . At Shiloh the tabernacle received its first permanent home. . . . This established Shiloh as the [Israelites'] main sanctuary of worship. (Lockyer, Sr. 981-82)

Shiloh is also associated with Christ because of a prophecy Jacob made concerning his son Judah (see Genesis 49:10 and Dummelow 44-45).

Now back to Joshua:

> . . . [the congregation] set up the tabernacle of meeting there. And the land was subdued before them.
>
> But there remained among the children of Israel *seven* tribes which had not yet received their inheritance.
>
> Then Joshua said to the children of Israel: "How long will you neglect to go and possess the land which the Lord God of your fathers has given you?
>
> "Pick out from among you *three* men for each tribe, and I will send them; they shall rise and go through

> the land, [and] survey it according to their inheritance. (18:1-4; italics added)

Besides the symbolism of Shiloh, the numbers 7 and 3 are appropriate in making a comparison to the walls of the Gallery, as is Joshua's reminder to the Israelites to take action, which is similar to the symbols in the Gallery that function as reminders to seek nourishment for the whole man and the whole woman. The matter of an inheritance is also appropriate in making a comparison since the Gallery leads to the King's Chamber, which represents the inheritance of the saints in the celestial kingdom.

* * *

A few more numbers in the Gallery deserve attention. For the diagonal groove that represents an altar or a table, Lemesurier lists a width of 8 inches (97). The 8 is for Christ. For the width of the inset stones above the holes in the ramps, Lemesurier gives the figure of 13 inches (97). This 13 is one more link to Christ and the Twelve Apostles.

Lepre has told us that the "smaller cavities within which the cement was placed" are at a 45-degree angle. This angle was chosen because the Ark of the Covenant was 45 inches long. Associated with Moses' tabernacle and Solomon's Temple, the Ark or chest "was the most important sacred object of the Israelites during the wilderness period." The chest's gold cover represented the throne of God. Inside the chest were the stone tablets that contained the 10 commandments, "considered to be the basis of the covenant between God and His people Israel" (Lockyer, Sr., *Nelson's Illustrated Bible Dictionary* 97-99).

The ceiling is 1836 inches long. This number, divided by 12, yields 153 (Lemesurier 99). The maker of the Ark of the Covenant is called *Bezalel* in Exodus 37:1. In Hebrew the letters and their numerical values are Beth—2, Çadhe—90, Lamedh—30, Aleph—1, and Lamedh—30. The sum of the numbers is 153 (see Strong 331, entry # 1212).

Taking one more look at the floor, we can compare its 153 feet to the 53 feet of the dead-end passage in the subterranean chamber. The difference between the two figures is exactly 100—a minus 100 for the dead-end passage. The Gallery, in conjunction with the Great Step, symbolizes members of the church on the correct path to performing at 100 percent and as a result meriting the celestial kingdom; the dead-end passage reflects just the opposite, that is, people with 100 percent failure and as a result they are cast out into outer darkness.

In a similar comparison, the 41-inch width of the Gallery's floor between the ramps and the 41-inch width of the ceiling, both of them being on a rise of 26 degrees, are meant to contrast with the dead-end passage, the floor of which "lies at a level 41 inches lower down than that of the" horizontal passage to the subterranean chamber (Rutherford, Book III, 1092).

These stark differences are additional evidence that what is below the base of the Great Pyramid, instead of having been abandoned, is a crucial part of its complete system of passages and chambers.

13. GODS

Then the Jews surrounded Him and said to Him, "How long do You keep us in doubt? If You are the Christ, tell us plainly."

Jesus answered them, "I told you, and you do not believe. The works that I do in My Father's name, they bear witness of Me.

"But you do not believe, because you are not of My sheep, as I said to you.

"My sheep hear My voice, and I know them, and they follow Me.

"And I give them eternal life, and they shall never perish; neither shall anyone snatch them out of My hand.

"My Father, who has given them to Me, is greater than all; and no one is able to snatch them out of My Father's hand.

"I and My Father are one."

Then the Jews took up stones again to stone Him.

Jesus answered them, "Many good works I have shown you from My Father. For which of those works do you stone me?"

The Jews answered Him, saying, "For a good work we do not stone You, but for blasphemy, and because You, being a Man, make Yourself God."

> Jesus answered them, "Is it not written in your law, 'I said, "You are gods"'?"
>
> (John 10:24-34)

The Great Step "lies on the east-west axis of the Pyramid," states Rutherford, who then adds,

> that is to say, it is exactly half way [sic] through the Pyramid from [the] north to south sides. [The] riser of the Great Step is also vertically above and in alignment with the east end of the apex of the Queen's Chamber's pointed roof. (Book III, 978)

This particular placement of the Great Step indicates a direct relationship with the Queen's Chamber, as does the width of the slots in the southeast and southwest corners at the top of the Step. That width is 5.8 inches (Rutherford, Book III, 979). It will be recalled that the height of the final 18 feet of the horizontal passage to the Queen's Chamber is 5 feet 8 inches. The duplication of the numbers 5 and 8 is intentional.

The vertical depth of the slots in the top of the Step is 5.3 inches (Rutherford, Book III, 979), which is a match for Petrie's measurement of the 5.3-inch vertical joint in the Gallery's side at the mouth of the well shaft.

The length of the slots is 20.6 inches or one royal cubit (Rutherford, Book III, 979). This length was intended to represent those who are of the royal priesthood line. (See 1 Peter 2:9 where Christ's chief apostle calls his fellow priesthood holders "a chosen generation, a royal priesthood".)

What Rutherford calls the riser of the Great Step—the north face—"closely approximates 36 inches" high (Book III, 978). The altar for burning incense in the tabernacle that Moses built was two cubits high, which, using the common cubit of 18 inches, is 36 inches (Exodus

30:2). In the present-day temples of the Church of Jesus Christ of Latter-day Saints, the altars in the sealing rooms measure nearly 36 inches high. And butted against the altars are kneeling benches. In the Great Pyramid, the south ends of the ramps where they butt against the Step function symbolically as kneeling benches.

In the *Book of the Dead*—which should actually be called by its Egyptian title, *Coming Forth by Day*, and which provided "the passwords necessary for admittance to certain stages of Tuat or the Underworld" (Margaret Bunson 47)—36 maxims govern "the conduct of the honest individual toward the gods" (Antelme and Rossini, *Becoming Osiris* 75). These maxims are at the beginning of Chapter or Spell 125 and include declarations of innocence such as:

> I have not impoverished my associates,
> I have not deprived the orphan of his property,
> I have not killed,
> I have not commanded to kill,
> I have not lessened food supplies.
> (Faulkner 29 and 31)

Instructions at the end of Chapter 125 direct the candidate who hopes to enter into the presence of Osiris to "utter this spell pure and clean and clad in white garments" (Faulkner 33).

It is interesting to find that course number 125 of the Great Pyramid's exterior measures 25 inches thick (Lemesurier, chart on page 377). Twenty-five is another number associated with Enoch since he was ordained at that age by Adam. It is also interesting that according to Lemesurier,

> Legend has it that the original of the so-called *Book of the Dead* [or *Coming Forth by Day*] was written by Thoth [Enoch],the great founding-father of Egypt. (32; footnote)

Certainly the concern with not being guilty of impoverishing others, of not cheating orphans out of their property, and of not diminishing food supplies, as indicated by the maxims, is in keeping with the statement in "The Book of Moses" that there were no poor among Enoch's people (7:18).

The top of the Step—which becomes a platform of "squared limestone"—is 5 feet north-to-south and 7 feet east-to-west (Lepre 85). These figures link the Step to the 3rd granite block in the ascending passage with its current length of 5 feet and its former length of 7 feet. In a related matter, this quote from *Nelson's Illustrated Bible Dictionary* is offered:

> All of the pre-flood ages [as given in Genesis] are either a multiple of *five* or a multiple of *five plus seven*. Scholars are not sure why this phenomenon exists, and they do not know what it means. . . .
>
> Many times seven is important as a symbol rather than a number. It is used almost 600 times in the Bible. (Lockyer, Sr. 763-64; italics added)

Does not the Great Pyramid solve this mystery?

The 5-feet-by-7-feet dimensions of the top of the Great Step are also a link to the Gallery; however, Rutherford makes a case for the Step being

> separate and distinct from the design of the Grand Gallery; it is the initial feature of the King's Chamber complex, for its horizontal surface is on the same level as the entire complex, which extends from the front of the step to the far side of the King's Chamber. (Book III, 979)

True, the Great Step is connected to the King's Chamber by way of the antechamber, but it is also connected to the Gallery, so Rutherford's analysis is too limiting. The "entire complex" suggested by Rutherford can actually be traced all the way back to the original entrance of the

Great Pyramid and beyond, since we should be on one continuous path which, at birth, begins downward because of the separation from our Father, but once we reach the age of accountability, which is 8 years old for children whose development is normal (*Doctrine and Covenants* 68:27), if we are then baptized and confirmed members of the Church of Jesus Christ of Latter-day Saints and receive the gift of the Holy Spirit, we immediately begin moving upwards, recovering lost ground, so to speak, and if we don't fall away, our progression will continue upwards until we find ourselves symbolically at the horizontal entrance to the King's antechamber.

If the Great Step—the altar—was removed, there would be a step-up of 5 inches from the central floor of the Gallery to the floor of the antechamber's entrance. This contrasts with the 5-inch downward step at the beginning of the horizontal passage to the Queen's Chamber (Lemesurier 108).

In addition, the floor beneath the Great Step, from its northern base to its southern edge at the top, is 5 feet 7 inches long (Lemesurier 99). Five feet 7 inches is 67 inches. When Jacob moved his family to Egypt, his sons—excluding Joseph—together with his grandchildren, numbered 66 (Genesis 46:26). If Joseph is included, the number is 67.

The first low passage into the King's antechamber is 44 inches high (Lepre 86) and 41 inches wide (Rutherford, Book III, 985). Rutherford says the passage is 41 inches square, but the height is definitely greater than the width. That the dimensions of 44 and 41 are correct seems to be supported by the fact that course number 44 is 41 inches thick (Lemesurier, chart on page 377).

The length of the passage is 52 inches (Lemesurier 110). When Abraham went to Egypt he was 62 years old ("The Book of Abraham" 2:14 and 21), and since he was 10 years older than his wife Sarah (Genesis 17:17), that means she was 52. So we have, in effect, in this part of the Great Pyramid, Abraham and Sarah accompanied by their grandson Jacob and his family.

Incidentally, the base walls of the Grand Gallery are 90 inches high (7½ feet x 12 inches), and Sarah was 90 when she gave birth to

Isaac, the promised heir who would ensure the fulfillment of the Lord's covenant with Abraham that through his descendants he would become the "father of many nations" (Genesis 17:5). And now, with Abraham being the 20th patriarch, we know why the ramps are 20 inches wide, and, with Isaac being the 21st patriarch, we know why the perpendicular height of the ramps is 21 inches (Lemesurier 98), and with Joseph being the 23rd patriarch we also know why the slots in the ramps alternate from 20 inches to 23 inches.

We can make some additional points concerning the number 52. For instance, it is 2 x 26, which provides a link with the descending and ascending passages, which in turn indicates that lifelong members of the church who are faithful in living the commandments are to be joined by those who had once been living on the telestial level but who have turned their lives around and have become worthy of going to the temple.

Fifty-two is also 4 x 13, and these 2 numbers represent the combination of the Quorum of the Twelve plus Christ being established in all lands in order to bless those who are to become patrons of the House of the Lord.

At the end of the 52 inches of the first low passage, which, like the Grand Gallery, is composed of limestone, the King's antechamber suddenly opens up with the ceiling expanding from 44 inches to 149 inches, an increase of 105 inches (Petrie 26). The width also expands from 41 inches to 48 inches, an increase of 7 inches (Piazzi Smyth 209).

The limestone floor continues on for another 13 inches past the point where the antechamber's height and width open up, but then, at a total distance of 65 inches, it changes to granite (Rutherford, Book III, 987). Ten inches more, at a total length of 75 inches, the walls change from limestone to granite (Petrie 26).

The granite floor is elevated ¼ inch higher than the limestone portion. Farther on, at the entrance to the King's Chamber, the floor rises an additional ¾ inch (Lepre 89). Rutherford attributes these changes in the floor to "thrusting caused by earthquake and subsidence movements in the masonry" (Book III, 987), but Lepre disagrees, maintaining that these "rises are not attributed to any roughness in the floor itself—for that floor is very finely leveled and smooth—but to a deliberate adjustment by the architect" (89).

Lepre is correct, and the reason for these alterations will be explained before this chapter concludes.

In the high middle section of the antechamber, the floor is 116 inches long, with 103 of these inches (exactly 5 royal cubits) being composed of granite (Rutherford, Book III, 987).

In this section there are a number of features that need to be described. For instance, above the first granite stone in the floor is the feature known as the Granite Leaf, which consists of "two blocks, one resting on the other" (Piazzi Smyth 584). The Granite Leaf extends from the east wall to the west wall and is "cemented into rectangular grooves" on each side (Lemesurier 111), but it does not extend from the ceiling to the floor; instead, its horizontal bottom, along with the grooves, is at the same level as the ceiling of the first low passage into the antechamber (Hancock 328).

The top of the Granite Leaf is rounded and slopes down on the south side for 5 inches. North to south, the Granite Leaf varies in thickness from 15¾ inches to 16¾ inches, depending on whether or not the one-inch vertical rebates on the north face of the Granite Leaf are included. These rebates run along the east and west edges of the 2 stones (Rutherford, Book III, 988).

In the upper stone, there is a "Boss or Seal" that Rutherford says "resembles a horse-shoe in outline, except. . . it is not hollow in the middle" (Book III, 988). Lepre regards this boss as "the strangest feature by far" in the antechamber. He describes it as "a chiseled protrusion" shaped somewhat like a protractor which "juts out from the face of the block by a full inch at its lowest, horizontal level, to zero degrees tolerance at its highest, arched level." He gives its dimensions as 4 inches high by 5 inches wide (89).

In Lemesurier's view, the boss "resembles a bas-relief of the sunrise or of the rainbow". He lists its surface dimensions as 3 inches in height and 5 inches in width (111) and says it is 5 inches above the joint that divides the 2 blocks, but 33½ inches above the bottom of the lower stone (112), which means the lower stone is 28½ inches high. Rutherford gives the upper stone a maximum height of 23½ inches (Book III, 988), therefore, if we add 28½ to 23½ we get a maximum height of 52 inches for the Granite Leaf—an obvious match for the 52 inches of the limestone flooring. (For an "[e]xploded isometric projection" of the antechamber see page 116 of Lemesurier's *The Great Pyramid Decoded*.)

Since the distance from the floor to the bottom of the Granite Leaf is 44 inches, if we add that figure to the 52 inches, we have 96 inches from the floor to the top of the upper stone. Next, if we subtract 96 inches from 149 inches, we find that from the top of the upper stone to the ceiling is 53 inches—a match number-wise with the 53 feet of the dead-end passage connected to the subterranean chamber, but these 53 inches are of course in a totally different setting.

We'll come back to the above figures, but first, Rutherford, providing more details about the boss, comments that it "is not in the centre of the Granite Leaf's north face, but is one inch to the west of it" (Book III, 988).

On the south side of the Granite Leaf, the east and west walls have "a retaining granite pilaster", that is, a narrow rectangular column (Lemesurier 113). On the south side of the pilasters, the east wall has a wainscot (a facing or paneling) that measures 103 inches high—a match for the 103 inches of granite flooring—while the west wall also has a wainscot, this one with a height of 112 inches.

Above the wainscots, says Rutherford, the walls have been moved back 12 inches, so that the width of the antechamber at the top of the east wainscot is 53 inches—another match number-wise with the dead-end passage—however, because the west wainscot is 9 inches higher, the width at that level is 65 inches (Book III, 993 and 995)—and so we have a match for the 65 inches of limestone flooring as well as another link with Enoch.

Rutherford's description continues:

> Each wainscot has. . . three full-length grooves on both sides. . . [and the grooves] are each 21.5 inches wide and 3.25 inches deep, [while] the vertical pilasters separating the grooves have a mean width of about 5.3 inches [another match for Petrie's 5.3-inch joint in the upper mouth of the well shaft and for the 5.3-inch depth of the 2 slots in the top of the Great Step], but the pilasters which retain the Granite Leaf on the south are only 3.75 inches wide. The three full-length grooves in the Wainscot on the west side of the passage have semi-circular hollows with a diameter of 17.25 inches carved out of the top. . . . [but] the tops of the grooves in the east Wainscot are quite plain and flat. (Book III, 995)

Lemesurier notes that the full-length grooves in the east and west walls descend below the level of the floor by 3 inches (113).

The south wall of the antechamber's middle section has 4 vertical grooves that are 3½ inches wide (Lepre 87). These grooves, Rutherford says, extend

> from the beginning of the roof of the Second Low Section of the King's Chamber Passage right up to the roof of the High Central Section. . . .
>
> These grooves are 2.8 inches deep from the top down to within 8 inches of the bottom where they originally terminated in a tapering rounded spoon-shape, becoming gradually shallower and finally ending in an unbroken flat surface over the doorway. Though the lower ends were thus rounded, the grooves themselves were cut square. (Book III, 995)
>
> The 4 grooves divide the wall into 5 equal spaces between them in that portion which is between the two wainscots. (Book III, 996)

The numbers 4 and 5 should remind us of the well shaft with its 4 sections containing 5 directions.

The grooves in the south wall are 105 inches long—a match for the 105-inch increase in height in the antechamber's mid-section—but their "full-depth portion" is 97 inches or 8 feet 1 inch. The entrance to the second low passage connected to the King's antechamber is directly below the grooves and, like the first low passage, measures 44 inches high. This figure, combined with the top 12 inches of the south wall, which revert back to limestone (Lemesurier 117), means the granite part of the wall is 93 inches in length.

The roof of the antechamber is composed of 3 large slabs, each being of red granite (Lemesurier 110), and each running east to west (Rutherford, Book III, 987).

The second low passage, which leads directly into the King's Chamber, is 101 inches long (Lemesurier 118). Adding these 101 inches to the 116 inches of the middle section and to the 52 inches of the first low passage yields a total floor length of 269 inches or 22.42 feet.

With this rather complete description of the antechamber, we'll now turn to explanations of its various features, and we'll start by asking why the entrance to the antechamber is so small, especially when it comes after the impressive size of the Grand Gallery.

Tom Valentine replies:

> All your effort [spent in climbing up the Grand Gallery] has brought you, finally, to the floor of the temple. . . . [O]nce you pass through the "Chamber of the Triple Veil" before you, you need never incarnate to the physical level again—your Egoic growth will be accomplished on higher levels of existence from this point on.
>
> The Chamber of the Triple Veil obviously has three parts to it. According to the *Book of the Master* [meaning the *Book of the Dead* or *Coming Forth by Day*], the first part is "inner conflict," the second part is "truce

> in chaos," and the third part is "final tribulation and humility."
>
> . . . After the magnificent ascent in the Grand Gallery, it's no wonder one wants to balk a little before stooping to enter the narrow, confining corridor. It's certainly symbolic of inner conflict. You only crawl for a few feet in this first "veil," and [then] you can stand up inside a small antechamber. You get a break in the confinement, and you can reflect on your reaction to the confining entrance. You are also standing directly above the Chamber of Chaos [the subterranean chamber] hundreds of feet below, and perhaps as you are getting this second "veil" of "truce," you can reflect on the millions of Egos, exactly like you, who have yet to make the ascent. Ahead lies the third veil, and once again you are forced to crouch to enter, but beyond this final low passage lies the main chamber—the "Hall of Judgment," the chamber of the "open tomb." (Quoted in Noone 230)

Worth Smith takes basically the same approach as Valentine.

> In whatever stance one goes thru [sic] the bore [the entrance] there is a constant awareness of one uncomfortable fact, that a huge and low-hung stone is resting directly upon the shoulders and back. It is much the same as if one were actually bearing upon the back a very heaven [sic] burden; and one wonders if that might be the symbolism of the tube, that of signifying a terrific burden upon the back of humanity, beneath which, greatly humbled, it must creep forward in pain and sorrow.

With that, Smith resorts to dating, assigning "the mouth of the low bore" to "August 4-5th, 1914, the exact date of the outbreak of the calamitous World War [One]". At the end of the passage, he says, is the date "November 9-10th, 1918, the ending of the World War" (119)!

Continuing with the antechamber proper, he perceives it as symbolizing

> the fulfillment. . . of the prophecy of "the Truce in Chaos" [meaning the "Armistice which closed the World War"], including the period of "the Triple Veil", as defined in the very ancient "Book of the Dead"; it is also "the Place of the Screen before the Great Pyramid's Holy of Holies" (the King's Chamber), as outlined in the same writings. This "Screen" in "the Place of the Screen" is simply the Granite Leaf in the Ante-Chamber; and the Granite Leaf, as interpreted in both the Great Pyramid and the Book of the Dead, is analagous to the Veil in the Temple at Jerusalem which was "rent in twain" at the Crucifixion (Matt. 27:51). The Ante-Chamber symbolizes also the period of the *Unveiling of God's Purpose* in Its relation to the destiny of mankind. The Ante-Chamber typifies, still additionally, the "School of Christ", a school of consecration unto death, until the Purpose indicated is served. (140)

Not yet finished with this analysis, Smith, realizing that the Peace Treaty of Versailles that ended World War I "was deficient in love, charity, forgiveness and other tokens of Brotherhood as taught by Jesus", connects the failure of the treaty to the Granite Leaf, which then becomes "the *Stone of Futility*" (142).

The second low passage, for Smith, symbolizes man's being humbled by having "to go down on his knees to negotiate" the passage. Here, man

> is given, as it were, "a double-dose of its own bad medicine"; for that tube is nearly *twice as long* as the First Low Passage that indicated the Great War. . . .

> Hence mankind in its march down the present stage of the grand highway of the ages is crawling humbly, sorrowfully, despairingly along that portion of the trail that is proving its Via Dolorosa; and it will not emerge therefrom. . . until the date of September 16, 1936. (143)

The end of the second low passage, says Smith, assures us that Satan "will be *seven times descended*, indicating positively the *certain, complete dethronement of Satin* [sic] to be *imminent*" (146; Smith's italics)!

Smith's book, *Miracle of the Ages*, was copyrighted 1937. World War II began 2 years later. His prediction based on his understanding of the antechamber and its passages was obviously as uninspired as Rutherford's prediction that the millennium would begin in 1979.

Lemesurier offers two explications of the antechamber. In the first of these he provides a "reading" in which he calculates various dates for the passages and for some of the features in the middle section. In doing so, he ignores Rutherford's dictum that "chronology can never be portrayed in granite" (Book III, 997).

To summarize Lemesurier's thesis, he goes from 1845 for the Great Step to 1933 for the first low passage, that is, the entrance, then he moves up to 1985 for the beginning of the antechamber proper. Where the granite section of the floor begins, he leaps to 1999; the floor beneath the boss escalates to 2034. The north side of the granite leaf he dates at 2039, the south side at 2116. The north side of the grooves on the east and west walls is pegged at 2134, the south side at 2498; the south wall comes in one year later at 2499. The second passage, the entrance into the King's Chamber, generates 2989 (111-19).

For Lemesurier, what these various dates involve is "*a time of preparation for the new Messianic Age*", continual reincarnation for "*those who have achieved enlightenment*", the occurrence of "*spiritual or cosmic events. . . calculated to bring perfection to the very basis of reincarnating human life*", plus, in

> *early A.D. 1999 a Messianic era reflecting the new spiritual*

> *initiative will start to force man to base his life on spiritual instead of physical foundations. Then, in late A.D. 2034, the bow-like sign of the Great Initiate, the One-who-is to-come, will appear in the cosmos, and by the autumn of A.D. 2039 this messenger from eternity, full of Messianic perfection, will have taken up his physical role in the earth-planes.*

However, come

> *spring of A.D. 2116 this Messianic figure will depart. But in the summer of A.D. 2134 a new Messianic emissary of supreme spiritual perfection will arrive, his function being to relay the very foundations of human life and finally to shut off the enlightened from any possible relapse into blind mortality.*

However,

> *this figure too will depart in the autumn of A.D. 2238, only to begin a new cycle of physical existence just 25 years later, in the summer of A.D. 2264.*
>
> *Departing again in the autumn of A.D. 2368, this Messianic leader will make a third appearance in the summer of A.D. 2394, and with the end of his mission in early A.D. 2499 the era of the preparatory Messianic initiative will draw to a close.*

Afterwards,

> *the reincarnating enlightened ones will set out on the final spiritual path of ultimate reward, which will eventually result in the raising of the physical initiates to utter spiritual perfection through the catalysing experience of the earthly Millennium. The age of the four-fold Messianic*

> *initiative will lead directly to that Millennium, which will commence in the year A.D. 2989.* (118-119; all italics by Lemesurier)

Lemesurier's second explication of the antechamber will be presented after we have a look at the Egyptologists' reason for the grooves in the east and west walls.

Edwards, who can speak for his colleagues, advises us that the grooves, or slots, as he calls them,

> were intended to hold three granite portcullises [to block off the entrance to the King's Chamber]; a fragment of granite found by Petrie in the Descending Corridor, and now placed outside the entrance to the pyramid. . . , may have broken off the upper part of one of the portcullises. According to Borchardt, these portcullises, each weighing about 2¼ tons, were designed to be lowered by ropes which ran over cylindrical beams mounted above the slots. Three semicircular depressions, into which the lower halves of the ends of the beams fitted, are still to be seen at the top of the west wall, and also four long grooves on the face of the south wall of the chamber along which the ropes passed. Spanning the antechamber. . . there still remain two blocks of granite, one resting on the other; a third block may originally have filled the space between the upper block and the ceiling. (106)

Now we'll let another Egyptologist—Lepre—point out the obvious weaknesses in this theory. First, he says the "three blocking slabs have long since disappeared, probably broken asunder by the first defilers of the pyramid to reach this upper level, and then by subsequent vandals and souvenir seekers" (86).

This assumption raises a question: how did these supposed defilers" manage to break "asunder" these granite slabs? After all, according to the Egyptologists, the granite blocks at the beginning of the ascending passage were impervious to al-Mamun's tools and that is why he directed his team of workers to gouge out a tunnel through the softer limestone. And, according to the Egyptologists, the Great Pyramid was most likely "robbed of its contents some time between the end of the [sic] Khufu's reign and the collapse of the Old Kingdom (c. 2134 BC)" (Lehner 114). In other words, the pyramid was raided at a time when only primitive tools were available. So how was it possible to break apart the granite portcullises?

This question raises another one: just how hard is granite? Noone asked a similar question of Wilfred J. Gregson, "founder and past president of the Society of American Registered Architects" (108).

> **Noone**: [W]hy would only the King's Chamber [out of the three main chambers] have been constructed entirely of granite?
>
> **Gregson**: Well, granite is the hardest common stone known to man today. It is extremely hard to cut or move. If you hit it with a chisel, the hammer will bounce back off the chisel towards your forehead, hardly making a dent in the stone. It is only with our modern equipment that we can grind the stuff and get it smooth and polished. So how in the world these people [the ancient Egyptians] did it is beyond me. Carving granite is, to say the least of it, a very difficult, slow, and precise operation. Even breaking it out from the quarry is difficult.

During Noone's interview with Gregson they went outside the architect's home so he could show the author a pillar of granite he had in his possession.

> **Gregson**: When I attempted to cut a hole in this pillar, I was unable to do it. The steel rock-drill I used just bounced off of it without making any significant

> indentation. So since steel is a great deal tougher than anything the Egyptians used, I don't know how they were able to get this granite as smooth as they did. (122-123)

And yet the Egyptologists make it sound as if the granite blocks they believe once existed in the antechamber could have been easily disposed of—so easily, in fact, that there is no evidence in the antechamber itself that they ever existed. As Hancock said of the supposed raid on the King's Chamber, here is another absolutely clean sweep by thieves who were excessively neat.

But to continue with Lepre's comments:

> Rollers were thought to have traversed the chamber, having been set into the semi-hollows of the wainscots. This initiates the popular theory of a roller system for the manipulation of said slabs.
>
> Yet although the several parts come together rather cohesively, there is a very serious flaw in this hypothesis—a missing piece of the puzzle—which contradicts the supposed validity of the theory. For while the semi-hollows supposed to have received the wooden rollers are indeed present at the top of [the] west wainscot, they are missing on the east wainscot. The ledge of this east wainscot is entirely flat and therefore could not have received the edges of the rollers said to have spanned the width of the chamber. Not only this, but the west wainscot is nearly 9" higher than the ledge of the east wainscot.
>
> These facts seem to negate the only logical theory for the interaction of the various components of this strange little compartment. . . . Why the master architect designed the elements of this chamber in such

> a contradictory manner presents a unique and puzzling problem for all serious pyramid scholars. (87-88)

So much for Borchardt's theory.

And now for Dunn, who writes:

> Borchardt may not have been far off with his analysis of the mechanism that was contained within the Antechamber. After building the resonators and installing them inside the Grand Gallery, the ancient Egyptians would have wanted to focus a sound of specific frequency, that is, a pure or harmonic chord, into the King's Chamber. They would be assured of doing so if they installed an acoustic filter between the Grand Gallery and the King's Chamber. By installing baffles [i.e. "a partition that prevents interference between sound waves" (*The American Heritage College Dictionary* 102)] inside the Antechamber, sound waves traveling from the Grand Gallery through the passageway into the King's Chamber would be filtered as they passed through, allowing only a single frequency or harmonic of that frequency to enter the resonant chamber. Those sound waves with a wavelength that did not coincide with the dimensions between the baffles would be filtered out, thereby ensuring that no interference sound waves could enter the resonant King's Chamber to reduce the output of the system.
>
> To explain the half-round grooves on the west side of the Antechamber and the flat surface on the east, we could speculate that when the installation of these baffles took place, they received a final tuning or "tweaking." This may have been accomplished by using cams. By rotating the cams, the off-centered shaft would raise or lower the baffles until the throughput of sound was

> maximized. . . . The shaft suspending the baffles would have then been locked into place in a pillar block located on the flat surface of the wainscoting on the opposite wall. (173-74)

Earlier in his book, Dunn remarks: "the very idea that granite slabs were once in place in the Antechamber is pure speculation" (36). Is his proposal any different? Where is the physical evidence to back up his claims? It doesn't exist. But in addition, Dunn never brings up the boss on the Granite Leaf, or the fact that the Granite Leaf is composed of 2 stones instead of one, nor does he mention the fact that the east and west walls descend 3 inches below the floor. How would that feature support his theory?

Neither does he discuss the fact that part of the antechamber is limestone instead of granite; he especially omits the matter of the south wall having 12 inches of limestone across the top, and he says nothing about the 4 grooves in the south wall. And he also makes nothing of the fact that the 2 low passages have different lengths. So how is his proposal any more convincing than that of the Egyptologists?

Now back to Lemesurier, who maintains that the boss or seal

> speaks again and again of the Messianic presence and seems to represent either the sunrise or the rainbow with their respective symbolisms of a new age or an end to death. Or possibly we can see in it the Messianic aura or "halo" about the head of a man some 6 ft. 3 in. in height. In short, the boss invites identification as none other than the biblical "sign of the Messiah"—a notion which in turn equates the Granite Leaf with the Christian notion of the "second coming" and the long-awaited advent of the One-who-is-to-come.
>
> But. . . *perhaps the boss's most obvious resemblance is to the Egyptian hieroglyph. . . [for] a loaf of bread. . . .* [T]he Antechamber's seal could thus be held to represent

> some kind of Messianic "bread sent down from heaven" preparatory to the final Chamber of Resurrection. (120; italics added)

Petrie had a completely different understanding of the boss. He was under the impression that it had been left "for the purpose of lifting the blocks" (26), but Rutherford counters by asking us to

> imagine trying to lift the block[s] by one lug only, for there is no corresponding lug on the other side, and that one lug in a lopsided position at that and not balanced in the centre of the side! (Book III, 990)

Lepre concurs with Rutherford, pointing out that the boss

> does not extend out far enough to be of service as a typical boss. . . . Additionally, the horizontal, bottom lip of the standard construction boss is flat, so as to more readily receive a bar or a rope and minimize slippage. Yet the bottom edge of this particular protrusion is slanted, and would simply not function in the manner that a rough boss would. (89)

Lepre, referring to the boss as a "three-dimensional symbol", notes that it

> projects at eye level into a cramped space. . . . Standing quite confined in this space, the visitor contemplates the carving scant inches away from his or her face. Why should this 5″-wide by 4″-high object—so cunningly carved—be positioned in such a closed space in such a way? (89)

Monsieur Lepre, the answer is forthcoming—at long last—but first, let's back up to the entrance to the antechamber. Why is it only 3 feet 8 inches (44 inches) high instead of 28 feet like the Grand Gallery? For the answer we compare the width of the entrance to the width of the Gallery's floor and ceiling, and since they are identical we are able to realize that the representation of husband and wife progressing together is maintained.

But, symbolically, we are to understand that any couple faithful enough to reach this point is not going to be under any spiritual restriction. Because the width of 2 cubits is a continuation of the width of both the central floor and the ceiling of the Gallery, what we are to do is to add the 3 feet 8 inches of the entrance's height to the 28 feet of the Gallery, which would make the entrance 31 feet 8 inches high or about 18 royal cubits.

To repeat what has been said in a previous chapter about the significance of the number 31, in the Book of Joshua, 31 kings opposed the Israelites when they began their conquest of the land of Canaan, but all 31 were defeated. That victory made it possible for the Israelites to obtain their inheritance from the Lord (12:7-24). In like manner, the righteous members of the Church of Jesus Christ of Latter-day Saints can eventually defeat all their enemies and reap their reward.

The other association with the number 31 concerns Josiah, who

> was *eight* years old when he became king, and he reigned *thirty-one* years in Jerusalem. (2 Kings 22:1; italics added)
>
> Now before him there was no king like him, who turned to the Lord with all his heart, with all his soul, and with all his might. (2 Kings 23:25)

Of this king, *Nelson's Illustrated Bible Dictionary* says:

> The three decades of Josiah's reign were characterized by peace, prosperity, and reform. Hence, they were among the happiest years experienced by [the kingdom of] Judah. King Josiah devoted himself to pleasing God. . . . The Bible focuses almost exclusively on Josiah's spiritual

> reform, which climaxed in the *18th* year of his reign with the discovery of the Book of the Law [i.e. the law of God as delivered to Moses]. (Lockyer, Sr. 599; italics added)

So with this exemplary king we have a tie-in with the numbers 31, 8 and 18.

And now, here is the reason why the seal is "in such a closed space", that space being 21 inches according to both Piazzi Smyth and Graham Hancock (pages 175 and 328 respectively). First, these 21 inches, when linked to the 21-inch perpendicular height of the ramps in the Grand Gallery, let us know that Isaac, the 21st patriarch, is represented here as well as in the Gallery.

Second, with the Granite Leaf being 52 inches tall we have another representation of Isaac's mother Sarah, and with the bottom stone measuring 28 inches we have a representation of Abraham, who lived 28 years longer than his grandson Jacob (Abraham died at the age of 175 [Genesis 25:7] and Jacob died at the age of 147 [Genesis 47:28]; 175-147 is 28). Symbolically, then, we have mother, father, and son represented in this "closed space".

Third, in the temples of the Church of Jesus Christ of Latter-day Saints, patrons attending an endowment session end up at the veil where they are required to answer certain questions asked by the "Lord", who is represented by a high priest standing on the other side of the veil.

John D. Charles stresses that the veil

> symbolizes the separation between us and the presence of God. Only those who have been symbolically initiated into the highest priesthood may pass through the veil, and then only after having been symbolically granted the Lord's permission to do so. This reminds us that it is only through Christ's atonement that we are able to enter the celestial kingdom. Passing through the

> veil is a symbolic *pre-enactment* of passing the divinely appointed sentinels to enter the celestial kingdom.
>
> Thus the veil itself, and the process of passing through the veil, is symbolic of. . . the final judgment, and possessing the required knowledge of key words, signs and tokens to be able to pass by the sentinels placed to guard the way to God's presence. (93)

The patrons, both men and women, are brought up close to the veil where, using a small opening sewn into the veil, the "Lord" puts his hand through to take the hand of the patron. At this point, even though the veil is between them, the "Lord" and the patron are standing "face to face", just as anyone who stands up in the 21-inch space between the north wall and the Granite Leaf will be "face to face" with the "seal".

Before proceeding, it will be worthwhile to repeat another quote that was presented in the last chapter pertaining to the *Book of the Dead* or *Coming Forth by Day* where "we find password and countersign and all the magical material necessary to the existence of. . . a secret cult" (Spence 59).

In ancient Egypt, "magic" was synonymous with religion. To be more specific, magic meant

> the conduct of rituals and ceremonies in order to assume powers or to produce specific results. Magic was a traditional part of religious rites in Egypt, viewed as the enabling force by which man and gods alike succeeded in their endeavors. Magic was the binding force between the earth and other worlds, the link between mortals and the divine. (Bunson 154)

Knowing that the ancient Egyptians were taught such precepts by Enoch helps us to understand why, as Peter Tompkins tells us, several writers

> have expressed the opinion that there is a close

> connection between the Great Pyramid and what are known as the Egyptian mysteries, that is to say, the secret knowledge possessed by a hierarchy of initiates which was communicated to those who could prove their worthiness by passing a long period of probationary training and severe trials. (256)

Referring once again to Chapter 125 of the *Book of the Dead*, we read there how the divine tribunal of 42 judges

> subject the deceased to a simple interrogation. Satisfied, they then allow him to enter "by this door of this hall of the two Maats [Maat being associated with truth and justice and with the weighing of the deceased's heart to determine his innocence or guilt]. . . . It would seem therefore that the deceased speaks to them in an *antechamber of this hall*, whose architectural elements will not let him move forward until he has uttered the names of his judges.
>
> Last, he has to answer Thoth and prove again his purity and degree of initiation so that he can be admitted into the presence of Osiris, which, for the deceased, is the equivalent of being declared righteous and furnished with divine offerings [which equate with eternal nourishment]. Thoth says to him: "Go! You are announced (to Osiris). (Antelme and Rossini 78; italics added)

In Chapter 145 of the *Book of the Dead* the deceased has to cross 21 gates "on his path to the domain of Osiris" (Antelme and Rossini 91). With these parallels in hand, can there be any doubt that the *Book of the Dead* and the Great Pyramid are closely linked, or that both are linked to the Church of Jesus Christ?

Continuing now with the antechamber, the veil is represented by the design of the south wall where the grooves create the impression of a long curtain hanging from the ceiling, and by the rebates on the Granite Leaf. Between the rebates, of course, is the seal, which is a triple symbol.

First, it represents Christ. As evidence for this claim, consider that in addition to the descriptions already given, the seal is shaped not only like the hieroglyph for bread but it also looks like the actual bread baked by the ancient Egyptians. (For a photograph of 3 "small loaves of bread" see page 205 of *The Complete Tutankhamun* by Nicholas Reeves.)

The loaves were found in baskets in the so-called tomb of Tutankhamen (which should immediately call to mind the basket buried at the entrance to the niche in the Queen's Chamber). Reeves informs us that "the baskets and [a model] granary included among their contents barley. . . and emmer wheat. . . with some, presumably accidental, admixture of leguminous and other plant seed." Howard Carter, credited with the discovery of the tomb, described the loaves of bread

> as semi-circular in shape, varying in size from 9.5 to 13cm (3¾ to 5⅛ in) in length, and enclosed "in a mesh of rush-work"; a dozen or more were found. . . . [A]ccording to [Alfred] Lucas [a member of Carter's team], it [the bread] "is very cellular and has the appearance of petrified sponge". The composition of one trefoil-shaped loaf or cake. . . is described as "a mixture of meal and fruits". (Reeves, *The Complete Tutankhamun* 205)

A careful review of this information will reveal several connections with the Bible. For example, the "mesh of rush-work" is meant to resemble part of a fishing net, and the bread appears like "petrified sponge" in order to link it to the sea—in particular, the Sea of Galilee and its association with Christ and the apostles, "at least seven [of which] were fishermen" (Lockyer, Sr., *Nelson's Illustrated Bible Dictionary* 386).

Another connection with the Bible is the "barley. . . and emmer wheat. . . with some, presumably accidental, admixture of leguminous and other plant seed." The inclusion of "leguminous and other plant seed" was not accidental. *Leguminous* refers to "peas, beans, clover and other plants" (*The American Heritage College Dictionary* 776). Keeping this definition in mind, let's take a look at the Book of Ezekiel, where that prophet is told by the Lord,

> "lie. . . on your right side;. . . you shall bear the iniquity of the house of Judah forty days. . . .
>
> "Also take for yourself wheat, barley, beans, lentils, millet [a grass grown "for its grains"], and spelt [a "hardy wheat"]; put them into one vessel, and make bread of them for yourself. (4:6 and 9; the definitions are from *The American Heritage College Dictionary* 865 and 1309).

There is still more to link the tomb and the Bible together. For instance, "[t]he composition. . . described as 'a mixture of meal and fruits'" is matched by Ralph Gower's note in *The New Manners and Customs of the Bible* in which he says that breakfast in ancient Israel "was an informal meal taken some time after getting up—a cake of bread with something inside, such as. . . dried fruit" (42). What's more, meal was used along with flour to make bread (Lockyer, Sr., *Nelson's Illustrated Bible Dictionary* 190).

Consider also the fact that "a dozen or more" baskets of bread were found in the tomb's so-called annex. Now, how many loaves of bread were prepared for the tabernacle and the Temple of Solomon? Twelve, which is a dozen. But that isn't the only connection. On the occasion when Christ fed 5000 disciples by miraculously multiplying 5 loaves of bread and 2 fish, how much was left over? Enough to fill "twelve baskets full of the fragments that remained" (Matthew 14:20).

Additionally, a direct connection can be made between the bread in the tomb and the seal in the pyramid's antechamber. What was the size of the bread in the tomb? It varied from 3¾ to 5⅛ inches. What is the size of the seal in the antechamber? Lemesurier, as already indicated, gives its surface dimensions as 3 inches in height and 5 inches in width (111), while Lepre prefers 4 inches by 5 (89).

There is one more comparison we can make between the tomb of Tutankhamen and the antechamber. First, from Reeves' study of the tomb:

> thanks to the activities of the tomb robbers, Carter and his men found remains of Tutankhamun's funerary provisions scattered throughout the tomb. (205)
>
> [Regarding a number of boxes "of Prepared Food"] "out of ten items only three, or at most four, show an agreement between the outside marking and the contents—an amazing example of carelessness." (Jaroslav Cerny quoted in Reeves 206)

Now from Petrie, whose investigation of the Great Pyramid's antechamber revealed that the granite had

> never been dressed down flat, and defective stones are employed; where the limestone was very bad, it was roughly plastered over, and many parts are strangely rough.

From such indications Petrie concluded

> that the supervision was less strict as the work went on, owing to the death of the man who had really directed the superfine accuracy of the earlier work. (86)

See the similarities? Supposedly those who prepared the tomb of Tutankhamun were amazingly careless while the architect or the foreman of the masons who built the Great Pyramid must have died, otherwise how could the undressed granite, the defective stones and the use of plaster be explained?

Who prepared the tomb of Tutankhamun? Enoch did, and so there was no carelessness involved in its preparation—nor were there any tomb robbers. Everything in the tomb is a symbol. Nothing was placed there with the idea that the pharaoh would be "supplied with the raw materials for its manufacture in the afterlife" (Reeves, *The Complete Tutankhamun* 207; for those who are curious, "Tutankhamun" was buried, according to Reeves, about 1323 BC [see page 33], but he is off by more than 400 years, plus *tutankhamun* is not a name, it is an epithet, as will be demonstrated in another volume in this series titled *Building Bridges of Time, Places and People: Tombs, Temples & Cities of Egypt, Israel, Greece and Italy*).

The marked boxes that have different contents from what is indicated on the outside symbolize hypocrisy. How many of us appear to be one thing on the outside, but on the inside we're something else. In addition, we have with these symbols another connection with Christ, who soundly condemned the hypocrites he met during his ministry (see, for example, Matthew 15:7-9).

Another matter is important in this brief discussion of the tomb of Tutankhamen. Where were the baskets of bread found? In the room designated the annex. The annex was the smallest of the rooms in the tomb and the farthest away from the burial chamber. Reeves tells us that the annex, the stone floor of which "lay more than a metre [3.28 feet plus, or nearly 41 inches] below that of the antechamber", was extremely cluttered. He quotes Carter as saying, "the state of this inner room. . . simply defies description. . . everything was in confusion". Carter surmised that the room had apparently become a repository for anything that could not find a satisfactory home in the antechamber (*The Complete Tutankhamun* 89).

Because of the pile of furniture, baskets, and other items, "the excavators had to be suspended on ropes above the chamber floor", but as the clearance of the annex proceeded, Carter came to realize that the "distribution of the objects had been rather more ordered than" first thought (89). He later wrote:

> "nearly 40 pottery wine-jars were placed on the floor at

> the northern end of this Annexe; next to these were added at least thirty-five heavy alabaster vessels containing oils and unguents; stacked beside them, some even on top, were one hundred and sixteen baskets of fruits". (Quoted in Reeves, *The Complete Tutankamun* 89)

The directions of north and south have the same symbolism in the tomb of Tutankhamen as in the Great Pyramid. And the numbers? We saw in the discussion of the ascending passage how the number 35 represented the First Presidency of the church, and how the first 40 inches of the Grand Gallery's floor represented the temple endowment. And 116? That is the length in inches of the floor in the high central section of the King's antechamber. If that isn't enough, what was in the 116 baskets? Fruits. One biblical association with fruits that comes to mind is John the Baptist and his admonishment of those who came to see him baptizing in the wilderness: "bear fruits," he said, "worthy of repentance" (Matthew 3:8).

Another association, of course, is with Christ, who used "fruits" as a symbol:

> "Beware of false prophets, who come to you in sheep's clothing, but inwardly they are ravenous wolves.
>
> "You will know them by their fruits. Do men gather grapes from thornbushes or figs from thistles?
>
> "Even so, every good tree bears good fruit, but a bad tree bears bad fruit." (Matthew 7:15-17)

As for the wine jars—which could also serve as water jars—some of them have the same form as the water jar depicted in the ascending passage. (Compare, for instance, the jar tagged with the number 340 which can be seen in the photograph of selected items from the annex on page 161 of *Treasures of Tutankhamun*, edited by Katharine Stoddert Gilbert, Joan K. Holt and Sara Hudson, to the illustration of the water jar found on page 968 of Rutherford's *Pyramidology*, Book III.)

The "alabaster vessels containing oils and unguents [which are ointments]" have a parallel in the Gospel of Mark:

> being in Bethany at the house of Simon the leper, as He [Christ] sat at the table [the Greek word actually means to recline], a woman came having an alabaster flask of very costly oil of spikenard [an ointment]. Then she broke the flask and poured it on His head.
>
> But there were some who were indignant among themselves, and said, "Why was this fragrant oil wasted?
>
> "For it might have been sold for more than three hundred denarii and given to the poor." (14:3-5)

Christ rebukes those criticizing the woman and tells them, "She has come. . . to anoint My body for burial" (14:8).

The annex was prepared to appear as if everything in it had been piled either in haste or because the objects were regarded as having no special importance. When we recall that the annex is the farthest room away from the mummified body, and that its floor is nearly 41 inches lower than either the tomb's antechamber or the burial chamber—thus inviting a comparison with the entrance to the dead-end passage which is nearly 41 inches lower than the entrance to the subterranean chamber—we can see that the idea Enoch meant to convey was that the man buried in this tomb, like most people today, had little use for what was truly valuable; spiritual matters usually receive the least attention. As Carol Neiman and Emily Goldman recognize in *Afterlife: The Complete Guide to Life after Death*, our "secular culture. . . emphasizes material success and accumulation" (177).

This is an apt description of the figure still entombed in the Valley of the Kings. He was an evil man who was ruled by greed and who rejected all attempts to teach him about Christ. His identity—and he was not a boy-king, although he was a high ranking officer in the administration of the pharaoh who ruled Egypt in his day—will be revealed at another time.

* * *

Returning now to the business of the undressed granite and the other imperfect features in the King's antechamber, it was left that way because the antechamber, along with representing the veil in the House of the Lord, also represents Christ's tomb. Compare, for example, the fact that when Peter and John went to the tomb on the morning of the resurrection they had to stoop in order to peer inside (John 20:4-6) with the fact that, likewise, it is necessary to stoop in order to enter the King's antechamber.

The antechamber is also linked to Christ's having been "lifted up":

> "And as Moses lifted up the serpent in the wilderness [to save those who were being bitten by fiery serpents (see Numbers 21:6-9)], even so must the Son of Man be lifted up, that whoever believes in Him should not perish but have eternal life." (John 3:14-15)

The Granite Leaf represents Christ being lifted up as described, and that is another reason for its being composed of 2 stones, the 2 symbolizing the 2nd member of the Godhead.

Here is yet one more reason for the King's antechamber exhibiting imperfection. In the House of the Lord, as in the tabernacle built by Moses and in the temple built by Solomon, the veil is in the terrestrial room, which is the same as the holy place, and since the terrestrial kingdom is imperfect, so too is the antechamber.

Now back to the boss or seal and its additional symbolism.

Piazzi Smyth receives credit for realizing that the thickness of the seal "is 1-5th of its breadth" (206). In like manner, in Solomon's Temple "the lintel and door posts [for the most holy place] were one-fifth of the wall" (1 Kings 6:31).

The top part of the upper stone of the Granite Leaf is rounded off instead of being squared. Why was it shaped that way? To resemble a man's shoulders. The seal, in addition to representing Christ, also represents the human heart. The seal, we are told, is one inch to the west of the Granite Leaf's vertical center, which would be on the left side of the chest; similarly, the human heart is off-center and to the left. When a physician uses a stethoscope to check a patient's heartbeat, does he place the bell of the stethoscope in the center of the chest? No, he places it to the left of the patient's sternum and at the apex of the heart.

The veil, as represented by the one-inch rebates, is open, thus revealing the "Lord". This illustrates a statement made by Christ that is recorded in the *Doctrine and Covenants*:

> inasmuch as my people build a house unto me in the name of the Lord, and do not suffer any unclean thing to come into it, that it be not defiled, my glory shall rest upon it;
>
> . . . [A]nd my presence shall be there, for I will come into it, and all the pure in heart that shall come into it shall see God. (98:15-16)

The Granite Leaf is meant to be connected with the Great Step and its symbolic altar, which in turn is related to the altar in the tabernacle, for, as directed by the Lord, that altar was placed

> "before the veil that is before the ark of the Testimony, before the mercy seat that is over the Testimony, where I will meet with you." (Exodus 30:6)

In the temples of the Church of Jesus Christ of Latter-day Saints there is a similar altar before the veil. In addition, in the tabernacle the veil concealed the Holy of Holies, "which represented the visible presence of God in all His power and holiness" (Lockyer, Sr., *Nelson's Illustrated Bible Dictionary* 486). In today's temples, the veil conceals the celestial room, which represents the dwelling place of God.

To draw one more interesting parallel between the present and the past, Lewis Spence reports that in ancient Egypt, the priest who was on duty

> washed himself and proceeded to the Holy of Holies, where he repeated certain formulae, accompanying them by prescribed gestures, preparatory to breaking the seal which closed the sanctuary. [At that point he would be] face to face with the god [of the temple]. (53)

* * *

The granite floor begins, as we have learned, with an increase of ¼ inch over the limestone section. This increase occurs at the point where the feet of a temple patron would be as he or she stood at the veil as represented by the Granite Leaf; also at that point the feet of the high priest representing the Lord would be directly in front of those of the patron, who is poised to make the transition from the temporal world into the eternal world of the Lord. That is why the floor and the walls of the antechamber change from limestone to granite, the granite signifying, as Rutherford has stated, the presence of the divine.

Corroborating this understanding of the rise in the floor are the references in the Bible to the number ¼. In Exodus 29:40, Leviticus 23:13, Numbers 15:4, as well as Numbers 28:5, 7 and 14, ¼ is linked to various sacrificial offerings to the Lord; going to the temple for oneself or for the dead is a sacrificial offering (one of the sacrifices being the honest payment of tithing), but the reward is fellowship with the Lord.

Lemesurier points out that the "east wall and [the] granite floor [of the antechamber] mark out between them a square. . . of. . . 5 Royal Cubits" (119).

Tompkins reveals that

> Petrie also noted that the squares of the dimensions of the King's Chamber, Queen's Chamber, antechamber and subterranean chamber were all even numbers of cubits,

> nearly all multiples of ten [see page 94 of *The Pyramids and Temples of Gizeh*]. From this it followed that the squares of the diagonals were likewise multiples of 10 square cubits. And the King's and Queen's Chambers were so arranged that the cubic diagonals were in even hundreds of square cubits, or multiples of 10 square cubits. (103)

In the chapter titled "Temple of Secret Initiation", Tompkins reviews Tons Brunes' book *The Secrets of Ancient Geometry*, which ties in with the above information.

> Brunes says that Moses, who was also an Egyptian priest, had knowledge of the ancient [Egyptian] geometry, which he passed hermetically in his instructions for building the Tabernacle, data which eventually reached Jerusalem and were incorporated into holy teaching.

Tompkins goes on to say that the

> French archeologist and mathematician Charles Funk-Hellet, in his *La Bible et la Grande Pyramide d'Egypte* [*The Bible and the Great Pyramid of Egypt*], agrees that the cubit of the Bible can only be the Egyptian royal cubit. (262-63)

The biblical cubit meant in this instance is not the common cubit but rather the long cubit of about 21 inches (see Ezekiel 43:13 and accompanying notes in the New International Version of the Bible). Rutherford, who lists Enoch as the first to use the cubit, argues that the

> entire geometric design of the Great Pyramid is built upon the Enoch Circle—its circumference, diameter and radius, which are respectively 365.242, 116.26 and 58.13 geometric or Pyramid inches. So by geometric

> symbolism the representation of Enoch is stamped on the entire Pyramid from top to bottom, inside and outside. (Book I, 83)

To carry this discussion a little farther, the temple seen in vision by Ezekiel likewise includes Petrie's "even numbers of cubits, nearly all multiples of ten. . . and in even hundreds of square cubits, or multiples of 10 square cubits." Some of the figures for this temple have already been cited, but here are a few more that are applicable:

> And he [the celestial being in bronze] measured the court, one hundred cubits long and one hundred cubits wide, foursquare. (40:47)
>
> . . . [H]e measured the temple, one hundred cubits long; and the separating courtyard with the building and its walls was one hundred cubits long; also the width of the eastern face of the temple, including the separating courtyard, was one hundred cubits. (41:13-14)
>
> Now when he had finished measuring the inner temple, he brought me out through the gateway that faces toward the east, and measured it all around. . . . He measured it on the four sides; it had a wall all around, five hundred cubits long and five hundred cubits wide, to separate the holy areas from the common. (42:15 and 20)

By now there should be no doubts concerning the similarities between certain parts of the Great Pyramid and the Temple of Ezekiel, as well as the Temple of Solomon and the tabernacle.

And with that, it is time to explain the real purpose behind the grooves in the east and west walls of the antechamber. The key to that purpose is found in this declaration by Christ, which is recorded in the *Doctrine and Covenants*:

> if a man marry a wife by my word, which is my law, and by the new and everlasting covenant, and it is sealed unto them by the Holy Spirit of promise, by him who is anointed, unto whom I have appointed this power and the keys of this priesthood; and it shall be said unto them—Ye shall come forth in the first resurrection. . . and shall inherit thrones, kingdoms, principalities, and powers, dominions, all heights and depths. . . and if ye abide in my covenant and commit no murder whereby to shed innocent blood, it shall be done unto them in all things whatsoever my servant hath put upon them, in time, and through all eternity; and shall be of full force when they are out of the world; and they shall pass by *the angels, and the gods, which are set there*, to their exaltation and glory in all things, as hath been sealed upon their heads, which glory shall be a fulness and a continuation of seeds [meaning children] forever and ever. (132:19; italics added)

The grooves on the east wall, which have a flat ledge at the top—which ledge is lower than the semicircular hollows on the west wall—represent 3 angels; in particular, they represent the 3 angels who form the presidency of the lowest of the 3 heavens in the celestial kingdom.

The grooves on the west wall represent 3 gods; in particular, they represent the presidency of the middle heaven in the celestial kingdom. The fact that the west wall represents gods instead of angels is confirmed by the "semi-hollows". Their design can be compared to the ecclesiastical throne from the tomb of Tutankhamen (see the photo of the throne on page 52 of Christiane Desroches-Noblecourt's *Tutankhamen*; as an interesting side note, duplicates of the curved stools that were stored in the tomb of Tutankhamen can be found in the brides' rooms of the temples built by the Church of Jesus Christ of Latter-day Saints).

The 3 granite blocks that comprise the ceiling represent the godhead that rules the 3rd heaven, that is, the celestial kingdom. This godhead consists of the Father of our spirits, his son Jesus Christ, and the Holy

Spirit. The gods of the middle heaven and the angels of the lowest heaven serve under these 3 in a descending order of authority. In addition, the angels and the gods represented by the grooves in the east and west walls are single individuals and therefore are not on the same level as those married couples who qualify to become equal with Christ and the Father, and that is why the grooves descend below the floor of the antechamber by 3 inches.

While the angels and the gods who are single are members of the celestial kingdom, their glory cannot increase like that of married couples because they cannot have children.

"Wait one minute!" some reader is likely to exclaim, objecting to what has just been said. "Jesus told the Sadducees that people aren't married in heaven. They're all single, like the angels."

The reference in this objection is to a passage in the Gospel of Matthew:

> the Sadducees, who say there is no resurrection, came to Him and asked Him, saying: "Teacher, Moses said that if a man dies, having no children, his brother shall marry his wife and raise up offspring for his brother.
>
> "Now there were with us seven brothers. The first died after he had married, and having no offspring, left his wife to his brother.
>
> "Likewise, the second also, and the third, even to the seventh.
>
> "Last of all the woman died also.
>
> "Therefore, in the resurrection, whose wife of the seven will she be? For they all had her."
>
> Jesus answered and said to them, "You are mistaken, not knowing the Scriptures, nor the power of God.
>
> "For in the resurrection they neither marry nor

> are given in marriage, but are like angels of God in heaven.
>
> "But concerning the resurrection of the dead, have you not read what was spoken to you by God, saying,
>
> 'I am the God of Abraham, the God of Isaac, and the God of Jacob'? God is not the God of the dead, but of the living." (22:23-32)

On the surface, it does appear that Jesus is saying no one will be married in heaven, but let's not be too hasty. Instead, let's examine some of the key elements in this passage to find out exactly what is being said by both the Sadducees and by Jesus.

In his discussion of these verses, Dummelow, picking up on the fact that the Sadducees did not believe in the resurrection, realizes that they "sought to bring Jesus into contempt and ridicule with the multitude by asking Him a question which they thought He could not answer" (697).

Exactly. Since the Sadducees had no belief in the resurrection, they obviously had no real interest in learning whether or not they could be married in heaven. Jesus was no one of importance to them; they were simply out to have fun at his expense.

Something is to be learned, however, from the first part of their question, and that is the reference to the injuction by Moses "that if a man dies, having no children, his brother shall marry his wife and raise up offspring for his brother." If the dead brother would not be married after he was resurrected then what was the point in the second brother fathering children for him?

On the other hand, if Moses understood that the dead brother could, if he was sealed to his wife by the power of the priesthood, continue to be married in eternity, then the injunction to have children on his behalf would make sense, for then it would be possible for him to have a family once his wife and children were also resurrected.

Then too, if Jesus had not been teaching the possibility of being married in heaven, why did the Sadducees take that particular approach in their attempt to ridicule him? In fact, Jesus had already said, "a man shall. . . be joined to his wife, and the two shall become one flesh". And he had said, "So then, they are no longer two but one flesh [figuratively, of course, not literally]. Therefore what God has joined together, let not man separate" (Matthew 19:5-6).

On this subject, Dummelow points out that in the time of Jesus most of the Jews who were not Sadducees were

> inclined to a materialistic view of the resurrection. The pre-Christian book of Enoch says that the righteous after the resurrection shall live so long that they shall beget thousands. . . . The point raised by the Sadducees was often debated by the Jewish doctors [of theology], who decided that "a woman who married two husbands in this world is restored to the first in the next." (698)

Why didn't Jesus inform the Sadducees of the possibility of eternal marriage? He chose not to cast his "pearls before the swine". The Sadducees were not teachable. Like many people today, they thought they had things figured out, so why should they listen to an opposing point of view?

But the Savior's comments to the Sadducees do hold true. For them, for the unbelievers, there will be no marriage in heaven. But does that mean no one, including the apostles, will be married after the resurrection? We know that Peter was married. Did he have to give up his wife when he died? What if he had used the sealing power Christ had given him to bind his wife to him? Would Christ have decided not to honor the act? No, Christ himself probably sealed Peter to his wife, as well as to his children and to his mother and father.

We should remember that how Christ responded to a question depended on who was doing the asking. What he taught the people in general was not always the same as what he taught the apostles. The apostles were privy to instruction that was not given to the multitudes that followed Jesus wherever he went. The proof of this is in his use of parables, which he explained to the apostles and other disciples who believed in him, but not to everyone else.

The concept that men and women can become gods and goddesses by living righteously, and by observing their temple covenants, needs to be discussed at length since there will be many who will have never considered such a possibility, or who, on the other hand, may be familiar with the concept but have rejected it because their priest or pastor or minister or some other influential person has convinced them it is a false belief.

In the exchange between Jesus and a group that wanted to end his life—which is quoted at the beginning of this chapter—Jesus asks a question that can be found in the 82nd Psalm. That psalm begins: "God stands in the congregation of the mighty;/He judges among the gods." That declaration is followed by a plea to God to

> Defend the poor and fatherless;
>
> Do justice to the afflicted and needy;
>
> Deliver the poor and needy;
>
> Free them from the hand of the wicked.
>
> (Verses 2-4)

Two lines later we read: "I said, 'You are gods'".

That statement is followed by this one: "And all of you are children of the Most High" (verse 6).

"Most High" is one of the many titles for God the Father (Lockyer, Sr., *Nelson's Illustrated Bible Dictionary* 730). The concept that we are all "children of the Most High" was taught by Christ. For example, after his resurrection, when Mary Magdalene—the first person to see him after he left the tomb, according to the Gospel of John—started to touch him, he said,

> Touch me not; for I am not yet ascended to my Father:

> but go to my brethren, and say unto them, I ascend unto my Father, and your Father; and to my God, and your God. (KJV, John 20:17)

Dummelow, whose insight into the Bible is usually reliable, is unfortunately misleading in his interpretation of the 82nd Psalm. He claims that this particular Psalm "is an impeachment of unjust judges, who are officially called 'gods.'" To support his claim he refers us to the passage quoted at the beginning of this chapter (362). But what is there in either the Psalm or in Christ's response to his enemies that points specifically to earthly judges? There is, quite simply, nothing. Neither the psalmist nor Christ was talking about earthly judges.

This assessment is in keeping with a passage in *The Book of Enoch the Prophet* as translated by Richard Laurence:

> The earth deprived of her children [because of bloodshed and iniquity] has cried even to the gate of heaven.
>
> And now. . . the souls of men complain, saying [to Michael, Gabriel, and other angels], Obtain Justice for us with the Most High. Then they [the angels] said to their Lord, the King, Thou art Lord of lords, *God of gods*, King of kings. . . .
>
> What on account of these things ought we to do to them? (IX:2-3 and 14; italics added)

Like the quote from Christ and from the 82nd Psalm, this one from *The Book of Enoch the Prophet* makes no mention of earthly judges. The word "gods" means a plurality of gods.

That there are more gods than our Father—and, more importantly, that we can become like him—gains credence from this statement in the Epistle of Paul the Apostle to the Romans:

> The Spirit Himself bears witness with our spirit that we are children of God, and if children, then heirs—heirs

> of God and joint heirs with Christ, if indeed we suffer with Him, that we may also be glorified together. (8:16-17)

The term "joint heirs" means sharing equally in the inheritance.

Now consider also Paul's Epistle to the Philippians:

> Let this mind be in you which was also in Christ Jesus, who, being in the form of God, did not consider it robbery to be equal with God. (2:5-6)

In this letter to members of the church in Philippi, which was in Macedonia, Paul obviously had no qualms about urging his fellow saints to seek the highest goal possible—godhood—but so there would be no misunderstanding, Paul, in his first letter to the Corinthians, explained that even though "there are many gods and many lords. . . for us, there is but one God, the Father. . . and one Lord Jesus Christ" (8:5-6), and that is why we pray to the Father in the name of his firstborn son.

To carry this argument a little farther, in the beginning of Genesis the word *Elohim*, which is translated as "God", is actually "plural in form" (Dummelow 4). In addition, in Chapter 1 verse 6, we read: "Then God said, 'Let Us make man in Our image, according to Our likeness'".

Who was God talking to? Dummelow suggests the possibility of "a council of angelic beings, or the form of the word may indicate a plural of majesty" (5). But why not make sense of the statement—and of the similar use of "Us" in Genesis 3:22, 11:7, and Isaiah 6:8—by accepting the obvious inference: God the Father was talking to Christ, our elder brother, who, acting under the Father's direction, created this earth (see John 1:1-14 and Ephesians 3:9).

For some reason, many people who call themselves Christians and who are students of the Bible seem to be unable to understand such straightforward declarations as our being in the image of God. The tendency is to claim that what is meant is the *spiritual* image of God, but the word *spiritual* is not in the quoted passage.

Christ had no problem accepting the literalness of the statement in Genesis, as is evident in this encounter with Philip, who was one of the apostles:

> "If you had known Me, you would have known My Father also; and from now on you know Him and have seen Him."
>
> Philip said to Him, "Lord, show us the Father, and it is sufficient for us."
>
> Jesus said to him, "Have I been with you so long, and yet you have not known me, Philip? He who has seen Me has seen the Father; so how can you say, 'Show us the Father'?" (John 14:7-9)

No, Jesus was not saying he was the Father; he was saying he looked like the Father. He was in the image of the Father—and so are we. His remark to Mary Magdalene and the statements by the psalmist and by Paul mean that we are the literal spirit children of our Father in Heaven.

Confusion seems to arise frequently from Christ's saying, "my Father and I are one". What did he mean by "one"? In the 17th chapter of John, Christ prays for his disciples: "Holy Father, keep through Your name those whom You have given Me, that they may be one as We are" (verse 11). Was Christ praying that his disciples would become one entity, one being? Were he and the Father one entity, one being? No, of course not. Christ was praying that the disciples would be one in purpose, that they would have the same desire to bring to pass the "immortality and eternal life of man" as he and the Father had.

Joseph Smith, breaking with the ministers of his day, boldly asserted,

> I have always declared God to be a distinct personage, Jesus Christ a separate and distinct personage from God the Father, and that the Holy Ghost was a distinct

> personage and a spirit: and these three constitute three distinct personages and three Gods.
>
> . . . [T]he doctrine of a plurality of Gods is as prominent in the Bible as any other doctrine. It is all over the face of the Bible. (Joseph Fielding Smith, *Scriptural Teachings of the Prophet Joseph Smith* 417-18)

Incidentally, Petrie's statement that in the King's antechamber "many parts are strangely rough" is reminiscent of Joseph Smith's description of himself:

> I am like a huge, *rough stone* rolling down from a high mountain; and the only polishing I get is when some corner gets rubbed off by coming in contact with something else, striking with accelerated force against religious bigotry, priestcraft, lawyercraft. . . all hell knocking off a corner here and a corner there. Thus I will become a smooth and polished shaft in the quiver of the Almighty. . . while these smooth-polished stones with which I come in contact become marred. (Joseph Fielding Smith, *Scriptural Teachings of the Prophet Joseph Smith* 339; italics added)

* * *

Continuing with the discussion concerning the plurality of gods, the ancient Egyptians took a view compatible with that of the Bible and of Joseph Smith. As Werner Forman and Stephen Quirke point out in *Hieroglyphs & the Afterlife*, Egyptian funerary texts are meant "to transfigure the dead, to make human beings into immortal gods" (7).

Similarly, William Kingsland affirms that the "ultimate goal of initiation [for the Egyptians] was 'the full realization of the essential *divine nature of man*, the recovery by the individual of the full knowledge and powers of his divine spiritual nature'" (quoted in Tompkins 284).

Colin Wilson speaks along the same lines when he notes that "for the Egyptians, the stars were not merely seasonal indicators. They were also the home of the gods who presided over life and death" (79).

Nicholas Reeves and Richard H. Wilkinson, co-authors of *The Complete Valley of the Kings*, observe that

> the deceased king was not simply assimilated into the line of his predecessors; he joined them into becoming one with Osiris and Re—an aspect, as it were, of these pre-eminent gods. At an even more abstract level, the king was believed to become one with the heavens and the earth—with the cosmos itself—while maintaining his own individuality as a distinct god. (47)

And Dimitri Meeks and Christine Favard-Meeks write in *Daily Life of the Egyptian Gods*: "some gods could eventually become 'more divine' than others" (37)

Despite the Egyptians' apostasy from the Lord's teachings as introduced by Enoch and his people, enough of the truth remains to see where the Egyptians' religious beliefs sprang from. This is especially true when we look at their attitude toward marriage and the family. According to Rosalie David, the "Egyptians appear to have been devoted to their families and to have loved their children." She also notes that "after death, the wife could expect the same eternal life as her husband" (*Handbook to Life in Ancient Egypt* 321).

At this point we might observe that the Hebrew word rendered as *Elohim* is not only plural but the ending is also feminine, not masculine, and so *Elohim* incorporates both gods and goddesses.

Lionel Casson in *Ancient Egypt* finds that the

> walls of many tombs depict the life the ancient Egyptians hoped to lead in the hereafter, and it was an extension of the life they led on earth. The wealthy are shown boating on the Nile, fowling in the marshes, picnicking with their families. (35)

In *People of the Pharaohs* Hilary Wilson begins the 3rd chapter this way:

> The ancient Egyptian civilization supported one of the most humane societies of all time, a society based on the family unit and the institution of legal marriage which was considered to have been ordained and sanctified by Osiris. (52)

Three pages later she writes, "children were to be cherished. . . . Children were a man's insurance for the afterlife" (55). And in *Understanding Hieroglyphs*, another book by Hilary Wilson, she adds that in

> ancient Egypt it was thought that the only proper way for people or gods to exist was within a family group. Each temple was seen as the home of a triad of deities, representing the unit family of husband, wife and child. (84)

In the same vein, Arthur Wallace states that in King "Sety's temple at Abydos, Ramses II had portraits of his children sculptured onto the temple walls so that they would be an eternal family" (30).

The granite floor in the antechamber's midsection measures 103 inches long because when Jacob was 103 years old his 12th son Benjamin was born and that made his family complete (see "The Testament of Benjamin", Chapter I verse 4, where Benjamin says he was born 12 years after Joseph, and since Jacob was 91 when Joseph was born, 91 + 12 = 103, Jacob's age at Benjamin's birth).

And the granite walls begin 75 inches into the antechamber because Abraham was 75 when he left Egypt to return to the land of Canaan (Genesis 16:3 and 16), the land promised to his descendants, and it was there that Isaac was born.

To explain why the granite walls begin 10 inches deeper into the antechamber than the granite floor, we first combine the 28-foot height of the Grand Gallery with the 11-foot-5-inch height of the antechamber's south wall, which gives a sum of 39 feet 5 inches. Joseph was 39 when he was finally reunited with his father and brothers. That reunion came about because the year before, Joseph's 10 older brothers had come to Egypt to buy grain during the first year of the 7-year famine. Furthermore, when Benjamin first came to Egypt with his brothers, Joseph had all 11 of them join him in order to "eat bread", but "Benjamin's serving was five times as much as" what the other 10 brothers received (Genesis 43:25 and 34).

As we continue to focus on Joseph a little longer, we're going to see that symbols can have multiple meanings, for this Christ-like figure is also represented by:

- the 7-inch increase in the antechamber's width, for it symbolizes the 7 years of abundance;
- the 9-inch increase in height of the west wainscot over the east wainscot, for Joseph was in his 9th year of ruling Egypt when his father and brothers moved there permanently—and they came from the east to the west;
- the 11-foot-5-inch height at which the 12-inch section of limestone begins on the south wall, for Joseph was Jacob's 11th son, and after his brothers moved to Egypt Joseph took 5 of them to meet the pharaoh (Genesis 47:2);
- the 13-inch section of limestone flooring that separates the end of the first low passage and the beginning of the granite flooring, for Joseph had been in Egypt for 13 years when he became the pharaoh's joint-ruler;
- the 14 feet (168 inches) from the beginning of the first low passage to the south wall (Petrie 26), for they represent the 14 years of the pharaoh's dream as interpreted by Joseph;
- the 17-inch width of the grooves that the Granite Leaf is cemented to;
- the 17-inch semicircular hollows in the west wall, and the total length of the granite floor, which is 17 feet (204 inches), for they represent Joseph's rule of Egypt while he

enjoyed the company of his father for the last 17 years of his life (Genesis 47:28);

- the 21-inch wide grooves in the east and west walls, for Joseph had been in Egypt for 21 years when his brothers came looking for grain;
- the 23 inches from the end of the first low passage to the beginning of the granite walls, for Joseph was the 23rd patriarch;
- the 23-inch height of the Granite Leaf's top stone, for the same reason; and
- the 37 inches from the top of the west wainscot to the ceiling, for Joseph was 37 at the culmination of the 7 years of abundant crops and herds.

Now, if we take another look at the height of the first low passage into the midsection of the antechamber, we can understand why it was set at 44 inches. Joseph was 44 when the famine ended; he and his family had survived, because like the 5 wise virgins of Christ's parable, they had prepared ahead of time so that when the moment of crisis came they were ready.

* * *

Regarding the use of both limestone and granite in the antechamber, Rutherford contends that the combination of the two kinds of stone was necessary "for symbolic reasons. In the Great Pyramid, chronology is portrayed in limestone only, never in granite" (Book III, 997). He equates the 65 inches of limestone flooring with 65 years And those 65 years result in the year 1979, the same date he assigns to the Queen's Chamber, the date supposedly for "the beginning of the Millennium" (Book I, 164). However, it is only the flooring that Rutherford considers; the 12 inches of limestone that run across the top of the south wall are bypassed entirely.

Lemesurier makes a stab at explaining the reason for this isolated level of limestone by including it in his conjecture that

> the reincarnating enlightened ones will set out on the final spiritual path of ultimate reward, which will eventually result in the raising of the physical initiates to utter spiritual perfection through the catalysing experience of the earthly Millennium. (119)

His conjecture has no validity. The limestone at the top of the south wall of the antechamber represents a poorer level of performance in comparison to those who have been endowed, sealed to their spouses, their children and their parents, and have remained faithful. But it is also a warning that if the covenants made in the House of the Lord are not honored the promised blessings may be withdrawn.

There is more to be said about the limestone on the south wall, but further discussion will delayed until the shafts in the King's Chamber are examined in detail.

Like the 18-foot-long passage to the Queen's Chamber, the 2nd low passage that leads to the King's Chamber represents paradise, but that part of paradise that is on a higher spiritual plane. Paradise, it must be understood, is not the same as heaven. Paradise, *The Revell Bible Dictionary* informs us, is a "loan word from the Persian, which originally meant 'park' or 'enclosed garden'. . . . In first-century Judaism, [paradise referred to] the location of the righteous dead" (Lawrence O. Richards 756).

Paradise is where Christ and the repentant thief on the cross went upon their deaths. In marked contrast to the spirit prison, paradise is a beautiful realm of lakes and rivers, trees and fields of grass and brightly colored flowers, and cities with magnificent buildings and large parks. Many near-death experiencers have described such scenes and have resisted leaving them to return to their bodies, as in this case of a 9-year-old girl who developed a fever of 106 degrees or higher and suddenly found herself free of her physical body and moving through a tunnel, at the end of which

> "was a lovely vista spread out before me. There were all fields with flowers and there was a nice road over on my

right and the trees were painted white halfway up and there was a white fence. It was lovely.

"And there were the most gorgeous horses I had ever seen in the pasture off to the right. I would have to cross two fences to get to these horses but since I was nine years old there was no doubt where I was going.

"I started off that way and after a little while there was a white kind of light, a presence beside me that was friendly and not at all threatening. The presence said: 'Where are you going?' And I said: 'I'm going over there.' And he said: 'That's great. We'll come along.'

"There were a lot of flowers I had never seen before and I was asking him their names and picking them as we went along. . . .

"I had just gotten my leg over the top rail of the fence and into the horse pasture when this voice out of nowhere said: 'What is she doing here?' And the light answered: 'She came to have the horses.' And the voice said: 'It's not right. It's not her time. She has to go back.'

"At this point I was clutching the rail because I didn't want to go back. That was the last thing I wanted to do. . . . So I threw a tantrum. I pitched a royal fit. I grabbed on to the rail of the fence and wrapped my arms and legs around it and I wouldn't let go. The voice just laughed. 'Look, you can have it later, but this is not the time. And throwing a tantrum is not going to do you any good.'

"I found myself floating over the field and going back down into the tunnel. . . and I popped back into

> my body." (Quoted in Morse and Perry, *Transformed by the Light* 54-55)

In this brief account it is interesting to note the symbolism that is consistent with that of the Great Pyramid. Which direction was the road that led to the horses? It was to the right. And where was the pasture in relation to the road? It was to the right. The right symbolizes movement toward God and toward genuine happiness that is found in loving God's creatures.

And the trees? They were painted white halfway up. That is reminiscent of the 6-inch-wide groove that divides the Grand Gallery's walls at the halfway point. And there was a white fence that is reminiscent of the Gallery's white walls.

How many fences did the 9-year-old have to cross to get to the horses? Two. The number 2 is prominent in the Gallery. There were also unfamiliar flowers along the way, just as there are unfamiliar (at least to most people) holes and inset stones along the ramps of the Gallery.

Some people who have a near-death experience are able to recognize that symbolism is involved in what they are permitted to see. For instance, Renee Zamora, whose NDE is presented in Arvin S. Gibson's *Echoes from Eternity*, realized that seeing the same groups of people after several visits to a park "had symbolic meaning beyond the outward appearances of the events themselves" (214). And in the same book, a woman named Mary was visited by her dead sister, who was wearing "a brown dress with a white collar. Her dress. . . seemed to symbolize scholarship" (186).

The use of symbolism in near-death experiences should not be surprising since such experiences bring into play the Lord's servants who are working on the other side, and those servants belong to the same church as Enoch and his people.

But what else do we know about paradise? One thing is certain: while music is often heard by those who are granted a glimpse of that realm, there are not a lot of spirits passing time playing harps. Undoubtedly, the most important activity in paradise is teaching and learning. The experience of James A. LeSueur, as told in *The Journey*

Beyond Life by Michele R. Sorensen and Dr. David R. Willmore, is instructive in this matter.

James relates how his spirit left his body one evening and he was met by a personage who identified himself as James' guardian angel. The angel, says James, conducted him to

> a large city which I knew to be a city where the spirits of those who had passed away were detained while awaiting. . . the resurrection. . . . We passed through the streets. . . and then came before a four-story building which covered an entire block.

Entering the building, James saw an audience of "about ten thousand" spirits.

> There was a look of expectancy upon their faces as though they were awaiting something to begin. . . . Presently, I heard a person begin speaking and I looked toward the speaker and listened to a sermon on the first principles of the gospel [which include faith in Christ and repentance]. The speaker explained the principles just as I had heard missionaries [of the Church of Jesus Christ of Latter-day Saints] present them, excepting baptism, which he said was an earthly covenant that should be attended to while in mortality. However, inasmuch as they had died without being baptized, the ordinance could be attended to for them by proxy, someone living in mortality could take their name and act for them. He explained that there were temples erected upon the earth where kinsmen and friends were being baptized vicariously for the dead; and that if they accepted the baptism and confirmation that was done for them, it would be as valid as if they had attended to it in person while in mortality.

> When this speaker had finished he turned around and looked up at me, and I saw that it was my brother, Frank [who had died at about the age of 20]. He looked supremely happy and I felt that I would be willing to go through any sacrifice if I could live to be worthy of such happiness. Then he bowed and smiled at me so joyously that a wonderful thrill passed through me. I shall never forget it.

James' account could satisfactorily end here, but it does not. He has something else extremely important to report.

> A young lady was standing beside him [James' brother]. . . . She bowed and smiled at me in recognition of my visit, and I looked at her very carefully, wondering who she was. The angel said,
>
> "The young lady standing by and assisting your brother is to be his wife." (150-52)

Just as relationships are formed in mortality, so too are they formed in paradise. And young people who die will be given the opportunity to obtain every blessing they may have missed out on as a result of not living a full life. This is one of the main reasons why this interim state exists. There would be no justice on the Lord's part if, as is taught by many Christians, we died and immediately received a final judgment.

Erwin W. Lutzer's 1997 publication titled *One Minute After You Die* is representative of what many believe regarding the afterlife. This book begins:

> One minute after you slip behind the parted curtain, you will either be enjoying a personal welcome from Christ or catching your first glimpse of gloom as you have never known it. Either way, your future will be irrevocably fixed and eternally unchangeable. (11)

Fortunately, Lutzer's point of view is based on speculation, not on fact. Instead of what he claims, a preliminary judgment is made when we die and we are then assigned a place in the spirit world where, if we choose, we can continue to progress (Crowther, *Life Everlasting* 86-87).

One of the obvious differences between paradise and the spirit prison is the peace and love that pervade paradise. Nearly everyone who has had an NDE that included contact with this part of the spirit world has remarked on how powerful both elements were. But also prevalent is the sense of purpose that exists in paradise. In addition to missionary work, there are many engaged in genealogical research (Crowther 78-79 and 101). The results of that research will be made available during the millennium when vicarious work for the dead will be stepped up in the Lord's temples and there will be contact between the people here in mortality and the people in the spirit world.

* * *

Before closing out this discussion of the 2nd low passage in the antechamber, 2 more points need to be made. One is the length of the passage, which is 101 inches; 101 inches equal 8.42 feet. Compare this 8 feet to the 29 feet of the subterranean horizontal passage that represents the spirit prison. The difference is 21 feet. The number 21, as already noted, occurs in the King's antechamber in the width of the grooves on the east and west walls. Is there any significance in that figure besides what has been said in this chapter about the number 21? We will see.

The other point to be made about the 2nd low passage is the difference between its 8 feet and the last 18 feet of the horizontal passage to the Queen's Chamber, which represents that part of the spirit world where those living on a terrestrial level reside. This difference of 10 feet is the approximate length of the antechamber's midsection (both Lepre and Hancock round out that length to an even 10 feet; see Lepre 86 and Hancock 329). The message is, the people on the terrestrial level will be without the blessings of the temple.

But in addition, these comparisons emphasize the fact that the people in the higher spiritual plane of paradise will spend much less time in the spirit world than those living on the lower levels, and that means they are going to be resurrected much sooner than those who will inherit the terrestrial and telestial kingdoms.

The number 42 in the figure of 8.42 feet for the 2nd low passage, and its equivalent of 3½ when we're talking about months and years, occur elsewhere, for instance,

- the grooves in the south wall are 3½ inches wide;
- the 12-inch section of limestone at the top of the south wall begins at a height of 11.42 feet;
- the distance between the top of the Granite Leaf and the ceiling is 4.42 feet;
- the maximum height of the antechamber's midsection is 12.42 feet;
- the total length of the antechamber's floor is 22.42 feet.

The numbers 42 and 3½ pertain to Christ's sacrifice on the cross which made it possible to overcome death and to bring about the exaltation of the righteous.

We can see a similar meaning in the 2.8-inch depth of the 4 grooves on the south wall: 2 is for Christ, the 2nd member of the Godhead, and 8 is for the new beginning brought about by his resurrection.

* * *

Six numbers are repeated twice in the King's antechamber: 12, 52, 53, 65, 103 and 105. The significance of this repetition can be determined by applying Joseph's explanation as to why the pharaoh dreamed twice of the 7 fat cows and the 7 thin cows.

> "The dream was repeated to Pharaoh twice because the thing is established by God, and God will shortly bring it to pass." (Genesis 41:32)

We can be certain of the appropriateness of this comparison by remembering that Joseph had been in prison for 6 years when he was set free after correctly interpreting the pharaoh's dream.

More significance can be detected in the number 53 when we convert it to 4 feet 5 inches, for once again we have a connection with the well shaft's 4 sections and 5 directions. And more significance can be found in the number 105, for *The Book of Enoch the Prophet* has precisely 105 chapters, the last verse of which reads:

> to the faithful shall he [the Lord] give faith in the habitations of uprightness. . . . [T]he righteous shall be at rest. Sinners shall cry out, beholding them, while they exist in splendour and proceed forwards to the days and periods prescribed to them.

Another significant number not included in the above list is 153, which was included in the treatment of the Grand Gallery. The combined length of the 2 low passages is 153 inches (52 inches + 101 inches). The vertical distance from the Great Pyramid's pavement to the roof at the south end of the King's antechamber is 153 feet (Petrie 31). Counting from the granite floor of the antechamber to the "Pyramid's summit-platform" there are "153 courses of masonry" (Lemesurier 111). Moreover, course number 153 is 22 inches thick (Lemesurier, chart on page 377). With course number 153, then, we have a link with the total length of the antechamber's floor, which, as stated above, is 22.42 feet. Jacob was the 22nd patriarch, plus Joseph, after 22 years, was united once more with his father and brothers, just as the 153 fish caught by 7 of Christ's apostles were united in the net that brought them safely to shore.

* * *

There is still another point to be made about the 2nd low passage, and that is the rise of ¾ of an inch at the entrance to the King's Chamber. This ¾ of an inch has a parallel in the Grand Gallery, as does the ¼ inch at the beginning of the granite floor in the antechamber. It will be recalled that in the Gallery the grooves in the two walls appear "5¼ inches above the third overlap from the bottom" and they have "a mean depth of ¾ of an inch" (Rutherford, Book III, 975).

Add the ¾ and the ¼ and the result is one. This one is included in the thickness of the rebates on the vertical edges of the Granite Leaf, which rebates represent a link with the veil depicted on the south wall. One is also included in the seal's placement to the west of the Granite Leaf's vertical center, as well as in the thickness of the seal. What is the significance of the one?

The significance lies in husband and wife becoming one as a result of their being sealed for time and for all eternity. But one also represents Paul's declaration in his letter to the Ephesians, in which he urges the members of the church

> to keep the unity of the Spirit through the bond of peace. There is one body and one Spirit—just as you were called to one hope when you were called—one Lord, one faith, one baptism; one God and Father of all, who is over all and through all and in all. (NIV, 4:4-6)

The oneness of Christ and his disciples—male and female, past, present and future—is what is at work here. This oneness, this unity, will be evident in the King's Chamber as we will see shortly.

And finally, just as the height of the entrance passage to the antechamber is supposed to be added to the total height of the Grand Gallery, so too is the 2nd low passage, which provides one more sharp contrast between this passage and the 2 passages connected to the subterranean chamber and the Queen's Chamber.

Paradise offers, in addition to everything else that has been said so far, a wonderful sense of freedom that will carry over into the celestial kingdom for those who are worthy of that highest degree of glory.

14. HEAVENS

> Then little children were brought to Him that He might put His hands on them and pray, but the disciples rebuked them.
>
> But Jesus said, "Let the little children come to Me, and do not forbid them; for of such is the kingdom of heaven."
>
> (Matthew 19:13-14)

The heaven that Jesus was referring to in this quote is the celestial kingdom, and the celestial kingdom is represented by the King's Chamber, which is built entirely of "polished red granite blocks" (Toth and Nielsen 72). According to Hancock, an even 100 of these blocks make up the walls of the chamber (330; see Lemesurier, page 123, and Rutherford, Book III, page 1001 for the same figure).

The number 100 is significant, as is evident from its occurrence in other places both inside and outside the Great Pyramid. For instance, in addition to the 100-foot section of the well shaft, the subterranean chamber lies "about 100 feet below the ground level above it" (Rutherford, Book III, 1084); al-Mamun's men tunneled into the pyramid for 100 feet before hearing the prism stone drop; and Bill Schul and Ed Pettit mention that the exterior casing of the Great Pyramid measured 100 inches thick (26).

The number 100, as indicated in earlier chapters, is also significant in the Bible, and certain passages are directly related to the King's

Chamber. For example, in Genesis 21:5 we're told that "Abraham was one hundred years old when his son Isaac was born to him", and Isaac, after he had married, moved to Gerar because of famine in the land of Canaan. Gerar was in the Negev, the southern desert of Palestine (Lockyer, Sr., *Nelson's Illustrated Bible Dictionary* 415). While he was there, "Isaac sowed in that land, and reaped the same year a *hundredfold*; and the Lord blessed him" (Genesis 26:1 and 12; italics added).

Isaac became the father of Jacob, who in turn became the father of 12 sons whose descendants became the 12 tribes of Israel, and from one of those tribes—the tribe of Judah—came Christ. And Christ declared that "many will come from east and west, and sit down with Abraham, Isaac, and Jacob in the kingdom of heaven" (Matthew 8:11).

There is more. The verses in Matthew that pertain to the 100 sheep (18:12-13), which were cited in the chapter on the well shaft, also apply to the King's Chamber, as does the Parable of the Sower and its reference to people who receive the teachings of Christ and then produce thirty, sixty and a hundredfold (Mark 4:20).

Similarly, another verse in Matthew is appropriate:

> "And everyone who has left houses or brothers or sisters or father or mother or wife or children or lands, for My name's sake, shall receive a *hundredfold*, and inherit eternal life." (19:29; italics added)

It is possible to misunderstand what Christ is saying here; it is possible to think he is encouraging the breakup of families, which is the approach taken by Colleen McDannell and Bernard Lang, who write in *Heaven, A History*:

> Jesus and his followers Paul and John of Patmos completely remodelled the received versions of heaven [as favored in "Jewish or Hellenistic beliefs"]. Their new perspective on eternal life was shaped by two main ideas found throughout their teachings: the priority of orientation toward God with direct experience of the

> divine, and the rejection of ordinary society structured by kinship, marriage, and the concomitant family concerns. (44)

This is not what Christ intended. While he hung on the cross one of his last utterances revealed his concern for his mother's welfare:

> When Jesus. . . saw his mother, and the disciple whom He loved [who is the same John of Patmos named by McDannell and Lang]. . . He said to His mother, "Woman, behold your son!"
>
> Then He said to the disciple, "Behold your mother!" And from that hour that disciple took her to his own home. (John 19:26-27)

The compassion Christ had for family members is evident in his restoring the widow's son to life (Luke 7:11-15); raising the 12-year-old daughter of Jairus from her death bed (Mark 5: 22-24 and 35-42); the healing of the daughter of "a woman of Canaan" (Matthew 15:22-28); the healing of the nobleman's sick son (John 4:45-53); casting out the evil spirit from the lunatic son (Mark 9:14-27); healing Peter's mother-in-law (Matthew 8:14-15; and calling Lazarus from the tomb after he had been dead for 4 days (John 11:1-46), during which Christ wept for his friend and for the love that the sisters of Lazarus had for their brother.

Besides these incidents, Christ's emphasis on his being the son of God and on his eventual return to his Father, as well as his teaching us to pray to *our* Father in Heaven, combined with his declaration that little children will be in the kingdom of heaven, should be conclusive evidence of the importance he placed on family relationships, both in mortality and in eternity.

Contrary to the opinion of McDannell and Lang, Christ's goal is to save as many families intact as he can; however, the people who are taught by authorized missionaries and who receive a witness from the Holy Spirit that what they have been taught is true but then decline being baptized because of opposition from a parent or some other member of the family, will be denied the richest of blessings. On the other hand, those who receive the truth and, despite opposition from family members, enter the waters of baptism, will receive the hundredfold in blessings promised by Christ, so long as they remain faithful to the end of their mortal lives—and if they do remain faithful they will have the opportunity to unite other family members by going to the House of the Lord to participate in sealings in their behalf after they have entered the spirit world.

Another biblical reference that contains the number 100 has to be included here.

> Joseph of Arimathea, being a disciple of Jesus. . . asked Pilate that he might take away the body of Jesus; and Pilate gave him permission. So he came and took the body of Jesus.
>
> And Nicodemus. . . also came, bringing a mixture of myrrh and aloes, about a *hundred* pounds. (John 19:38-39; italics added)

Christ's presence is throughout the King's Chamber, and especially so in the sarcophagus, which will be discussed later in this chapter. But for now, we need to recall that the temple described in the Book of Ezekiel measures 100 cubits (41:13-15), and the temple is certainly applicable to the King's Chamber since the holy of holies corresponds to the King's Chamber.

At this point it should be mentioned that not everyone agrees with the count of 100 blocks in the chamber's walls. Lepre comes up with a count of 101 (92). Apparently he is including one special block in his figure, whereas Hancock is not. Lepre specifies that this block is different in that it comprises

> two, rather than one, courses of masonry. It is, by far, the largest of all the wall stones—and understandably so, as it is positioned directly over the entrance. (102)

Lepre believes it was put in that position in order to "support the stress bearing down on that particular aperture" (102). That, however, is not the real reason for this stone's taking up two courses instead of one. It represents the sealing of husbands and wives who then figuratively become one. In this respect, it is to be compared to the Granite Leaf with its dividing joint, for there is, in Petrie's words, "a remarkable diagonal drafted line across the immense block of granite over the doorway" (28).

Rutherford gives the dimensions of this huge stone as 94 inches high by 113 inches long (Book III, 1001). Joseph lived to be 110 years old (Genesis 50:26). If we start with 17, the age at which he was taken to Egypt, and count up to 110 we will find that he lived in Egypt for 94 years—a match for the height of the stone. The significance of the length can be determined by noting that course number 113 is one royal cubit thick (Lemesurier, chart on page 377). Furthermore, 113 can be expressed as 100 plus 13, and we know what those numbers mean.

Coming back to Lepre, he comments that

> this massive stone. . . contained the fundamental dimensions of the 3-4-5 or Pythagorean Triangle. (102)

He also observes that

> this 3-4-5 sequence is similarly manifested within the basic dimensions of the King's Chamber itself. For as the length of this chamber is 34'4", its width 17'2" and its height 19'1", so its short (east or west) wall diagonal is 25'9", and its long central diagonal (which cuts directly through the chamber obliquely) is 42'11". In simpler terms we have:
>
> 3 = 25'9" = 309"
> 4 = 34'4" = 412"
> 5 = 42'11" = 515"

> Thus, 309″ is to 412″ is to 515″ as 3 is to 4 is to 5. (102)

Previously, in the 19th century, Petrie had

> established to his satisfaction that the walls [of the King's Chamber] had been constructed on the basis of the [pi] proportion which ruled the exterior of the building. Its length was to the circuit of its side wall as 1 is to [pi].
>
> This value was not immediately evident, because the floor of the chamber had been inserted between the walls so as to cut off a fraction at the bottom. But the cut was cunning in that it thus incorporated in the chamber. . . the 3-4-5 Pythagorean triangles. (Tompkins 101-02).

As a result of such findings, Hancock writes:

> The huge room had an endless capacity to generate indications of mathematical game-playing. For example, its height (19 feet 1 inch) was exactly half of the length of its floor diagonal (38 feet 2 inches). Moreover, since the King's Chamber formed a perfect 1 x 2 rectangle, was it conceivable that the pyramid builders were unaware that they had also made it express and exemplify the "golden section"?
>
> Known as *phi*, the golden section was another irrational number like *pi* that could not be worked out arithmetically. [David Furlong puts it another way: pi, he says, "produces a string of decimal places that stretches to infinity with no apparent repetition" (77).] Its value was the square root of 5 plus 1 divided by 2, equivalent to 1.61803. This proved to be the "limiting value of the ratio between successive numbers beginning

> 0, 1, 1, 2, 3, 5, 8, 13—in which each term is the sum of the two previous terms."
>
> . . . This proportion, which had been proven particularly harmonious and agreeable to the eye, had supposedly been first discovered by the Pythagorean Greeks, who incorporated it into the Parthenon at Athens. There is absolutely no doubt, however, that *phi* was illustrated and obtained at least 2000 years previously in the King's Chamber of the Great Pyramid at Giza. (336-337)

Hancock states that the "Egyptologists considered all this was pure chance. Yet the pyramid builders had done *nothing* by chance. Whoever they had been, I found it hard to imagine more systematic and mathematically minded people" (338).

Hancock is correct. Pi, phi, and the Pythagorean Triangle were purposefully incorporated into the dimensions of the King's Chamber by Enoch to illustrate the fact that in the celestial kingdom husbands and wives will enjoy an eternal increase in children and that creativity throughout the universe is also eternal, "for there is no space in the which there is no kingdom; and there is no kingdom in which there is no space" (*Doctrine and Covenants* 88:37), and space is, in fact, infinite.

The 1 by 2 rectangle formed by the King's Chamber suggests a correlating passage in the Book of Jeremiah:

> "I [the Lord] will take you one from a city and two from a family, and I will bring you to Zion.
>
> "And I will give you shepherds according to My heart, who will feed you with knowledge and understanding. . . .
>
> "In those days the house of Judah shall walk with the house of Israel, and they shall come together out of

> the land of the north to the land that I have given as an inheritance to your fathers." (3:14-15 and 18)

The House of Israel includes members of the Church of Jesus Christ of Latter-day Saints, if not by direct descent then by adoption (Brooks 187).

* * *

The blocks that make up the walls are "laid in five courses" (Hancock 330). While the number 5 has already received considerable attention, a reminder of its significance as it applies particularly to the King's Chamber is not out of order.

Turning once again to John Anthony West, we learn that 5 is "the number of life" (40). Furthermore, in "ancient Egypt, the symbol for a star was drawn with five points. The ideal of the realised man was to become a star, and to 'become one of the company of Ra'" (40-41). Five is also "the key to the vitality of the universe, its creative nature"; 5 is "the number of 'potentiality'"; 5 is "the number of eternity and of the principle of eternal creation, [and of the] union of male and female" (42).

The "entire top course" of the 5 courses, Noone writes, is "constructed of only *seven* granite blocks—a number symbolizing perfection in the ancient world" (171)—and a number we have seen in the Grand Gallery.

Noone further observes that the joints between the blocks in the Grand Gallery "are precision-cut. The joints are almost invisible. It is impossible to insert a needle anywhere" (170). This precision is one more factor in establishing the oneness of husbands and wives in the celestial kingdom, as well as the oneness with the Godhead.

To ensure that the message would be detected, Enoch and his people built a similar precision into other areas of the pyramid. Consider, for example, that while inspecting the monument's exterior,

> Petrie found the workmanship on the original casing stones, some of which weighed over 15 tons, quite as

> remarkable as Howard-Vyse had described it. The faces were so straight and so truly square that when the stones had been placed together the film of mortar left between them was on the average no thicker than a man's nail, or 1/50 inch over an area of 35 square feet.
>
> Petrie found that the mean variation of the casings from a straight line and a true square was but 1/100 inch on a length of 75 inches. This [was] staggering accuracy. . . .
>
> As Petrie remarked, "Merely to place such stones in exact contact would be careful work, but to do so with cement in the joint seems almost impossible: it is to be compared to the finest opticians' work on a scale of acres."
>
> So fine was the texture of the cement that after millennia of exposure to the elements, the stones shattered before the cement would yield. (Tompkins 105)

Lepre is equally impressed by the cement or mortar used in the Grand Gallery. Here, the L-shaped stones above the ramps are

> cavities filled in with mortar. Yet this is not mortar in the typical sense of the word, but an incredibly solid and durable type which is certainly as strong as the surrounding limestone. It is indeed the very same cement which was used extensively by the original builders throughout the external portions of the monument to obtain a more solidified bond between the huge blocks of coarse, nummulitic limestone. (83)

The mortar used in the Great Pyramid symbolizes the sealing power exercised in the House of the Lord. Just as the pyramid was built to last, so will marriages performed in the temples last so long as the husbands and wives are faithful to each other and to the Lord while in mortality.

For the floor, Lepre lists 21 stones, "most of which are of a formidable size". The number 21 is clearly meant to match the 21-inch width of the vertical grooves in the east and west walls of the antechamber, the 21-inch space between the antechamber's north wall and the north face of the Granite Leaf, and the 21-inch perpendicular height of the ramps in the Grand Gallery, which also means a connection with Isaac, the promised heir, who was patriarch number 21 of the Genesis period. (Soon, we will see the number 21 in use elsewhere in the pyramid.)

Lepre's book *The Egyptian Pyramids* is copyrighted 1990, and at that time 2 of the 21 stones had been "lifted from their original positions and set on top of some of the other still-intact floorstones [sic]." Lepre proposed that these

> two stones were removed long ago so that tomb robbers could tunnel through the softer limestone beneath in search of possible treasure which they surmised might lie under the floor of the chamber in the immediate area of the sarcophagus. Two other floorstones were also once removed, but no longer exist, evidently having been broken asunder by vandals.
>
> As a result, a huge chasm of a sort has been dug out here to *a depth of some 30 feet.* Its width varies greatly, but it more or less forms a cavernous excavation approximately 6-10′ wide. (101; italics added)

The 2 stones that remained in the chamber were not taken up by anyone looking for treasure; they were taken up by Enoch for symbolic reasons. The same applies to the 2 stones that were uprooted from the floor and disappeared. All 4 stones will receive special attention in the last part of this chapter.

As for the 30-foot-deep "chasm", alert readers should have already thought of comparing it to the one in the subterranean chamber, which, according to Schul and Pettit, "was carved to *a depth of 30 feet*" (27; italics added). In addition, the "diagonal of the [subterranean] Pit shaft at the top is 100 inches" (Rutherford, Book III, 1089). One hundred inches is 8.33 feet, which fit within the range of Lepre's figure of 6 to 10 feet for the width of the King's pit.

The floor of the Queen's Chamber is at the level of the pyramid's 25th exterior course (Petrie, diagram between pages 95 and 96). The floor of the King's Chamber is at the top of the 50th course—25 doubled (Lemesurier 123). The chamber was constructed at this level because the number 50 ties in with Noah's ark, which was 50 cubits wide (Genesis 6:15); the exodus of the Israelites from Egypt, after which they were to "consecrate the fiftieth year, and proclaim liberty throughout all the land"; the 50th year was to be a jubilee for them, during which the Lord told them, "each of you shall return to his possession, and each of you shall return to his family" (Leviticus 25:10); the Levites, who were released from serving in the tabernacle at the age of 50 (Numbers 8:25).

Salvation, freedom and the reunion of families are clearly associated with the number 50 as it occurs in the Old Testament.

The thickness of the 50th course is 28 inches. The shaft in the southern wall of the King's Chamber currently exits at the 102nd course, which is 28 inches thick. The ceiling of the chamber is at the base of the 60th course, which is also 28 inches thick (Lemesurier 45). Making another comparison with the Queen's Chamber, the ceiling there on the north and south sides is at the 30th course, which is 28 inches thick (Lemesurier 44). With the number 28, then, we have another bridge between the 2 chambers, as well as the 28-inch-square dimensions of the well shaft and the 28-foot height of the Grand Gallery.

Would it not be absurd to think that the repetition of all the numbers that have been discussed is purely accidental?

* * *

In agreement with Petrie's observation that the walls extend lower than the floor—which creates another obvious connection with the King's antechamber—Rutherford indicates that "the lowest wall course dips 5 inches below the floor level" (Book III, 1001). He also indicates that the length of the King's Chamber is 4 times that of the antechamber's middle section; furthermore, the square that is formed in the middle section by the length of the floor and the "height of the East Wainscot" prefigures 8 such squares in the King's Chamber, where each square "has an area of 25 square Royal Cubits" (Book III, 1001).

The walls extending lower than the floor serve the same purpose as those in the antechamber: they reflect the presence of angels and gods who are on a different level from the men and women who will inherit the 3rd heaven of the celestial kingdom. However, in the antechamber the 3 inches are linked to resurrection—because Christ was resurrected on the 3rd day—while the 5 inches in the King's Chamber represent fellowship throughout eternity.

The increase in size in the King's Chamber over the antechamber is an obvious indication of what can be expected by the people who inherit the celestial kingdom. But who will those people be? The *Doctrine and Covenants* provides important details concerning this matter, details that will add to what has already been related in previous chapters:

> concerning. . . the resurrection of the just—
>
> They are they who received the testimony of Jesus, and believed on his name and were baptized after the manner of his burial, being buried in the water in his name, and this according to the commandment which he has given—
>
> That by keeping the commandments they might be washed and cleansed from all their sins, and receive the Holy Spirit by the laying on of the hands of him who is ordained and sealed unto this power;
>
> And who overcome by faith, and are sealed by the

Holy Spirit of promise, which the Father sheds forth upon all those who are just and true.

They are they who are the church of the Firstborn.

They are they into whose hands the Father has given all things—

They are they who are priests of the Most High, after the order of Melchizedek, which was after the order of Enoch, which was after the order of the Only Begotten Son.

Wherefore, as it is written, they are gods, even the sons of God—

Wherefore, all things are theirs, whether life or death, or things present, or things to come, all are theirs and they are Christ's, and Christ is God's. . . .

These shall dwell in the presence of God and his Christ forever and ever. . . .

These are they who shall have part in the first resurrection. . . .

These are they who are come unto Mount Zion, and unto the city of the living God, the heavenly place, the holiest of all.

These are they who have come to an innumerable company of angels, to the general assembly and church of Enoch, and of the Firstborn.

These are they whose names are written in heaven, where God and Christ are the judge of all. . . .

These are they whose bodies are celestial, whose glory is that of the sun, even the glory of God, the

> highest of all, whose glory the sun of the firmament is written of as being typical. (76:50-59, 62, 64, 66-68, and 70)

Section 137 provides additional insight into the celestial kingdom:

> The heavens were opened. . . and I [Joseph Smith] beheld the celestial kingdom of God, and the glory thereof. . . .
>
> I saw the transcendent beauty of the gate through which the heirs of that kingdom will enter, which was like unto circling flames of fire;
>
> Also the blazing throne of God, whereon was seated the Father and the Son.
>
> I saw the beautiful streets of that kingdom, which had the appearance of being paved with gold.
>
> I saw Father Adam and Abraham; my father and my mother; my brother Alvin, that has long since slept [a synonym for "died"];
>
> And marveled how it was that he had obtained an inheritance in that kingdom, seeing that he had departed this life before the Lord had set his hand to gather Israel the second time [that is, to restore the Church of Jesus Christ], and had not been baptized for the remission of sins.
>
> Thus came the voice of the Lord unto me, saying: All who have died without a knowledge of this gospel, who would have received it if they had been permitted to tarry [another word for "live"], shall be heirs of the celestial kingdom of God;
>
> Also all that shall die henceforth without a

> knowledge of it, who would have received it with all their hearts, shall be heirs of that kingdom;
>
> For I, the Lord, will judge all men according to the desire of their hearts.
>
> And I also beheld that all children who die before they arrive at the years of accountability [that is, the age of 8] are saved in the celestial kingdom of heaven. (Verses 1-10)

After receiving this revelation, Joseph Smith taught that children who die before the age of 8 "will come forth from the grave as children, be raised to maturity by worthy parents, and be entitled to receive all the ordinances of salvation that eventuate in the everlasting continuation of the family unit" (Millet and McConkie 119). The 8 squares in the King's Chamber, then, are linked both to Christ and to these little children.

The vision cited above was granted to Joseph Smith in 1836. Since then a number of near-death experiencers have been permitted to see part of what he saw many years earlier. Maurice S. Rawlings recounts two such NDEs in *To Hell and Back.* The first of these concerns a

> retired and well-to-do accountant [who] was a Christian-turned-cold following the death of his mother several years previously when her leg was amputated. In spite of his most fervent prayers, she died and he concluded, "God is as deaf as a stone idol. He has no use for me, nor I for him." Subsequent to that time, the patient himself got into trouble.
>
> In the hospital elevator, I actually felt my heart stop and then I stopped breathing. I remembered saying, "So this is it."
>
> The next thing. . . I was going through this dark passage. . . and at the other end I walked out into an

> open field. On the far side was this endless white wall which had three steps leading to a doorway. . . .
>
> On the other side of the door I was amazed to find a brilliantly lit city, reflecting what looked like the rays of the sun, only diffused and suspended with particles of radiance. The roads were all made of gold. Some sort of shining metal covered the domes and steeples in beautiful array and the walls were strangely smooth, not quite like marble, but made of something I had not seen before. . . .
>
> Then I saw two figures walking toward me and I knew immediately who they were. My mother and father who had died years ago. My mother was an amputee at the time of her death, but now she had two legs and was walking! (55-56)

If this Christian-turned-cold had been an informed member of the Church of Jesus Christ of Latter-day Saints he would not have been surprised to see that his mother's spirit was whole and that she had both her legs, for Joseph Smith taught that the spirit is eternal. He also taught that it is indestructible, and even though "the spirit is substance. . . [and] it is material,. . . it is [also] more pure, elastic and refined matter than the body", and therefore whatever might happen to the body, the spirit that quickens it is not affected in a physical sense (Joseph Fielding Smith, *Scriptural Teachings of the Prophet Joseph Smith* 235; see also Brent L. Top and Wendy C. Top, *Beyond Death's Door* 34).

Here is the second NDE from Rawlings' book:

> In the late 1970s Assistant Secretary of the Navy James E. Johnson was in his car waiting on a traffic light in Washington, D.C. . . . [when] the car was rear-ended at high speed, hurling him into the steering column, wedging him into the dash. Everything went black. A

> moment later he found himself floating toward a light which was as dazzling as a brilliant sunrise. . . .
>
> [Johnson relates:]
>
> I flew headlong through a dark tunnel at accelerating speed toward the shimmering light I sensed was Christ. . . .
>
> Inside this light was a celestial city, like a castle in the sky. The translucent golden streets glowed with the brilliance that illuminated the whole city. (56-57)

James E. Johnson's description is reminiscent of George Ritchie's experience in *Return from Tomorrow* when his guide, Jesus, took him off the earth:

> we seemed to have left the earth behind. I could no longer see it. Instead we appeared to be in an immense void, except that I had always thought of that as a frightening word, and this was not. Some unnameable promise seemed to vibrate through that vast emptiness.
>
> And then I saw, infinitely far off, far too distant to be visible with any kind of sight I knew of. . . a city. A glowing, seemingly endless city, bright enough to be seen over all the unimaginable distance between. The brightness seemed to shine from the very walls and streets of this place, and from beings which I could now discern moving about within it. In fact, the city and everything in it seemed to be made of light, even as the Figure at my side was made of light.
>
> . . . Could these radiant beings, I wondered, amazed, be those who had indeed kept Jesus the focus of their lives? Was I seeing at last ones who had looked for Him in everything? Looked so well and so closely that they

> had been changed into His very likeness?. . . Even as I asked the question, two of the bright figures seemed to detach themselves across that infinity with the speed of light.
>
> But as fast as they came toward us, we drew away still faster. The distance increased, the vision faded. Even as I cried out with loss, I knew that my imperfect sight could not now sustain more than an instant's glimpse of this real, this ultimate heaven. He had shown me all He could; now we were speeding far away. (Ritchie and Sherrill 72-73)

The city of light that Ritchie was permitted to view momentarily was the City of Enoch, which will return to the earth in the near future. More will be said about this city when the compartments above the King's Chamber are examined.

Before concentrating on another part of the King's Chamber, a word of caution needs to be issued. While near-death experiences are enlightening in many respects and provide fascinating glimpses into the spirit world—and it is the spirit world that is involved in nearly every instance, despite claims from near-death experiencers that they saw heaven—some ideas that have been derived from NDEs are misleading and have the potential to do great harm to the faith of many people.

This is especially true regarding the belief that there will be no judgment when we die. The following encounter with a being of light and the conclusion drawn from that encounter, which is taken from Raymond Moody's *Life After Life*, is all too typical:

> He [the being of light, who was a celestial personage] showed me [in a life review] some instances where I had been selfish to my sister, but then just as many times where I had really shown love to her and had shared with her. He pointed out to me that I should try to do things for other people, to try my best. There wasn't any accusation in any of this, though. When he came across

> times when I had been selfish, his attitude was only that I had been learning from them, too. (67)

The implication that the being of light, who is frequently identified as Jesus, is completely loving and nonjudgmental is similar to a concept explored by Mally Cox-Chapman in *The Case for Heaven*:

> Modern Christian theologians tend to dismiss hell. They make grand statements about God's love being stronger than any sin a person can commit. They argue that God could not be so cruel as to condemn a person to eternal damnation. Whatever their thinking, scholars do not seem to think it [hell] is a subject worthy of their time. (53)

There is a failure here to realize that the being of light knows that the near-death experiencer is going to return to mortality and so it would be completely inappropriate to pass judgment on a life that is not yet over. The final judgment, as Brent L. Top and Wendy C. Top confirm, will not be made until we have been resurrected (204). However, as stated previously, when we die a preliminary judgment is made to determine which part of the spirit world we will reside in.

Bill Pacht, a "manager of engineering and computer services at a large aerospace company", learned this was true when he had a near-death experience at the age of 41. While his spirit was out of his body he saw his mother, who had died earlier. Bill asked her "where she had been."

> She said, "I live in Chicago now." [In mortality, she had lived in New York.] Bill said, "Why are you living there?" His mother replied, "You don't get to choose where you go. You're assigned." (Cox-Chapman 122-23)

Christ, like our Father in Heaven, loves us unconditionally, nevertheless he is bound to execute justice. This is one of the points he made when he chastised those who opposed him:

> "Woe to you, scribes and Pharisees, hypocrites! For you pay a tithe of mint and anise and cumin [all herbs], and have neglected the weightier matters of the law: justice and mercy and faith. These you ought to have done, without leaving the others undone." (Matthew 23:23)

Paul the Apostle makes a similar declaration when he advises members of the church:

> Do not be deceived, God is not mocked; for whatever a man sows, that he will also reap. . . .
>
> And [so] let us not grow weary while doing good, for in due season we shall reap if we do not lose heart. (Galatians 6:7 and 9)

Raymond Moody, in his second book, *Reflections on Life After Life*, deals with this subject in a chapter titled "Judgment".

> In discussing *Life After Life*, one reviewer stated:
>
> The area sure to provoke controversy among religious groups is a section dealing with models of the afterlife. Most of the individuals interviewed did not experience any reward-punishment crisis—the traditional model of being reviewed by a St. Peter type before being admitted to the afterlife. (31)

Moody responds to this observation by noting that people who are granted a life review during their NDE feel "extremely repentant" when they see "any selfish acts which they [have] done", and so the people are judging themselves (32). Moody adds:

> One other feature of this [life] review which might

> be mentioned is that some report that in addition to their acts, they can see portrayed before them the consequences of their acts for others. As one man put it most graphically:. . . everything in my life just went by for review, you might say. I was really very, very ashamed of a lot of the things that I experienced because. . . the light was showing me what was wrong, what I did wrong. . . .
>
> It was like there was a judgment being made. . . . That's the part that has stuck with me, because it showed me not only what I had done but *even how what I had done had affected other people.* And it wasn't like I was looking at a movie projector because I could feel these things;. . . I found out that not even your thoughts are lost. . . . Every thought was there. . . . Your thoughts are not lost. (34-35)

As a result of such comments Moody is able to discern that there "may well be a Final Judgment; near-death experiences in no way imply the contrary. Indeed, many of the persons whom I have interviewed have mentioned their belief that this will take place" (37).

With his eye on the topic of hell, Moody offers this thought:

> One final remark, with respect to the question of what might happen to persons such as the perpetrators of the Nazi horrors [during World War II]. If what my subjects have reported happens to everybody, imagine for a moment what would happen to them during this [life] review, especially if, as some say, they see not only selfish acts but also the consequences of those acts for others. Those who engineered the Nazi atrocities seem to have been people whose lack of love was so complete that they willed the deaths of millions of innocent persons. This resulted in countless individual tragedies. . . . It

> resulted in innumerable long, lingering deaths and fast brutal ones. It resulted in awful degradations, in years of hunger, tears, and torment for their victims. If what happened to my subjects happened to these men, they would see all these things and many others come alive, vividly portrayed before them. In my wildest fantasies, I am totally unable to imagine a hell more horrible, more ultimately unbearable than this. (38-39)

Certainly one of the most persistent themes in *The Book of Enoch the Prophet* is that of a final judgment and our being rewarded or punished for what we do during mortality; the same is true of Egyptian texts that deal with the afterlife, and the same is true of the book of Revelation, where John states:

> And I saw the dead, small and great, standing before God, and books were opened. And another book was opened, which is the Book of Life. And the dead were judged according to their works, by the things which were written in the books. (20:12)

Bruce R. McConkie, a 20th-century apostle, advises us that the

> *book of life* is the record of the acts of men as such record is written in their own bodies. It is the record engraven on the very bones, sinews, and flesh of the mortal body. That is, every thought, word and deed has an effect on the human body; all these leave their marks, marks which can be read by Him who is Eternal as easily as the words in a book can be read. (Quoted in *Beyond Death's Door* by Brent L. Top and Wendy C. Top, page 203)

But in addition to the record within ourselves there is also a record being kept by celestial beings, a record that includes every single individual we come into contact with during our lives, and as already indicated, all our words, actions, thoughts and emotions can be recalled immediately, as can everyone else's, and that fact insures that our judgment will be honest and fair.

Another problem area associated with near-death experiences is brought up by Mally Cox-Chapman's suggestion that if "experiencers were atheists before, they are believers afterward. If they had a firm commitment to one particular religion before, they believe any religious path leads to God afterward" (10).

If it is true that "any religious path leads to God", and by inference to heaven, then Christ's stipulation that we must enter the strait gate and stay on the narrow path in order to inherit heaven is a lie.

Mally Cox-Chapman makes one more statement that fits in with this subject, and that has to do with NDEs tending "not to conform to any one religious tradition" (156). Moody makes a similar statement in *The Light Beyond*:

> People who undergo an NDE come out of it saying that religion concerns your ability to love—not doctrines and denominations. . . .
>
> A good example of this is an elderly woman in New Hampshire who had an NDE after a cardiac arrest. She had been a very religious and doctrine abiding Lutheran since she was a child. But after the NDE, she loosened up and became a more joyous person. When members of her family asked her to account for the change in her personality, she said simply that she understood God after her episode and realized that He didn't care about church doctrine at all. (88)

Such attitudes are not shared by members of the Church of Jesus Christ of Latter-day Saints, who, as demonstrated in this book, find impressive support for their beliefs in near-death experiences when the meaning of those experiences is interpreted correctly.

While Moody's *Life After Life*, first published in 1975, popularized the subject of NDEs, 8 years earlier, in 1967, Duane S. Crowther published *Life Everlasting*, a collection of NDEs reported by numerous members of the church, some of them dating back to the 1800s. Crowther's work established such basic NDE events as the spirit leaving the body, being met by a being who often identifies himself as the person's guardian angel, entering the spirit world, enjoying a reunion with dead relatives and friends, and having a life review, but in addition, his work established that

> there exists a divine plan of salvation which gives meaning to life and death. . .
>
> that God has often revealed knowledge to the leaders and members of The Church of Jesus Christ of Latter-day Saints concerning the future estates of life. . .
>
> [and] that the personal manifestations cited do not conflict with the scriptures, nor with the words of the prophets. (xv-xvii)

Crowther sets the stage for the body of his book by quoting Joseph Smith:

> All men know that they must die. And it is important that we should understand the reasons and causes of our exposure to the vicissitudes of life and death, and the designs and purposes of God in our coming into the world, our sufferings here, and our departure hence. What is the object of our coming into existence, then dying and falling away, to be here no more? *It is but reasonable to suppose that God would reveal something in reference to the matter, and it is a subject we ought to study more than any other. We ought to study it day and night, for the world is ignorant in reference to their true condition and relation. If we have any claim on our Heavenly Father for anything, it is for knowledge on this important subject.* (xvii)

Other NDE studies published by Latter-day Saint writers and researchers include *The Journey Beyond Life* by Michele R. Sorensen and David R. Willmore, and Arvin S. Gibson's two books, *Glimpses of Eternity* and *Echoes from Eternity.*

Sorensen and Willmore emphasize the importance of family in the afterlife. They allege that the "consistent theme in experiences dealing with spirits is the predominance and concern family members beyond the veil [which separates the living from the spirit world] have for us" (41). They also report that during interviews with Latter-day Saints, these NDErs "generally describe the being of light as a deceased family member" (48).

Getting down to a particular case, perhaps the most memorable and most meaningful NDE in *The Journey Beyond Life* is the account of a woman who says she "began to pray with fervent desire" to know whether or not she had been forgiven of those things she had repented of (89). In her own words,

> I was. . . seeing a play before me on stage that looked like the book of life, and I was the main character. In it, I saw some things for which I felt sorry. I had been seeking forgiveness, and seeing these things made me ask the Lord more fervently, "Hast Thou truly forgiven me of this?" Then a huge page of the book-of-life came right over the top of the scene I was worried about and I heard the words, "*Thy sins are forgiven thee; remember them no more.*" (90)

This graphic description involving the Lord's forgiveness recalls the statement quoted earlier from the *Doctrine and Covenants*: the inheritors of the celestial kingdom will be those who have been baptized and "washed and cleansed from all their sins" (76:51-52).

Gibson's *Glimpses of Eternity* contains the personal story of Gary Gillum, who was born in 1944 in Indiana. Raised in the Lutheran Church, Gary decided as a young man "to study for the ministry" (191). But in 1963, while riding in a car that was struck head-on, he suffered life-threatening injuries. Taken to a hospital, he was declared clinically dead. It was then that he had his first NDE.

He was told by a personage he believed to be his paternal grandfather that if he returned to his body and resumed his life he would someday "find the truth" (193). A few days later, he had another out-of-body experience, during which he

> "saw a building with tall spires, and I saw people in a room dressed in white clothing. The people were involved in a strange ceremony. I didn't understand any of it. It was totally foreign to my experience, and I didn't know what it symbolized, if anything." (195)

Gary eventually recovered, then in

> "1969, six years after the accident, I was going with a girl who happened to be LDS [a Latter-day Saint]. She was 'the angel' who was sent to help me find the truth. As a result of our mutual interest in each other, I listened to the missionaries". (195)

Even though he knew his parents would be disappointed in him, Gary was baptized and confirmed a member of the Church of Jesus Christ of Latter-day Saints. He also married the LDS girl he was dating and 2 years later, as they drove toward a temple where they planned to be sealed, Gary saw the same spires he had seen during his 2nd NDE. Then, inside the temple, when he saw the officiators and patrons all dressed in white, he "recognized the whole scene from [his] previous [near-death] experience" (197).

In Gibson's 2nd book, *Echoes from Eternity*, Elane Durham tells a similar story. She was raised in a "fundamental Christian faith", had her NDE in 1976, and when she was met by a being of light she identified as Jesus, she asked a number of questions, among which was, "what was the correct Bible? [and] what was the true church" (66-67)?

Another being came forward to answer her questions. He told Elane

> "that our Bible was only a small portion of the history of the people and the King James version was the most accurate. He said that more records had been found, and there were still more records to be found." (69)

Concerning the true church, Elane's instructor

> "let me know that when I found the church here on earth that believed in the history of the people (as described in the King James version of the Bible) and believed that there was additional history that had been found—and that there was still more to be revealed—I would recognize that church by the same spirit I felt there with him. He also told me that The Church had Apostles and Prophets but that they weren't accepted any more today than they had been in ancient times when Christ was here". (69-70)

After several years had passed, Elane was introduced to a pair of full-time missionaries by a friend she had hired to mow her lawn. She was attracted by the "family aspect of the LDS Church"—due in part because of her NDE, during which she was joined by one of her grandmothers who had died when Elane was only 9, as well as by her mother's step-dad who had been dead since Elane "was sixteen or seventeen", and by an aunt who had recently died.

Elane thought she was going to surprise the young missionaries by informing them "that there were three heavens, and that there were different levels in each of the three"—this she had been taught during her NDE—but the missionaries were more amused than surprised (76).

Elane concludes:

> "as I listened to those young Elders it was as if I were hearing an echo of the spiritual being I had met on a high place in a different world. An enormous sense of deja vu hit me as I listened to them." (76)

Elane was baptized in 1991 (76).

In the appendix to *Echoes from Eternity*, Gibson provides statistical data on the 70 people he interviewed for both of his books. Part of that data includes in one column the religion of the individuals at the time of their NDE, or, if they were atheist or agnostic, that is also listed. The next column indicates whether or not a change had occurred in the individuals' religious beliefs at the time of their interview.

Out of the 70 people involved, one atheist had become an agnostic; another atheist had become a pastor in the Church of Christ (not to be confused with the Church of Jesus Christ of Latter-day Saints). Three people listed as Christians had become members of the Church of Jesus Christ of Latter-day Saints. Four who were Protestants became LDS. Thirty-eight who were LDS at the time of their NDE were still LDS at the time they talked to Gibson. None of the LDS changed to another religion.

Such statistics, of course, do not provide a definitive response to claims that NDEs do not "conform to any one religious tradition" or that God doesn't "care about church doctrine at all", however, they do offer evidence that such claims can be successfully challenged.

McDannell and Lang make a similar point. First, they note that the "motifs of the modern heaven—eternal progress, love, and fluidity between earth and the other world—while acknowledged by pastors in their funeral sermons, are not fundamental to contemporary Christianity." Then they qualify their comment by specifying that there is one "major exception to this caveat"—and that is the Church of Jesus Christ of Latter-day Saints.

> The modern perspective on heaven—emphasizing the nearness and similarity of the other world to our own and arguing for the eternal nature of love, family, progress,

> and work—finds its greatest proponent in Latter-day Saint (LDS) understanding of the afterlife. While most contemporary Christian groups neglect afterlife beliefs, what happens to people after they die is crucial to LDS teachings and rituals. (313)

McDannell and Lang might have added that the "modern heaven" of the Latter-day Saints is basically the same heaven that was sought after by the ancient Egyptians, who, according to Ruth Schumann Antelme and Stephane Rossini, had

> knowledge of experiences on death's door, these experiences including separation of body and "spirit," journeys through a black and terrifying region inhabited by tormenting entities, a flash of images from one's life up to that point, a region awash in light and love, and various friendly encounters, followed by a return to the physical body while retaining a memory of these events. (110-111)

Somewhat perplexed by the Egyptians' familiarity with the near-death experience, the authors ask, "How and by whom have these ideas been acquired" (112)?

The answer is, Enoch, whose heaven was identical to the "modern heaven" of the Latter-day Saints.

* * *

One remarkable feature of the King's Chamber is its acoustics; it resonates "with every murmur and footstep" (Lehner 14). Hancock tells of a personal experience in relation to this feature:

> I folded my hands across my chest and gave voice to a sustained low-pitched tone—something I had tried out several times before at other points in the King's Chamber. On those occasions, in the centre of the floor,

> I had noticed that the walls and ceiling seemed to collect the sound, to gather and to amplify it and project it back at me so that I could sense the returning vibrations through my feet and scalp and skin. (334)

He observed a similar effect with the sarcophagus; however, sound inside the sarcophagus seemed "amplified and concentrated many times over. It was like being in the sound-box of some giant, resonant musical instrument designed to emit for ever [sic] just one reverberating tone" (335). (In Volume 2 of *Books Written in Stone* we will see a completely opposite effect in one of the underground chambers of the 3rd pyramid on the Giza plateau, which is the smallest of the 3 major pyramids. We will also see a tie-in between the acoustics in the King's Chamber and the compartments above it.)

Dunn claims that the sarcophagus was originally positioned between the north and south shafts where it "served to amplify the microwave signal that entered the resonant cavity" from the northern shaft (186-87). In his view, the entire chamber, like the sarcophagus, was composed of granite so it could be "tuned to resonate in harmony with the fundamental frequency of the Earth and the Pyramid" (157)! However, he goes on, the

> hydrogen in the power center [the King's Chamber] for some inexplicable reason exploded in an awesome ball of fire, and the power plant suffered a "meltdown." The King's Chamber was affected in a disastrous way. Its walls were pushed out nearly an inch and the ceiling beams cracked. (209)

Dunn is echoing information found in Petrie's *Pyramids and Temples of Gizeh*, where the Egyptologist says of the King's Chamber:

> On every side the joints of the stones have separated, and the whole chamber is shaken larger. . . . I also observed, in measuring the top near the W., that the

> width from N. to S. is lengthened .3 [of an inch] by a crack at the S. side.
>
> These openings or cracks are but the milder signs of the great injury that the whole chamber has sustained, probably by an earthquake, when *every* roof beam was broken across near the South side. (27)
>
> In the King's Chamber the masonry is very fine, both in its accuracy of fitting and in the squareness and equal height of the blocks [with the exception of the monolithic stone over the entrance]; but the builders were altogether wrong in their levels, and tilted the whole chamber over to one corner, so that their courses are 2¼ inches higher at the N.E. than at the S.W., a difference much greater than that in the whole base of the Pyramid. An error like this, in putting together such a magnificent piece of work, is astonishing; for the walls are composed of nearly 1/10 of a mile length of granite blocks about 4 feet high, and probably as thick. . . with an average variation of only 1/20 of an inch. (86)

Responding to Petrie's assumption that an earthquake caused the damage to the King's Chamber, Dunn asks,

> Why would an earthquake seek out one lonely chamber in a giant complex of masonry, passages and chambers? The Queen's Chamber seems to have been unaffected by this catastrophic event. The Descending Passage. . . is remarkably precise. No unusual disturbances were noted inside the Grand Gallery; even the Antechamber does not show the extent of damage suffered by the King's Chamber. More important, it is the specific characteristics of the disturbance that give rise to serious misgivings about the earthquake theory. Something caused the King's Chamber to expand! (40)

Dunn's assessment of the situation is quite valid; no actual earthquake caused the expansion of the chamber, but then neither did a meltdown of the type envisioned by himself. However, the chamber was constructed to appear as if it had been struck by an earthquake. Why? In order to simulate the destruction that took place when Christ died on the cross. At that time "the veil of the temple was torn in two from top to bottom [and this is another reason why in the King's antechamber some of the stones are defective and "many parts are strangely rough"]; and the earth quaked, and the rocks were split" (Matthew 27:51).

But the condition of the King's Chamber also reflects the results of a climactic event that was prophesied nearly 2000 years ago and that will soon be realized. That event will be detailed shortly.

In the southeast corner of the ceiling in the King's Chamber, Petrie noticed that "for about five feet on each side, the joint is all daubed up with cement [i.e. plaster] laid on by fingers" (28).

Dunn asks,

> what purpose does a thin layer of plaster serve? It is doubtful that it would lend any structural improvement to the granite complex, for what could a thin layer of cement do to prevent one of the forty-five- or seventy-ton granite beams above the King's Chamber from collapsing? Would the cement have been added to the cracked beams for some other purpose? (41)

The answer is yes. The plaster serves a definite purpose, and that is to lead us to a particular passage in the Book of Deuteronomy.

> Moses and the elders of Israel commanded the people: "Keep all these commands that I give you today. When you have crossed the Jordan [River] into the land the Lord your God is giving you, set up some *large stones and coat them with plaster*. Write on them all the words of this law [meaning the law of Moses] when you have crossed over to enter the land. . . flowing with milk

> and honey, just as the Lord, the God of your fathers, promised you." (NIV, 27:1-3; italics added)

As indicated by Dunn, besides the *large* stones in the walls of the King's Chamber, the granite beams in the ceiling are also large.

While Moses' instructions to write on the plaster do not specify using fingers that is probably what was intended since the commandments were involved and the commandments as first given to Moses were "written with the finger of God". Furthermore, they were written on 2 stone tablets (Exodus 31:18), and on "*both sides*" (Exodus 32:15; italics added), just as the cement or plaster was spread with fingers on both sides of the ceiling in the King's Chamber.

Christ linked the finger of God with the Kingdom of God when he told the Jews, "if I cast out demons with the finger of God, surely the kingdom of God has come upon you" (Luke 11:20). And Christ, of course, emphasized the need to keep the commandments in order to inherit the heaven of heavens: "if you want to enter into life," he said, meaning eternal life, the kind of life the Father has, "keep the commandments" (Matthew 19:17). Notice the chapter number and the verse number for this quote—19 and 17; as listed earlier in this chapter, the height of the King's Chamber is 19 feet and the width is 17 feet.

When he examined the east side of the King's Chamber, Petrie was able to discern that the

> crack across the Eastern roof-beam has been also daubed with cement, looking, therefore, as if it had been cracked *before* the chamber was finished. (28)

What is the meaning of this feature? The meaning is found in the fact that the "Lord God planted a garden eastward in Eden, and there He put the man whom He had formed" (Genesis 2:8). The man was Adam, the first of all men to come to this earth to experience mortality. He and his wife Eve transgressed while they were in the garden for they broke the commandment not to eat the fruit "of the tree of knowledge of good and evil" (Genesis 2:17), and as a consequence they were driven from the garden (Genesis 3:23). However, they repented, they were baptized, and they were redeemed ("The Book of Moses" 5:9-11; 6:64-65 and 68).

The "crack across the Eastern roof-beam" symbolizes the expulsion from the garden of Eden. In Egyptian mythology, the creator-god withdrew into the heavens due to "the revolt of the human race". Dimitri Meeks and Christine Favard-Meeks recognize that this "moment of separation was a crucial one; indeed, it structured the new world" (26). In the account of Adam and Eve the same separation occurred. After their transgression, the Father withdrew so that they could no longer enjoy his immediate presence; all future contact with the Father would have to be through a mediator—namely, his firstborn son, Jesus Christ.

The cement or plaster on the eastern side of the King's Chamber symbolizes this repair in the disruption of direct communication with the Father. It also symbolizes the redemption of Adam and Eve, an act made possible by Christ's sacrifice in the garden of Gethsemane and on the cross, for that sacrifice reaches back in time to Adam and Eve. Just as bringing back "lost sheep" to the Lord is a means of covering "a multitude of sins" (James 5:19), so the plaster covers up defects in the King's Chamber.

* * *

The exterior measurements for the sarcophagus in the King's chamber incorporate numbers that have been seen in other parts of the Great Pyramid. For example, the length is 7 feet 6 inches or 90 inches (Lepre 277), which is a match for the 90-inch height of the base walls in the Gallery and therefore another match for Sarah's age when Isaac was born, and as pointed out before, Isaac prefigured Christ's sacrifice.

The exterior width of the sarcophagus is 3 feet 3 inches or 39 inches (Lepre 277; Edwards 287). From the beginning of the ascending passage to the end of the contiguous girdle stones is 39 feet (15 feet for the 3 granite blocks and 24 feet for the contiguous girdle stones), and these 39 feet include the basic principles of Christ's teachings—that is, faith, repentance, baptism, and the gift of the Holy Spirit—plus the lesser priesthood and the greater priesthood.

The exterior height of the sarcophagus is 41.31 inches (Petrie 30; Hancock 330). The number 41 is a direct link to the width of the central floor and the ceiling in the Gallery plus the width of the 2 low passages in the antechamber, and since we're dealing with the height of the sarcophagus we have confirmation that the 2 passages in the antechamber are to be added to the height of the Gallery. The 31 in 41.31 is another link to the 31-inch height of the short section that connects the descending passage to the well shaft and to Josiah, the Christ-like king of Jerusalem.

Hancock lists the interior length of the sarcophagus at "6 feet 6.6 inches" (330). The three 6s should immediately catch the Bible student's attention since it is "the number of the beast" or antichrist as recorded in Revelation 13:18. The "beast" is a satanic figure who personifies deceit and death and so his association with the sarcophagus is perfectly appropriate, for the sarcophagus represents Christ's death at the hands of antichrists. But because the sarcophagus is empty it also represents his resurrection and his ultimate triumph over deceit and death and over all antichrists of the past, present and future.

Petrie's figure for the interior width of the sarcophagus is 26.81 inches (30). The number 26 needs no further comment at this time; 81 is related to a lance or a spear, the weapon used to pierce Christ's heart, for *cain* in Greek means "lance" or "spear", and the name is spelled Kappa, which = 20, Alpha, which = 1, Iota, which = 10, and Nu, which = 50, and these numbers add up to 81 (see Strong 39, entry # 2535 under the heading "CAIN").

Petrie's measurement for the interior depth or height of the sarcophagus is 34.42 inches (30). The 34 matches the 34 feet in the length of the chamber. Thirty-four times the Hebrew word *chayah* occurs in the King James Version of the Old Testament; *chayah* means "to live" or "to revive" (Strong 9, entry # 2421 under the heading "ALIVE").

The number 42 brings to mind the number of months in Christ's earthly ministry, but 42 also figures in Matthew 1:17 where we're told that

> all the generations from Abraham to David are fourteen generations, from David until the captivity in Babylon are fourteen generations, and from the captivity in Babylon until the Christ are fourteen generations.

Fourteen + 14 + 14 = 42.

Petrie supplies another important number associated with the sarcophagus when he reveals that it is "1/5th the scale of the chamber" (94). Here is the reason for this particular scale. Five Roman soldiers carried out the crucifixion of Jesus. One of the five, namely the centurion who was in command, came to the realization that Christ "was the Son of God" (Mark 15:39).

Hancock cites Petrie's discovery that the sarcophagus "must have been cut out of its surrounding granite block [of bedrock] with straight saws '8 feet or more in length'" (331). In his examination of the sacophagus, Livio Catullo Stecchini established the fact that the number 8 is definitely written into its design, for "the contents of the coffer is [sic] 8 cubic royal cubits". Moreover, he says, "the walls were given a thickness such that the outside volume of the coffer is twice that of the contents, that is, 16 [8 x 2] cubic royal cubits" (322).

Both the 8 and the 16 can also be found in "one of the wall blocks located on the west wall of the chamber, at its lowest course". This block, Lepre says,

> has three open joints surrounding it. Its right side joint is open 1/4"; its left side, 1/8"; and its top joint, 1/16".

Lepre follows up this information by pointing out that the

> original builders, who were for some strange reason fond of plastering certain joints throughout the pyramid, used this method on the three open joints surrounding

> this particular stone. The plaster application on this lower corner stone. . . was partially removed from certain areas by my using a sharp pen knife. When I noted the open joints which had been hidden by that mass of plaster. . . the idea of a possible western entrance came to mind.
>
> That there may be a second, western entrance at this point in the King's Chamber is not such an improbable idea as it may seem. For in the Bent Pyramid. . . at Dahshur [a few miles south of Giza], there is a western entrance as well as the standard one on the north side. (103)

The Bent Pyramid "is so named because the angle of the outer walls alter abruptly part way [sic] up. The lower part is a steep 54 degrees, while the upper part [is] 43 degrees" (Hobson 70). According to Egyptologists, this pyramid was one of the first true pyramids and was built at a time when "there was as yet no blueprint for a true pyramid" (Lehner 102). As a result, or so Egyptologists claim, pyramid building was in a stage of experimentation and evolution, which eventually culminated in the Great Pyramid (Lepre 51). But even with the Great Pyramid, some Egyptologists such as Edwards, who is unable to perceive the symbolic purpose behind such features as the girdle stones, finds what he thinks is evidence that the ancient "builders were engaged on an operation which lay outside their experience" (290).

Just the opposite is true. The Great Pyramid was the first pyramid built in Egypt; all others followed it. There was no experimentation or evolution involved because Enoch and his people had perfected their construction skills while building the city of Zion and establishing colonies in other countries. In addition, all the pyramids that were reputedly built by different pharaohs during what is termed the Old Kingdom were built by the Lord's elect, and they all depict one or more of the degrees of glory as well as other concepts taught in the scriptures.

But Lepre does deserve to be credited with correctly deducing a connection between the Great Pyramid and the Bent Pyramid. However, he failed to notice other connections that could have been made between the 2 pyramids. For instance, the number 54 in the slope of the bottom half of the Bent Pyramid is a match for the 54 sockets or slots in the Grand Gallery's ramps—and it is a match for the number of years that Joseph lived and continued to rule Egypt after his father Jacob died.

The number 43 is matched by the number of granite beams that can be counted in the King's Chamber ceiling plus the ceilings of the 4 compartments above (Dunn 153; Tompkins, illustration of the 5 ceilings on page 62).

Lepre, like other Egyptologists, ascribes the Bent Pyramid to the pharaoh Sneferu, and Sneferu, he says, was the 7th and last pharaoh of the 3rd Dynasty who supposedly reigned for 24 years, from 2813 to 2790 BC (47). We can see these same numbers in Joseph's life, for after serving Potiphar for 7 years, he was cast into prison at the age of 24; he was eventually freed from prison as a result of interpreting the chief butler's dream which involved the restoration to his former post after 3 days.

According to Lawton and Ogilvie-Herald, the Bent Pyramid "is about 80 per cent of the size of the Great Pyramid" (28). It is this size because it was meant to be associated with Joseph's 80-year rule of Egypt, which was from 1751 to 1671 BC. We have, then, from 2813 to 1751, a discrepancy of 1,062 years.

The Bent Pyramid, like the Great Pyramid, is a symbolic structure. The lower half represents Joseph's attempt to build a perfect spiritual kingdom in Egypt after the pattern of Enoch's and Melchizedek's success; the upper half represents the apostasy that took place after Joseph's death, its 43-degree slope symbolizing imperfection and incompletion.

Along with the 3 open joints discovered in the King's Chamber by Lepre, Stecchini's numbers of 8 and 16 can be compared to this quote from Exodus, which includes part of the Lord's instructions for the design and construction of the tabernacle:

> "For the far side of the tabernacle, westward, you shall make six boards.
>
> "And you shall also make two boards for the two back corners of the tabernacle. . . .
>
> "So there shall be *eight* boards with their sockets of silver—*sixteen* sockets—two sockets under each of the boards." (26:22-23 and 25; italics added)

The sarcophagus, like the boards and the sockets for the tabernacle, is "westward" in the King's Chamber. But the similarities don't end there. Other comparisons can be made between the sarcophagus and information gleaned from the Bible. Bullinger, for example, observes that

> the "Holy of Holies," both in the Tabernacle and in the Temple [of Solomon], were *cubes*. In the Tabernacle it was a *cube* of 10 cubits. In the Temple it was a cube of 20 cubits. (201)

What does the King's Chamber measure in cubits? The answer, as reported by Stecchini, was first supplied by Sir Isaac Newton, the English scientist and mathematician: it "measures 10 by 20 cubits" (323).

There is at least one more 8 associated with the sarcophagus that has yet to be mentioned. In *Secrets of the Great Pyramid*, we learn that in order to

> measure the bottom of the coffer and to see if there were any secret opening beneath it, Petrie had its 3 tons raised about 8 inches, but found no sign of any opening. (Tompkins 103) [Note the correlation between the 3

> tons and the period of 3 days that Christ's body was in the tomb.]

Making the assumption that the sarcophagus was originally perfect and squared off, Lehner writes that the people

> who first violated the stone box and robbed the royal mummy probably made the prominent break in the corner of the sarcophagus in order to lift the heavy lid. (114)

Lepre, with a different point of view, thinks the sarcophagus

> bears the scars and chippings of hordes of visitors and souvenir-seekers; [and so] its once straight edges are rounded down, and its southeast corner is very much fractured" (92).

Neither claim is valid. First of all, as Tompkins points out, "no trace of the lid has been found", therefore Lehner's claim is unsupported speculation. Second, Tompkins informs us that the sarcophagus consists "of feldspar, quartz and mica" and its granules "are even harder than those of the chamber walls" (17). In that case, Lepre needs to tell us just how visitors or souvenir seekers might have managed to chip away the southeast corner of the sarcophagus.

The sarcophagus appears scarred and broken in places because it was intended to simulate the tomb of Joseph of Arimathea, which "was hewn out of the rock," (Luke 23:53). The sarcophagus, in like manner, was "hewn from a single block of granite" (Lepre 92).

To secure this point, let's compare more description of the sarcophagus by Lepre to descriptions of Joseph's tomb from the Bible and one or two additional sources.

> **Lepre**: "The lid, which is now missing, is calculated to have weighed over two tons" (92).

Bible: "Now when the Sabbath was past, Mary Magdalene, Mary the mother of James, and Salome. . . came to the tomb when the sun had risen.

"And they said among themselves, 'Who will roll away the stone from the door of the tomb for us?'

"But when they looked up, they saw that the stone had been rolled away—for it was very large" (Mark 16:1-4).

Like the missing sarcophagus lid, the stone that had been used to seal off the tomb's entrance "had been taken away from the tomb" (John 20:1).

Lepre: "Traces of angled grooves and three pinion holes used, along with a resinous glue, for the fastening of the lid are still barely discernable at the top edges of the sarcophagus" (92-93).

"For the sarcophagus, on its flat unbeveled top edge has three almost imperceptible circles, each the size of a quarter, finely inscribed into it. These three circles, upon even closer scrutinization, prove to be drill holes which have broken granite pinions, or bolts, firmly embedded into them; and these granite bolts prove that the lid of the sarcophagus was sealed not only by being slid into the beveled grooves of the sarcophagus and shut tight, but also by this additional locking device" (280).

Bible: "a rich man from Arimathea, named Joseph. . . rolled a big stone in front of the entrance to the tomb. . . .

"The next day. . . the chief priests and the Pharisees went to Pilate. 'Sir,' they said, 'we remember that while he was still alive that deceiver [meaning Jesus] said, "After three days I will rise again." So give the order

> for the tomb to be made secure until the third day. Otherwise, his disciples may come and steal the body and tell the people that he has been raised from the dead. . . . '
>
> "'Take a guard,' Pilate answered. 'Go, make the tomb as secure as you know how.' So they went and made the tomb secure by putting a seal on the stone and posting the guard" (NIV, Matthew 27:57-65).

> ***The New Manners and Customs of Bible Times***: "[In Jerusalem, the] mouth of the tomb was sealed either with a disc-shaped stone that ran in an inclined groove in front of the cave or with a boulder that fell into the access hole beneath it. Either way, the stone was extremely difficult to move once it was in place" (Gower 72-73).

In order to secure the stone that blocked the entrance to the tomb, the chief priests and scribes would have had mortar applied to the stone's edges, cementing it to the exterior of the tomb, then the mortar would have been officially sealed by using "a device such as a signet ring or cylinder, engraved with the owner's name, a design, or both" (Lockyer, Sr., *Nelson's Illustrated Bible Dictionary* 960). In this case, the seal would have belonged to Pilate, and most likely it would have been used at both sides and at the top of the stone.

A seal the size of a signet ring would have been about the same size as an American quarter. A number of such seals were found in the tomb of Tutankhamen (Reeves, *The Complete Tutankhamun* 112-13).

The damaged corner of the sarcophagus reflects the damage that occurred to the tomb when

> there was a great earthquake; for an angel of the Lord descended from heaven, and came and rolled back the stone from the door. (Matthew 28:2)

These are not the only similarities between the sarcophagus and important passages in the Bible. Consider, for example, Noone's report that the sarcophagus contains "an extremely high percentage of quartz crystals." A "high percentage of quartz crystals" is also part of the composition of the blocks in the walls, along with mica and feldspar, but whereas the walls seem to absorb the light, the "box sparkled with an almost incandescent light as if it held something ancient and sacred" (171-172).

With this mention of crystals, we have a tie-in with the Revelation of John, for the throne of God has before it "a sea of glass, like crystal" (4:6); furthermore, "the holy Jerusalem, descending out of heaven from God," has light "like a precious stone, like a jasper stone, clear as crystal" (21:10-11); and "a pure river of water of life, clear as crystal, [proceeds] from the throne of God and of the Lamb" (22:1).

* * *

In the antechamber, the number 9 occurs frequently. For instance, at the beginning of the middle section, the height increases by nearly 9 feet over the height of the entrance passage; the west wainscot is 9 inches higher than the east wainscot; the south wall is divided into 9 vertical sections; and the 3 grooves on the east wall, plus the 3 on the west wall and the 3 stones that make up the ceiling, add up to 9.

From the antechamber, the number 9 has been carried over to the King's Chamber where the flat ceiling is comprised of 9 granite beams (Rutherford, Book III, 1004). John Anthony West remarks, "there can be no mistaking the importance attached to the number Nine by Egypt" (54). He also maintains that 9 "is extremely complex, and practically insusceptible of precise verbal expression" (54). Even so, Richard H. Wilkinson asserts that "[m]ost commonly, the number [9] appears in conjunction with the enneads or groups of nine gods." He also says that 9 might "represent all the gods" (*Symbol and Magic in Egyptian Art* 137 and 146).

The 3 angels, the 3 gods and the Godhead represented in the antechamber are duplicated in the ceiling of the King's Chamber.

Regarding the Godhead, David Furlong makes a comment that should be considered:

> in their religion, the ancient Egyptians held special reverence for trinities—made up of a god, his consort and their son. This "triune" concept is almost certainly the inspiration behind the origin of the Christian Trinity, of Father, Son and Holy Ghost. In the pyramid age, the religious centre of Egypt resided at Heliopolis, now part of modern Cairo. The priests there worshipped three main gods: Osiris, Isis and their son Horus. (73)

Furlong, of course, doesn't realize that the Egyptian trinity developed from Enoch's original teachings that the Godhead consisted of the Father, the Son and the Holy Spirit. In the trinity listed by Furlong, Osiris represents Christ; Isis, the bride of Osiris, represents the church; and Horus—who is a child or youth in some cases and an elderly man in others—represents Joseph and Jacob (for Horus as a child, see Meeks and Favard-Meeks, *Daily Life of the Egyptian Gods*, pages 77, 97, and 106; for Horus as a blind, elderly "god" see the same source, pages 72 and 214, note # 177; for Jacob's blindness in his old age see Genesis 48:10).

Lepre writes that the ceiling beams "which traverse the chamber from north to south, actually extend beyond the walls upon which they are set by 5 feet on either side" (92). The Queen's Chamber, as we saw earlier, has a similar arrangement of its ceiling; however, there is a difference in that the stones in the Queen's Chamber extend 10 feet past the walls and the ceiling is gabled.

There is also a contrast between the ceiling in the King's Chamber and its antechamber, not just in the number of beams involved but in the direction they are laid. The antechamber, with its representation of passing through the veil in the House of the Lord, has its ceiling oriented east to west because the tabernacle and the temple of Solomon, as well as the temple that existed in Jerusalem at the time of Christ's ministry, were oriented east to west. The King's Chamber, representing the celestial kingdom, has its beams running north and south in order to indicate a direct link with the Father of our spirits.

Rutherford describes each beam in the ceiling of the King's chamber as having

> a depth of about 7 feet. The width of these varies from 45 inches to nearly 63 inches. It will be observed that the depth is greater than the width. One of these great granite stones is 27 feet long, 7 feet deep and 5 feet wide and weighs about 72 tons and, so far as is known, it is the largest stone in the entire Pyramid.

After posting these impressive figures, Rutherford adds that "this is the weight of some modern railway locomotives", and then he exclaims with a sense of wonder, "what a feat to raise this huge block of granite over 160 feet from the ground and place it in position" (Book III, 1004)!

This singularly large stone represents Christ, for it weighs an estimated 72 tons and 3 days equal 72 hours.

The number 27 deserves further discussion, especially since all 9 of the stones in the ceiling measure 27 feet long (Lepre 92), plus there are 27 stones in the lowest course of the chamber when all 4 walls are included, there are 27 stones in the 2 lowest courses of the east and south walls, and there are 27 stones in the north wall when the huge stone over the entrance is counted as one stone (see Lepre's diagram of the King's Chamber on page 98).

In the tabernacle, the table for the showbread was 27 inches high—1.5 cubits x 18 inches (Exodus 25:3). The showbread "symbolized the continual presence of the Lord. . . and the people's dependence on God's provision for their spiritual and physical needs" (Lockyer, Sr., *Nelson's Illustrated Bible Dictionary* 987).

The framework for the tabernacle consisted of frames that measured 27 inches wide and that had "three vertical arms joined by three cross pieces" so that the center of the frame formed a Greek cross (Tenney,

The Zondervan Pictorial Encyclopedia of the Bible, vol. 5, 574; see also Exodus 36:20-21 and 31-33).

In the temple of Solomon, there were 10 stands or carts that held basins or lavers supported by pedestals; the outside diameter of the lavers was 1½ cubits—27 inches—and the 4 wheels that the carts were mounted on had a diameter of 1½ cubits—27 inches (1 Kings 7:27, 29-32).

In both the tabernacle and the temple of Solomon, the Ark of the Covenant was placed inside the holy of holies. The Ark was 1½ cubits wide and 1½ cubits high—27 inches by 27 inches (Exodus 31:1).

At the heart of the New Testament is Christ—and the New Testament consists of 27 books.

* * *

The width of the 27-foot-long stone described by Rutherford is 5 feet, the depth 7 feet. Once again we have the combination of 5 and 7, a combination seen in the 3rd granite block in the ascending passage, in the Great Step, in course number 5 (the top course) of the King's Chamber with its 7 stones, and, to add to these, Lepre says the narrow shaft in the north wall has a height of 5 inches and a width of 7 inches (95). One significant point to make about this combination is that 5 x 7 = 35, the number that represents the First Presidency of the church, and the First Presidency represents Christ.

Regarding the 2 shafts in the north and south walls, Rutherford, who calls them "ventilators" or "air-channels", notes that their "top edge. . . is at the same level as the top of the entrance doorway and only about 5 feet to the west of it." He also remarks that because

> the King's Chamber lies south of the Pyramid's east-west axis, the north air channel is longer than the southern one, the latter being somewhat under and the former somewhat over 200 feet out to the exterior of the building. (Book III, 1004)

Hancock and Bauval add to this information, writing that the shafts

> are all inclined to the horizontal plane of the Pyramid and their angles of slope vary from 32 degrees 28 minutes [for the northern shaft] to 45 degrees 14 minutes [for the southern shaft]. The shafts were constructed in a step-by-step manner as the Pyramid rose in height (i.e. they were not drilled through the masonry as some have supposed) and they reveal the use of very complex and sophisticated engineering and levelling techniques. (53)

After explaining in detail just what was involved in order to construct the shafts the way they are, the authors observe:

> If ventilation was really the objective then the question that must be asked is this: why opt for such complications and difficulties when an effective flow of air could have been provided for the chambers in a much simpler way? From an engineer's point of view the obvious solution would have been to leave a masonry joint open—say 20 cms—running horizontally. . . right to the outside of the monument. (55)

As is, the

> northern air channel's upper end [meaning its point of exit] is in the 101st course (the bottom or floor being on the top of the 100th course) of core masonry as it presently exists. (Rutherford, Book III, 1005)

The 100th course is 35 inches thick (Lemesurier 45); the girdle joint at the top end of the ascending passage, which represents the First Presidency of the church, is 35 feet. The 101st course is 33 inches thick (Lemesurier 45); the girdle stone that represents the high priests is 33 inches thick, plus Christ, who lived to be 33, was—and is—the great high priest (see the 7th chapter and the 1st verse of Chapter 8 of Hebrews).

The southern shaft exits at course number 102, which is 28 inches thick (Lemesurier 45). Altogether, 11 of the Great Pyramid's courses measure 28 inches thick (see Lemesurier's chart on page 377). As a reminder, Joseph was the 11th son of Jacob and he was 28 when he interpreted the dreams of the butler and the butcher, and in so doing demonstrated his prophetic powers.

The interior wall courses in the King's Chamber are arranged so that a number of combinations can be made. To begin with, the maximum total of 101 stones matches the 101st course; count the monolithic stone over the entrance as a single stone and the total of 100 stones matches the 100th course. Count the huge stone twice—which is certainly appropriate since it takes up 2 courses—as a single stone and a double stone and the chamber has 102 stones, a match for the 102nd course.

Because of the exceptionally large granite block over the chamber's entrance, the north wall can be said to contain 26 or 27 or 28 stones, depending on whether or not that singular block is omitted from the count or taken as a single stone or as 2 stones. All 3 numbers have been shown to be extremely important in the pyramid's symbolic functions.

For those who are interested, a diagram of the walls of the King's Chamber can be found on page 98 of Lepre's *The Egyptian Pyramids* (this diagram, however, was first drawn by Piazzi Smyth; see Plate # XVII in Smyth's *The Great Pyramid: Its Secrets and Mysteries Revealed*).

Returning our attention to Joseph, he is represented by the east wall, where the 4 courses up from the floor contain 17 stones. On the north wall, the 2nd and 3rd courses up from the floor contain 11 stones when the one huge stone is included. On that same wall, the 1st course contains 7 stones, as does the 4th course, so that we have two 7s separated just as the 7 years of abundance were separated from the 7 years of famine.

If we omit the one huge stone in the north wall, then the 2nd and

3rd courses have 10 stones, a match for Joseph's 10 older brothers who sold him into slavery. Above these 10 stones in the north wall, there are 9 more: 7 in the 4th course and 2 in the 5th course. The 7 represents the 7 years of abundance. The 2 represents the 2nd year of famine, when Joseph was reunited with his family. The 5th course represents the 5 years of famine that still remained; at the same time it represents the hand of fellowship that Joseph extended to his family in order to save them both temporally and spiritually—and it is for this reason that the young "god" Horus became a "Savior" (Meeks and Favard-Meeks 106).

When the east and west walls are combined, they have a total of 37 stones. The 5 courses in the south wall altogether contain 37 stones. Joseph was 37 during the last year of the 7 years of abundance, plus we saw in an earlier chapter how the number 37 is linked to Christ.

If the monolith over the entrance is left out, the 2nd course up from the floor consists of 22 stones (this is counting all 4 walls). Joseph lived apart from his father for 22 years. If the monolith is included, then the number of stones increases to 23. Joseph was patriarch number 23.

The first 4 courses in the south wall consist of 34 stones, a match for the length of the King's Chamber. Interestingly, both Piazzi Smyth (page 443) and Rutherford (Book III, page 1001) prefer the more precise length of 34 feet 34 inches over the usual figure of 34 feet 4 inches (Lawton and Ogilvie-Herald round out the number to 34 feet, dropping the 4 inches [22]). The 34 feet 34 inches is, in fact, more preferable since Jacob and Joseph spent 34 years together, and so one of the 34s represents Jacob while the other 34 represents Joseph.

Thirty-four is, of course, 17 + 17. Within the confines of the King's Chamber, we have 9 ceiling stones that measure 17 feet; 9 x 17 = 153, and, as a reminder, the gematria of the phrase "Sons of God", when written in Hebrew, is 153 (Bullinger 275).

More remains to be revealed about the northern channel or shaft of the King's Chamber, but first we should deal with the fact that there are 19 stones in the west wall of the King's Chamber and there are 19 feet in the chamber's height. The number 19 leads to a significant link with the Book of Joshua, where we learn that the descendants of Naphtali,

Jacob's 6th son, inherited land that included "nineteen cities with their villages" (19:32-38). That land also included Galilee, which became "a focal point of [Christ's] ministry" (Lockyer, Sr., *Nelson's Illustrated Bible Dictionary* 746).

To add to our understanding of the importance of 19, Bullinger points out that it is "a combination of 10 and 9, and would denote the perfection of *Divine order* [signified by the number 10] connected with *judgment* [signified by the number 9]." In addition, 19 "is the *gematria* of Eve" (262), who is "the mother of all living" (Genesis 3:20).

John Anthony West provides the following on the number 19:

> The Egyptian decision to base a grid upon nineteen squares was based upon an understanding of the complex role played by nineteen in all questions of manifestation in time and space. (43).

The Giza plateau was laid out in a grid pattern, and so 19 plays an important role both inside and outside the pyramid.

And now, Bauval and Gilbert provide more details about the northern shaft by drawing on the experience of Rudolf Gantenbrink, a German engineer who designed a remote-controlled mini-robot and in 1993 sent it up the northern shafts in the Queen's and King's Chambers. The robot was equipped with a video camera so it was able to send back pictures of the shafts' interiors. Accordingly, it was learned that since

> the Grand Gallery is in the direct path of the shafts, both had to be given a pronounced "kink" westward to bypass the Gallery. . . . Moreover, these shafts had been given more gentle kinks as they ran past the Grand Gallery and then reverted to their original course.
>
> What was not realized. . . was that the shafts, with their kinks, appeared to be shaped in the form of the sacred adze. . . .

> It now seemed certain that the ceremony for the opening of the mouth had been performed, perhaps, several times, inside the Queen's Chamber. (209-210; an illustration on page 209 of *The Orion Mysery* depicts what the 2 authors are describing)

Supposedly part of the mortuary liturgy performed by Egyptian priests, the opening of the mouth is said to have involved "a small metal cutting instrument, similar to a carpenter's adze" (Bauval and Gilbert 205).

A "knife-sharp tool", the adze was used to symbolically "restore the body's vital functions for the afterlife" (Casson 78). This ritual is depicted in a wall painting in the burial chamber of the tomb of Tutankhamen, where a high priest wearing a leopard skin holds an adze before the pharaoh's face. (A photo of this scene can be found on page 25 of *The Mummy in Ancient Egypt* by Salima Ikram and Aidan Dodson. A close-up view of the table and the images above it reveals a finger, which never seems to generate any curiosity on the part of Egyptologists.)

What could have been the original source for "this rather bizarre ceremony", as Bauval and Gilbert call it (205)?

The answer is in the command the Lord gives to his authorized servants to open their mouths and declare his word to those they are sent to. We find a rather typical example of this in the Book of Isaiah, where the prophet writes:

> I saw the Lord sitting on a throne, high and lifted up, and the train of His robe filled the temple.
>
> Above it stood seraphim. . . .
>
> Then one of the seraphim flew to me, having in his hand a live coal which he had taken with the tongs from the altar.
>
> *And he touched my mouth with it*, and said:

> "Behold, this has touched your lips;
> Your iniquity is taken away,
> And your sin purged."
> Also I heard the voice of the Lord, saying:
> "Whom shall I send,
> And who will go for us?"
> Then I said, "Here am I! Send me."
> And he said, "Go, and tell this people:
> 'Keep on hearing, but do not understand;
> Keep on seeing, but do not perceive.'"
> (6:1-2 and 6-9; italics added)

In a similar manner Jeremiah's mouth was touched:

> the word of the Lord came to me, saying:
>
> > "Before I formed you in the womb I knew you;
> > Before you were born I sanctified you;
> > I ordained you a prophet to the nations."
>
> Then said I:
>
> > "Ah, Lord God!
> > Behold, I cannot speak, for I am a youth."
>
> But the Lord said to me:
>
> > "Do not say, 'I am a youth,'
> > For you shall go to all to whom I send you,
> > And whatever I command you, you shall speak.
> > Do not be afraid of their faces,
> > For I am with you to deliver you," says the Lord.
>
> *Then the Lord put forth His hand and touched my mouth*, and the Lord said to me:
>
> > "Behold, *I have put My words in your mouth.*
> > See, I have this day set you over the nations and over the kingdoms,

> To root out and pull down,
> To destroy and to throw down,
> To build and to plant."
> (1:4-10; italics added)

Any complete Bible concordance will include several columns of verses that pertain to the mouth of man and of God.

The ancient Egyptian ritual of the opening of the mouth can be associated with Christ's "opening his mouth" while he was in the spirit world where he organized his church and established a missionary force to take his message to the spirits in prison.

As for the leopard skin depicted in the tomb of Tutankhamen, its symbolism is the same as the temple garments worn by members of the Church of Jesus Christ of Latter-day Saints who have been endowed. Both are symbols of the "garments of skin" God made for Adam and Eve to cover their nakedness (meaning their spiritual nakedness) after they partook of the forbidden fruit (NIV, Genesis 3:21). Moreover, the leopard is a panther, and the

> belief that the panther always slept three days after feeding and returning to its cave, and only upon waking sent forth its "fragrant" voice. . . contributed to associating it symbolically with Christ. (Biedermann 254)

The form of the northern shaft of the King's Chamber, as determined by its relationship to the Grand Gallery, does not resemble an adze as much as it does a sickle—and a sickle is what the shape of the shaft was meant to depict. 'lhe reason for the sickle shape will be revealed in the next few pages.

* * *

The 76th section of the *Doctrine and Covenants* has more important verses that have not yet been quoted; here is what they say, starting first with those who will be in the terrestrial kingdom:

> These are they who receive of the presence of the Son, but not of the fulness of the Father. (Verse 77)

And now for the telestial kingdom:

> These are they who shall not be redeemed from the devil until the last resurrection, until the Lord, even Christ the lamb, shall have finished his work.
>
> These are they who receive not of his fulness in the eternal world, but of the Holy Spirit through the ministration of the terrestrial;
>
> And the terrestrial through the ministration of the celestial.
>
> And also the telestial receive it of the administering of angels who are appointed to minister for them, or who are appointed to be ministering spirits for them; for they shall be heirs of salvation. (Verses 85-88)

These additional details about the two lower kingdoms have a bearing on the symbolic function of the shafts in the King's and Queen's Chambers, and they have a bearing on 4 blocks of granite that receive considerable attention from Lepre, who refers to them as "*blocks* of fractured stone, or *squared* 'fragments'" (91).

One of the 4 blocks is outside the pyramid, "just beyond the point of the original entrance" (Lepre 89). It measures

> 38″ long by 21″ thick by 29″ high. (90)
>
> [This particular "fragment" has] three holes [that measure 3½″]. . . drilled into the block, and they are exactly 6½″ apart—the precise distance between the vertical channels cut into the south wall of the [King's] antechamber. (91)

According to Edwards, this granite block was originally found by Petrie in the descending passage (105-106). However, while Petrie described the block he discovered as "large", the only measurement he cited for it was a thickness of 20.6 inches, and he specified that it had "on one edge a part of an old Egyptian tubular drill hole, which had been cut right through the mass." Other than adding that it was a puzzle as to what part of the pyramid the block had come from and that there was "nothing like it, and no place for it, is known", Petrie had nothing else to say about it (see page 8 of *The Pyramids and Temples of Gizeh*).

He never stated that he or anyone else removed the block from the descending passage to a position just outside the entrance, nor did he state that it came from the King's antechamber as theorized by Edwards. Clearly, since Petrie's block had only one hole drilled in it, it is not the same block described by Lepre.

Another granite fragment can be found in the pit in the subterranean chamber. This fragment measures

> 30″ long by 21″ thick by 12″ high. (90)
>
> [It is about] 10′ down from the top of the shaft [on a ledge]. . . .
>
> [And it] is finely hewn and polished and has two large drill holes, 3½″ in diameter, running through it. (114)

A 3rd fragment rests inside the small antechamber located in the horizontal passage to the subterranean chamber. This fragment has no holes drilled in it. It is

> 18″ long by 21″ thick by 18″ high. (90)

The 4th fragment can be found "in the center of the Grotto". It contains one

> 3½″ drill hole bored through it; its dimensions are 21″ by 18″ by 17″. (118)

Since this fragment has just one hole like the one described by Petrie it is possible that they are one and the same, but in that case who went to the trouble to transport it from the descending passage to the grotto? It most certainly would not have been Petrie, who would have avoided doing anything that might lead to further speculation on the part of the pyramidologists. Chances are, the one in the grotto is a different stone, which would leave the whereabouts of Petrie's stone unknown.

Lepre tells us that the 4 granite blocks are not "set into masonry, but are loosely set on portions of limestone." And they are a mystery because "they are in areas where there is no other granite" (90).

Lepre attempts to solve this mystery by suggesting that they are fragments from the 3 portcullis blocks that were supposedly installed at one time in the 21-inch wide grooves in the east and west walls of the King's antechamber, and that, he reasons, is why the fragments are 21 inches thick.

But, in that case, how did the fragments "come to rest at such disparate locations both inside and outside the pyramid" (91)? Lepre, again, thinks he has the answer. The fragments, he contends, "became the objects of revelry for groups of delinquents who needed to let out their frustrations at not having found anything of value in their search of the pyramid" (92).

Fleshing out this scenario, Lepre continues:

> It is not very difficult to visualize how groups of such men could have *rolled* the two granite fragments now found in the pit of the subterranean chamber and the niche preceding it from the antechamber, down the Grand Gallery, first ascending corridor and descending passage to the above-mentioned locations. Admittedly, the locations of the third and fourth granite fragments do present something more of a problem. For the block located just outside of the original entrance of the

> pyramid, after having been *playfully rolled* down the Grand Gallery and first ascending passage, would then have [had] to be pushed up—and with great labor I might add—that 50′-section of the descending passage which runs from the terminus of Al Mamoun's [sic] Passage where it breaks into the west wall of that descending passage, to the aperture of the original entrance. [Based on Petrie's figures, Lepre needs to add another 42 feet to his 50 in order to make the correct total of 92 feet.] Why vandals would have devoted so much effort to positioning this granite block at that point may at first seem puzzling. Yet if one considers the pitch and fervor of the moment, and the great enthusiasm which usually accompanies such acts of frenzy and impetuousness, the resulting behavior is quite comprehensible.
>
> With the repositioning of the fourth and final stone the reasoning of such actions can likewise be understood. But here, the method employed is even more unusual. This fragment was *rolled* down the Grand Gallery, as were the other fragments. From here it was lowered down the well shaft and placed inside the grotto. But it could not have been rolled down the well shaft, which is vertical at its upper end; rather; it had to be lowered, having been first fastened with a rope—an activity which must have presented no small difficulty. (92; italics added)

The fragments were *playfully rolled* down the Grand Gallery? How? As Lepre makes clear, the fragments are squared. How is it possible to roll an object that is squared? And what about the weight? The 3 missing portcullis blocks that Lepre speaks of would have been, according to his own estimate,

> 48½″ wide by 48½″ high by 21″ thick; this is specifically

> determined by the width of the chamber where the slabs were to have been set into place, the width of the grooves located in the side walls, and the height of the passage leading from the antechamber to the King's Chamber. (90)

Ludwig Borchardt conjectured that each portcullis would have weighed "about 2¼ tons", or 4500 pounds (Edwards 106). Using that figure, the smallest of the 4 fragments, measuring 17 inches by 18 inches by 21 inches, would weigh over 1000 pounds, which would not make for easy handling. And yet Lepre expects us to go along with his contention that the four fragments were *playfully* transported from the King's antechamber to their current locations by "groups of delinquents" who were so frustrated at not having found any treasure inside the Great Pyramid that this was the best course of action they could think of to work off their frustration. It seems fair to ask, what kind of satisfaction might these frustrated delinquents have obtained by such insane behavior?

The truth is, there never were 3 portcullises in the King's antechamber; the 4 blocks are in their current locations for symbolic reasons, and here, one by one, is what they symbolize.

The block just outside the original entrance to the pyramid has to do with our spirits being accompanied by 2 of the Lord's servants at the time we come to the earth to be born into mortality. The 3½-inch diameter of the holes links us to Christ, our elder brother, while at the same time it symbolizes—along with the 6½-inch separation between the holes—the fact that as spirits we are incomplete.

The dimensions of the block itself—21 inches x 29 inches x 38 inches—must be considered since 2 out of the 3 numbers are found in the King's Chamber. As we recall, there are 21 stones in the floor, plus the 3rd course consists of 21 stones when the huge stone over the entrance is included. As for the number 38, the stone with 3 open joints uncovered by Lepre in the bottom southwest corner of the west wall measures 38 inches wide (270).

Because 21 is 3 x 7 it can represent not only Isaac but also Enoch.

If all 4 fragments were stacked on top of each other they would have a combined thickness of 84 inches (4 x 21), and in gematria the phrase "the seventh from Adam" adds up to 84 (Bullinger 194). The 7th from Adam is Enoch.

The number 38 was discussed in connection with the beginning of the Grand Gallery's floor where its association with Christ was made explicit. That same association applies to the width of the ascending passage at its lower end and to the block of squared granite just outside the pyramid's original entrance.

Lepre mistakenly places the entrance at the 13th course (see page 89); instead, it is at the 17th course (Lawton and Ogilvie-Herald 19). When the exterior casing was intact, the entrance was at the 19th course. And how thick is the 19th course? It is 38 inches (Petrie16-17; Lemesurier 51; Rutherford, Book III, 949). In contrast, the 17th course is 11 inches thinner, being 27 inches thick (Lemesurier, chart on page 377). In the King's Chamber, we have not only the 9 stones in the ceiling that run 17 feet, but the top stones in the east and west walls cover the same distance, so there are actually 11 stones that measure 17 feet. It borders on being amusing, this combination of numbers that so plainly tie in with Joseph.

Now that we have seen the numbers 17, 19, 21, 27, and 38 take on symbolic significance in the King's Chamber there should be no reason to doubt that the link between it and the placement of the pyramid's original entrance and the granite block with its 3 holes—which can be compared not only to the south wall of the King's antechamber but also to the 3 pinion holes of the sarcophagus—was according to a preconceived plan and not to some pharaoh's inexplicable change of mind as to where he wanted to be buried.

The number 29 that is associated with the block at the pyramid's entrance figures in the horizontal passage to the subterranean chamber, and that passage, as previously noted, represents the spirit prison where the majority of mankind will end up before the final judgment, but we also need to be reminded that 29 is included in the 129 feet of the ascending passage, which leads to both the Queen's Chamber and the

King's Chamber. All mankind, then, is accounted for in the block's 3 numbers.

The 2 holes in the granite stone positioned on the ledge in the pit of the subterranean chamber represent two sentinels standing guard over the sons of perdition, preventing their escape. The measurements of this stone—12 by 21 by 30—again link it to the King's Chamber with its floor of 21 stones, but there is also a link to the King's antechamber. Remember the 12 inches of limestone at the top of the south wall in the antechamber? Here is the connection. If granite represents the divine—and it does—then Limestone represents the earthly, or to put it another way, the lack of perfection. That certainly applies to the symbolism of the pit in the subterranean chamber.

In addition, remember the pit that is sunk 30 feet beneath the floor in the King's Chamber? The number 30 is a key factor in Judas Iscariot's betrayal of Christ, for he received 30 pieces of silver from the chief priests for turning traitor (Matthew 26:15). About Judas, Christ said, "woe to that man by whom the Son of Man is betrayed! It would have been good for that man if he had never been born" (Mark 15:21). Having been one of the Twelve Apostles and therefore knowing that Christ was the son of God and the promised messiah, Judas's betrayal, added to his taking his own life (Matthew 27:5), makes him a prime example of those who will be cast into the pit.

The relationship between the stone in the subterranean chamber's pit and the features in the King's Chamber and antechamber is so evident as to be undeniable.

In a related matter, in the antechamber to the burial chamber of the tomb of Tutankhamen, there stood

> two life-sized figures of a king in black, facing each other like sentinels, gold kilted, gold sandalled, armed with mace and staff. . . .
>
> These [Howard Carter wrote] were the dominant objects that caught the eye at first. (Quoted in Reeves' *The Complete Tutankhamun* 78)

The traditional explanation for the presence of these 2 statues, these "divinities in human form" (Casson 176), is that they were meant to protect the pharaoh and his burial chamber. But what if they were meant instead to keep the pharaoh imprisoned inside the chamber? That would put an entirely different slant on things, would it not?

As already observed, there are clear signs in the tomb that the man buried there was evil-minded. Among these signs is the fact that he

> was locked away at the center of a series of cases, each fitting inside another like Chinese boxes—four outer shrines of gilded wood; then a sculptured stone sarcophagus; then three inlaid coffins, the innermost, weighing 242 pounds, of solid gold. (Casson 178)

Significantly, the outer coffin was "so tight a fit that its extrication was a problem. Moreover, it seemed unbelievably heavy" (Hobson 113). Additionally, the 3 coffins were not identical. The outer two were not of solid gold but of gilded wood (Reeves and Wilkinson, *The Complete Valley of the Kings* 123).

The coffins were not designed to be identical because they represent the 3 degrees of glory. The smallest of the coffins is the innermost one made of solid gold. It represents the celestial glory. It represents what the man in the tomb could have attained if he had been righteous.

The tomb of Tutankhamen is the smallest of the so-called royal tombs in the Valley of the Kings. How many chambers does it contain? Four. Furthermore,

> Eight distinct types of large seal impressions [were used] to stamp the plastered outer surfaces of the blockings erected at either end of the corridor and at the entrances into the Burial Chamber and the Annexe. (Reeves, *The Complete Tutankhaum* 92)

The tomb is entered by descending a staircase. How many steps in the staircase? Sixteen (Hobson 111).

These elements indicate a connection between the tomb and the open joints of the stone in the southwest corner of the King's Chamber.

At the bottom of the staircase is a descending passage which leads to the tomb's antechamber. Along with the 2 sentinels, the antechamber housed a wooden lion, "standing six feet long, [and] designed as a bier" (Casson 174). This lion exhibits a distinctly sad expression; it is, in fact, weeping. Why was it depicted as weeping if the man in the tomb was a pharaoh who was going to become a god? On the other hand, if the man's heart was not pure, if he was evil-minded, then he would be consigned to the lowest of the heavens, or perhaps even be condemned as a son of perdition. In that case, the lion would have reason to weep.

The lion, by the way, represents Christ, who is called in the book of Revelation "the Lion of the tribe of Judah" (5:5). And in "The Book of Moses" Christ weeps over the evil "residue of the people" (7:28).

Resuming the discussion of the 4 granite fragments, the one in the niche or antechamber to the subterranean chamber has no holes, which sets it apart from the other 3; however, its dimensions—18 by 18 by 21—link it to the King's Chamber, where the east wall is composed of 18 stones (Rutherford, Book III, (106), plus one of the 2 missing floor stones had a depth of 18 inches (Lepre 90).

From other sources, we have important ties to this unusual fragment. For instance, in *The Book of Enoch the Prophet*, the leaders or chiefs of the fallen angels number 18 (Laurence VII:9), and in the Old Testament a series of passages revolve around the same number.

> And the children of Israel. . . did evil in the sight of the Lord. So the Lord strengthened Eglon king of Moab against Israel. . . .
>
> So the children of Israel served Eglon king of Moab eighteen years. (Judges 3:12 and 14)
>
> Then the children of Israel again did evil in the sight of the Lord. . . .

> So the anger of the Lord was hot against Israel; and He sold them into the hands of the Philistines and into the hands of the people of Ammon.
>
> From that year they harassed and oppressed the children of Israel for eighteen years. (Judges 10:6-8)
>
> In the eighteenth year of King Jeroboam the son of Nebat, Abijam became king over Judah. . . .
>
> And he walked in all the sins of his father, which he had done before him; his heart was not loyal to the Lord his God. (1 Kings 15:1 and 3)
>
> Now Jehoram the son of Ahab became king over Israel at Samaria in the eighteenth year of Jehoshaphat king of Judah. . . .
>
> And he did evil in the sight of the Lord. (2 Kings 3:1-2)
>
> Jehoiachin was eighteen years old when he became king, and he reigned in Jerusalem three months. . . .
>
> And he did evil in the sight of the Lord, according to all that his father had done. (2 Kings 24:8-9)

In the New Testament, Christ issues a warning that involves the number 18:

> "[Of] those eighteen on whom the tower in Siloam fell and killed them, do you think that they were worse sinners than all other men who dwelt in Jerusalem?
>
> "I tell you, no; but unless you repent you will all likewise perish." (Luke 13:4-5)

In the same chapter of Luke we have a more positive association with the number 18:

> there was a woman who had a spirit of infirmity eighteen years, and was bent over and could in no way raise herself up.
>
> But when Jesus saw her, He called her to Him and said to her, "Woman, you are loosed from your infirmity." And He laid His hands on her [to bless her], and immediately she was made straight, and glorified God. (Luke 13:11-13)

Looking back to the Old Testament for a moment, we learn in the First Book of the Chronicles that 18 able men served as gate-keepers in the House of the Lord (26:9 and 12).

Bonnie Gaunt teaches that the "number 18 is often used for the combined concept of the Deity and the work of creation and redemption" (74). Her teaching in this matter is sound.

The presence of the granite fragment in the antechamber to the subterranean chamber brings to mind a scene described in *Return from Tomorrow*. Concerning the plain where he saw "hordes of ghostly discarnate beings. . . locked in what looked like fights to the death," George Ritchie says:

> Gradually I was becoming aware that there was something else on that plain of grappling forms. Almost from the beginning I had sensed it, but for a long time I could not locate it. When I did it was with a shock that left me stunned.
>
> That entire unhappy plain was hovered over by beings seemingly made of light. It was their. . . blinding brightness that had prevented me at first from seeing them. Now that I had, now that I adjusted my eyes to take them in, I could see that these immense presences were bending over the little creatures on the plain. Perhaps even conversing with them.

> . . . I clearly saw. . . that not one of these bickering beings on the plain had been abandoned. They were being attended, watched over, ministered to. And the equally observable fact was that not one of them knew it. (Ritchie and Sherrill 63 and 66)

Ritchie reveals that this plain, which is part of the spirit prison, is here on the earth (63).

Now, why are there no holes in the fragment located in the antechamber to the subterranean chamber? There are no holes because the number of celestial servants attempting to redeem the people in the spirit prison is unlimited. For every person in the spirit prison there is a servant of the Lord available to bring that spirit up to a higher level if he or she ever becomes teachable.

But, there are also no holes in the block because the people in the spirit prison are, as Ritchie indicated, blind to the help that is being offered. Unlike the other 3 blocks, if this one was held up to the light no light would pass through. The symbolism involved is applicable to the spiritual darkness of the spirit prison.

The 4th stone, which is in the grotto, has almost the same dimensions as the one just discussed, however, instead of being 18 by 18 it is 18 by 17, with the standard thickness of 21 inches, and it has a single 3½-inch hole.

This single hole has a number of associations, the most important being the one way to achieve exaltation, which is by and through Jesus Christ. He is the one gate, the one door to the celestial kingdom.

For the numbers 18 and 17, there is an important incident recorded in the Book of Jeremiah that relates directly to both.

> The word that came to Jeremiah from the Lord in the tenth year of Zedekiah king of Judah, which was the *eighteenth* year of Nebuchadnezzar.
>
> For then the king of Babylon's army besieged Jerusalem, and Jeremiah the prophet was shut up in

the court of the prison, which was in the king of Judah's house.

For Zedekiah king of Judah had shut him up, saying, "Why do you prophesy and say, 'Thus says the Lord: "Behold, I will give this city into the hand of the king of Babylon, and he shall take it; and Zedekiah king of Judah shall not escape from the hand of the Chaldeans, but shall surely be delivered into the hand of the king of Babylon"'?"

And Jeremiah said, "The word of the Lord came to me, saying, 'Behold, Hanamel the son of Shallum your uncle will come to you, saying, "Buy my field which is in Anathoth. . . for the right of inheritance is yours, and the redemption yours; buy it for yourself." [Anathoth, which was about 3 miles north of Jerusalem, was Jeremiah's birthplace.] Then I knew that this was the word of the Lord.

"So I bought the field from Hanamel. . . and weighed out to him the money—*seventeen* shekels of silver. . . .

"Then I charged Baruch [Jeremiah's scribe]. . . saying, 'Thus says the Lord of hosts, the God of Israel: "Take these deeds, both this purchase deed which is sealed and this deed which is open, and put them in an earthen vessel, that they may last many days."

'For thus says the Lord of hosts, the God of Israel: "Houses and fields and vineyards shall be possessed again in this land."'

"Now when I had delivered the purchase deed to Baruch the son of Neriah, I prayed to the Lord, saying, 'Ah, Lord God! . . . You are great in counsel and mighty in work, for your eyes are open to all the ways of the

> sons of men, to give everyone according to his ways and according to the fruit of his doings. You have set signs and wonders in the land of Egypt, to this day'". (32:1-4; 6-9; 13-17; and 19-20; italics added)

Nelson's Illustrated Bible Dictionary explains the significance of this incident by pointing out that (1), the name Anathoth means "answered prayers" [notice the inclusion of the name *Thoth* in Ana*thoth*], and (2), Jeremiah's purchase of the field "was to serve as a sign of God's promised redemption of Israel" (Lockyer, Sr. 47).

Another 17 that has not yet been mentioned has a bearing on the granite stone in the grotto. The number 153, as we have seen, is an important factor in the Grand Gallery, the King's antechamber, and the King's Chamber, and 153, as Lemesurier notes, is "the sum of the numbers 1 to 17" (30; footnote), so by association we are back to the gathering of the fish, or in other words, the salvation of man as brought about by Christ and his authorized servants.

And that is what is represented by the granite fragment in the grotto.

* * *

A detailed discussion of the 4 narrow shafts in the King's and Queen's Chambers will be left for the 2nd volume in this series, but before leaving the subject it should be pointed out that the celestial kingdom's ministration to the terrestrial kingdom and the terrestrial kingdom to the telestial provides the explanation for the connections that have been demonstrated between the King's Chamber and the Queen's Chamber and between the Queen's Chamber and the subterranean chamber, along with their connecting passages. In addition, there are connections between the King's Chamber and the subterranean chamber because the celestial kingdom has the overall responsibility for all kingdoms and for maintaining control over the outer darkness and the sons of perdition.

To give just one more example of these connections, the floor of the dead-end passage is 41 inches lower than the floor of the horizontal passage to the subterranean chamber; the depth of the niche in the Queen's Chamber is 41 inches; and the exterior height of the sarcophagus in the King's Chamber is 41 inches.

And now the time has come to discuss the 2nd cataclysmic event that is reflected in the open joints and cracked ceiling beams in the King's Chamber—as well as in the fact that "two different kinds of plaster show that repair work to the fissures [or cracks in the King's Chamber and in the upper compartments] took place twice" (Lawton and Ogilvie-Herald 134). This event, which is recorded in the Revelation of John the Beloved, revolves around the assault on Jerusalem that will be carried out in the near future.

Petrie, in his examination of the King's Chamber, discovered a total of 11 joints that had been opened (27). In Chapter 11 of Revelation we read of 2 prophets who, after defending Jerusalem for 3½ years, will be killed by "the beast that ascends out of the bottomless pit" (verse 7). Whereas the pit in the subterranean chamber represents the prison from which Satan will be released (Revelation 20:7), the one that descends 30 feet below the floor of the King's Chamber represents the beast's bottomless pit.

As we continue with Chapter 11 we learn that the prophets'

> dead bodies will lie in the street of the great city which spiritually is called Sodom and Egypt. . . .
>
> Then those from the peoples, tribes, tongues, and nations will see their dead bodies three-and-a-half days, and not allow their dead bodies to be put into graves. (Verses 8-9)

These verses tie in with the uprooted floor stones in the King's Chamber. Regarding these stones, Lawton and Ogilvie-Herald report "that as of March 1999" they have "been replaced as part of the ongoing restoration of the edifice by the authorities, so that the floor is once again complete" (264, note # 26).

This restoration is part of the fulfillment of Peter's prophecy that all things would be restored before Christ returned (Acts 3:19-21). In keeping with this prophecy, we learn from Lepre that one of the missing stones had been 58 inches long while the other was 33 inches (page 90); 58 represents the elders and 33 the high priests of the Church of Jesus Christ, but in addition, 58 + 33 = 91, Jacob's age when Joseph was born, and Joseph's key mission in life was to restore the church in Egypt, which he did.

The 2 previously missing stones measured 21 and 31 inches wide, and 21 + 31 = 52, a match for the length of the 1st low passage in the King's antechamber. Likewise, the 101 stones that comprise the walls of the King's Chamber match the 101-inch length of the 2nd low passage in the antechamber, and both contrast with the 101 feet (1213 inches) that make up the vertical distance from the Great Pyramid's pavement to the south end of the subterranean chamber's dead-end passage (Petrie 31).

Petrie gives a slightly different measurement for the vertical distance from the pyramid's pavement to the beginning of the dead-end passage. That figure is 1219 inches or 101.5833 feet (31). What were the lengths of the 2 missing stones? They were 58 and 33 inches.

The combined depth of the 2 missing stones is also important. Together they came to 46 inches—18 inches + 28 inches (Lepre 90). The west and north walls of the King's Chamber have a combined total of 46 stones (Lepre, diagram on page 98). The southwest corner stone with the 3 open joints is 46 inches high (Lepre 270). And the subterranean chamber is 46 feet east to west (Lawton and Ogilvie-Herald 19).

The number 46 is emphasized in the following exchange between Christ and a group of Jews who opposed him.

> Now the Passover of the Jews was at hand, and Jesus went up to Jerusalem.
>
> And He found in the temple [meaning the temple grounds, not inside the temple itself] those who sold oxen and sheep and doves, and the money changers doing business.

> When He had made a whip of cords, He drove them all out of the temple, with the sheep and the oxen, and poured out the changers' money and overturned the tables.
>
> And He said to those who sold doves, "Take these things away! Do not make My Father's house a house of merchandise!"
>
> . . . So the Jews answered and said to Him, "What sign do You show to us, since You do these things?"
>
> Jesus answered and said to them, "Destroy this temple, and in three days I will raise it up."
>
> Then the Jews said, "It has taken *forty-six* years to build this temple, and will You raise it up in three days?"
>
> But he was speaking of the temple of His body.
>
> (John 2:13-16 and 18-21; italics added)

What we need to grasp here is the relationship between Christ's death and resurrection and the floor stones that were restored to their former positions in March 1999. March is the 3rd month; Christ was resurrected on the 3rd day. Earlier in this chapter the number 19 was associated with Christ; 99 is also associated with him, not just because of his parable concerning the 99 sheep and the one that went astray but because the gematria for *Amen* is 99 (Gaunt 17).

Amen—which is also spelled Amon or Amun—was the great Egyptian god who was called by a name that meant "*the hidden*". "Little is known of his original character," says Veronica Ions, and that is why he was given this unusual name (93). Amen exemplified "the dynamic force of life." His symbol was the ram (Bunson 19-20).

It should not be necessary to list any more details about Amen for most readers to realize that Amen was another name for Christ, whose life was also hidden in that we know nothing of his activities from the age of 12 until he began his ministry at the age of 30. That is a period of 18 years—and a link to the granite blocks in the grotto and in the niche of the horizontal passage to the subterranean chamber.

Confirmation of Christ's identification with Amen can be found in Revelation 3:14, where Christ is called "Amen, the Faithful and True Witness, the Beginning of the creation of God".

Like Christ, the 2 prophets who will defend Jerusalem are called witnesses (Revelation 11:3). Their dead bodies lying in the street of the city were meant to be represented by the 2 stones that were removed and placed on top of other stones in the floor. Their unused graves were represented by the holes that were created when the stones were lifted out.

The 2 floor stones that went missing for many years represented the 2 prophets who went missing when they were translated during the Old Testament period. The restoration of the stones signifies their "return", and the 11 open joints, which can be related to Christ's declaration that "it is the eleventh hour, and the last time that I shall call laborers into my vineyard" (*Doctrine and Covenants* 33:3), warn us that the time is imminent.

In Revelation 11:9 the list of "peoples, tribes, tongues, and nations" adds up to 4, which is a match for the height of the blocks in the King's Chamber. But in addition, *Nelson's Illustrated Bible Dictionary* points out that 4 is a repeating number in the book of Revelation; for instance, there are "four living creatures, four horsemen and four angels" (Lockyer, Sr. 916).

The 4 living creatures—or beasts, as they are called in some translations—are associated with 24 elders who are seated around the throne of the Lord (Revelation 4:4 and 6). In the King's Chamber the 4th course up from the floor contains 24 stones, which parallels the arrangement in John's vision. The 24 elders represent the 12 patriarchs of the 12 tribes of Israel and the Lord's Twelve Apostles (Draper 46), but the number 24 is also a link to the occurrence of that number in the distance that the original entrance to the Great Pyramid is offset to the east and to the 24 feet of contiguous girdle stones.

In the book of Revelation there are other sets of 4 in earlier chapters; for example, in Revelation 6:8 we read:

> I [John] looked, and there before me was a pale horse! Its rider was named Death, and Hades was following close behind him. They were given power over a fourth of the earth to kill by sword, famine and plague, and by the beasts of the earth. (NIV)

The set of 4 in this instance is the series of "sword, famine and plague, and. . . beasts".

Now, notice something else about Revelation 6:8. We have Death and Hades, which are 2, and associated with them is the number ¼. What did Petrie say about the King's Chamber?

> [T]he builders were altogether wrong in their levels, and tilted the whole chamber over to one corner, so that their courses are 2¼ inches higher at the N.E. than at the S.W.

The builders were not wrong, but Petrie's understanding was. Had he realized why the King's Chamber exhibited such anomalies he would not have been astonished at what he perceived as an error on the part of the ancient builders. The 2 and ¼ in his quote represents Death and Hades personified and their power to destroy ¼ of the earth, and the chamber was tilted because the earth's axis is going to be tilted as it was in the days of Noah (see Laurence's translation of *The Book of Enoch the Prophet*, Chapter LXIV, verse 1).

Related to these catastrophic events is the image of a sickle created by the course changes of the northern shaft in the King's Chamber. From the 14th chapter of Revelation we have:

> Then I looked, and behold, a white cloud, and on the cloud sat One like the Son of Man, having on His head a golden crown, and in His hand a sharp *sickle.*

> And another angel came out of the temple, crying with a loud voice to Him who sat on the cloud, "Thrust in Your sickle and reap, for the time has come for You to reap, for the harvest of the earth is ripe."
>
> So He who sat on the cloud thrust in his sickle on the earth, and the earth was reaped. (Verses 14-16; italics added)

This reaping is the separation of the Lord's "wheat", meaning the righteous, from the tares, i.e. the wicked or those living on a telestial level (see Matthew 13:24-30).

Now we turn again to the 11th chapter of Revelation:

> after the three-and-a-half days the breath of life from God entered them [the 2 prophets], and they stood on their feet, and great fear fell on those who saw them.
>
> And they heard a loud voice from heaven saying to them, "Come up here." And they ascended to heaven in a cloud, and their enemies saw them.
>
> In the same hour there was a great earthquake, and *a tenth* of the city fell. (Verses 11-13; italics added)

Compare the 1/10 in verse 13 to the "1/10 of a mile length of granite blocks" observed in the King's Chamber by Petrie. Furthermore, his statement that the width of the chamber "is lengthened .3 by a crack in the south wall" is paralleled by Revelation 16:18-19.

> And there were noises and thunderings and lightnings; and there was a great earthquake, such a mighty and great earthquake as had not occurred since men were on the earth.
>
> Now the great city [Jerusalem] was divided into *three parts*. (Italics added)

Petrie also recorded the following important observation about the King's Chamber and the 5 compartments associated with it:

> Not only has this wreck overtaken the chamber itself, but in every one of the spaces above it are the massive roof-beams either cracked across or torn out of the wall, more or less, at the South side; and the great Eastern and Western walls of limestone, between, and independent of which, the whole of these construction chambers are built, have *sunk bodily*. (27; italics added)

Compare the conclusion of this quote to the conclusion of the sentence cited above from Revelation:

> . . . and the cities of the nations *fell*. (Italics added)

It is the fall of cities and nations that is represented by the sunken condition of the limestone walls that enclose the compartments above the King's Chamber.

Let's go back momentarily to Revelation 6:8 where Death and Hades have the power to kill "a fourth of the earth". This 4th is part—but not all—of the people who will be living on the telestial level or lower at the time of Christ's second coming. Some of these people will end up in the outer darkness represented by the subterranean chamber's dead-end passage, which can be linked to Revelation 6:8 by Petrie's discovery that the sides of the passage "wind 6 or 8 inches in and out" (20).

Now, a few questions arise.

First: why was the King's Chamber, which represents the celestial kingdom, designed to simulate the effects of 2 earthquakes? Shouldn't the chamber be perfect to mirror the perfection of the highest kingdom of heaven?

Answer: in his discussion of the last days Christ told his disciples, "the powers of the heavens will be shaken" (Matthew 24:29). This is precisely why the King's Chamber appears to have been shaken so forcefully.

Incidentally, it should have been noticed by now how the acoustic qualities of the King's Chamber have their counterpart in the multitude of sounds associated with the second coming.

Another question: why does the south wall of the King's Chamber show signs of suffering the most damage?

Answer: during the preexistence, Satan, who is also known as Lucifer, said in his heart

> "I will ascend into heaven,
> I will exalt my throne above the stars of God;
> I will also sit on the mount of the congregation
> On the farthest sides of the north. . .
> I will be like the Most High."
> (Isaiah 14:13-14)

God's abode is in the north, consequently, when Lucifer fell from heaven (Isaiah 14:12), he fell to the south. The end of the subterranean chamber's dead-end passage is the farthest point south in the Great Pyramid. South is associated with evil. In addition, the south is emphasized in a revelation given to the prophet Ezekiel that concerns the house of Israel:

> "Son of man, set your face toward the south; preach against the south and prophesy against the forest land, the South, and say to the forest of the South, 'Hear the word of the Lord! Thus says the Lord God: "Behold, I will kindle a fire in you, and it shall devour every green tree and every dry tree in you; the blazing flame shall not be quenched, and all faces from the south to the north shall be scorched by it."'" (20:46-47)

In *The Book of Enoch the Prophet*, winds from the south are hot and they bring "blight and destruction" (Laurence, LXXV:6 and 8). And in the Book of Zechariah we're told that all nations will be gathered

> to battle against Jerusalem. . . .
> Then the Lord will go forth
> And fight against those nations. . .
> And in that day His feet will stand on the Mount of Olives,
> Which faces Jerusalem on the east.
> And the Mount of Olives shall be split in two,
> From east to west,
> Making a very large valley;
> Half of the mountain shall move toward the north
> And half of it toward the south.
> (14:2-4)

The King's Chamber with its simulation of great catastrophes should be correlated with the first section of the *Doctrine and Covenants*:

> the voice of the Lord is unto all men, and there is none to escape; and there is no eye that shall not see, neither ear that shall not hear, neither heart that shall not be penetrated.
>
> And the rebellious shall be pierced with much sorrow; for their iniquities shall be spoken upon the housetops, and their secret acts shall be revealed.
>
> And the voice of warning shall be unto all people, by the mouths of my disciples. . . .
>
> And the anger of the Lord is kindled, and his sword is bathed in heaven, and it shall fall upon the inhabitants of the earth.
>
> And the arm of the Lord shall be revealed; and the day cometh that they who will not hear the voice of the Lord, neither give heed to the words of the prophets and apostles, shall be cut off from among the people. (Verses 2-4 and 13-14)

The message built into the King's Chamber is also linked to Malachi 4:5:

> Behold, I will send you Elijah the prophet
>
> Before the coming of the great and dreadful day of the Lord.

During Elijah's mortal ministry "heaven was shut up *three years and six months*, and there was a great famine throughout all the land" (Luke 4:25; italics added). Elijah will exercise that divine power once more, for he will be one of the 2 prophets to stand against Jerusalem's enemies before the great and dreadful day comes.

Who will be the other prophet?

He will be the 7th from Adam, he who was not for the Lord took him.

He will be Enoch the Seer.

15. HWFW

> Someone asked him, "Lord, are only a few people going to be saved?"
>
> He said to them, "Make every effort to enter through the narrow door, because many, I tell you, will try to enter and will not be able to."
>
> (NIV, Luke 13:23-24)

In the 4 uppermost compartments above the King's Chamber, hieroglyphs or quarry marks, as the Egyptologists call them, can be seen on some of the stones. On one of them, according to Ahmed Fakhry, the marks

> record the seventeenth year of Khufu's reign, showing that the building had reached this stage at that time. These are the only places where Khufu's name occurs inside the pyramid. (120)

While there is no factual information to back up Fakhry's supposition that the number 17 is to be equated with that particular stage of construction, it has nevertheless been accepted as a fact by other Egyptologists as well as pyramidologists such as Rutherford, who praises Fakhry's book *The Pyramids* as a "fine work". Rutherford comments:

> This reveals that Khufu was still living in the 17th year of his reign and that the King's Chamber was completed

> and sealed-over [sic] a certain time before that. We learn from the ancient records that Khufu reigned 23 years and with this the leading Egyptologists are in agreement. (Book III, 967).

Rutherford is correct in regard to the Egyptologists' acceptance of a 23-year reign for Khufu (see, for example, page 8 of Lehner's *The Complete Pyramids* and page 138 of Margaret Bunson's *Dictionary of Ancient Egypt*; both list the dates of 2551-2528 BC, which is 23 years).

Seventeen and 23? Aren't these numbers associated with Joseph, the son of Jacob? Yes, Joseph was 17 when he was taken to Egypt by the Ishmaelite traders who bought him from his brothers, and he was patriarch number 23 from the Genesis period.

But, did Joseph build the Great Pyramid? No, of course not. When Joseph arrived in Egypt in 1764 BC the Great Pyramid was more than 1100 years old. The Great Pyramid, along with all the other pyramids at Giza, was built by Enoch and his people. However, because of the all-encompassing vision he had been granted of the earth's pre-history, Enoch knew of Joseph, knew that he would be the living image of the Lord just as Seth had been the living image of Adam (see Genesis 5:3), and so Joseph's presence was incorporated into the exterior and interior features of the Great Pyramid, as we have seen in the preceding chapters.

Now, if Joseph is the same as Khufu, how did he receive this name? This is a viable question since we're told in Genesis 41:45 that once he had made Joseph his co-ruler, the pharaoh called him Zaphnath-Paaneah. But there is a difference here—Khufu is not a name. What Khufu really means will be explained by starting with some basic information about ancient Egyptian hieroglyphs.

According to virtually all Egyptologists, the word *hieroglyph*—which is actually Greek—means "sacred writing" and,

> [a]bove all, the hieroglyphic script was associated with Thoth. . . . It has even been suggested that the hieroglyphic system may have originated with the

> temple administration of the cult of this particular god. (Wilkinson, *Symbol & Magic in Egyptian Art* 149-50)

This suggestion is partly right. Many hieroglyphs were a part of the temple administration as established by Christ after Adam and Eve's repentance and after they covenanted with him to obey his commandments, and so hieroglyphs are Adam's "pure and undefiled" written language ("The Book of Moses" 6:6). However, there was no cult to worship Thoth/Enoch, and even though he exercised great power during his mortal ministry, he could not be said to be a god until after he was translated, at which time he was given the authority to stand in for Christ when Christ could not be on the earth himself.

Enoch's knowledge of the temple endowment and his translation—along with those who joined him—account for the following observations taken from various sources:

> **Colin Wilson**: "ancient Egypt. . . was basically a *religious* civilization, bound together in total unity" (327).
>
> **Patrick Boylan**: "[Thoth could] read the secrets of men's hearts" (99; compare to Acts 1:24, the King James Version, where Christ knows "the hearts of all men").
>
> "To make clear the function of Thoth. . . we must here examine briefly the applications of the term *hike* as a substantive [i.e. a noun] in Egyptian.
>
> "In the Pyr[amid] texts, and in the oldest texts of the Book of the Dead *hike* appears as a power (or quality) which is possessed by the gods, and by all the deified dead. It is something which is needed to make divinity complete. . . . It seems, thus, to resemble, somehow, other qualities, or endowments needed for the full perfection of the glorified dead—something, that is, on the same plane as the so-called Kas of Re" (126).

"It is Thoth. . . who pronounces the formulae of 'glorification'" (136).

Meeks and Favard-Meeks: "Normally, the gods were not affected by old age. This was notably the case, we are told, with Thoth" (79).

Boylan: "Re says to Thoth. . . 'thou shalt be in my place. . . thou shalt be called Thoth, the "Substitute for Re"'". (81)

Christiane Desroches-Noblecourt: "[After the solar god departs] for celestial horizons, [he]. . . is replaced by Thoth, the divine scribe, god of the moon, who from the sky governs the world in his stead" (264).

Meeks and Favard-Meeks: "The gods themselves did not hesitate to pass some of their secrets on to people by letting a providential manuscript fall from the heavens. Writing was, plainly, the instrument of revelation; it provided access to the world of the gods" (7).

Lemesurier: "the great Thoth himself (under his Greek name of Hermes Trismegistus) was credited specifically by the Egyptian priest-historian Manetho with having produced 36,525 books of ancient wisdom—*a figure identical to the number of Primitive Inches in the Great Pyramid's designed perimeter* [the "primitive inch" equals 1.00106 standard inches]" (10 and 16; italics by Lemesurier).

If we remove the comma from the number 36,525 and then separate 365 from 25 we have 2 numbers associated with Enoch; he lived 365 years after he began building the city of Zion and he was ordained by Adam at the age of 25.

The *ka* mentioned in the quote from Boylan is the Egyptologists' translation of a hieroglyph that represents a pair of arms and hands raised in the air. They, of course, do not realize that this representation comes from the temple endowment and that it is therefore related to exaltation in the celestial kingdom, and so their interpretation of this hieroglyph is anything but precise and consistent.

For example, Karl-Theodore Zauzich finds *ka* to be "an untranslatable religious concept, meaning something like a person's immortal soul" (21), while Nancy Jenkins in *The Boat Beneath the Pyramid* says *ka* is

> confusingly often translated as "soul", but in a more general sense as a vital animating spirit. The *ka*, which was created at birth, was shown hieroglyphically as two arms extending upward, symbolizing a protective embrace. (146)

Werner Forman and Stephen Quirke have a more lengthy definition of *ka* in their text *Hieroglyphs and the Afterlife in Ancient Egypt*:

> The principle of sustenance throughout eternity receives expression in the Egyptian word *ka*, sometimes used simply for "food", but most often in the innumerable hieroglyphic inscriptions appealing for offerings from king to gods to be handed on to the *ka* of a named individual. Since kingship must endure forever, there would always be a king offering to the gods, giving a perpetual source of sustenance, if only the person could secure a share in it for his own life after death.
>
> Yet the *ka* was not simply a ghost to be conjured after death. It expresses the very essence, we might say loosely spirit, of living. In the concept of *ka* that energy so mundanely present as calories in a diet rises to a level which we consider abstract and spiritual. Our analytical thinking imposes insistently binary models on the word with pairings such as body and soul, physical and spiritual. The *ka* defies modern habits of thought,

> presenting at once "physical" food and "spiritual" energy, and thereby preserves the unity of our earthly existence. (27-28)

After reading this exegesis of *ka* we can appreciate the observation made by Dimitri Meeks and Christine Favard-Meeks that

> contrary to what might be supposed, we do not know the Egyptian language well enough to be perfectly sure of the exact meanings of words. In every religious text—indeed, in practically every line—uncertainty and doubts arise. (4)

Ka should not be translated as "soul", nor was it created at birth. Since *ka* is included in the signs of the priesthood as given in the House of the Lord it can be said to be "without beginning of days" as is said of the priesthood itself (*Doctrine and Covenants* 84:17). And the hieroglyph translated as *ka* does not symbolize "a protective embrace". As for Forman and Quirke, when they write that the "*ka* defies modern habits of thought" they are not speaking for those Latter-day Saints who have been endowed, for the Saints know that the *ka* hieroglyph represents a plea to God to hear what is being said.

Lawton and Ogilvie-Herald, in their discussion of ancient Egyptian texts, come to the conclusion that "hieroglyphs may well contain all sorts of hidden meanings" (230). Zauzich, the author of *Hieroglyphs without Mystery*, makes basically the same point when he notes that numerous hieroglyphic "inscriptions, especially those on temple and tomb walls, were intended 'for eternity'" (29), and when it comes to interpreting these inscriptions, a

> scribal custom with a religious explanation creates difficulties in the reading of royal names and many names of private individuals. Such names usually consist of several words and frequently form a complete sentence. (30)

At the end of the paragraph just quoted Zauzich takes something of a defensive stance, claiming that the

> correct reading of royal and private names in which gods' names occur can only be determined by someone with a thorough knowledge of the Egyptian language,

but then he suddenly adopts a different position, saying

> and even then the readings are not always certain, since Egyptologists themselves differ over how some names should be read. (31)

John Anthony West takes a similar tack. He writes:

> Translation of the hieroglyphs is fraught with technical problems. But beyond these technical problems there is a much greater philosophical and theological problem. The sacred texts of Egypt are part of an initiatic religion, and are comprehensible only within that context.

West compares ancient Egyptian records to the 4 gospels in the New Testament, which "are initiatic texts; they are handbooks to a higher state of consciousness" (136). He charges that the "inevitable consequence of this is that, to Egyptologists, an accurate translation of sacred texts is almost impossible."

But West goes a little too far when he contends that "as translated and accepted by Egyptologists, the sacred texts of Egypt are meaningless" (136). Actually, there are times when the Egyptologists' renderings are quite serviceable, as has been demonstrated in this volume—and yet, they are working under a genuine burden by not being familiar with the temple endowment and by making false assumptions that result in totally misleading translations.

One of these false assumptions is that hieroglyphs enclosed by what is called a cartouche always spell out the name of a pharaoh. Hilary

Wilson describes a cartouche as an "oval shape, in the form of a loop of rope" (*Understanding Hieroglyphs* 14).

Does she or any other Egyptologist know why a loop of rope was used? The reason can be found in *The Book of Enoch the Prophet* where Enoch sees ropes given to angels. He is informed that the angels use the ropes to measure the righteous and to strengthen their words, and that the "measures shall reveal all the secrets in the depth of the earth" (Laurence, LX:1-3 and 5-6).

One of the secrets contained within the cartouches is that not all of them enclose names. Let's take *Khufu*, for instance. There are 4 hieroglyphs that the Egyptologists translate as *Khufu*. These hieroglyphs depict a disk with several horizontal lines drawn across it, a quail chick, a horned viper and a second quail chick.

Page 91 of Zauzich's H*ieroglyphs without Mystery* has a drawing of this cartouche, but it is better to see the photo of the cartouche on page 25 of Nancy Jenkins' *The Boat Beneath the Pyramid*. Her photo is of a stone that contains the actual cartouche.

An important detail left out by Zauzich's drawing is the number of lines across the disk. Zauzich has 3, the photo shows 6. What is the significance of 6? It represents man antagonistic to God. How does that apply here? We will see.

Egyptologists are stumped by this disk with its 6 lines. Zauzich, for instance, on page 119 of his work includes the disk along with other "Signs of Doubtful Origin" and after the disk he has written "Placenta" followed by a question mark. Mark Collier and Bill Manley, authors of *How to Read Egyptian Hieroglyphs*, also have "placenta" with a question mark in parenthesis, but willing to make another guess, they include beneath the single word "placenta" the phrase "ball of string", again followed by a question mark in parenthesis (138). Christine Hobson in *The World of the Pharaohs* has "sieve", followed by a question mark (159). Samuel Mercer's *Handbook of Egyptian Hieroglyphs*, revised and expanded by Janice Kamrin, simply identifies the hieroglyph as a disk; there is no mention of the lines across its face (4).

Here is what the disk is related to:

[Following a plague of locusts, after which the pharaoh still refused to set the Israelites free,] the Lord said to Moses, “Stretch out your hand toward heaven, that there may be darkness over the land of Egypt, darkness which may even be felt.”

So Moses stretched out his hand toward heaven, and there was thick darkness in all the land of Egypt three days. (Exodus 10:21-22)

Behold, the day of the Lord comes,
Cruel, with both wrath and fierce anger,
To lay the land desolate:
And he will destroy its sinners from it.
For the stars of heaven and their constellations
Will not give their light:
The sun will be darkened in its going forth,
And the moon will not cause its light to shine.
(Isaiah 13:9-10; italics added)

“Immediately after the tribulation of those days *the sun will be darkened*, and the moon will not give its light”. (Matthew 24:29; italics added)

Now it was about the *sixth hour* [of Christ’s crucifixion], and there was darkness over all the earth until the ninth hour.

Then *the sun was darknened.* (Luke 23:44-45; italics added)

Then the fifth angel sounded: and I saw a star fallen from heaven to the earth. To him was given the key to the bottomless pit.

And he opened the bottomless pit, and smoke arose

> out of the pit like the smoke of a great furnace. So *the sun and the air were darkened* because of the smoke of the pit. (Revelation 9:1-2; italics added)

The disk with lines across its face represents the sun being darkened because of the wickedness of the people who reject Christ. (Incidentally, the "moon will not give its light" after the tribulation of the last days because the moon represents Enoch and for 3½ days Enoch will be dead, his "light" completely extinguished on the earth during that time.)

Now, what do we make of the horned viper that is represented in the cartouche? What did Christ call the generation he tried to teach during his mortal ministry? "Brood of vipers! How can you, being evil, speak good things" (Matthew 12:34)? "Serpents, brood of vipers! How can you escape the condemnation of hell" (Matthew 23:33)?

And the chicks?

> "O Jerusalem, Jerusalem, the one who kills the prophets and stones those who are sent to her! How often I wanted to gather your children together, as a hen gathers her chicks under her wings, but you were not willing!" (Matthew 23:37)

Like the number 153, chicks are referred to only once in the entire Bible, and that makes this reference rather special. Notice that Christ says "Jerusalem" twice and that can be related to the 2 chicks, but in addition, since Egypt was so much like Israel in its rejection of the prophets sent to minister to her, the 2 chicks also represent the 2 lands.

Now we need to return to Zauzich, for he reveals some essential information that has a bearing on the correct translation of the cartouche that combines the 2 chicks, the horned viper and the symbol of the darkened sun.

Zauzich makes it clear that "no one knows exactly how ancient Egyptian words sounded" (7). That being the case, why do Egyptologists list rule after rule as to how to pronounce the ancient Egyptian language? Zauzich himself, starting with page 11 of his text, presents his version of the ancient Egyptian alphabet accompanied by the pronunciation of the letters. To do so is perhaps acceptable as long as we understand that the suggested pronunciation is based on conventions agreed on by Egyptologists and therefore it is "*totally artificial*" (7; italics added).

On page 91 of *Hieroglyphs without Mystery*, Zauzich presents several cartouches that are regarded by Egyptologists as the names of some of the early pharaohs. Included, of course, is the cartouche rendered as *Khufu*. The disk with its 6 lines is transliterated as the letter H, the horned viper as the letter F, and the 2 chicks as Ws, and their order is given as HWFW.

Now, the Egyptologists, apparently uncertain as to what to make of these 4 letters, add a K before the H and they change each W to a U, and that is how they come up with *khufu*. They justify the addition of the K by claiming that the disk should be pronounced like a "soft kh; [or like the] German *ich*" (Zauzich 12)—but remember, such rules of pronunciation are "totally artificial" and therefore are ultimately worthless.

There is no need to add the letter K or to change each W to a U when translating the 4 hieroglyphs. However, since Egyptian hieroglyphs do not include vowels (Mercer 5)—that is, the letters A, E, I, O, and U—what is needed is to add one or more vowels in order to turn the consonants of HWFW into meaningful English words. But which vowels?

Hilary Wilson informs us that in "cases where vowels are necessary to pronunciation the modern convention is to insert the letter 'e'" (30).

Zauzich, however, stresses that

> words using only the vowel *e* do not have a particularly attractive sound. For this reason, other pronunciations that do not follow these rules have long been used for many royal names. Thus the king's name that would

> be vocalized Imenhetep by Egyptological convention occurs in the [Egyptologists'] literature as Amenhotep, Amunhotpe, Amenhetep, and so on. . . . Out of curiosity, someone once took the trouble to count all the renditions in modern publications of the name *Ii-m-ḥtp*, who was the chief architect of King Djoser: he found thirty-four different forms. (8)

In other words, Egyptologists play fast and loose with their own rules, so we should not be criticized for using 2 different vowels in order to make sense of HWFW. Let's go ahead and use an E between the last 2 of these consonants; for the other 2 we'll use an O. The result is: *HOW FEW.*

As stated before, the 4 hieroglyphs under discussion do not spell out a name; in short, there was no pharaoh by the name of Khufu. And as already stated, not all cartouches contain the names of Egyptian kings.

But why did Enoch write the phrase *HOW FEW* in one of the compartments above the King's Chamber? What do these words signify? The answer is in the scriptures.

This chapter began with a quote from Luke 13:23-24 in which the question is asked, will only a *few* people be saved? Christ's reply was basically the same as his declaration recorded in Chapter 7 of Matthew:

> "Because narrow is the gate and difficult is the way which leads to life. . . there are *few* who find it." (Verse 14; italics added)

The word *few* is also stressed in the 9th chapter of Matthew when Christ says:

> "The harvest [of souls] is truly plentiful, but the laborers are *few*." (Verse 37; italics added)

And in Matthew 20:16 Christ advises his disciples that "many are called [to serve the Lord], but few [are] chosen [for exaltation in the celestial kingdom]." Regarding this pronouncement, Joseph Smith provides the following commentary:

> why are they not chosen? Because their hearts are set so much upon the things of this world, and [they] aspire to the honors of men, that they do not learn this one lesson—that the rights of the Priesthood are inseparably connected with the powers of heaven, and that the powers of heaven cannot be controlled nor handled only upon the principles of righteousness. . . .
>
> We have learned by sad experience that it is the nature and disposition of almost all men, as soon as they get a little authority, as they suppose, they will immediately begin to exercise unrighteous dominion. Hence many are called, but few are chosen. (Joseph Fielding Smith, *Scriptural Teachings of the Prophet Joseph Smith* 162)

How few will listen to the missionaries sent to them by the Lord; *how few* will be gathered; *how few* will be exalted in the final judgment, for the generation of vipers that surrounded Christ during his ministry was not unique. Joseph, the son of Jacob, faced a similar generation. Listen to what he says in his own testament:

> my brethren hated me, but the Lord loved me:
>
> They wished to slay me, but the God of my fathers guarded me. . .
>
> I was in prison, and my God showed favour unto me;
>
> In bonds, and He released me;

> Slandered, and He pleaded my cause;
>
> Bitterly spoken against by the Egyptians, and He delivered me;
>
> Envied by my fellow-slaves, and He exalted me. . . .
>
> And I struggled against a shameless woman, urging me to transgress with her; but the God of Israel my father delivered me from the burning flame. (Platt, Jr., "The Testament of Joseph" I:5-6, 13-17, and 19)

When Jacob arrived in Egypt, Joseph introduced him to the pharaoh and the pharaoh

> said to Jacob, "How old are you?"
>
> And Jacob said to Pharaoh, "The days of the years of my pilgrimage [on the earth] are one hundred and thirty years; *few and evil* have been the days of the years of my life, and they have not attained to the days of the years of the life of my fathers in the days of their pilgrimage." (Genesis 47:8-9; italics added)

In light of the foregoing scriptures, could any phrase more appropriate than *how few* have been chosen for placement in the Great Pyramid where the subterranean chamber—the representative of the lowest of the 3 degrees of glory—is larger than the other 2 chambers combined?

* * *

Volume 2 in this series will examine the other pyramids at Giza; the temples; the Sphinx; the so-called trial passages, which are underground and on the east side of the Great Pyramid; an ancient boat that had been dismantled and hidden on the south side of the Great Pyramid; and the iron plate with traces of gold.

The procedure in Volume 2 will be similar to the procedure displayed in Volume 1, except that the pyramidologists will no longer be involved; that is because their only interest is in the Great Pyramid. They have failed to recognize that the other pyramids on the plateau are part of a single plan, and that is because they have accepted the Egyptologists' view that the other pyramids were constructed by different pharaohs at different times. Volume 2 will establish the fallacy of this view.

What will Egyptologists think of Volume 1? The chances are they will never become aware of its existence, but if any of them do, all that should be expected is for them to dismiss it without reading so much as a single page. Egyptologists by and large seem to regard the Bible as no more than myth and so the scriptures that have been cited would mean nothing to them, plus, no matter how much evidence is presented to the contrary, they are not likely to alter their belief that the Great Pyramid was built as a tomb for a pharaoh they insist on calling Khufu.

At any rate, this book was not written for them, nor was it written exclusively for members of the Church of Jesus Christ of Latter-day Saints, for the author already knows that some of them will not believe that Christ and Enoch were responsible for the Great Pyramid. No, this work is aimed primarily at people who know little if anything at all about the church but who are interested in the Great Pyramid and who have an open mind about what its purpose might be. These people, if they are also favorable toward the Bible and believe that it is an authentic history instead of myth, may find themselves convinced that the claims made here are well supported and deserve honest and sincere consideration.

Most readers who reject the thesis of *Books Written in Stone* will do so as a result of accepting the Egyptologists' histories of ancient Egypt as the truth. At the heart of the Egyptologists' histories is the assumption that the ancient Egyptians who built the Great Pyramid used, as Lehner puts it, nothing but "simple tools—such as plumb bobs, string, rope, wood, stone hammers, sledges, copper chisels and saws" (*The Complete Pyramids* 210).

Because a similar attitude toward ancient civilizations in general prevails in our schools, most people are highly skeptical about claims that there was at least one pre-flood civilization that had a technology greater than what we have today. As for the possibility that hundreds of thousands of people from that civilization were translated—changed so that they could live indefinitely without aging, without suffering from disease—and that they are among us today. . . *how few will believe.*

Nevertheless, the day will come when the skeptics, be they Egyptologists or Latter-day Saints or of any other camp, will be convinced that such claims are valid, that Enoch and his people did in fact build the Great Pyramid to represent the 3 degrees of glory, and that they have been on the earth for thousands of years. And that day is not far off, as is evident from the ongoing restoration of ancient structures throughout Egypt, restoration that is being supervised by the prophet and seer whose own writing was for a future generation—which generation is the one inhabiting this planet at the beginning of the 21st century.

WORKS CITED

Abbott, Lyman. Introduction. *The Book of Enoch the Prophet*. Translated by Richard Laurence. 1976. San Diego, CA: Wizards Bookshelf, 1995. iii-xlviii.

Alder, Vicki. *Mysteries in the Scriptures: Enlightenment Through Ancient Beliefs*. Sandy, UT: Wellspring, 1991.

The American Heritage College Dictionary. Third edition. New York: Houghton Mifflin, 1993.

Antelme, Ruth Schumann, and Stephane Rossini. *Becoming Osiris: The Ancient Egyptian Death Experience*. Translated by Jon Graham. 1995. Rochester, Vermont: Inner Traditions, 1998.

Atwater, P. M. H. *Beyond the Light*. 1994. New York: Avon, 1995.

Baines, John, and Jaromir Malek. *The Cultural Atlas of the World: Ancient Egypt*. Alexandria, VA: Stonehenge Press, 1990.

Bauval, Robert, and Adrian Gilbert. *The Orion Mystery*. New York: Crown Trade Paperbacks, 1994.

Biedermann, Hans. *Dictionary of Symbolism*. Translated by James Hulbert. New York: Meridian, 1994.

"The Book of Abraham." *The Pearl of Great Price.* 1902. Salt Lake City, UT: The Church of Jesus Christ of Latter-day Saints, 1997.

The Book of Enoch the Prophet. Translated by Richard Laurence. 1976. San Diego, CA: Wizards Bookshelf, 1995.

"The Book of Moses." *The Pearl of Great Price.* 1902. Salt Lake City, UT: The Church of Jesus Christ of Latter-day Saints, 1997.

Boylan, Patrick. *Thoth: The Hermes of Egypt.* 1922. Chicago: Ares, 1987.

Breasted, James Henry. *Ancient Records of Egypt.* Volume 1. 1906. New York: Russell and Russell, 1962. 5 volumes.

Brewster Jr., Hoyt W. *Behold, I Come Quickly: The Last Days and Beyond.* Salt Lake City, UT: Deseret, 1994.

Brooks, Melvin R. *L.D.S. Reference Encyclopedia.* Salt Lake City, UT: Bookcraft, 1960.

Brunton, Paul. *A Search in Secret Egypt.* Revised edition. 1984. York Beach, Maine: Samuel Weiser, 1995.

Budge, E. A. Wallis. *The Egyptian Heaven and Hell.* 3 volumes. 1905. Mineola, New York: Dover, 1996.

Budge, E. A. Wallis. *An Introduction to Ancient Egyptian Literature.* 1914. Mineola, New York: Dover, 1997.

Budge, E. A. Wallis. *Osiris and the Egyptian Resurrection.* 2 volumes. 1911. New York: Dover, 1973.

Bullinger, E. W. *Number in Scripture.* Grand Rapids, MI: Kregel, 1967.

Bunson, Margaret. *A Dictionary of Ancient Egypt.* 1991. New York: Oxford University Press, 1995.

Casson, Lionel. *Ancient Egypt.* Revised edition. Alexandria, VA: Time-Life, 1977.

Ceram, C. W. *The March of Archaeology.* 1958. New York: Alfred A. Knopf, 1970.

Charles, John D. *Endowed from On High: Understanding the Symbols of the Endowment.* 1997. Bountiful, Utah: Horizon, 1998.

Charlesworth, James H., editor. *The Old Testament Pseudepigrapha.* Volume 1. New York: Doubleday, 1983.

Clark, R. T. Rundle. *Myth and Symbol in Ancient Egypt.* London: Thames and Hudson, 1959.

Clayton, Peter. *Great Figures of Mythology.* New York: Crescent, 1990.

Clemishaw, J. Introduction. *The Great Pyramid: Its Divine Message.* By D. Davidson and H. Aldersmith. Revised edition. London: Williams and Norgate, 1925. v-xii.

Collier, Mark, and Bill Manley. *How to Read Egyptian Hieroglyphs.* Berkeley and Los Angeles: University of California Press, 1998.

Comay, Joan. *The Temple of Jerusalem.* New York: Holt, Rinehart and Winston, 1975.

Constable, George, ed. *Mystic Places.* Alexandria, VA: Time-Life, 1987.

Cottrell, Leonard. *The Mountains of Pharaoh.* London: J. Hale, 1956.

Cox-Chapman, Mally. *The Case for Heaven.* 1995. New York: Berkley, 1996.

Crowther, Duane S. *Life Everlasting.* 1967. Salt Lake City, Utah: Bookcraft, 1987.

"Dating the Pyramids." *Archaeology* September/October 1999: 26-33.

David, Rosalie. *Discovering Ancient Egypt.* 1993. New York: Facts on File, 1994.

David, Rosalie. *Handbook to Life in Ancient Egypt.* New York: Facts on File, 1998.

Davidovits, Joseph, and Margie Morris. *The Pyramids: An Enigma Solved.* New York: Hippocrene, 1988.

Davidson, D., and H. Aldersmith. *The Great Pyramid: Its Divine Message.* Revised edition. London: Williams and Norgate, 1925.

Davreu, Robert. "The Lost Empire of the Indus Valley." *The World's Last Mysteries.* Pleasantville, NY: Reader's Digest, 1978.

Dersin, Denise, editor. *What Life Was Like: On the Banks of the Nile.* Richmond, VA: Time-Life, 1997.

Desroches-Noblecourt, Christiane. *Tutankhamen.* 1963. Boston: New York Graphic Society, 1978.

The Doctrine and Covenants of The Church of Jesus Christ of Latter-day Saints. Salt Lake City, UT: The Church of Jesus Christ of Latter-day Saints, 1997.

Draper, Richard D. *Opening the Seven Seals: The Visions of John the Revelator.* Salt Lake City, UT: Deseret, 1991.

Dummelow, J. R. *A Commentary on the Holy Bible.* 1908. New York: Macmillen, 1975.

Dunn, Christopher. *The Giza Power Plant: Technologies of Ancient Egypt.* Santa Fe, New Mexico: Bear & Company, 1998.

Eadie, Betty J. *Embraced by the Light.* 1992. New York: Bantam, 1994.

Edwards, I. E. S. *The Pyramids of Egypt.* Revised edition. New York: Penguin, 1993.

Evans, Humphrey. *The Mystery of the Pyramids.* New York: Thomas Y. Crowell, 1979.

Fakhry, Ahmed. *The Pyramids.* Chicago: The University of Chicago Press, 1961.

Faulkner, R. O., translator. *The Ancient Egyptian Book of the Dead.* Edited by Carol Andrews. 1972. Austin, Texas: University of Texas Press, 1997.

Forman, Werner, and Stephen Quirke. *Hieroglyphs and the Afterlife in Ancient Egypt.* Norman, OK: University of Oklahoma Press, 1996.

Freedman, David Noel, editor. *The Anchor Bible Dictionary.* Volume 6. New York: Doubleday, 1992. 6 volumes.

Furlong, David. *The Keys to the Temple.* 1997. London: Judy Piatkus, 1998.

Gaster, Theodore. "Enoch, Books of." *The Encyclopedia Americana: International Edition.* 1998.

Gaunt, Bonnie. *Jesus Christ: the Number of His Name.* Kempton, IL: Adventures Unlimited Press, 1998.

Gibson, Arvin S. *Echoes from Eternity.* 1993. Bountiful, UT: Horizon, 1995.

Gibson, Arvin S. *Glimpses of Eternity.* 1992. Bountiful, UT: Horizon, 1997.

Gilbert, Katharine Stoddert, Joan K. Holt, and Sara Hudson, editors. *Treasures of Tutankhamun.* Washington, D.C.: The Metropolitan Museum of Art, 1976.

Gower, Ralph. *The New Manners and Customs of Bible Times.* Chicago: The Moody Bible Institute of Chicago, 1987.

Greyson, Bruce, and Nancy Evans Bush. "Distressing Near-Death Experiences." *The Near-Death Experience: A Reader.* Edited by Lee W. Bailey and Jenny Yates. New York: Routledge, 1996.

Guggenheim, Bill, and Judy Guggenheim. *Hello from Heaven*! New York: Bantam, 1995.

Hancock, Graham. *Fingerprints of the Gods.* New York: Three Rivers Press, 1995.

Hancock, Graham, and Robert Bauval. *The Message of the Sphinx.* New York: Three Rivers Press, 1996.

Hawass, Zahi. "*The Pyramids and Temples of Gizeh*: An Update." *The Pyramids and Temples of Gizeh.* By W. M. Flinders Petrie. 1883. London, England: Histories & Mysteries of Man, 1990. 96-135.

Hayes, Michael. *The Egyptians.* New York: Rizzoli International, 1996.

Hobson, Christine. *The World of the Pharaohs: A Complete Guide to Ancient Egypt*. New York: Thames and Hudson, 1987.

Holes, Brook P. "Statistical Report, 2010." *Ensign*. May 2011: 29.

Holy Bible: Authorized King James Version. 1979. Salt Lake City, UT: The Church of Jesus Christ of Latter-day Saints, 1996.

Holy Bible: New International Version. Grand Rapids, MI: Zondervan Bible Publishers, 1984.

Holy Bible: The New King James Version. Nashville, TN: Thomas Nelson, 1982.

Howick, E. Keith. *The Miracles of Jesus the Messiah*. Salt Lake City, UT: Bookcraft, 1985.

Ikram, Salima, and Aidan Dodson. *The Mummy in Ancient Egypt: Equipping the Dead for Eternity*. London: Thames and Hudson, 1998.

Ions, Veronica. *Egyptian Mythology*. 1965. Feltham, England: Hamlyn, 1968.

Jenkins, Nancy. *The Boat Beneath the Pyramid*. New York: Holt, Rinehart and Winston, 1980.

Kimball, Spencer W. *The Miracle of Forgiveness*. 1969. Salt Lake City, UT: Bookcraft, 1992.

Knight, Christopher, and Robert Lomas. *The Hiram Key*. Rockport, MA: Element Books, 1997.

Knight, Christopher, and Robert Lomas. *The Second Messiah*. Boston, MA: Element Books, 1997.

Larson, Anthony E. *And There Shall Be a New Heaven and a New Earth.* Vol. 3. Orem, Utah: Zedek Books, 1985. 3 vols.

Laurence, Richard, translator. *The Book of Enoch the Prophet.* 1976. San Diego, CA: Wizards Bookshelf, 1995.

Lawton, Ian, and Chris Ogilvie-Herald. *Giza: The Truth.* London: Virgin, 1999.

Lehner, Mark. *The Complete Pyramids.* New York: Thames and Hudson, 1997.

Lemesurier, Peter. *The Great Pyramid Decoded.* Revised edition. New York: Barnes and Nobel, 1996.

Lepre, J. P. *The Egyptian Pyramids: A Comprehensive Illustrated Reference.* Jefferson, NC: McFarland, 1990.

Lockyer, Herbert, Sr. *All about the Second Coming.* Editor Herbert Lockyer, Jr. Peabody, Mass.: Hendrickson, 1998.

Lockyer, Herbert, Sr., editor. *Nelson's Illustrated Bible Dictionary.* Nashville, TN: Thomas Nelson, 1986.

Lundahl, Craig R., and Harold A. Widdison. *The Eternal Journey.* New York: Warner, 1997.

Lutzer, Erwin W. *One Minute After You Die.* Chicago: Moody Press, 1997.

McDannell, Colleen, and Bernhard Lang. *Heaven, A History.* New Haven and London: Yale University Press, 1988.

McGeveran, Jr., William A., Editorial Director. *The World Almanac and Book of Facts: 2004.* New York: World Almanac Books, 2004.

Meeks, Dimitri, and Christine Favard-Meeks. *Daily Life of the Egyptian Gods*. Translated by G. M. Goshgarian. 1993. London: Pimlico, 1999.

Mendelssohn, Kurt. *The Riddle of the Pyramids*. New York: Praeger, 1974.

Mercer, Samuel A. B. *The Handbook of Egyptian Hieroglyphs*. Revised and expanded by Janice Kamrin. New York: Hippocrene, 1998.

Mertz, Barbara. *Temple, Tombs and Hieroglyphs: A Popular History of Ancient Egypt*. 1964. New York: Peter Bedrick, 1978.

Metzger, Bruce M., and Michael D. Coogan, editors. *The Oxford Companion to the Bible*. New York: Oxford University Press, 1993.

Millet, Robert L., and Joseph Fielding McConkie. *The Life Beyond*. 1986. Salt Lake City, UT: Bookcraft, 1987.

Moody, Raymond A. *Life After Life*. 1975. New York: Bantam, 1988.

Moody, Raymond A. *The Light Beyond*. 1988. New York: Bantam, 1989.

Moody, Raymond A. *Reflections on Life After Life*. 1977. New York: Bantam, 1989.

Morse, Melvin, and Paul Perry. *Transformed by the Light*. 1992. New York: Ivy, 1994.

Neiman, Carol, and Emily Goldman. *AfterLife: The Complete Guide to Life after Death*. New York: Viking Studio, 1994.

Netton, Ian Richard. *A Popular Dictionary of Islam*. Atlantic Highlands, NJ: Humanities Press International, 1992.

New Larousse Encyclopedia of Mythology. 1959. Translated by Richard Aldington and Delano Ames. New York: Prometheus Press, 1973.

Nibley, Hugh. *Enoch the Prophet.* Salt Lake City, UT: Deseret, 1986.

The NKJV Greek-English Interlinear New Testament. Translated by Arthur J. Farstad, et al. Nashville, Tennessee: Thomas Nelson, 1994.

Noone, Richard W. *5/5/2000.* Revised edition. New York: Three Rivers Press, 1995.

Petrie, W. M. Flinders. *The Pyramids and Temples of Gizeh.* 1883. London, England: Histories & Mysteries of Man, 1990.

Platt, Rutherford H., Jr., editor. "The Book of the Secrets of Enoch." *The Lost Books of the Bible and The Forgotten Books of Eden.* World Bible Publishers, 1926-1927.

Platt, Rutherford H., Jr., editor. "The Second Book of Adam and Eve." *The Lost Books of the Bible and the Forgotten Books of Eden.* World Bible, 1926-1927.

Platt, Rutherford H., Jr., editor. "The Testament of Benjamin." *The Lost Books of the Bible and The Forgotten Books of Eden.* World Bible, 1926-1927.

Platt, Rutherford H., Jr., editor. "The Testament of Gad." *The Lost Books of the Bible and The Forgotten Books of Eden.* World Bible, 1926-1927.

Platt, Rutherford H., Jr., editor. "The Testament of Joseph." *The Lost Books of the Bible and The Forgotten Books of Eden.* World Bible, 1926-1927.

Platt, Rutherford H., Jr., editor. "The Testament of Levi." *The Lost Books of the Bible and The Forgotten Books of Eden.* World Bible, 1926-1927.

Platt, Rutherford H., Jr., editor. "The Testament of Reuben." *The Lost Books of the Bible and The Forgotten Books of Eden.* World Bible, 1926-1927.

Potter, Charles Francis. *Did Jesus Write This Book*? New Hyde Park, NY: University Books, 1965.

Putnam, James. *Egyptology*. New York: Crescent, 1990.

Quirke, Stephen, and Jeffrey Spencer, eds. *The British Museum Book of Ancient Egypt*. 1992. New York: Thames and Hudson, 1996.

Rawlings, Maurice S. *To Hell and Back*. Nashville, TN: Thomas Nelson, 1993.

Reeves, Nicholas. *The Complete Tutankhamun*. 1990. New York: Thames and Hudson, 1993.

Reeves, Nicholas, and Richard H. Wilkinson. *The Complete Valley of the Kings*. New York: Thames and Hudson, 1996.

Richards, Lawrence O., editor and writer. *The Revell Bible Dictionary*. New York: Wynwood, 1990.

Richards, LeGrand. *A Marvelous Work and a Wonder*. Revised edition. Salt Lake City, UT: Deseret, 1976.

Ritchie, George G., with Elizabeth Sherrill. *Return from Tomorrow*. Waco, Texas: Chosen, 1978.

Ritmeyer, Leen and Kathleen. *Secrets of Jerusalem's Temple Mount*. Washington, D. C.: Biblical Archaeology Society, 1998.

Robinson, John J. *A Pilgrim's Path: Freemasonry and the Religious Right.* New York: M. Evans, 1993.

Robinson, O. Preston, and Christine H. Robinson. *Christ's Eternal Gospel.* Salt Lake City, UT: Deseret, 1976.

Romer, John and Elizabeth. *The Seven Wonders of the World.* New York: Henry Holt, 1995.

Rutherford, Adam. *Pyramidology.* 4th edition. Book I. London: C. Tinling, 1957. 5 vols.

Rutherford, Adam. *Pyramidology.* Book II. London: C. Tinling, 1962.

Rutherford, Adam. *Pyramidology.* Book III. London: C. Tinling, 1966.

Schiffman, Lawrence H. *Reclaiming the Dead Sea Scrolls.* Philadelphia and Jerusalem: Jewish Publication Society, 1994.

Schul, Bill, and Ed Pettit. *The Secret Power of Pyramids.* 1975. New York: Fawcett Gold Medal, 1987.

Sellier, Charles E. *Mysteries of the Ancient World.* New York: Dell, 1995.

Sitchin, Zechariah. *The Cosmic Code.* New York: Avon, 1998.

Sitchin, Zechariah. *The Stairway to Heaven.* 1980. New York: Avon, 1983.

Skousen, W. Cleon. *The First 2000 Years.* 1953. Salt Lake City, UT: Bookcraft, 1974.

Skousen, W. Cleon. *The Third Thousand Years.* 1964. Salt Lake City, UT: Bookcraft, 1973.

Smith, Joseph Fielding, editor. *Scriptural Teachings of the Prophet Joseph Smith.* Revised edition of *Teachings of the Prophet Joseph Smith*, 1976. Salt Lake City, UT: Deseret, 1993.

Smith, Worth. *Miracle of the Ages: The Great Pyramid of Gizeh.* New York: W. H. Wise, 1937.

Smyth, Mrs. Piazzi. "Biographical Notice of John Taylor of 'The Great Pyramid.'" *The Great Pyramid: Its Secrets and Mysteries Revealed.* By Piazzi Smyth. 1880. New York: Gramercy, 1978. 637-52.

Smyth, Piazzi. *The Great Pyramid: Its Secrets and Mysteries Revealed.* 1880. New York: Gramercy, 1978.

Sorensen, Michele R., and Dr. David R. Willmore. *The Journey Beyond Life.* Orem, UT: Family Affair, 1988.

Spence, Lewis. *Egypt.* London: Senate, 1994.

Stecchini, Livio Catullo. Appendix: "Notes on the Relation of Ancient Measures to the Great Pyramid." *Secrets of the Great Pyramid.* By Peter Tompkins. 1971. New York: Galahad, 1997. 287-382.

Strong, James. *The New Strong's Complete Dictionary of Bible Words.* Nashville, TN: Thomas Nelson, 1996.

Talmage, James E. *The House of the Lord.* Revised edition. Salt Lake City, UT: Deseret, 1971.

Talmage, James E. *Jesus the Christ.* Salt Lake City, UT: Deseret, 1962.

Tenney, Merrill C., editor. *The Zondervan Pictorial Encyclopedia of the Bible.* Grand Rapids, MI: Zondervan Publishing House, 1975. 5 volumes.

Terrien, Samuel. "Enoch." *The Encyclopedia Americana: International Edition*. 1969.

Terrien, Samuel. "Enoch, Books of." *The Encyclopedia Americana: International Edition*. 1969.

Tompkins, Peter. *Secrets of the Great Pyramid*. 1971. New York: Galahad, 1997.

Top, Brent L., and Wendy C. Top. *Beyond Death's Door*. Salt Lake City, UT: Bookcraft, 1993.

Toth, Max, and Greg Nielsen. *Pyramid Power*. New York: Warner Destiny, 1976.

Turkkan, Fatma. Foreward. *The Great Pyramid: Its Secrets and Mysteries Revealed*. By Piazzi Smyth. 1880. New York: Gramercy, 1978. v-vi.

VanderKam, James C. *Enoch: A Man for All Generations*. Columbia, SC: University of South Carolina, 1995.

Von Daniken, Erich. *The Eyes of the Sphinx*. New York: Berkley, 1996.

Walker, Barbara G. *The Woman's Dictionary of Symbols and Sacred Objects*. New York: HarperCollins, 1988.

Wallace, Arthur. *LDS Roots in Egypt*. Los Angeles: LL Company, 1981.

Watson, F. Michael. "Statistical Report, 1999." *Ensign*. May 2000: 22.

West, John Anthony. *Serpent in the Sky*. 1979. Wheaton, Illinois: The Theosophical Publishing House, 1993.

Wilkinson, Richard H. *Symbol & Magic in Egyptian Art.* 1994. New York: Thames and Hudson, 1999.

Wilson, Colin. *From Atlantis to the Sphinx.* New York: Fromm International, 1996.

Wilson, Hilary. *People of the Pharaohs: From Peasant to Courtier.* London: Michael O'Mara, 1997.

Wilson, Hilary. *Understanding Hieroglyphs.* London: Michael O'Mara, 1995.

Wilson, Ian. *Jesus: The Evidence.* 1996. London: Phoenix Illustrated, 1998.

Wright, G. Ernest. "In the Days of Israel's Glory." *Everyday Life in Bible Times.* Editor Merle Severy. Washington, D.C., National Geographic Society, 1968. 220-255.

Zauzich, Karl-Theodor. *Hieroglyphs without Mystery: An Introduction to Ancient Egyptian Writing.* Translated by Ann Macy Roth. 1992. Austin: University of Texas Press, 1996.

Made in the USA
Middletown, DE
10 August 2016